Michael Kofler

Scripting

Automation with Bash, PowerShell, and Python

Editor Megan Fuerst
Acquisitions Editor Hareem Shafi
German Edition Editor Christoph Meister
Translation Winema Language Services, Inc.
Copyeditor Yvette Chin
Cover Design Graham Geary
Photo Credit Shutterstock: 2197648801/ © Dima Zel, iStockphoto: 165687831/ © enjoynz
Layout Design Vera Brauner
Production Graham Geary
Typesetting III-satz, Germany
Printed and bound in Canada, on paper from sustainable sources

ISBN 978-1-4932-2556-9

1st edition 2024
1st German edition published 2023 by Rheinwerk Verlag, Bonn, Germany

Library of Congress Cataloging-in-Publication Control Number: 2023056495

Contents at a Glance

Contents

3 Bash and Zsh 49

Preface

A script is a small piece of code to solve a specific problem or automate a tedious task. You don't need a development environment or a compiler to develop a script—an editor is enough. When it comes to scripting, minimalism is the name of the game, and its goal is achieving maximum impact with minimal resources. To put it casually, scripting is the art of solving IT problems in ten lines of code.

In my work environment, scripts are ubiquitous. I use scripts to set the power saving mode for my laptop, to create a PDF file of this book from Markdown files, to automate backups to servers, to watermark e-books, to set up new customers in a web application, to scan dozens of databases for logical errors, to create virtual machines for teaching, to sort photos, and more.

Bash, PowerShell, or Python?

The "classic" scripting language is Bash. Its full name, *Bourne Again Shell*, is a pun. The predecessor was the Bourne shell, which was widely used on Unix. The license for the Bourne shell was unsuitable for Linux, which is why a new project was created. Today, Bash is the dominant Linux shell, both in interactive mode for executing commands and for script programming. macOS relies on the largely compatible Zsh, which is also gaining more and more followers on Linux.

Bash is popular, but its antiquated syntax doesn't win any beauty contests. On the contrary, Bash scripts sometimes look awful. For this reason, Microsoft did not even try to adapt Bash for Windows. Instead, with PowerShell, Microsoft has combined the basic ideas of a classic Unix shell with the concepts behind object-oriented programming languages and created a completely new language, which turned out surprisingly well! Not without reason, Windows administrators love PowerShell.

Python is actually not a typical scripting language. Depending on the intended use, Python is the basis for AI developments, a tool for (natural) scientists, or a first language for entry-level programming. Probably no other language is used as universally as Python! The elegance of Python's syntax and its almost inexhaustible supply of extension modules have led to Python also being used for system administration, converting files between different formats, as a database tool or for hardware control (for the Raspberry Pi). Python plays to its strengths the more complex the task.

About This Book

Because no single perfect scripting language exists, this book starts in Part I with crash courses for the Bash, PowerShell, and Python languages. If you want, you can focus on one of these three languages to get started and gradually increase your language vocabulary.

Part II of this book introduces you to tools and working techniques typically used in scripts: These topics include commands for processing text files, cmdlets for applying regular expressions, and functions for handling JSON and XML files. I'll show you how to run scripts regularly and automatically, how to run code or copy files to other machines via SSH, and how to combine version management for your code and scripting via Git. Many practical examples round off the information I provide throughout this book.

Finally, Part III deals with concrete applications: Key topics include backups, image processing, web scraping, using REST APIs, databases, using the cloud, and virtual machine administration.

I have tried as much as possible to design this book in a modular way. Thus, you don't need to read all the chapters from start to finish, but instead, you can search specifically for the information important to you at a specific moment. All chapters in Parts II and III begin with a brief information box that summarizes the prerequisites for that chapter.

Scripting and AI Tools

Recently, ChatGPT has ushered in a sea change in many professions. As often is the case, your perspective will determine whether you see the glass as half full or as half empty: AI tools are far from perfect today, but they are definitely (already and likely even more so in coming years) a tool that will revolutionize software development.

If you ask ChatGPT or GitHub Copilot in VS Code for a PowerShell script to read a JSON file and store the data it contains in a PostgreSQL database, the solution will output a plausible-looking script in seconds.

Ideally, the script will work right away. In my experience, however, the code is rarely ideal—all the less so the more complex the problem is. Often, the generated code contains unique errors, such as options or commands that don't exist. Sometimes, logical errors also exist that are more difficult to detect. With some scripting experience, most problems can usually be fixed quickly. You can even ask the AI tool specifically to improve a certain aspect of the code.

My personal impression is that the more solid your prior knowledge is, the better you can use AI tools. An AI tool plus an experienced developer or an experienced programmer—in my view, that's the dream team of the future. This book provides exactly the foundation needed, without dwelling on too many encyclopedic details. For the programming of the future, you don't need to know a hundred syntax variants for certain regular expressions by heart. But you do need to know that regular expressions exist, the basics of how they work, and where pitfalls exist. This kind of knowledge is precisely the focus of this book.

Scripting as a Core Competence for Efficient IT Work

No matter in which branch of the IT industry or on what kind of projects you're currently working on, even just a little scripting knowledge will go a long way to making you more efficient in your work. Focus on the essentials; leave tedious side tasks to scripts. I wish you every success in this endeavor!

–Michael Kofler (*https://kofler.info*)

Downloadable Files

All the sample files for this book can be downloaded at *https://rheinwerk-computing.com/5851*.

PART I

Scripting Languages

Chapter 1
Scripting: Doing One Thing

This short introductory chapter addresses the question, "What is scripting?" We'll cover the differences between "full-fledged" programming languages and classic scripting languages and show you right away how these boundaries (especially with Python) are fluid.

In this chapter, I want to go into a bit of the background and philosophy of scripting. I think this background is especially important if you've previously developed code using a language like Java or C#. You have learned to use the correct data types and to structure your code in an object-oriented way. You've followed all the rules of the art as best you can.

At this point, you might be wondering: What is wrong with also developing a backup script or a test program for a REST API in a strictly typed programming language? What are the advantages of a syntactically much more generous script language like Bash, which knows strings as the only data type? Why make friends with PowerShell when it uses the same .NET foundation as C#? We'll be answering these questions as we discuss the benefits of each scripting language in the coming sections.

1.1 What Does Scripting Mean?

Scripting means the following:

- You can write 20 lines of code to create a backup of your database once a day, including encrypting and uploading this data to cloud storage.
- With a tiny program, you can reduce countless wedding photos to a maximum resolution of 1024×768 pixels, including watermarking and uploading the files to a hidden directory on your web server so that your customers can view and select their favorite images via your website.
- You can easily scan all the computers on your local network for a specific security vulnerability or an outdated software version.
- You can capture, for instance, the volume of gas stored in Germany, the price fluctuations of the next notebook you want to buy, or the latest COVID-19 case numbers from public websites and represent this data in charts.
- You can filter out the 20 error messages relevant to you from a log file of 50,000 lines.

1.1.1 Scripting versus Programming

Scripts, too, are "only" programs. However, they differ from large software projects in the way they are programmed, the tools/components used, and their objectives:

- Typically, scripts perform manageable, relatively simple tasks. They often help automate administrative tasks or at least perform them more efficiently.
- Scripts are used in text mode (in the terminal) or executed automatically in the background. No graphical user interface (GUI) exists.
- Special script languages are used for programming, which make uncomplicated, efficient development possible. Script languages require neither elaborate development tools nor compilers. The syntax is minimalistic (sometimes, unfortunately, also outdated and it can take some getting used to). Central principles familiar from large projects, such as object orientation or strict type control of variables, play a subordinate role or cannot be implemented at all.
- Popular script languages are characterized by huge offering of commands or extension modules. This diversity helps to perform basic operations (read and evaluate files, set up users, perform network operations, etc.). When it comes to scripting, you don't have time to reinvent the wheel! You should rather make use of a huge toolbox of existing components and building blocks as best you can.
- The code size of scripts is small, typically under 100 lines (not counting comments and strings).

In large software projects, an extremely important goal is that code be developed "cleanly"—that is, the code can be understood by all members of the team and later extended or modified. In other words, all guidelines of modern software design are observed.

Scripting, on the other hand, is about solving a small problem quickly and pragmatically (*getting things done*). Of course, you shouldn't go out of your way to develop sloppy scripts! Scripts should also use meaningful variable names, be documented with comments, contain basic error protection, and so on. But the priorities and development goals of a script that should be ready within a day if possible are quite different from the priorities and development goals for a software project whose code may need to be maintained for a decade.

1.1.2 Glue Languages and Glue Code

In the context of scripting, sometimes, you'll hear talk of "glue code." Accordingly, scripting languages are sometimes referred to as "glue languages." What do these terms mean?

In larger projects, the proverbial *glue* is often necessary to connect independent or incompatible software components. In the simplest case, a script calls some external commands that in themselves have nothing to do with each other: One creates a backup of a database, the second encrypts the resulting file, the third transfers the file to another server via HTTP, and so on. Each of the commands used was developed independently of all the others. But by connecting the commands through your script, a new meaningful component is created.

Glue code is sometimes also necessary to efficiently apply modern software development tools. For example, let's say your team is developing a large project in JavaScript using tools like Git (version control) and Docker (containers for local testing environments). Each time a team member completes ("checks in") a new test version, the current code should be transferred ("deployed") to an external test server. This step could be performed by a small script.

Theoretically, you can perform such tasks with any programming language. However, scripting languages are particularly well suited for these tasks because of their simple syntaxes, minimal development overhead, and the fact that scripts create few (or even no) new project dependencies.

1.1.3 Do One Thing and Do It Well

Unix programs were developed according to the motto "*Do one thing and do it well,*" formulated by Doug McIlroy, and these programs are still assessed by this standard today. When Unix became Linux and macOS, what was then called a "program" is now called a "command." But the principle has not changed: A command like `ls`, `grep`, or `find` is expected to perform a very specific task and to do that task really well.

What does Unix's motto have to do with scripting? On Linux and macOS, when you develop scripts in the Bash or Zsh languages, you do so on a foundation of several hundred commands that meet the Unix recommendation. You would be well advised to adopt the motto for your own projects as well. Write scripts that perform *one* task neatly.

1.2 Scripting Languages

In purely formal terms, scripting languages differ from other, "higher-level" programming languages in that the code is interpreted. Thus, the code is formulated in a text file and then executed directly by an interpreter in Bash, PowerShell, or Python. The code does not need to be compiled (i.e., converted to a binary representation) beforehand.

This concept has an advantage in that scripts can be executed immediately without lengthy preparation work, which speeds up the development process.

However, using an interpreter has a disadvantage in that scripts usually run somewhat more slowly than compiled programs. For this reason, a scripting language is rarely the ideal choice for developing computationally intensive algorithms. Since many scripts consist mainly of calls to other commands, the loss of efficiency due to the missing compiler does not matter at all.

All Linux shells are considered "classic" scripting languages, such as Bourne Shell, the Korn Shell, Bash, and Zsh. A shell is actually a command interpreter, that is, a program that accepts and executes commands. If several such commands are stored in a text file, the original form of a script is created.

Over time, countless scripting languages were developed that offered more syntactic options than traditional shells and were often optimized for specific tasks. These other languages include, for example, JavaScript, Python, PHP, and Tcl.

In the Windows world, the unspeakable *cmd.exe* program originally took over the role of the shell. Even now, **.bat* files based on this program are still in use today despite their extremely modest scripting capabilities. This program was followed by VBScript, the VBA language optimized for Microsoft Office, and finally PowerShell, which brought Microsoft the success they had been hoping for: PowerShell is now considered *the* language when it comes to maintaining and administering large Windows network installations.

Compilers for Scripting Languages

The interpreter/compiler criterion was established in the past to distinguish between scripting and other languages, but this distinction is obsolete today. Compilers now exist for many languages whose code was initially executed by an interpreter. These compilers are often *just-in-time compilers* that compile the code immediately before execution and are thus unnoticed by users. This invisibility is true for JavaScript, PHP, and Python, among others.

1.2.1 Bash and Zsh

Obviously, I cannot cover all popular scripting languages in this book. I'll instead focus on three (with Zsh, four) languages that are most important for administrative tasks and in DevOps environments. In the following sections, I'll briefly introduce these languages to you.

The name *Bash* is an abbreviation for *Bourne Again Shell*. The Bourne shell was immensely popular for Unix more than 30 years ago. However, this program was not available in an open-source license, which led to the development of the largely compatible Bash, which later became the standard shell for most Linux distributions.

When *scripting* is mentioned in the context of a Linux environment without further explanation, the scripting language is almost always Bash. Whether server processes are being started, network connections set up, or firewall rules changed, quite often

Bash scripts are already used at the operating system level for this purpose. Therefore, also running your own tasks using Bash makes sense.

The widespread use of Bash sometimes makes one overlook the fact that its roots and syntax are old. Accordingly, the syntax of the language is sometimes inconsistent, sometimes simply atrocious. Instead of simple functions, countless special characters must be used to perform quite trivial tasks (e.g., edit strings or perform calculations). Besides strings and arrays, no other data types exist. Object orientation is an unknown concept in Bash anyway.

On the plus side, an almost limitless selection of Unix tools can be used and combined in scripts. So, the strength of Bash lies not in its linguistic capabilities but in its commands, which you can easily call in scripts. (And as mentioned earlier, these commands were developed based on the motto "*do one thing....*")

However, I must mention also that beginners can find becoming accustomed to the world of Bash and Linux commands quite difficult. While (almost) every command is well documented on its own, no central overview exists.

Bash versus Zsh

Zsh is largely compatible with Bash. With regard to script programming, the differences are minimal, and of course, you can call the same commands in both shells. However, when used interactively, Zsh stands out for its many advantages and better extensibility. Thus, Zsh is gaining more and more fans in the Linux world and is even used as the default shell by some distributions. (For other distributions, Zsh can be installed in a few simple steps.)

macOS switched from Bash to Zsh in 2019. Apple's motivation had less to do with technical merits and more to do with licensing issues: Current versions of Bash use the GPL 3 license, which is avoided by Apple. Zsh, on the other hand, has a more liberal, BSD-like license.

As far as this book is concerned, whether you prefer Bash or Zsh doesn't matter much. I'll provide a brief overview of their main advantages and disadvantages in Chapter 3, Section 3.4.

1.2.2 PowerShell

Microsoft has long relied on GUIs, not only in the Microsoft Office area, but also for server administration. At first glance, this reliance seemed to be an advantage compared to Linux: A few mouse clicks are easier to understand than dubious configuration files.

For administrators, however, this choice has turned into a nightmare: The main problem is that configuration work does not scale. You need ten times longer to administer ten servers with a single mouse click than to administer just one server. In contrast to Linux, hardly any way existed to automate such work.

This limitation changed with the launch of PowerShell 2006. Microsoft used this opportunity for a new beginning well: Compared to Bash, PowerShell scores major points with a much more logical syntax. From a technical point of view, the most interesting feature of PowerShell is that data is transported from one command to the next, not in text form, but as full-fledged objects. This new approach enables far-reaching ways of processing by reading properties and calling methods. However, the object-oriented approach only works with commands specially optimized for PowerShell, which Microsoft refers to as *cmdlets*. (Calling traditional commands is also possible but is subject to restrictions.)

Another success factor for PowerShell can be found in its environment: Microsoft has started to make many Windows components and server services fully configurable through cmdlets. In the past, only basic settings could be changed via scripts, and other options could only be reached via mouse click. Now, the emphasis is on *PowerShell first*.

In addition to the cmdlets provided by default, countless extension modules with cmdlets for specific tasks are available on the internet. An active community has grown up around PowerShell. Since 2018, PowerShell has also been an open-source project and can also be installed on Linux and macOS. However, the cmdlet offerings available outside the Windows world is much smaller. Typical admin tasks (setting up users, changing network configuration, etc.) only work on Windows. Across platforms, PowerShell can only be used for tasks that are not Windows specific.

1.2.3 Python

The first Python version was released in 1991. Thus, Python is almost as old as Bash, the first version of which appeared in 1989. But unlike Bash, Python hardly shows its age: Python is characterized by an elegant, well-designed syntax that still sets standards today.

Python is a scripting language in that its code was originally executed by an interpreter. In current versions, however, the code is first compiled into an intermediate binary format (called *byte code*) for performance reasons. You won't notice any of this effort when using Python. In other words, Python behaves like an interpreted language, but it very much uses a compiler behind the scenes.

Python was not primarily designed to automate administrative operations but instead is rather extremely general purpose. You can equally learn to program or solve AI problems with Python!

A basic concept behind Python is that the language core is very compact. For this purpose, the language can be easily extended by modules, and these modules are exactly why Python is so popular today (also) as a scripting language in the sense of this book.

Over time, more and more extension modules have emerged to use cloud services, apply network functions, access databases, and more. For almost any admin task imaginable, a suitable Python module can be installed in no time!

However, Python is only moderately suitable for calling existing commands. In this respect, the modules are both a curse and a blessing. While you may already be familiar with the commands required for a Bash script, you'll need to learn about an adequate Python module with similar functions. Several modules might be eligible, and you may not clearly see which module is more suitable or which one will be maintained in the future. In this respect, the use of Python is worthwhile especially when the task is reasonably complex, when the advantages of Python compensate for the disadvantage of a longer familiarization with a particular additional module.

1.2.4 Many Similarities, Even More Differences

Describing *three* scripting languages in one book is admittedly an intellectual challenge—for the author as well as for you, the reader! Of course, all three languages are characterized by many similarities, especially true Bash and PowerShell. At the same time, however, countless syntactic variations can make rapid switching between languages tedious. Thus, one tip: You should use an editor that supports the respective scripting language well because then the editor will detect most errors or syntax mixups before your first test runs.

1.3 The Agony of Choice

If you're just entering the world of scripting, you'd probably prefer it if I would tell you now, "Learn language Xxx, it's good for everything." Unfortunately, the IT world is not that simple. Which scripting language is the most suitable or the ideal solution for you depends greatly on the task and the operating system on which your script is supposed to run, for instance:

- For scripts to administer Windows computers and networks, PowerShell is definitely the best choice. Many Windows-specific functions are best controlled by PowerShell's own commands and modules.
- Similarly, Bash (or, almost equivalently, Zsh) is the ideal language if you want to run administrative scripts on Linux machines or servers and on macOS.
- For tasks that are platform-independent and do not depend on operating system-specific libraries, PowerShell, Bash, and Python are equally suitable. In that case, I pragmatically recommend the language you know best or whose environment (commands, extension modules) you know best.
- The greater the complexity of the task; the more elaborate the control of the code (loops, branches, functions, etc.); and the more extensive the expected amount of

code and the greater the number of variables and data structures required, the stronger my tendency is towards Python.

- If your script runs the risk of turning into a "real" program, with several hundred lines of code, the advantages of Python (with its clearer syntax and better development tools) outweigh its disadvantages. However, we're then moving well beyond the scope of this book.

You must start somewhere: If you're at home in the Windows environment and want to run your scripts there, I would start using PowerShell. Similarly, I advise Linux and macOS fans to first learn the basics of Bash and Zsh, respectively. (This recommendation also applies if you use Windows as your working environment, but you want your scripts to run on Linux servers. While this juggling sounds contradictory, in real life, this scenario is absolutely common. Microsoft's own *Azure* cloud runs more Linux instances than Windows ones. Nothing wrong with combining the benefits of Windows on the desktop with those of Linux on the server.)

Once you're somewhat familiar with Bash or PowerShell, you should get acquainted with Python. Python scores major points with its impressively elegant syntax and is miles superior to Bash as well as PowerShell in this respect. However, these advantages are more effective for complex, platform-independent tasks. In this respect, Python is not quite a "classic" scripting language but has a much more universal objective. If your script is primarily intended to call elementary Linux tools (such as `find`, `grep`, `adduser`, and `gzip`) or to perform basic Windows admin tasks, Bash or PowerShell are better suited for this purpose than Python, despite all their syntax peculiarities.

Ultimately, the key is simply to start programming. In this context, don't let yourself be influenced by the order in which the chapters appear in this book but instead start with whatever chapter seems most logical to you. When writing, I tried extremely hard to conceive all the chapters as independently as possible. The PowerShell chapter does not assume any knowledge of Bash, or vice versa!

To conclude these first reflections, I have made a very personal, thoroughly subjective evaluation of the languages presented in this book in Table 1.1. You'll notice that Python performs very well in this regard. This high score doesn't change the fact that, for simple tasks, depending on the operating system, Bash or PowerShell are the tools that will accomplish your goals the fastest and are therefore probably the ones you'll use most often. (At least, that's how I feel.)

Criterion	Bash/Zsh	PowerShell	Python
Suitable for Windows	4	10	10
Suitable for macOS	10	3	10
Suitable for Linux	10	3	10

Table 1.1 Personal Rating of Selected Script Languages (0 = Miserable; 10 = Great)

Criterion	Bash/Zsh	PowerShell	Python
Operating system-specific administrative tasks	10	10	5
Platform-independent tasks	7	5	10
Consistent syntax	3	6	10
Simple call of external commands	10	9	5
Toolbox size (commands, modules, etc.)	9	5	10
Development tools/debugging	2	5	8
Help system/documentation	2	6	8
Simple, "classic" scripts	8	8	3
Complex code	2	4	10

Table 1.1 Personal Rating of Selected Script Languages (0 = Miserable; 10 = Great) (Cont.)

Chapter 2
Ten Times Ten Lines

The next few chapters lay the foundation for script programming. Depending on the language you want to work in and your previous knowledge, you might skip some of these chapters. But if you prefer linear reading, there are many pages describing theory and syntax before the much more exciting scripts follow. That's why in this chapter I'm going to present ten short scripts, each a maximum of ten lines of code, as an appetizer, so to speak.

If you're at the start of your scripting career, you won't understand, or will only begin to understand, how these scripts work. But that does not matter! Each script ends with a cross-reference to a chapter in which a similar script or a more extensive variant is explained. At this point, the sole purpose is to prove to you what great possibilities even tiny scripts can offer.

I know from many years of experience: Nothing is duller than imparting knowledge where the goal is unclear. This problem is exactly what I want to avoid. The knowledge from this book should enable you to solve everyday IT tasks with minimal code effort—just like the ten examples in this chapter!

Longer Scripts

Don't get me wrong! Of course, "real" scripts are often much longer and often contain 100 or 200 lines. Such scripts then perform more complex tasks, validate the input parameters, display help texts, and. I just want to illustrate in this chapter how far you can get with only ten lines of code and without special functions for code minimization, which make code difficult to understand.

2.1 Markdown Spell Checker (Bash)

I don't write my books in Microsoft Word but use Markdown syntax and work in an editor without a spell checker. This approach may seem old-fashioned to you, but I can assure you that my writing process is quite efficient.

However, certain typos and spelling errors keep happening to me. So that I don't drive my proofreaders to despair, before I start proofreading, I apply a script that replaces certain words in all chapter files.

The following Bash script reads the entries from the *corrections.txt* file line by line in the first loop and forms a `sed` command for each entry (see Chapter 9, Section 9.3). In the second loop, the script applies `sed` to all files passed to the script. This loop creates a backup of the original file (`-i.bak` option).

```
#!/bin/bash
# Sample file correct.sh
sedcmd=""
while read -r findtxt replacetxt; do
    sedcmd+="s/$findtxt/$replacetxt/g;"
done < corrections.txt
for filename in $*; do
    echo "Correct file $filename"
    sed -i.bak "$sedcmd" $filename
done
```

The call of the script looks as follows:

```
$ ./correct.sh *.md
```

If you like, you can convince yourself of the function's correctness by calling `diff test.md test.md.bak`. The *corrections.txt* file simply contains search and replace words separated by spaces, with the wrong spelling in the first column and the correct spelling in the second one:

```
Addin           Add-in
Github          GitHub
commited        committed
diffrence       difference
acommodate      accommodate
calender        calendar
...
```

2.2 Sorting Images by Date (PowerShell)

Recently, I received several thousand photos from my siblings to create a photo album. Fortunately, most of the photos came from the digital age: For this reason, most photos were image files that contained exchangeable image file format (Exif) information with the date they had been taken. To enable a quick overview of the photos across time, I wanted to move the images into different directories based on the month in which the photos had been taken (e.g., `2015-03` for photos taken in March 2015).

This task can be performed by a PowerShell script that requires the ExifTool program to be installed first (see Chapter 16, Section 16.2).

The first loop goes through all the parameters passed to the script, for instance, `*.jpg` and `*.jpeg` if the script was started in the form `.\sort-images.ps1 *.jpg *.jpeg`. The second loop processes the files corresponding to the pattern, uses ExifTool to determine the date they were taken, and formats this information in the form `yyyy-mm`. If necessary, `New-Item` creates the corresponding directory. Finally, `Move-Item` moves the image file to that directory.

```
# Sample file sort-images.ps1
foreach ($arg in $args) {
    foreach ($file in Get-Item $arg) {
        $yearmonth = exiftool -s3 -d '%Y-%m' `
                              -DateTimeOriginal $file
        if ($yearmonth) {
            $targetdir = New-Item -ItemType Directory `
                                  -Path $yearmonth -Force
            Move-Item $file $targetdir
        }
    }
}
```

2.3 Converting a JSON File to XML Format (Python)

Let's say we have a file called *employees.json*, which is a JSON file with the following structure:

```
[
  {
    "emp_no" : 10001 },
    "birth_date" : "1953-09-02",
    "first_name" : "Georgi",
    'last-name': "Facello",
    ...
  }, ...
```

We need to form an XML file from the JSON file, and the XML file should look as follows:

```
<?xml version="1.0"?>
<employees>
  <employee no='10001' birth_date='1953-09-02'>Georgi
    Facello</employee>
  ...
</employees>
```

This scenario is exactly the kind of task Python is designed for! The `with` keyword opens the source file and the target file. The code `json.load` reads the JSON file and turns it into a Python list of dictionaries (where each list entry is a dictionary with employee data). The for loop runs through all list elements and brings the employee number, date of birth, and name into the desired XML format.

```
# Sample file json2xml.py
import json
fmt = "  <employee no='%s' birth_date='%s'>%s %s</employee>\n"
with open('employee.json', 'r') as jsonfile, \
     open('employee.xml', 'w') as xmlfile:
    data = json.load(jsonfile)
    xmlfile.write('<?xml version="1.0"?>\n<employees>\n')
    for item in data:
        xmlfile.write(fmt % (item['emp_no'],
          item['birth_date'], item['first_name'],
          item['last_name']))
    xmlfile.write('</employees>\n')
```

For basic principles on handling JSON and XML files, see Chapter 10.

2.4 Daily Server Backups (Bash)

Let's say we have a web application running on a LAMP server (Linux, Apache, MySQL/MariaDB, PHP). In this scenario, the contents of the database and the directory containing the web application files should be backed up once a day. This process can be performed automatically via the following brief Bash script:

```
# Sample file lamp-backup.sh
dbfile="/localbackup/sql.gz"
mysqldump -u backupuser --single-transaction dbname | \
  gzip -c > $dbfile
htmlfile="/localbackup/html.tar.gz"
tar czf $htmlfile -C /var/www/html/applicationdir .
```

The mysqldump command requires the existence of a /root/.my.cnf configuration file in which the password for the backup user is stored. To run the script every night at 4:30 am with root privileges, you must add the following line to /etc/crontab (see also Chapter 11, Section 11.1):

```
# in /etc/crontab
30 4 * * * root /path/to/lamp-backup.sh
```

Basic principles and tips for designing backup scripts are described in Chapter 15. I will show you how to encrypt your backups and upload them to the cloud in Chapter 20, Section 20.2.

2.5 Web Scraping (Python)

Web scraping is the art of extracting information from a web page, such as the current price from a product page. In this script, we'll extract the current version number from a webpage (in our case, the Git homepage at *https://git-scm.com*) and extract the link to the release notes as well.

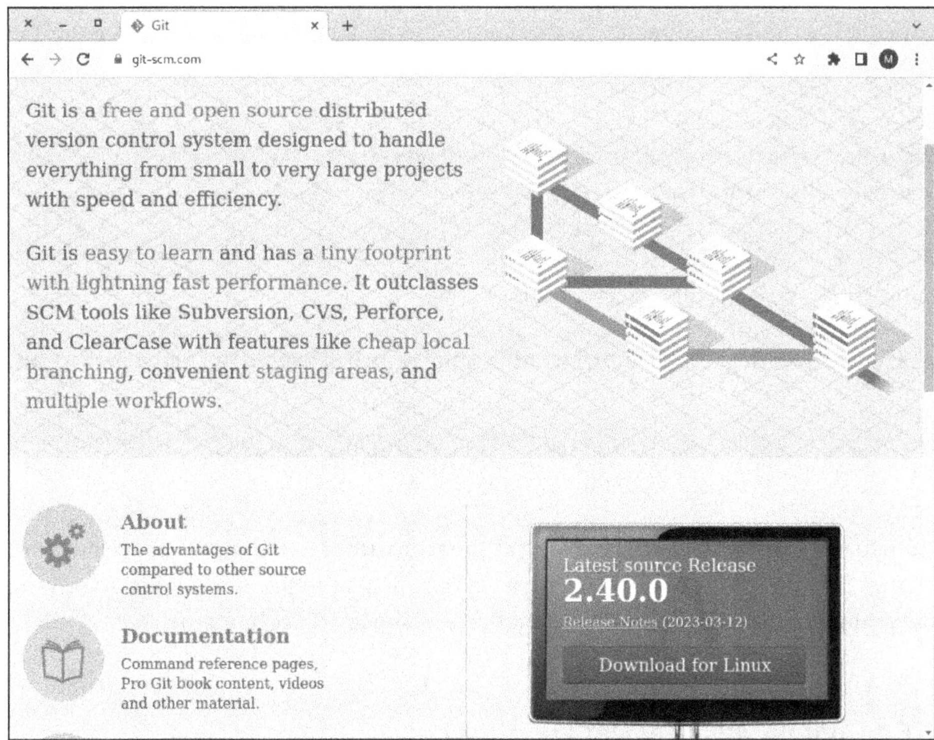

Figure 2.1 Git Homepage Showing the Current Version Number in the Bottom-Right Corner

A look into the HTML code of the web page reveals the following code snippet:

```
...
<div class="monitor">
  <h4> Latest source Release </h4>
  <span class="version">
      2.40.0
  </span>
  <a href="https://raw.github.com/git/git/master/Documentation/\
           RelNotes/2.40.0.txt">Release Notes</a>
  ...
```

Our next Python script requires that you install two modules beforehand. Depending on your operating system, you'll need to use `pip` or `pip3` for this step:

```
$ pip install requests
$ pip install beautifulsoup4
```

The mini program downloads the HTML code and uses the *Beautiful Soup library* to look for the span tag. Its text property returns the desired version number. To determine the link to the release notes, parent accesses the layer above it (in this case, the div tag with the monitor class), while find looks for the first a tag in it.

```
import requests
from bs4 import BeautifulSoup
response = requests.get("https://git-scm.com/downloads")
dom = BeautifulSoup(response.content, 'html.parser')
version = dom.find('span', class_='version')
print("Git version:", version.text.strip())
url = version.parent.find('a')
print("What's new:", url.attrs['href'])
```

As I finished writing this chapter, I ran this script, which delivered the following output:

```
Git version: 2.40.0
What's new: https://raw.github.com/git/git/master/Documentation/\
            RelNotes/2.40.0.txt
```

Note that this script only works as long as the structure of the Git project page does not change. I'll discuss this basic problem of web scraping as well as various programming techniques in the Bash, PowerShell, and Python languages in Chapter 17.

2.6 Logging Weather Data (Python)

On countless sites on the internet, you can discover interesting data via what are called *REST APIs*. Many services require you to register first, however, and free use is often limited, as with *https://www.weatherapi.com*.

The following script determines the weather in Graz, Austria, and logs this information into a file called weather.csv, which has the following structure (using a semicolon as the delimiter):

```
2023-04-14 11:30;Light rain;5.0
2023-04-14 12:13;Light rain;6.0
...
```

In this example, the three columns contain the time, a short description of the weather and the temperature. The associated script performs a GET request and turns the resulting JSON data into a Python data structure. The desired data can then be easily extracted from this data structure. Like the previous example, this script also requires the requests module.

```
# Sample file log-weather.py
import requests
key = "7901xxxx"
location = "Graz"
base = "https://api.weatherapi.com/v1/current.json"
url = base + "?key=" + key + "&q=" + location
data = requests.get(url).json()
temp = data['current']['temp_c']
condition = data['current']['condition']['text']
time = data['location']['localtime']
with open("weather.csv", 'a') as f:
    f.write("%s;%s;%s\n" % (time, condition, temp))
```

You also now have the option of automating the periodic invocation of this script using cron or the Microsoft Windows Task Scheduler (see Chapter 11). You should prefix the filename weather.csv with an absolute path. For instructions on how to use REST APIs in Python and PowerShell scripts, see Chapter 18.

2.7 Microsoft Hyper-V Cleanup (PowerShell)

If you use Microsoft Hyper-V as a virtualization system, you run the risk of accumulating old snapshots that will eat up storage space. The following PowerShell script deletes all snapshots older than 30 days:

```
# Sample file delete-old-snapshots.ps1
$days = 30
$aMonthAgo = (Get-Date).AddDays(-$days)
foreach ($snapshot in Get-VMSnapshot -VMName *) {
    if ($snapshot.CreationTime -lt $aMonthAgo) {
        $vmname = $snapshot.VMName
        $snapname = $snapshot.Name
        Write-Output "Delete '$snapname' of VM '$vmname'"
        Remove-VMSnapshot -VMName $vmname -Name $snapname -Confirm
    }
}
```

The script assumes that Hyper-V is installed with all the administration tools on your Windows machine, which automatically makes the Hyper-V PowerShell module available as well. The script also requires admin rights: In other words, you must first open a PowerShell terminal as an administrator before you can run the script in it.

To be on the safe side, the cleanup script will ask for your confirmation before deleting each snapshot. These queries are omitted if you remove the -Confirm option. More examples of virtual machine administration with Hyper-V are described in Chapter 21, Section 21.3.

2.8 Statistical Analysis of a Logging File (Bash)

The starting point for this example is a log file of a web server that has been anonymized for privacy reasons. Each line of this file is structured in the following way (text wrapped for space reasons):

```
160.85.252.207 - - [05/Feb/2023:00:00:26 +0100]
  "GET /research/business/only HTTP/1.1" 200 25158
  "https://example.com/less/response/edge/policy"
  "Mozilla/5.0 ..."
```

In each case, the first column indicates the IP address from which the website was contacted. The script, which is unparalleled in its brevity, creates a list of the 20 most common IP addresses. The $1 character combination is the first parameter passed to the script.

```
# Sample file ip-address-statistic.sh
cut -d ' ' -f 1 $1 | sort | uniq -c | sort -n -r | head -n 20
```

When you analyze the sample.log file using this script, you'll get the following result:

```
$ ./ip-address-statistics.sh

   6166  65d3:f5b9:e9e5:4b1c:331b:29f3:97c1:c18f
   6048  3547:0b26:4c84:4411:0f66:945e:7741:d887
   5136  186.107.89.128
   4620  d741:a4ea:f6e1:6a17:78b1:1694:f518:c480
    ...
```

Therefore, 6,166 requests originated from IPv6 address 65d3:f5b9:...:c18f, etc. For a detailed explanation of how the cut, grep, uniq, sort, and head commands in this script work, see Chapter 8, Section 8.1.

2.9 Uploading Files to the Cloud (PowerShell)

The task for our penultimate example is to upload all image files in the current directory that have changed since the last time the script was run or that have been added since then to a bucket on the Simple Storage Service (S3) cloud service from Amazon Web Services (AWS).

This PowerShell script assumes that the AWS.Tools.Common and AWS.Tools.S3 modules are installed and that the access data for the bucket has been stored with Set-AWSCredential for profile name MyProfile (see also Chapter 20, Section 20.3).

The if construction tests whether the last-run file exists. If this file exists, the time of the last change will be read. Then, the LastWriteTime property is updated with the current time. If the file does not exist, it will be created. This script takes into account all image files since January 1, 2000.

Next, Get-ChildItem determines all image files in the current directory. Where-Object filters out files that are new or have been modified. Write-S3Object uploads these files to an S3 bucket.

```
# Sample file upload-images-to-aws.ps1
if (Test-Path -Path "last-run") {
    $lastRunTime = (Get-Item -Path "last-run").LastWriteTime
    (Get-ChildItem "last-run").LastWriteTime = Get-Date
} else {
    $lastRunTime = New-Object DateTime(2000, 1, 1)
    New-Item "last-run" | Out-Null
}
Get-ChildItem -Path "*.jpg", "*.jpeg", "*.png" |
Where-Object { $_.LastWriteTime -gt $lastRunTime } |
ForEach-Object {
    Write-S3Object -BucketName "my.aws.bucket" `
      -ProfileName "MyProfile" -File $_.Name -Key $_.Name
}
```

I must admit a little reluctantly that this script just barely exceeds the ten-line promise I made for this chapter.

2.10 Cloning Virtual Machines (Bash)

The last example is from server administration. One of my Linux servers is running the Kernel-based Virtual Machine (KVM) virtualization system. At the beginning of each semester, I create virtual machines with sequential numbers for all students attending my Linux course. For example, the ./make-vms.sh 20 44 command results in 25 clones of my base system being created, numbered vm20 through vm44.

```
# Sample file make-vms.sh
orig='vm-base'    # Name of the base VM to clone
for (( nr=$1; nr<=$2; nr++ )); do
    echo "create vm-$nr"
    disk=/var/lib/libvirt/images/vm-$nr-disk.qcow2
```

```
    virt-clone --name "vm-$nr" --original $orig \
       --mac 52:54:00:01:00:$nr --file $disk
done
```

Although this script respects the ten-line rule, I cheated a little. The "real" version of this script tests whether two parameters were really passed to the script, shuts down the source virtual machine that may still be running, sets up multiple disks and multiple network interfaces for each exercise VM, and more.

For basic principles and more details, refer to Chapter 21, Section 21.1.

Chapter 3
Bash and Zsh

3

Bash (Bourne Again Shell) is the default shell of most Linux distributions. It performs two tasks: On the one hand, it accepts commands in the terminal, executes these commands, and displays their results. On the other hand, Bash is considered *the* classic scripting programming language. In this chapter, I will only briefly discuss the interactive application; instead, I'll focus on introducing you to the main concepts behind Bash.

As an alternative to Bash, Zsh is gaining momentum. While the differences compared to Bash in script programming are negligible, Zsh scores points with many small improvements in interactive operations. Popular extensions (such as one called *Oh My Zsh*) make Zsh even more comfortable and improve its appearance. On macOS, Zsh has been the default shell since 2019. On Linux, the switch from Bash to Zsh can be made in a minute if necessary.

3.1 Terminal, Shell, and Bash

So far, some terms have appeared that I want to explain again briefly now. Let's start with the terminal: In this program, you can execute text-based commands. On Linux and macOS, the existence of the terminal was always a matter of course. While a *terminal* program is available on macOS, there are countless programs to choose from on Linux. The most common ones include `gnome-terminal`, the new console of the GNOME Project (program name `kgx`), as well as `konsole`. Even on Windows, the *Windows Terminal* is available now.

Inside the terminal, the shell is running: This shell is a program that takes your text input, executes the resulting command, and displays the result back in text form. The shell also provides a lot of additional features that are not obvious at first glance: It can redirect the results of a command to a file, link several commands together, and so on.

In the early history of Unix and Linux, shells have been developed multiple times: Bourne Shell, C Shell, Bash, Dash, Zsh, and so on. However, this chapter only deals with the two currently most popular shells—Bash and Zsh.

Why the Separation between Terminal and Shell?

The nesting of terminal and shell seems confusing at first sight. This separation stems from the fact that the terminal is only necessary when you work on a graphical desktop system. But most operating systems can also be controlled in text mode or via a network connection (SSH)—then the shell runs *without a* terminal!

The separation between terminal and shell has a further advantage in that you can combine your favorite terminal with your favorite shell, deviating from the default settings of Linux or macOS. This freedom is especially important to Linux professionals.

3.1.1 Determining the Current Shell

To determine which shell is running on your machine, you must run the `echo $SHELL` command, which displays the contents of the `$SHELL` variable that specifies the path to your account's default shell. If the shell running is Bash, you can access its version number with the second command, `bash --version`.

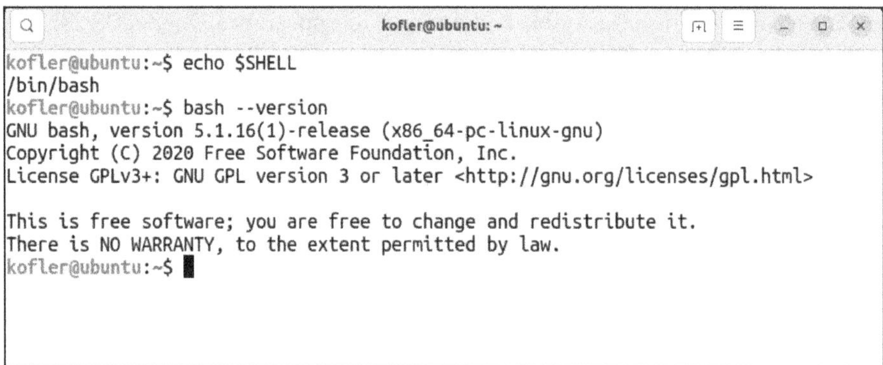

Figure 3.1 Computer Running Bash Version 5.1

3.2 Installation

Almost all Linux distributions have Bash preinstalled. Thus, if you work on Linux, this section is unnecessary. If your distribution uses Zsh, I recommend you keep using it for its interactive features. However, to develop scripts that are as portable as possible, the parallel installation of Bash is recommended. This parallel installation can be achieved with the package management command for your distribution; for example, on Debian and Ubuntu, you would use `sudo apt install bash`.

On macOS, Bash is only available in the outdated version 3.2. In future versions of macOS, Bash is expected to be removed entirely. In this respect, Zsh represents a compatible, and in many ways even better, replacement. If you prefer Bash or use it for script programming, the best approach is to set up the *Homebrew* package manager first (see *https://brew.sh*). Then, you can install Bash in the terminal using the `brew install bash` command. To start Bash, run `/opt/homebrew/bin/bash`.

The installation of Bash is only difficult on Windows. In this section, we'll present different ways you can use Bash on Windows. All of these options have their benefits and drawbacks. But let me say this first: No variant is really ideal.

3.2.1 Using Bash in a Virtual Machine

Perhaps the most straightforward way to using Bash is to install a common Linux distribution (e.g., Ubuntu) in a virtualization program (i.e., in Oracle VM VirtualBox, VMWare, or Microsoft Hyper-V). Inside the virtual machine, you'll then have Bash available in the terminal window.

For learning Bash, this solution is ideal. However, you cannot access the Windows file system via your scripts. For example, if you develop a script that processes image files, you can apply the script only to files within the Linux file system. (Some virtualization systems allow you to share a directory between Windows and the Linux virtual installation. Especially with VirtualBox, however, the procedure is quite cumbersome.)

Another disadvantage of the virtualization solution is that you're actually no longer working on Windows, but on Linux. You'll have to get used to an unfamiliar desktop and get at least a little bit into Linux administration. But you do want to learn Bash though, don't you? (From my very personal point of view, using Linux is an advantage, not a disadvantage. But I don't plan to elaborate the virtues of Linux here.)

Another argument speaks against the virtualization solution: The free and therefore correspondingly popular VirtualBox program, in my experience, often causes trouble on computers that are used for software development. This problem stems from the fact that various Hyper-V functions are active on such computers. Theoretically, VirtualBox should be compatible with it, but in real life, that's more often not the case.

3.2.2 Windows Subsystem for Linux

From my point of view, the best solution for using Bash on Windows is provided by the *Windows Subsystem for Linux (WSL)*. This function allows Linux to be run in a terminal window. What's great about this approach is that you can access your Linux files in Windows and your Windows files just as easily in WSL. (In current WSL versions, you can even run Linux in graphics mode. But for our purposes that isn't necessary at all.)

The latest version of WSL is available free of charge from the Microsoft Store. After installation, followed by a mandatory Windows restart, you must search again for *Ubuntu 22.04 LTS* (or from April 2024 for the then current version 24.04) in the Microsoft Store. The installation process and your first start should take about two minutes. You'll have to enter a password twice, and you must make sure you remember this password! You'll need it later when you want to install additional software components using sudo. (Besides Ubuntu, other distributions are also available in the Microsoft Store, including AlmaLinux, Debian, openSUSE, and Oracle Linux. Use the one you're most familiar with.)

Subsequently, you can open a window via Bash at any time in the Windows Terminal or in the **Start** menu (program name *Ubuntu n.n*).

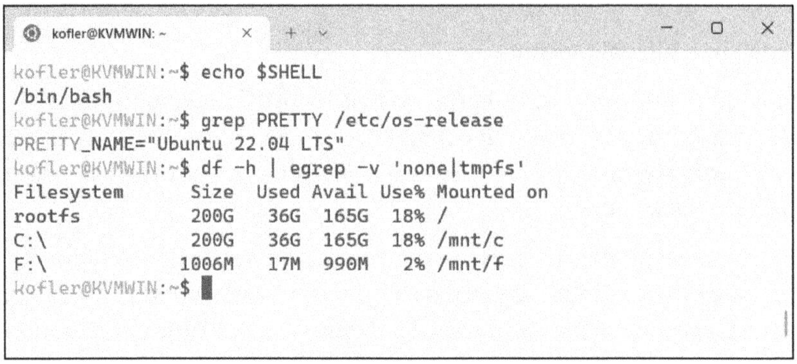

```
kofler@KVMWIN:~$ echo $SHELL
/bin/bash
kofler@KVMWIN:~$ grep PRETTY /etc/os-release
PRETTY_NAME="Ubuntu 22.04 LTS"
kofler@KVMWIN:~$ df -h | egrep -v 'none|tmpfs'
Filesystem      Size  Used Avail Use% Mounted on
rootfs          200G   36G  165G  18% /
C:\             200G   36G  165G  18% /mnt/c
F:\            1006M   17M  990M   2% /mnt/f
kofler@KVMWIN:~$
```

Figure 3.2 Ubuntu with Bash in a Terminal Window on Windows

Within Bash, you can access your Windows user directory via the following path (assuming your Windows installation is on the *C:* drive):

```
/mnt/C/Users/<name>
```

Conversely, you can find your Linux/Bash user directory in Windows Explorer via the **Linux** entry at the bottom of the sidebar or via the following address:

```
\\wsl.localhost\Ubuntu-22.04\home\<name>
```

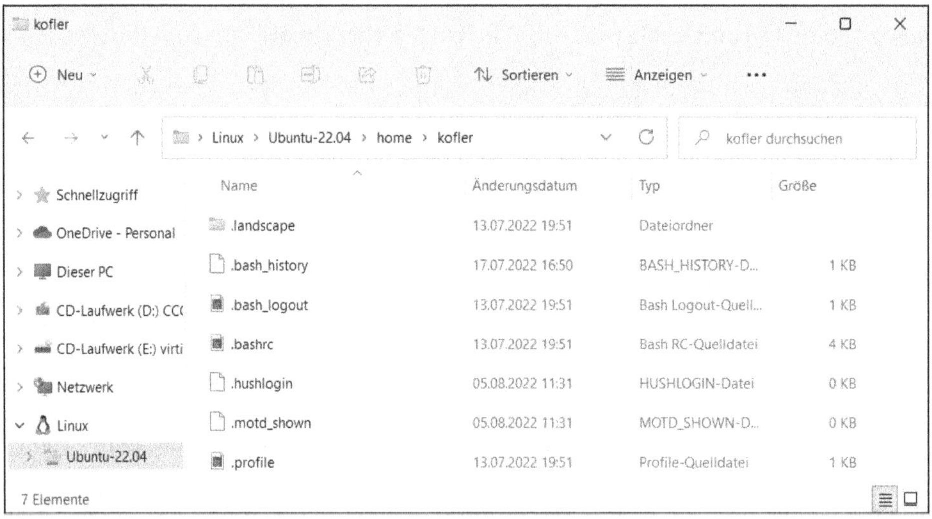

Figure 3.3 Easy Access to the Linux Home Directory in Windows Explorer

3.2.3 Git Bash

The Git version management program provides a rather elegant entry point into Bash. When you install Git on Windows (see *https://git-scm.com/download/win*), Git Bash is installed at the same time. If you work in software development, you most likely already have Git installed anyway. (You don't work without Git, do you?) Then, you can run *Git Bash* from the **Start** menu, which will open a terminal window running Bash version 4.4, which is not the latest version, but it is sufficient for our purposes.

Git Bash uses the Windows file system directly. In the Git Bash window, the most important commands are available that are also commonly used on Linux or macOS, namely, `ls`, `cat`, `less`, `more`, `find`, and `grep`, among others.

The problem with Git Bash is that you cannot install any other commands. Sooner or later (more likely sooner), you'll get to the point where you want to call a command in your script that is not part of the basic Git Bash. As far as Bash programming is concerned, you'll then hit a dead end.

3.2.4 Docker

Provided you're familiar with the Docker container system, you can also run Bash scripts in a Docker container. However, this approach is more suitable for professionals to share scripts. To learn Bash interactively, Docker is not the ideal way.

3.2.5 Bash Configuration (/etc/profile and .bashrc)

Several files affect the behavior of Bash. Most important are */etc/profile* with its global settings and *.bashrc* in your home directory with individual options. Note that when running scripts outside your account, only */etc/profile* is considered.

For normal use, you do not need to make any changes to either file. The most common reason to change one of the files after all is to call commands or programs that have been installed away from the usual directories. For this task, you must extend the `PATH` environment variable. The following example shows how you can include `/my/own/scripts` in addition to the default directories:

```
# at the end of .bashrc or /etc/profile
export PATH=/my/own/scripts:$PATH
```

3.3 Running Commands Interactively

If you're already familiar with the terminal, regardless of the operating system, you can safely skip this section. Otherwise, a good idea is to first become a little familiar with the interactive execution of commands and with the operation of the terminal before you start using your first script.

Also, later it will be the case that you try out individual commands in parallel to your script editor in a terminal window. Only when the commands work the way you want them to should you incorporate them into your script.

In the following example, you first go to the `Downloads` directory using `cd` (*change directory*) and then use `ls` (*list*) to see which files are stored in that directory:

```
$ cd Downloads
$ ls

  00a_intro_pn.pdf
  00b_about_pn.pdf
  00c_next_pn.pdf
  ...
```

`ls` with the `-l` option (*long*) shows more details about each file such as the access rights, the owner and group assignment, the size and the time of the last modification, among other things:

```
$ ls -l

  -rw-r--r-- 1 kofler kofler  674076 ... 11:49  00a_intro_pn.pdf
  -rw-r--r-- 1 kofler kofler  943948 ... 11:53  00b_about_pn.pdf
  -rw-r--r-- 1 kofler kofler  714852 ... 11:58  00c_next_pn.pdf
  ...
```

If you want to know how many files there are in the directory, you should pass the output of `ls` to `wc` (*word count*). The command returns three numbers. The first one indicates the number of lines, the second the number of words, and the third the number of characters. Since `ls` prints each file on a separate line, only the number of lines is relevant. The `wc` option `-l` (*lines*) reduces the output accordingly.

```
$ ls | wc

  116      159     3194

$ ls | wc -l

  116
```

With these trivial commands you have already learned a lot:

- The most commonly used commands in Bash have very short names. At first, these names are not very intuitive. However, once you get used to it, the typing effort is minimal.
- The behavior of commands can be controlled by options. Many options consist of only one letter, and they are preceded by a hyphen. Often, an alternative long form

exists that is preceded by *two* hyphens. For example, `wc --lines` and `wc -l` are equivalent.

- Commands can be linked with the pipe operator (|). I will discuss this operator in more detail later in Section 3.7.2. In short, `command1 | command2` means that `command1` does not display its text output but passes it to `command2` for processing.

3

The Prompt

The "prompt" is the string that is displayed to the left of the cursor when new commands are entered. On Linux, it is common for the prompt to end with the $ character for ordinary users. If, on the other hand, the system administrator `root` is working, the prompt ends with #.

The prompt is adjustable (environment variable `PS1`) and can therefore look quite different depending on the distribution and configuration. Often, the current directory and/or hostname are displayed before the $ or # character.

In this book, commands to be executed in Bash or Zsh are preceded by the $ character. (It should be clear to you by now that this character must *not* be entered.) PowerShell commands are preceded by the > character because the Windows prompt uses this character.

This chapter is a special case: Since it is clear anyway that the examples refer to Bash, I often omit the prompt altogether. I especially omit the prompt when presenting techniques that work equally well interactively in the terminal or as code in a script.

3.3.1 Operating the Terminal

You have probably already noticed that the mouse is largely useless in the terminal. You cannot use it to change the cursor position as in other programs. Entries can only be made in the last line of the terminal. (On Linux, you can mark text with a mouse and paste it with the middle mouse button at the current cursor position without copying the text to the clipboard.)

This poor mouse support is compensated by many keyboard shortcuts that enable you to edit the current input line and revert to past input (see Table 3.1).

Shortcut	Meaning
Tab	Completes a command or a name
Ctrl + A	Places the cursor at the beginning of the line
Ctrl + C	Aborts the input or stops a running command
Ctrl + D	Deletes the character at the cursor position
Ctrl + E	Places the cursor at the end of the line

Table 3.1 Keyboard Shortcuts in the Terminal

Shortcut	Meaning
Ctrl + K	Deletes everything up to the end of the line
Ctrl + R abc	Searches for a previously executed command abc
Ctrl + Y	Inserts the last deleted text again
Alt + Backspace	Deletes a word backwards

Table 3.1 Keyboard Shortcuts in the Terminal (Cont.)

The Tab shortcut is particularly useful as it saves a lot of typing: You only need to specify the first letters of a command, directory, or file, then press Tab. If the command, directory, or filename is already clearly recognizable, it is completed in full; otherwise, only until several options are eliminated. Pressing Tab twice displays a list of all possible completion values.

3.3.2 Online Help

Commands like `ls` or `wc` do not have a help menu. But help texts for these commands are available that can be read via other commands. As a first attempt, you should call `<command> --help` (for example, `ls --help`). This command will usually give you a list of all the options along with a brief explanation of what they mean.

`man <command>` displays a longer info text for many commands. Thus, `man ls` explains how to use the `ls` command and what options are available. You can navigate through the multi-page text using the cursor keys. The space bar scrolls down an entire page. Using / you can search for an expression in the help text. N jumps to the next search result if necessary, and Q closes the help interface.

3.3.3 Command Reference

Throughout this book, I will introduce you to a lot of Linux commands. A good starting point in this regard is Chapter 6.

3.4 Zsh as an Alternative to Bash

I mentioned at the start of this chapter, for the core topic of this book (i.e., for programming scripts), Zsh plays only a minor role. For compatibility reasons, a better approach is to use Bash for programming scripts, and even to forgo the use of some Bash-specific extensions over other shells. In this way, you can make your scripts really work in almost any environment.

The appeal of Zsh lies rather in its interactive application: Zsh takes an even smarter approach than Bash when expanding command, file, and directory names when you press Tab. You don't have to specify the initial letters; instead, a combination of letters that occurs somewhere in the name is sufficient. In addition, Zsh provides more configuration options and extension modules. Since I've gotten to know the comfort of Zsh in combination with the Oh My Zsh extension, "ordinary" Bash is no longer good enough for me!

3.4.1 Installation

macOS as well as selected Linux distributions already rely on Zsh by default. For all other Linux distributions, you can install Zsh effortlessly with the respective package management tool. On Debian and Ubuntu, you would use the following commands:

```
$ sudo apt update
$ sudo apt install zsh
```

In the next step, you can activate Zsh for your account:

```
$ chsh -s $(which zsh)
```

For this change to take effect, you must log out and log back in. Now, when you open a terminal for the first time, a configuration script runs once:

```
This is the Z Shell configuration function for new users,
zsh-newuser-install. (...) You can
(q) Quit and do nothing.  The function will be run again next
    time.
(0) Exit, creating the file ~/.zshrc containing just a comment.
    That will prevent this function being run again.
(1) Continue to the main menu.
(2) Populate your ~/.zshrc with the configuration recommended
    by the system administrator and exit.
```

You're not doing anything wrong if you simply take the default settings suggested by the script or the default configuration file *.zshrc* (point 2) provided by your distribution in the manual configuration (point 1). If necessary, you can repeat and adjust the configuration later via `zsh-newuser-install`.

To use Zsh on Windows, the same recommendations apply as for Bash: Install Linux in WSL or as a virtual machine and run Zsh there! The switch from Bash to Zsh can be done as we've described here.

3.4.2 Zsh Configuration (/etc/zshrc and .zshrc)

Similar to Bash, Zsh also evaluates some configuration files at startup. The most important ones are */etc/zshrc* for global settings and *.zshrc* in your home directory.

3.4.3 Oh My Zsh

For Zsh, many plugins are available on the internet that provide additional functionality, as well as themes that change the look of the command prompts. *Oh My Zsh* is a script that helps manage such extensions. Various plugins and themes are included right away and more can be added later.

To install, download a small script from the project page *https://github.com/ohmyzsh/ohmyzsh* and run it. The script requires that the `git` command from the package of the same name is available. Instead of typing the following command, you should copy the code from the Oh My Zsh GitHub page:

```
$ sh -c "$(curl -fsSL https://raw.githubusercontent.com/ohmyzsh/\
                        ohmyzsh/master/tools/install.sh)"
```

During the installation, the *.zshrc* file will be overwritten. The previous content ends up in a backup file named *.zshrc.pre-oh-my-zsh*. Oh My Zsh will test for updates at startup in the future. Accordingly, when you open a new terminal window, you're often prompted to update Oh My Zsh.

In the basic configuration, the prompt has the `robbyrussell` theme by default. As the only active plugin, `git` contributes countless aliases that help with the operation of Git. A guide to the many functions and tips for further configuration of Oh My Zsh can be found, for example, at *https://ohmyz.sh* or in the following blog: *https://stackabuse.com/pimp-my-terminal-an-introduction-to-oh-my-zsh*.

3.5 The First Bash Script

After this short excursion to Zsh, we'll now return to Bash. Before I introduce you to the syntax of Bash including various programming and working techniques in this chapter, I want to use this section to explain what a script actually is. As a matter of fact, this is quite simple: A script is a text file in which you formulate the same commands that you enter interactively in the terminal. Only two special features distinguish a script from just commands: The first line of the script must contain what's called a *shebang*, and the file must be marked as an executable using `chmod`.

3.5.1 Hash Bang (Shebang)

The first line of a script to be executed on Linux or macOS must start with the characters, `#` ("hash" or "sharp") and `!` ("bang") as well as the path of the interpreter. "Shebang" is a linguistic shortening of "sharp bang."

The interpreter is the program that reads and processes the script file, and in this chapter, that interpreter is Bash (or in exceptional cases Zsh). However, other programming languages can also be used as interpreters, such as Python or Perl.

On Linux, the Bash program is predominantly installed in the /bin directory. Thus, a Bash script starts with the following line:

```
#!/bin/bash
```


3.5.2 Shebang Variants

Depending on which distribution or Unix-like system you're working in, Bash may be installed in a different directory, such as /usr/bin. Using which bash, you can determine the location on your computer as in the following example:

```
$ which bash

  /usr/bin/bash
```

Links often make sure that both /usr/bin/bash and /bin/bash work. A general-purpose hash bang formulation that works regardless of the location uses the /usr/bin/env command. This command searches all common locations:

```
#!/usr/bin/env bash
```

If Bash is not installed on your machine at all and you're using Zsh, you'll want to replace /bin/bash with /bin/zsh (or the location where Zsh is installed on your machine):

```
#!/bin/zsh
```

If you want your script to work regardless of whether Bash or Zsh is available, the following hash bang will get you there:

```
#!/bin/sh
```

sh is a link that points to the default shell on most Linux systems. However, you must be aware that different shells will be used from now on when your script is run, depending on the computer/distribution. For example, on Debian and Ubuntu, the speed-optimized Dash will be executed. When formulating your scripts, you must be careful not to use any Bash-specific extensions that are not available in other shells.

What Now?

I know it's annoying that, in the IT world, for every rule there are three exceptions and then five special cases. Unless there are compelling reasons not to, you should always use #!/bin/bash as the hash bang. The sample files for this book also use this code.

3.5.3 Making the Script Executable (chmod +x)

All Unix-like systems including Linux and macOS store some access bits along with each file that provide information about who is allowed to read, write, and execute the file. For scripts, the execute bit (x for short) is crucial. Only with this bit can a script be executed later like a command.

To set the execute bit, you need to run the following command once in the terminal. Note that the chmod variant of macOS does not understand the +x short notation. You must explicitly specify for whom the execute bit is set. a means "for all."

```
$ chmod +x my-script-file.sh     (Linux, Git Bash)
$ chmod a+x my-script-file.sh    (macOS)
```

Thus, chmod is used to change the access bits. The command supports quite diverse syntax variants. (You can run man chmod if you're interested in the details). For us, only the chmod +x variant is relevant, for setting the execute bit.

The .sh Identifier

All Bash sample files in this book end with .sh. Although this file extension is common, using it is by no means mandatory. Bash scripts can work without an identifier (and even with a wrong identifier), provided the hash bang is correct.

Since this book covers PowerShell (.ps1) and Python (.py) in addition to Bash, the identifier helps with the assignment of the sample files.

3.5.4 Hello, World!

To write your first script, you want to launch your favorite editor: Visual Studio Code (VS Code) is a good choice, but any editor is fine, including the minimalist nano program that you can run directly in a terminal. Then, enter the following two lines:

```
#!/bin/bash
echo "Hello, World!"
```

Save this file as hello-world.sh. By using chmod, make the script executable, with the following command:

```
$ chmod  +x hello-world.sh    (Linux, Git Bash)
$ chmod a+x hello-world.sh    (macOS)
```

To check if a script works, you need to type its name and press Enter. Note that you must prefix the name with ./. In this way, you tell Bash to look for your script in the current directory. (. is a short notation for the currently active directory.)

```
$ ./hello-world.sh
  Hello, World!
```

If Script Execution Does Not Work

If the execution of a script triggers an error, various reasons may be the cause:

- Did you specify the filename correctly?
- Did you use chmod +x?
- Did you specify the hash bang line correctly?
- Is Bash not installed on your computer at all? If you want to run the script using Zsh, you need to change the hash bang to #!/bin/zsh or #!/bin/sh.

3.5.5 Elementary Syntax Rules

Besides the hash bang, you must follow a few other rules in your scripts:

- Lines beginning with # are comments and are not evaluated.
- You can use the \ character for long commands that run across multiple lines. The \ character must be placed exactly at the end of the line, and no more spaces may follow!
- Code indentation is allowed but is optional.
- Bash is extremely picky about the use of spaces in code. s="abc" is correct; the variants s ="abc" or s= "abc" as well as s = "abc" are all wrong and will trigger errors!

  Conversely, in some cases, spaces are required before or after parentheses for Bash to recognize the construct correctly. If your script does not work as expected and the error messages are vague or misleading, you should first check the use of spaces!

3.5.6 A "Real" Example: Backup Script

Of course, you're not reading this book to run "Hello World!" scripts. This second example is a bit longer, but it performs a real task: It creates a compressed backup of all files in your documents directory and stores the backup in the mybackups directory:

```
#!/bin/bash
# Sample file backup-documents.sh
# Save the contents of this directory
documentdir=~/documents
# Backup location
backupdir=~/mybackups
# Create backup directory
mkdir -p $backupdir
# returns e.g., date=27 for 2023-03-27
day=$(date '+%d')
# Create backup, save as documents-<day>.tar.gz
echo "Backup file: $backupdir/documents-$day.tar.gz"
tar czf $backupdir/documents-$day.tar.gz -C $documentdir .
```

This script requires some explanation:

- `documentdir=~/documents` stores the name of your documents directory in the `documentdir` variable. ~ is a short notation for your home directory (e.g., `/home/kofler` on Linux, but `/Users/kofler` on macOS).

  Depending on the operating system or distribution you use, you'll need to use the English word `Documents`. When macOS displays `Documents` in the Finder with a German language setting, the real directory name is actually `Documents`!
- `backupdir=~/mybackups` stores the desired backup location in another variable.
- `mkdir -p $backupdir` creates the backup directory. The `-p` option prevents error messages if the directory already exists (which is the case after the second execution of the script at the latest).
- `day=$(date '+%d')` stores the day of the month in the `day` variable. `date` is a command which normally returns the whole date including time. Using the additional parameter `+%d` you supply only the day of the month (`01` to `31`) instead.

  The notation `$(...)` means: Execute the command contained in the parentheses and return the result.
- The `echo` command outputs the exact path of the new backup file on the screen. The output is just feedback for you to understand that the script works as intended.

  Note that you must specify variable names without `$` when assigning them but prefix them with `$` when reading them. This is one of the many strange syntax rules of Bash.
- Finally, the `tar` command creates a backup of all files in the `$documentdir` directory. The syntax of this command is also weird:
  - `czf` specifies what the command is supposed to do (*create, zip, file*). The next parameter specifies the location of the backup file, for example, `/home/kofler/documents-27.tar.gz`.
  - `-C` determines which directory is to be active during the execution of `tar`. In this example, it should not be the currently active directory, but the directory where the files to be backed up are located.
  - A `.` at the end of the command means that the entire contents of the directory must be backed up (and not just selected files, which would also be conceivable).

  A more detailed description of the important `tar` options follows in Chapter 6, Section 6.3.

If you run this script once a day, after some time, you'll have 31 backup versions in the `mybackups` directory, from `documents-01.tar.gz` to `documents-31.tar.gz`. While this script is a bit wasteful, it does give you the ability to recover any documents that were mistakenly overwritten or deleted within the last month. (I'll show you how to automate daily backups in Chapter 11. I describe other variants for performing backups in Chapter 15.)

For starters, this example might have been bit much all at once. But don't worry, a lot of basic information follows in the course of this chapter, which makes this code easier to understand. My primary goal in this example was simply to show you what "real" scripts look like.

Sample Files

This script, along with all the other longer listings, can be found in the sample files for this book. You can download these files at *https://rheinwerk-computing.com/5851.*

3.5.7 Running Scripts without ./

Do you find it annoying that you always must prepend ./ when running scripts (or even the full path if you're currently in a different directory)? There is a solution to this!

- **Custom script directory**
  First, you need to set up a separate directory for your scripts, for example, `myscripts` in your home directory.
- **Extend the PATH variable**
  Second, you want to add the full path for this directory to the `PATH` environment variable. By default, `PATH` contains various directories in which Bash searches for commands. So, when you run `ls`, Bash searches all the directories contained in `PATH` in sequence. If `PATH` also contains `myscripts`, then this directory will also be searched.

  To change `PATH`, you can use an editor to open the `.bashrc` file in your home directory (or `.zshrc` if you use Zsh). At the end of this file, you must add the following line:

  ```
  # at the end of .bashrc or .zshrc
  ...
  export PATH=/home/kofler/myscripts:$PATH
  ```

  Instead of `/home/kofler/myscripts`, you must of course specify the full path to your own script directory. Also pay attention to the correct syntax! No spaces must exist before and after `=` and :. Note also that `PATH` is written without the `$` character the first time, but with the `$` character the second time.

  For this change to take effect, you must log out and log back in. From now on, you can run scripts stored in this directory simply by naming them.

3.6 Running Commands

Now that you've had a chance to get a little acquainted with Bash or Zsh, the next sections will cover the basics. I am generally referring to Bash, but almost all of the information applies in the same way to Zsh.

One more note before things really get going: All the techniques explained in the following sections apply equally to the interactive use of Bash as well as to scripting!

3.6.1 Serial Execution

In the simplest case—as in the backup example in the previous section—a script consists of a sequence of commands that are executed in sequence:

```
# Execute commands one after the other
command1
command2
command3
```

You can also specify multiple commands, separated by semicolons, on a single line. This approach saves space and is especially handy when using Bash interactively, when you want to complete several time-consuming tasks in succession without typing a new command each time:

```
# equivalent
command1; command2; command3
```

3.6.2 Conditional Command Execution

Each command returns a normally invisible error code. 0 means that no error has occurred. Any other value indicates an error or a negative result. The term "error" is actually too strong, depending on the context: For instance, if a condition formulated with the `test` command does not apply or if the `grep` filter command does not find the search term, the command is considered unsuccessfully executed and returns a return code not equal to 0.

Bash allows you to make the execution of the second command dependent on the result of the first one. The first variant uses the character combination `&&`. It expresses that the second command should be executed only if the first one was successful. (Similarly, you can of course link three or more commands in this way.)

```
# Run command 2 only if command 1 was successful
command1 && command2
```

Using `&&` makes sense, for example, when the first command runs a test (does the file exist?) and the second command should run only on a positive test result.

Another example: You want to perform an update. First, you update the package sources (via `apt update` in Debian or Ubuntu). Not until this process succeeds without errors will the actual update be performed in the second step (`apt full-upgrade`). If, on the other hand, an error occurs during `apt update`, for example, because the internet disconnects for a moment, executing the second command is pointless.

```
# tests whether data.csv exists and then
# returns a corresponding message from
test -f data.csv && echo "data.csv exists"

# Update package sources;
# if successful, then perform the
# actual update
apt update && apt full-upgrade
```

As an alternative to &&, you can also link two commands via ||. In that case, an inverse logic applies: Command 2 does not get executed until command 1 causes an error:

```
# Execute command 2 only if command 1 fails
command1 || command2
```

Instead of && and ||, you can of course use `if` constructs, which I am going to introduce in Section 3.11 on branching. However, && and || allow you to formulate more compact code that is more similar to the style of traditional shell scripts.

3.6.3 Running Commands in the Background

Usually, the execution of a command blocks the terminal or the script. The subsequent command cannot be started until the preceding command is finished. What can help you in this case is `command &` to run a command in the background (i.e., asynchronously).

The asynchronous execution of commands is rarely useful in scripts. Much more often, you'll need % during interactive operation in the terminal. For example, you can use `command &` to start a program with a graphical user interface (GUI), such as the Firefox web browser, without blocking further input in the terminal.

A process running in the background can be made a foreground process again using `fg`. Conversely, a time-consuming command can be interrupted via `Ctrl` + `Z` and then continued in the background using `bg`.

3.6.4 Running Commands in a Subshell

By placing multiple commands in parentheses, you can start a new shell process for their execution and run the commands there. This subshell can be created in a single line using `(c1; c2; c3)`. In scripts, you can place the brackets wherever you like:

```
command1   # run in main shell
(          # run the following commands in a subshell
command2
command3
command4
)
command5   # in the main shell again
```

Within the subshell, all previously defined variables are still available. However, subshells have an advantage in that variables defined and changed within a subshell only apply in that subshell and then loses its validity or resumes its previous value. Likewise, a directory changed by using `cd` is only valid within the subshell. When the subshell ends, the previously valid directory becomes active again.

Subshells can be used to better structure the code. When you run `exit` within a subshell, you only exit the subshell, not the script running in the main shell.

3.7 Standard Input and Standard Output

In Bash, there are three "channels" that use commands for input and output:

- **Standard output (`stdout`)**
  Results of a command are directed to the what's called the "standard output." When you run `ls`, the result of this command is the list of all files in the local directory. This result is output as text and is typically displayed in the terminal.
- **Error messages (standard error = `stderr`)**
  Usually, error messages are also displayed in the terminal. Internally, however, error messages are routed to a different channel, resulting in the possibility of treating normal output and error messages differently.
- **Standard input (`stdin`)**
  Many commonly used variables process text files whose name is passed as a parameter. If this specification is missing, the command expects the text to be processed from the standard input. So, you must enter text in the terminal, which the command then receives. To express that the input is complete, press [Ctrl] + [D] in this case.

At first glance, the three standard channels seem to be self-evident: Where else than in the terminal should a command display its results, where else than by your input should a command receive input?

3.7.1 Redirecting Input and Output

One highlight of Bash is its ability to redirect input and output. Using the `command > file` call, you can save the result of a command in a text file. Caution: If the file already exists, it will be overwritten.

Similarly, `command < file` reads the data to be processed from a text file instead of waiting for terminal input. Table 3.2 summarizes the syntax for some other variants. I will discuss heredoc and herestring syntax in more detail in Section 3.10.

Command	Function
`command > out.txt`	Saves the standard output to the file
`command >> out.txt`	Adds the output to the end of the file
`command 2> errors.txt`	Stores error messages in the file
`command &> all.txt`	Stores outputs and errors in the file
`command >& all.txt`	As above
`command >&2`	Redirects the standard output to the error channel
`command < in.txt`	Processes the file
`command << EOF`	Considers all lines up to end of file (EOF) as standard input (heredoc)
`command <<< $var`	Considers the content of the variable as standard input (herestring)

Table 3.2 Operators for Redirecting Input and Output

In the simplest case, output redirection is used to store results permanently:

```
ls  > filelist.txt
```

Input redirection is useful for interactive commands. For example, the MySQL client `mysql` typically expects SQL commands to be entered. In the following applications, these commands are read from a text file, for example, to restore a database from a backup:

```
mysql < backup.sql
```

The `cat` command, which normally simply prints a text file to the screen, can be used to create a new file (ending with a key combination to stop the input):

```
cat > newfile.txt
  first input line
  second input line
  <Ctrl>+<D>
```

Because `cat` is missing the parameter with the file to be output, the command expects interactive input at the terminal. This input is redirected to the `newfile.txt` file. Using this trick, you can create small text files without launching an editor.

Caution

However, you cannot read and write a file at the same time. The `sort < file > file` command does not sort the contents of the text file and then save the result, but instead deletes `file` because `> file` is run first.

Heredoc Syntax

A special case of input redirection is the heredoc syntax. I'll discuss this topic separately in Section 3.10.

3.7.2 The Pipe Operator

We are not quite done with input and output redirection yet. Perhaps the coolest feature is still missing: By using `command1 | command2`, `command1` produces a result. However, this result is not displayed but redirected to `command2`. The pipe operator `|` thus makes the standard output of `command1` the standard input of `command2`. The pipe operator can be applied multiple times, each time passing the output of one command to the next command.

The pipe operator results in such a wide range of options for analyzing and processing text files that I have dedicated Chapter 8 to this topic. At this point, a few simple examples will have to suffice, which in this case refer to the Linux-specific `/etc/passwd` file. This file contains information about all accounts of the system. I will explain the `grep`, `cut`, `sort`, and `head` commands in more detail in Chapter 8, Section 8.1.

```
# displays all lines from /etc/passwd that contain 'nologin'
grep nologin /etc/passwd

# extracts the first column
# with the account name from the resulting lines
grep nologin /etc/passwd | cut -d ':' -f 1
# sorts the names
grep nologin /etc/passwd | cut -d ':' -f 1 | sort

# and displays the first five results
grep nologin /etc/passwd | cut -d ':' -f 1 | sort | head -n 5
```

3.7.3 Redirecting and Displaying Outputs at the Same Time

The `tee` command duplicates the standard input, displays it in the standard output, *and* redirects it to a file. Thus, using the following command, the result of `command` is displayed in the terminal *and* stored in the `out.txt` file.

```
command | tee out.txt
```

3.8 Globbing, Brace Extension, and Handling File and Directory Names

What happens if you pass `*.txt` or `directory??/*.pdf` to a command because you want to process all text files or all PDF files in a couple of subdirectories? The term "globbing" describes the mechanisms Bash provides for such tasks. Table 3.3 summarizes the meaning of Bash's "wildcard characters." (These characters are a simplified variant of the "regular expressions" that you'll get to know in Chapter 9.)

Character	Meaning
?	Any character
*	Any number (also zero) of any characters
**	Recursive globbing (globstar)
[aeiou]	One of the specified characters
[a-z]	Character range
[a-zäöüß]	All lowercase letters (in German)
[A-Fa-f0-9]	One hexadecimal digit
[!a-f]	None of the characters from a to f
[^a-f]	None of the characters from a to f

Table 3.3 Globbing Characters

What is crucial about these wildcards is that globbing is the responsibility of Bash and not of the respective command. So, for example, if you run `cp *.jpg some/directory/` to copy some images to a subdirectory, Bash—*not* the `cp` command—determines the list of files to copy. This situation makes sense because otherwise almost every command would need corresponding code. But because Bash is responsible, the analysis of characters like * or ? is done centrally and always according to the same rules: Bash first analyzes all globbing characters, matches them with the filenames in the current directory, and then passes the completed list of parameters to the relevant command. `cp` thus never sees `*.jpg`, only the completed list of filenames, such as `img_1.jpg`, `img_2.jpg`, and `img_3.jpg`.

If you're unsure about which filename list is returned by a globbing expression, you should run `echo <expression>`, for example:

```
echo img_*.raw
  img_23433.raw img_23434.raw img_23435.raw
```

Zsh is even more convenient in this respect: There, you can simply press Tab to replace the globbing expression with the filenames that match in the current directory.

If you want to prevent globbing, you should put the character combination in simple quotation marks. Perhaps you have created a file whose filename is ???. (Not a good idea, but an allowed filename.) To delete this file, run `rm '???'`.

No Globbing Results

Globbing only works if there is at least *one* matching file. If there is no JPG file at all in the current directory, then the evaluation of `*.jpg` is useless. Bash then passes the original string to `cp`. The command searches for a file that's exactly named `*.jpg`. This file cannot be found, so `cp` returns the error message, *file not found*.

You can prevent such errors using `shopt -s nullglob`. The `nullglob` option causes the pattern to be removed if no files match. However, `cp *.jgp some/path/` triggers an error even then, this time because only one parameter was passed to the command (there must be at least two).

3.8.1 Recursive Globbing

The ** character combination recursively covers all (sub)directories. Thus, `ls **/*.pdf` has a similar meaning as the search command `find . -name '*.pdf'`. Because recursive searching of all directories can take a lot of time, this behavior is disabled by default. Before you can use this function, you must activate it via `shopt -s globstar`. The following example copies all PDF files to the `all-my-pdfs` directory:

```
shopt -s globstar
mkdir all-my-pdfs
cp **/*.pdf all-my-pdfs
```

3.8.2 Access to Important Directories

Aside from globbing rules, short notations are available for accessing frequently needed directories (see Table 3.4).

Character	Meaning
.	The current directory
..	The parent directory
~	Your own home directory
~name	The home directory of name

Table 3.4 Short Notations for Important Directories

3.8.3 Brace Extension

In Bash, you can formulate enumerations separated by commas or ranges created via `..` in curly brackets. Before the command gets executed, all possible combinations are created, so the expression specified in parentheses is "expanded." Unlike globbing, however, the brace extension does not consider whether corresponding files already exist or not. The easiest way to understand the mechanism is by looking at some examples:

```
echo {a..f}.txt
  a.txt b.txt c.txt d.txt e.txt f.txt

echo /{etc,usr,var}
  /etc /usr /var

echo {1..3}{a,e,i,o,u}
  1a 1e 1i 1o 1u 2a 2e 2i 2o 2u 3a 3e 3i 3o 3u
```

At first glance, brace extensions seem like a gimmick. However, applications do indeed exist: Imagine you want to create a subdirectory for each month of the current year (determined via `date '+%Y'`). In Bash, this task is a one-liner:

```
mkdir -p $(date '+%Y')/{01..12}
```

In this case, `$(date ...)` returns the result of this command. Not only does the `-p` option with `mkdir` cause individual directories to be created, but also entire directory strings if required (for the year 2023, therefore, first `2023` and then `01`, `02`, etc.).

The brace extension can also be used to create loops, with `i` being a variable in this case. Basic principles about variables and loops will follow in Section 3.9 and in Section 3.12:

```
for i in {1..10}; do echo $i; done
  1
  2
  ...
```

3.8.4 Filenames and Directory Names with Spaces

In Bash, parameters passed to a command are separated by spaces. `cp a.txt b.txt /my/directory` copies the files `a.txt` and `b.txt` into one directory.

This behavior becomes an issue if files themselves contain spaces. (Die-hard Linux users do their best to avoid this case!) For instance, `cp filename with blanks.txt /my/directory` thinks you want to copy the three files `filename`, `with` and `blanks.txt`, and does not recognize that `filename with blanks.txt` is *one* file. To clarify this ambiguity, you need to put the name in question in quotation marks, such as:

```
cp "filename with blanks.txt" /my/directory
```

Although at this point it is again an anticipation of the loops that have not yet been discussed at all (Section 3.12): The quotation marks are also necessary if you process files automatically. Thus, the globbing expression `*.txt` may well provide filenames with spaces. The following loop, which should simply display detailed information about each corresponding file, then triggers errors:

```
# triggers errors if *.txt file contains spaces
for fn in *.txt; do ls -l $fn; done
```

The code does not work correctly until you enclose the fn variable in quotes in the ls command:

```
# correct variant of the previous example
for fn in *.txt; do ls -l "$fn"; done
```

The situation gets even more complicated if the parameters passed to a Bash script are to be analyzed and filenames with spaces exist. Correct processing will only succeed if you change the Bash variable IFS upfront (Section 3.9 and Section 3.12).

3.9 Variables

Dealing with variables in Bash takes some getting used to, especially if you have worked in other, "higher-level" programming languages. I want to start with three basic rules:

- Variable names must usually be preceded by a dollar sign when analyzed (when reading), but not when assigned (when writing). As you'll see, exceptions to this rule exist.
- With the myvar=value assignment, no blanks are allowed before and after the = character.
- Bash variables usually store strings. (Yes, Bash can also handle numbers and even supports arrays. But these are special cases, some of which require syntactic acrobatics.)

The first example illustrates the handling of variables. Explanations of the if construct with the -gt comparison operator (*greater than*) follow in Section 3.11.

```
myvar="123"
myvar='123'            # equivalent here
myvar=123              # equivalent here
echo $myvar            # output: 123
echo "Inhalt: $myvar"  # output: Content: 123
if [ $myvar -gt 100 ]; then
  echo "myvar is greater than 100"
fi
```

3.9.1 Initializing and Deleting Variables

When assigning variables, you can use var="abc" or also var='abc' to clarify the string character. Syntactically, quotes are only required if the expression to be stored contains spaces or other special characters, for example, for var="abc efg" or var='$x'.

I'll explain the difference between the two quotation marks in Section 3.10. In short, `"abc $myvar abc"` inserts the contents of the `myvar` variable (as in the previous `echo` command), while `'abc $myvar abc'` takes the string unchanged.

If you want to store the result of another command in a variable, you must use the notation `myvar=$(command)`. The somewhat bulky name for the `$(...)` expression is *command substitution* because the specified command is executed and replaced by its contents. Alternatively, the equivalent formulation with backticks is allowed (i.e., ``myvar=`command` ``).

To delete a variable, you can run `unset myvar` or simply assign no content (i.e., `myvar=`).

3.9.2 Declaring Variables

In Bash, you don't need to `declare` variables before using them—and yet a `declare` command exists. This command allows you to influence the behavior of variables, as in the following example:

```
# constant, cannot be changed later (r = readonly)
declare -r const="abc"

# myvar can only store integers (i = integer)
declare -i myvar
myvar="abc"    # no error, but myvar=0

# normal and associative array (details to follow)
declare -a myarray
declare -A mymap
```

3.9.3 Performing Calculations in Bash

Bash "thinks" in terms of character strings. Calculations or the analysis of mathematical expressions are only possible in a special context using `let` or within double parentheses (see Table 3.5). All mathematical calculations use only integers as a matter of principle.

Expression	Meaning
`((expression))`	Runs the contained mathematical expression
`$((expression))`	As above, but returns a result
`let myvar=expression`	Stores the result of the expression in a variable

Table 3.5 Mathematics in Bash

Mathematical Operators

Note that mathematical operators such as + and *, but also comparison operators such as < or >=, are only allowed in the context of the expressions listed in Table 3.5. In particular, < and > are usually used in Bash for input and output redirection.

The following lines contain some examples of mathematical expressions in Bash. In the process, some otherwise common rules have been softened. For example, within `((...))`, assignments also work with spaces before and after `=`. (But not with `let`!) In addition, you are permitted to omit the preceding $ character when reading variables.

```
x=2
y=$x+3              # caution, wrong: y contains "2+3"!
let y=x+3           # y=5, x can be analyzed without $
((y=x+3))           # equivalent
(( y = x + 3 ))     # equivalent, within (( ... ))
                    # spaces are allowed
y=$((x+3))          # equivalent
y=$(( x + 3 ))      # equivalent
(( y++ ))           # y=6
echo $(( y > 10 )) # does not apply (false)
  0
echo $(( y < 10 )) # applies (true)
  1
```

3.9.4 Arrays

Besides simple variables, Bash also can deal with arrays. Ordinary arrays use integers as index. Note the `${field(n)}` syntax for accessing the *n*th element, which differs from many other programming languages.

```
x=()              # Definition of an empty array
x[0]='a'          # assign array elements
x[1]='b'
x[2]='c'

x=('a' 'b' 'c')   # short notation for the above 4 lines

echo ${x[1]}      # read an array element
echo ${x[@]}      # read all array elements
```

Bash versus Zsh

I have pointed out several times in this chapter that Bash and Zsh are compatible with each other in their basic functions.

One of the few exceptions in this context concerns array indices. While these range from 0 to the total element count minus 1 in Bash, the first array element in Zsh has an index of 1! Index 0 is not allowed (unless you enable the KSH_ARRAYS option). You can find relevant background information on this topic at *https://stackoverflow.com/questions/50427449*.

You can use `mapfile` to read an entire text file line by line into the elements of an array. In the following example, `z` is the name of the variable:

```
mapfile z < textfile
```

To initialize the elements of an array with the columns of a line, the best approach is to use the `read` command via the `-a` array option. Details on `read` as well as on herestrings formulated with `<<<` follow in Section 3.10.

```
data="abc efg ijk opq uvw"
read -a myvar <<< $data
echo ${myvar[2]}  # output ijk
```

If the columns or "words" of a string are not separated by whitespace, you need to temporarily modify the *internal field separator* contained in the predefined `IFS` variable. By default, this variable contains a space character, a tab character, and a newline character (i.e., the three most important whitespace characters).

In the following example, however, the words are separated by the `:` character. Because the `IFS` declaration is made on the same line as the `read` command, the change applies only to that one command. As a result, afterwards, `IFS` has the default setting again. (This scenario is important because `IFS` has implications for many commands.)

```
data="abc:efg:ijk lmn:opq:uvw"
IFS=':' read -a myvar <<< $data
echo ${myvar[2]}  # output ijk lmn
```

Besides ordinary arrays, Bash also knows associative arrays. Instead of numbers, any character strings are allowed as indexes. Depending on the programming language, you may also know this data structure as a dictionary or map. To use associative arrays, you must explicitly `declare` the variable using `declare -A`.

```
declare -A y        # Definition of an empty associative array
y['abc']='123'      # Assign element of associative array
y['efg']='xxx'
y=( [abc]=123 [efg]=xxx )     # Short notation
echo ${y[abc]}                # Read an array element
```

3.9.5 Predefined Variables

Bash scripts can access predefined variables (see Table 3.6). These variables can only be read, but not changed. The abbreviation PID stands for *process ID* (i.e., the internal process number).

Variable	Meaning
$#	Number of parameters passed to the script
$0	Filename of the executed script
$1 to $9	Parameters 1 to 9
${10}, ${11}	Access to additional parameters
$* or $@	Totality of all passed parameters
$?	Return value of the last command
$!	PID of the last started background process
$$	PID of the current shell

Table 3.6 Predefined Bash Variables

In practice, the analysis of the parameters passed to a script is particularly important. Their number is indicated by `$#`. You can access the individual parameters via `$1`, `$2`, and so on. Examples of the analysis of many parameters in loops or via `case` constructs are included in Section 3.11 and Section 3.12.

3.9.6 Environment Variables

Ordinary variables lose their validity after the execution of a script. Environment variables declared or modified using `export myvar=...` are excluded from this rule. `printenv` lists all environment variables with their current value. Important environment variables (see Table 3.7) are preset in `/etc/profile`, in `.profile`, and in `.bashrc` or `.zshrc`.

Variable	Meaning
HOME	The home directory
LANG	Localization settings (i.e., language and character set)
PATH	Directories in which programs are searched for
PS1	Content/appearance of the command prompt
PWD	The current directory

Table 3.7 Important Environment Variables

Variable	Meaning
USER	The login name of the active user
SHELL	Name of the active shell
EDITOR	Name of the default editor (often vi or nano)
IFS	Internal field separator (decomposition of strings into words)

Table 3.7 Important Environment Variables (Cont.)

Unlike "ordinary" variables, environment variables can be changed using `ENVVAR=... command` only for the execution of a command. I gave an example of this earlier when reading parts of a string into an array:

```
# the modified IFS content applies only to read
IFS=':' read -a myvar
```

Another common use looks as follows:

```
# execute the command without the current language settings
LANG= command
```

This command deletes the `LANG` environment variable with the language settings only for the execution of `command`. `command` is therefore executed without the otherwise valid language settings and returns error messages in English if necessary. (English is the default language when `LANG` is empty. English error messages are useful when searching the internet for the cause of a problem.) `LANG` does not get permanently deleted, however, but is available again for the other commands.

No Temporary Change for Bash Flow Structures

The `ENVVAR=... command` syntax can only be used for ordinary commands, but not for loops or branches that you initiate using `if`, `for`, `while`, and so on.

3.10 Strings

Strings are the central data type of Bash—I already mentioned that several times. Nevertheless, the handling of strings sometimes seems strange. This section summarizes the most important functions with regard to strings.

3.10.1 Single versus Double Quotation Marks

In Bash, strings can be placed in both single and double quotation marks:

- 'abc$efg': In this case, the string will be transferred exactly.
- "abc$efg": In this variant, Bash replaces variables contained in the text ($efg in this case) with its contents and may also perform other substitution procedures, which I will explain later in this section.

In Bash, multiple strings can be concatenated without an operator. The only requirement is that Bash can recognize the strings as such, which is not the case in the first line of the following listing:

```
x=abc efg           # Error!
x=abc               # OK
x="abc"             # better
x='abc'             # here equivalent
y="123"$x"456"      # -> 123abc456
y='123'$x'456'      # -> 123abc456
y="123 $x 456"      # -> 123 abc 456
y='123 $x 456'      # -> 123 $x 456
y=123 $x 456        # Error!
```

You are allowed to distribute strings across multiple lines. To preserve the line breaks in the output via echo, you must enclose the variable in quotes (see also the following section):

```
myvar='1st Line
2nd Line'
echo "$myvar"
```

3.10.2 Outputting Strings (echo)

Of course, you already know the echo command for outputting strings:

```
myname="Michael"
echo "Hello, $myname!"
  Hello, Michael!
```

At this point, I would like to point out some peculiarities of echo. You can use the -n option to prevent echo from starting a new line after the output. In this way, you can distribute the output of one line across several commands, as in the following example:

```
echo -n "Hello, "
echo $myname
```

The -e option enables you to achieve that backslash sequences contained in the string are interpreted correctly (i.e., that the \ and n characters are recognized as line breaks):

```
myvar="abc\nefg"
echo $myvar
  abc\nefg
echo -e $myvar
  abc
  efg
```

The handling of real line breaks is also confusing. These line breaks can be replaced by blanks using `echo $myvar`. Only `echo "$myvar"` with quotes returns a multiline output:

```
myvar="abc
efg"
echo $myvar
  abc efg
echo "$myvar"
  abc
  efg
```

You redirect the error message to the `stderr` channel using `>&2`:

```
echo "Error message" >&2
echo >&2 "Error message"   # equivalent
```

printf

The `printf` function, known from many programming languages, is available as a command on Linux and macOS. The `printf` function is better suited than `echo` to format output. Syntax details can be shown via `man 1 printf`.

3.10.3 Colors

You can also output text in color. To change the color, you need to include what are called *ANSI escape sequences* in the output. To change the background color, you must replace `3n` with `4n`.

Color	Code	Color	Code
Black	0;30	Gray	1;30
Blue	0;34	Light blue	1;34
Green	0;32	Light green	1;32
Cyan	0;36	Light cyan	1;36

Table 3.8 ANSI Color Codes for Foreground Colors

Color	Code	Color	Code
Red	0;31	Light red	1;31
Purple	0;35	Pink	1;35
Brown	0;33	Yellow	1;33
Light gray	0;37	White	1;37

Table 3.8 ANSI Color Codes for Foreground Colors (Cont.)

Color codes must be placed between the control sequences `\033[` and `m`. To prevent your code from becoming completely unreadable, a best practice is to store the color codes in variables. `echo` processes color codes correctly only if you use the `-e` option. The notation `${var}` instead of `$var` is useful in this context to separate variable names from the rest of the text without spaces.

```
BLUE='\033[0;34m'
RED='\033[0;31m'
NOCOLOR='\033[0m'
echo -n -e "Text output in ${RED}Red${NOCOLOR} "
echo    -e "and ${BLUE}Blue${NOCOLOR}."
```

The actual appearance of the colors will vary depending on the terminal configuration. For instance, instead of displaying colors brighter (e.g., `1;34` for light blue), the output might be in the basic color, but with bold type, depending on the terminal. A reference for other codes that you can also use to change the cursor position can be found at *https://en.wikipedia.org/wiki/ANSI_escape_code* or at *https://tldp.org/HOWTO/Bash-Prompt-HOWTO/c327.html*.

Poor Readability, Difficult Further Processing

The use of colors has its disadvantages. On the one hand, readability may suffer as a result, especially since you cannot rely on a specific background color in the terminal. Many users use terminals with a dark background; others prefer a light or even white background.

In addition, color codes make further processing of text output more difficult. If you decide to use colors, you should provide an option to disable this feature if necessary.

3.10.4 Entering or Reading Character Strings (read)

The easiest way to perform interactive input redirection is to use `read`. For users to know what they need to enter, you should perform an output beforehand using `echo`. Adding `-n` causes the cursor to stop after the output, as in the following example:

```
echo -n "Please enter your name: "
read myvar
echo "The name is: $myvar"
```


`read` can also be used in combination with input redirection to read a file line by line. A corresponding example follows in the next section.

`read -a myarray` reads a line and stores its words in elements of the specified array variable.

Help for the read Command

`read` is an internal `bash` command. Details about the various `read` options are therefore provided by `help read` and not, as is usually the case, by `man read`.

3.10.5 Substitution and Expansion Mechanisms

Bash contains various "substitution or expansion mechanisms," although these terms are largely synonymous and are used inconsistently in the documentation. In any case, an expression introduced with `$` is replaced by its content or analysis:

- **`$myvar` or `${myvar}`**
  By far the most important one is *variable substitution*, which you have already seen in several examples. The alternate `${myvar}` notation is useful if the variable name is to be delimited from further text (e.g., `${myvar}txt`).
- **`$(command)` or `` `command` ``**
  In the case of *command substitution*, discussed earlier in Section 3.9.1, the command is executed and replaced by its result (i.e., standard output).
- **`$((mathexpression))`**
  In *arithmetic substitution*, the mathematical expression contained in double parentheses is analyzed and replaced by its result.
- **`${__var__}`**
  By means of the what's called *parameter substitution*, Bash provides some options to process the string contained in the variable. The expression returns the result. Instead of ___, you specify various special characters that are unfortunately difficult to memorize, which I will discuss through examples next.

3.10.6 Parameter Substitution

Bash lacks the string handling functions common in other programming languages. For this purpose, Bash has some quite efficient mechanisms under the term *parameter substitution*, which extract information from character strings that is stored in variables. Note that all constructs return a result, but never directly modify the specified variable:

- **${var:n}**
  Prints the string stored in var starting from the *n*th character, counting from 0:

  ```
  var="abcdefghij"
  echo ${var:3}        # output defghij
  ```

- **${var:offset:len}**
  Skips offset characters and then outputs len characters:

  ```
  var="abcdefghij"
  echo ${var:5:3}      # output fgh
  ```

- **${var:-default}**
  If the variable is empty, the construct returns the default setting as a result, otherwise the content of the variable. The variable does not get changed.

  ```
  var=
  echo ${var:-abc}     # output abc
  var=123
  echo ${var:-abc}     # output 123
  ```

- **${var:=default}**
  As above, but at the same, time the content of the variable will be changed if it was empty before.

- **${var:+new}**
  If the variable is empty, it remains empty. If, on the other hand, the variable is already being used, the previous content is replaced by a new setting. The construct provides the new content of the variables.

- **${var:?errormessage}**
  If the variable is empty, the variable name and the error message are output, and the shell program is then terminated. Otherwise, the construct returns the content of the variable.

- **${#var}**
  Returns the number of characters stored in the variable as a result or 0 if the variable is empty. The variable does not get changed.

  ```
  x='abcde'
  echo ${#x}         # output 5
  ```

- **${var#pattern}**
  Compares the beginning of the variable with the specified pattern. If the pattern is recognized, the construct returns the contents of the variable minus the shortest possible text that matches the search pattern. If, on the other hand, the pattern is not found, the entire contents of the variable are returned. The characters known from globbing can be used in the search pattern (i.e., *, ? and [abc]).

```
dat=/home/pi/images/img123.png
echo ${dat#*/}     # output home/pi/images/img123.png
echo ${dat#*.}     # output png
```

- **${var##pattern}**
  As above, but now, the largest possible string that matches the pattern is eliminated.

```
echo ${dat##*/}    # output img123.png
echo ${dat##*.}    # output png
```

- **${var%pattern}**
  Like `${var#pattern}`, but now the pattern matching is performed at the end of the variable content. The shortest possible string from the end of the variable is eliminated. The variable itself remains unchanged.

```
echo ${dat%/*}     # output /home/pi/images
echo ${dat%.*}     # output /home/pi/images/img123
```

- **${var%%pattern}**
  As above, but now, the largest possible string gets eliminated.

```
echo ${dat%%/*}    # no output (empty string)
echo ${dat%%.*}    # output /home/pi/images/img123
```

- **${var/find/replace}**
  Replaces the first occurrence of the `find` pattern with `replace`.

```
x='abcdeab12ab'
echo ${x/ab/xy}    # output xycdeaab12ab
```

- **${!var}**
  Returns the contents of the variable whose name is contained in the string.

```
abc=123
efg='abc'
echo ${!efg}       # output 123
```

Finally, I want to show you a typical application of a parameter substitution: Let's say you want to use `convert` or `magick` (see Chapter 16, Section 16.1) to convert some PNG files in the current directory into JPEG format. For this task, you must replace the `.png` identifier with `.jpg` in the `pngname` variable within the filename. The easiest way to perform this task is the following script:

```
#!/bin/bash
# Sample file png2jpg.sh
shopt -s nullglob
for pngname in *.png; do
    # Replace .png with .jpg
```

```
    jpgname=${pngname%.png}.jpg
    convert "$pngname" "$jpgname"
done
```

`shopt -s nullglob` avoids an error message if no `*.png` files exist in the directory at all. Details on how the `for` loop works will follow in Section 3.12. Note that the `pngname` and `jpgname` variables are enclosed in quotes when the `convert` command is called. These quotation marks are the only way to make a script work for filenames with spaces.

It's So Much Easier to Process Strings in Python!

Once you get used to the strange Bash mechanisms for editing strings, you can use it to solve a surprising number of problems. Nevertheless, for scripts where you need to manipulate many strings, you're better off using Python. I don't know of any language that provides such comprehensive yet easy-to-use functions for handling strings.

3.10.7 Heredocs and Herestrings

Here documents (heredocs, for short) are blocks of text embedded in the script that end with the character sequence specified by `<<` (often `EOF` for *end of file*). The following example illustrates the syntax very clearly. (The `mail` command is based on the assumption that a mail server is running on the machine.)

```
name="Michael"
amount=1200
to="spamvictim@spamforever.com"

mail -s "Invest safely" $to << EOF
Hello $name, enclosed is a great investment offer
without any risk. If you transfer $amount US$ to this account
you'll get ...
EOF
```

You can easily execute multiline text output via `cat`, as in the following example:

```
cat << EOF
This is
a long
help text
EOF
```

Internally, heredocs are a special type of input redirection. `mail` or `cat` expects the mail text from standard input. Instead, the following text lines are used, with the usual variable substitution (`$name`, `$amount`) taking place in the text.

Several syntax variants for heredocs exist:

- Leading tab characters are eliminated from the heredoc text in the form `<<- EOF`, which makes it possible to indent the text. Unfortunately, this text conversion does not work for spaces.
- `<< "EOF"` prevents variable substitution.
- `<<< $myvar` passes the contents of the variable as standard input. This process is known as *herestring*.

3.10.8 The Backslash

It feels like almost every special character in Bash has a special meaning. If you want to use the character as such in a string, you must put the string in simple quotes or precede it with a backslash as a quoting character:

```
echo \$myvar
  $myvar
```

You can also address files with spaces in their names with a backslash. Even easier, however, is the use of quotation marks, as in the following example:

```
touch filename\ with\ blanks.txt
ls "filename with blanks.txt"
rm 'filename with blanks.txt'
```

Unlike numerous other programming languages, Bash does not create a line break from `\n`. Instead, the characters `\` and `n` are output or stored separately. Only `echo -e` analyzes this character sequence as expected.

```
echo -e "Line 1\nLine 2"
```

Finally, you can use the backslash to spread long commands across multiple lines:

```
command --with --many --options and even \
  more parameters
```

3.11 Branches

As in almost any programming language, you can formulate branches using `if` in Bash. The syntax is as follows:

```
if condition1; then
    command1a
    command1b
[ elif condition2; then
    commands2 ]
```

```
[ else
    commands3 ]
fi
```

Consider the following concrete example:

```
if [ $# -ne 2 ]; then
    echo "Two parameters must be passed to the command!"
    exit 2  # error code for wrong parameters
else
    echo "Parameter 1: $1, Parameter 2: $2"
fi
```

I'll discuss the strange syntax for the actual condition in a moment. The indentations in the listing are optional but improve readability.

What's confusing about this syntax (and often forgotten) are the semicolons after the conditions. You can save the semicolons if you sacrifice a separate line for then. But that doesn't make the code any nicer, as shown in the following example:

```
if condition
then
    command1
    command2
fi
```

3.11.1 if Short Notation with && or ||

By placing semicolons correctly, you can formulate if constructs on a single line. If only a single command is to be executed in the context of an if construct, the conditional execution of commands with && or || is more elegant and saves space (see also Section 3.6). However, this notation makes the code harder to understand, especially for people who are not familiar with Bash.

```
if condition; then
    command
fi
# equivalent
if condition; then command; fi

# also equivalent: the command will be executed
# if the condition is met
condition && command

# inverse logic: the command will be executed
# if the condition is not met
inverse condition || command
```

3.11.2 Conditions

While the `if` syntax is simple, formulating conditions is already considerably more difficult. Bash provides several variants for this task, which are summarized in the following listing. I'll explain these concepts later. A preceding exclamation mark negates a condition.

```
x=5
test "$x" -gt 3  && echo "true"   # -> true
test "$x" -eq 2  && echo "true"   # (no output)
[ "$x" -gt 3 ]   && echo "true"   # -> true
[[ "$x" -gt 3 ]] && echo "true"   # -> true
(( x > 3 ))      && echo "true"   # -> true
! (( x > 3 ))    && echo "true"   # (no output)
```

Put Variables in Quotation Marks!

`test $x -gt 3` is syntactically correct, but only as long as the variable is not empty. If `$x` has no content, the result is `test -gt 3`. This statement is nonsensical and results in a syntax error. That's why you should get in the habit of always putting variables for comparisons in quotation marks!

In the most original form, the `test` command is used. It processes one or more parameters, where the condition is expressed with options. `-gt` stands for *greater than*, `-eq` for *equals*. You may wonder why `test $x > 5` does not work. This has to do with the fact that the `>` and `<` characters are reserved for input and output redirection.

Instead of `test condition`, the short notation `[ condition ]` exists (see Table 3.9). It is important that spaces must be placed before and after the square brackets! Note also that the comparison operators depend on the data type: `-eq` compares numbers, `=` compares strings. If variables occur in the test expression, their names must be prefixed with `$`. `dat` refers to strings with filenames.

Test Expression	Meaning
`[ var ]`	True if the variable is not empty
`[ -n var ]`	As above
`[ zk1 = zk2 ]`	True if the strings match
`[ z1 -eq z2 ]`	If the numbers are equal (*equal*)
`[ z1 -ne z2 ]`	If the numbers are not equal (*not equal*)
`[ z1 -gt z2 ]`	If `z1` is greater than `z2` (*greater than*)

Table 3.9 The Most Important Syntax Variants for Formulating Conditions Using [ ]

Test Expression	Meaning
`[ z1 -ge z2 ]`	If z1 is greater than or equal to z2 (*greater equal*)
`[ z1 -lt z2 ]`	If z1 is less than z2 (*less than*)
`[ z1 -le z2 ]`	If z1 is less than or equal to z2 (*less equal*)
`[ -d dat ]`	If dat is a directory (*directory*)
`[ -f dat ]`	If dat is a file (*file*)
`[ -r dat ]`	If the file may be read (*read*)
`[ -w dat ]`	If the file may be modified (*write*)
`[ dat1 -nt dat2 ]`	If file 1 is newer than file 2 (*newer than*)
`! [ ... ]`	Negates the condition

Table 3.9 The Most Important Syntax Variants for Formulating Conditions Using [ ] (Cont.)

`[ condition ]` is available in most shell variants. Bash and Zsh alternatively allow conditions to be placed between double square brackets, for instance, `[[ condition ]]` (see Table 3.10). In `pattern`, you can use the characters known from globbing (i.e., *, ? and `[a-z]`).

Test Expression	Meaning
`[[ zk = pattern ]]`	True if the string matches the pattern
`[[ zk == pattern ]]`	As above
`[[ zk =~ regex ]]`	True if the regular expression is true (see Chapter 9)
`[[ bed1 && bed2 ]]`	If both conditions are met (*and*)
`[[ bed1 || bed2 ]]`	If at least one condition is met (*or*)

Table 3.10 Bash-Specific Formulation of Conditions with [[ ]]

In the following example, `myvar` must contain a code like A17 or C99:

```
if [[ "$myvar" == [ABC][0-9][0-9] ]]; then
    echo "ok"
fi
```

Compatibility Concerns

The `[[ ]]` syntax is not supported by all shells (but by Zsh). You can increase the compatibility of your scripts if you omit `[[ ]]`. Some Bash-specific additional functions can be easily replaced: For instance, `[[ bed1 && bed2 ]]` corresponds to `[ bed1 ] && [ bed2 ]` and `[[ bed1 || bed2 ]]` corresponds to `[ bed1 ] || [ bed2 ]`.

The (( )) notation for mathematical expressions, introduced earlier in Section 3.9, can also be used for formulating conditions. Readable comparison operators like <, > or != are allowed. Inside the double brackets, you can omit the marking of variables with $, as shown in the following example:

```
x=5
(( x == 5 )) && echo "true"  # -> true
```

Make sure that you don't accidentally use = for comparisons: ((var = value)) performs an assignment and always returns "true"!

```
x=5
(( x = 6 )) && echo "true"  # -> true
echo $x                     # -> 6 !!
```

Caution is also advised when variables are not declared at all. Bash then assumes the value 0 and displays neither a warning nor an error:

```
# always true, Bash assumes emptyvar=0
if (( emptyvar < 100 )); then ...
```

3.11.3 Branches with case

Branches can also be formulated using case, which compares an expression (often simply the content of a variable) with different patterns. The patterns can contain the * and ? globbing characters as well as character ranges like [a-z]. As so often, the syntax of Bash takes some getting used to:

```
case expression in
    pattern1)
        command1a
        command1b
        ...
        ;;
    pattern2)
        command2a
        command2b
        ...
        ;;
    *)          # Default block (optional)
        ...
esac
```

The indentations and the start of a new line after pattern) are optional but improve readability. The double semicolons end the case construct. If you deliberately omit the semicolons or simply forget them, Bash defaults to the case construct. If Bash detects other applicable patterns, it also executes the assigned commands. The following lines show the analysis of a yes/no input, where the input is accepted in any case and in the short forms y (yes):

```
echo -n "yes/no? "
read answer
case $answer in
    [yY] | [yY][eE][sS] ) echo "yes";;
    [nN] | [nN][oO] )      echo "no";;
    *)                     echo "invalid input";;
esac
```

3.11.4 Parameter Analysis via case

In my own scripts, I mostly avoid case and prefer more readable if constructs. Sometimes, however, case is actually helpful. Let's consider another example: a simple analysis of parameters (*command-line arguments*) that are passed to a script.

The myoptions.sh script accepts three options (-a, -b, and -c), which can be specified in any order. In this case, -b and -c expect one parameter each. Following the options, any number of additional parameters can be passed. The following listing shows two calls of the script:

```
$ ./myoptions.sh -a -b lorem -c ipsum dolores est
  Option a
  Option b with parameter lorem
  Option c with parameter ipsum
  More parameters: dolores est

$ ./myoptions.sh -c lorem -b ipsum dolores
  Option c with parameter lorem
  Option b with parameter ipsum
  More parameters: dolores
```

To analyze the passed options and parameters, the script uses the Bash-internal getopts command, which you can use in the following way:

- getopts "abc" expects the options -a, -b, and -c in any order, even in combinations (i.e., -bc instead of -b -c).
- getopts ":abc" works as above but does not return any error messages for invalid parameters.
- getopts "ab:c:" with a colon after b and c expects one parameter for each of these options. During the analysis, the passed parameter can be read from the $OPTARGS variable.

- Each call analyzes *one* option. The analysis must therefore be performed in a loop. For this example, I used `while`. (Details on loops will follow in the next section.)
- During the processing of the options, `$OPTIND` references the next element of the parameter list.

  Provided that the options are passed first and then the parameters, all processed options can be removed from `$*` using `shift`. (`shift <n>` removes the first *n* elements from `$*`. But because `$OPTIND` already references the next element, only `$OPTIND -1` elements may be pushed out of the parameter list.)

```
# Sample file myoptions.sh
while getopts ":ab:c:" opt; do
    case $opt in
       a) echo "Option a";;
       b) echo "Option b with parameter $OPTARG";;
       c) echo "Option c with parameter $OPTARG";;
       ?) echo "Invalid option"
          echo "Usage: myoptions [-a] [-b data] [-c data] [...]"
          exit 2
          ;;
    esac
done
# remove processed options from $*
shift $(( $OPTIND - 1 ))
echo "More parameters: $*"
```

getopts versus getopt

`getopts` is a relatively simple command that can only handle 1-letter options, but not long options like `--search`. A more powerful alternative is the external `getopt` command, which is mostly included in the `util-linux` package on Linux. For an example of how to use this command and more tips on evaluating script parameters, see Stack Overflow, specifically *https://stackoverflow.com/questions/192249*.

3.12 Loops

Bash provides several commands to choose from for creating loops. In this section, I'll start with `for`, before I provide a brief introduction to `while` and `until`. The basic syntax of the `for` loop is shown in the following listing. Note the placement of the semicolon before and not after `do`! You can avoid this semicolon by starting a new line with `do`.

```
for myvar in mylist; do
  command1
  command2
done
```

```
# equivalent
for myvar in mylist; do command1; command2; done

# Example
for item in a b c; do echo $item; done
  a
  b
  c
```

The myvar loop variable thus runs through all values of the specified list. (You'll see momentarily that "list" is a fairly generic term: You can use for to loop through parameters, filenames, lines of a text file, etc.) Be sure you specify the name of the loop variable after for without $! This step is consistent in that the variable is changed at this point and not read.

The following lines contain some more examples of use, each of which is formulated in a single line to save space. Note that filenames can always contain spaces! You should therefore always enclose the loop variable in quotes to ensure that the file in question is processed correctly. A brace extension expression can also serve as a starting point for a loop (see the third example). Note the pattern nature of the examples. As long as you perform only a single operation, you can often do without loops altogether in Bash.

```
# outputs all parameters passed to the script
# (command line arguments)
for para in $*; do echo $para; done

# copy all *.jpg files into the images directory
for filename in *.jpg; do cp "$filename" images; done

# creates file-00.txt to file-99.txt
for fn in file-{00..99}.txt; do touch $fn; done

# equivalent commands to the above three loops
echo "$*"
cp *.jpg images
touch file-{00..99}.txt

# loop through array elements
myarray=("item" "other item" "third item")
for item in "${myarray[@]}"; do echo $item; done
```

In Bash, you'll rarely need a loop that numerically traverses a range of values. However, such loops are quite possible, as the following listing shows. Note in particular the last example, which corresponds to the classic for loop of the C programming language.

```
for i in {1..10}; do echo $i; done
# Output 1, 2, ..., 10

for i in {01..12}; do echo $i; done
# Output 01, 02, ..., 12

for ((i=1; i<=10; i++)); do echo $i; done
# Output 1, 2, ..., 10
```

3.12.1 Processing Filenames with Spaces

The above `for para in $*; do ...` example processes all parameters passed to a script. You should act with caution if filenames may contain spaces! Let's suppose you have a file named `account names.txt`, and you run `./myscript.sh *.txt` with the following code:

```
# processes filenames with spaces incorrectly
for filename in $*; do
  ls -l "$filename"
done
```

An error occurs twice in the process. The `ls` command does not find the `account` or `names.txt` file. For the script, it is not recognizable that `account names.txt` is *one* filename. The reason is that the parameters passed in the loop are separated by default at every *whitespace* character, which includes both whitespace and newline characters, which Bash uses to separate filenames.

To ensure the loop is processed correctly, you must prepend the statement `IFS=$'\n'`. This statement means that the decomposition into words is performed only in case of a newline character.

```
# processes filenames with spaces correctly
IFS=$'\n'
for filename in $*; do
  ls -l "$filename"
done
```

I already introduced you to the special `IFS` variable (internal field separator) in Section 3.9. The preceding dollar character ensures that `\n` is interpreted correctly.

3.12.2 while and until

The `while` loop is executed as long as the condition is met and uses the following structure:

```
while condition; do
  commands
done
```

```
# Example (output: 1, 2, 3, 4, 5)
i=1
while [ $i -le 5 ]; do
    echo $i
    (( $i++ ))
done
```

while loops can be excellently combined with an input redirection or with the pipe command through the following structure:

```
# Read file line by line
while read filename; do
    echo "$filename"
done < files.txt

# Process files
ls *.jpg | while read filename; do
  echo "$filename"
done
```

until loops work similarly to while loops. The difference is that the loop continues as long as the condition is *not* met:

```
# Output: 1, 2
i=1
until [ $i -eq 3 ]; do
  echo $i
  (( i++ ))
done
```

break and continue

The break and continue keywords work in Bash as they do in most programming languages: Using break, you can abort the execution of a loop prematurely. For nested loops, break n specifies how many loop levels are to be terminated.

continue skips the remaining commands in the loop block, but then continues the loop.

3.12.3 Loops over Text Files

A common scenario involves text files that are supposed to be processed. In Bash, two commonly used procedures for this purpose exist, but they are not exactly equivalent.

The following while loop reads one line from access.log with each loop pass. Note how this text file is used as default input for the entire loop construct due to the redirect character < with done!

```
# Process text file line by line
while read line; do
    echo $line
done < access.log
```

As an alternative, you can create a list via `$(cat file)` and then process it using `for`. This procedure is recommended only for small text files. In the loop, the list is split at each space, tab, or line separator. The text is thus processed word by word.

```
# Process text file word by word,
# Word separation at ' ', \t and \n
for word in $(cat words.txt); do
    echo $word
done
```

The points at which `for` splits the `cat` output into words are controlled by the `IFS` environment variable (internal field separator). In the following example, I have set `:` as a separator. In addition, the line break is *always* considered a separator. After the loop, the original state of `IFS` is restored.

```
# Process text file word by word, word separation at : and \n
OLDIFS=$IFS
IFS=':'
for word in $(cat words.txt); do
    echo $word
done
restore IFS=$OLDIFS  # IFS
```

3.13 Functions

The `function` keyword defines a function that can be called in the script like a command. The code of the function must be enclosed in curly brackets. Functions must be declared *before* they are called for the first time and are therefore often placed at the beginning of the script.

Parameters can be passed to functions. Unlike many programming languages, the parameters are not enclosed in parentheses. Within the function, the parameters can be taken from the `$1`, `$2`, etc. variables. A function processes parameters in the same way that the script processes *command-line arguments*. The following mini-script outputs *Hello World, Bash!*

```
#!/bin/bash
function myfunc {
    echo "Hello World, $1!"
}
myfunc "Bash"
```

The `function` keyword is optional. If you omit `function`, however, the function name must be followed by parentheses. Thus, the following function is equivalent to the previous example:

```
myfunc() {
    echo "Hello World, $1!"
}
```

Bash functions help you to clearly structure the code. You can also swap out blocks of code that are needed more than once, thus avoiding redundancy.

Using `return`, you leave a function prematurely. No option exists to return data. However, you can of course perform outputs via `echo` or change variables.

3.13.1 Local Variables

Usually, all variables are "shared" throughout the script, so they are also accessible in functions and can be changed there. The `local` keyword provides the option to define local variables.

```
function myfunc {
    a=4
    local b=4
}

a=3; b=3
myfunc
echo "$a $b"  # output 4 3
```

3.14 Error Protection

Bash has a decidedly casual way of dealing with errors: If a command in a script triggers an error, Bash simply continues the script with the next statement! This strange strategy has to do with the fact that the return code of many commands often does not indicate real errors at all, but merely that a condition was not met or that when searching for a file it was not found. This occurrence does not necessarily have to be a "real" error.

However, some exceptions exist. In case of obvious syntax errors, for instance, if quotes or brackets are missing or control structures are incomplete (no `fi` for `if`), the script will not be started at all.

3.14.1 Detecting Errors

The return code of each command is stored in `$?`. The value 0 means that everything is OK. Any other number indicates an error.

```
command_might_fail
errcode=$?
if [ $errcode -ne 0 ]; then
  echo "Errorcode $errcode"
fi
```

3.14.2 Canceling in Case of Errors

If you want your script to terminate on the first error, you need to add the `-e` option to the hash bang:

```
#!/bin/bash -e
```

In the case of interlinked commands, the overall result is valid. If `command1` fails in the following script—even if the command does not exist—`command2` will be executed. Only if this command also leads to an error will the script be aborted.

```
#!/bin/bash -e
command1 || command2
```

Instead of setting the error behavior in the hash bang for the entire script, you can enable strict error testing via `set -e` for some lines of code and disable it later using `set +e`.

Not Recommended

Most Bash manuals and FAQs advise against running Bash with the `-e` option or enabling the function via `set -e`. The damage is greater than the benefit, as the behavior of the script can become unpredictable, as described in *https://mywiki.wooledge.org/BashFAQ/105*.

3.14.3 exit

`exit (n)` terminates the script. The return value of the last command or the value `n` is returned.

Exit Code	Meaning
0	Okay, no error
1	General error
2	Error in the passed parameters (arguments)
3–255	Other command-specific or script-specific error

Table 3.11 Error Codes of Bash and Linux Commands

3.14.4 Responding to Signals (trap)

The concept of process management on Unix/Linux is that processes can be sent signals (see Table 3.12). Even more signals are listed by `kill -l`. For example, if you press [Ctrl] + [C] while executing a Bash script, the `SIGINT` signal is sent, and the script execution gets aborted.

Signal Name	Code	Meaning
SIGHUP	1	Prompt to re-read the configuration
SIGINT	2	Interruption via [Ctrl] + [C]
SIGKILL	9	kill signal; cannot be intercepted
SIGTERM	15	Prompt to exit the program

Table 3.12 The Most Important Signals

You can use `trap` to specifically respond to such signals. The syntax of `trap` is simple:

```
trap 'commands' signals
```

`commands` specifies one or several commands to be executed when one of the specified signals is received. The signals can be specified either by their names or by their codes. If you want to execute complex code in response to a signal, you should define the code in a function and specify the function name in the `trap` command.

`trap` is often used to perform cleanup operations prior to a program abort triggered by a signal. For example, you can delete a temporary file. The simple `trap '' 2` command allows you to make your script ignore [Ctrl] + [C].

3.14.5 Timeout

For commands that rely on network or database connections, it is not always clear whether an error has really occurred or whether the connection setup is too slow. Using `timeout <time> <command>`, you can execute a command with a given timeout. If the command takes longer than the expected time, the execution is aborted. The return value of `timeout` is 124 if a timeout occurs. The command knows some more special error codes (125, 126, 127, and 137; see `man timeout`). On the other hand, if `command` is terminated within the timeout, `timeout` returns the exit code of `command`. The following command tests whether a Git remote repository exists for the current branch (see also Chapter 14):

```
timeout 30s git ls-remote
```

Chapter 4
PowerShell

The oldest "shell" for Windows is the `cmd.exe` program, often called the "command prompt." `cmd.exe` represents the user interface (UI) of MS-DOS, the text-based predecessor of Microsoft Windows. Batch files (extension `*.bat`) allow simple script programming. However, `cmd.exe` is no longer a contemporary tool but a relic from the IT stone age.

In 2006, Microsoft introduced the first version of *Windows PowerShell* as a powerful successor to `cmd.exe`. Meanwhile, we have reached version 7.*n*. The program also runs on Linux and macOS; because the shell is thus no longer Windows specific, its name has been simplified to *PowerShell*. PowerShell is *the* scripting tool in the Windows world today. The language is irreplaceable if you want to administer Windows-related functions (e.g., Microsoft 365 cloud setups or Microsoft Active Directory).

The biggest technical achievement of PowerShell compared to other shells is its object-oriented approach. PowerShell commands do not return text, but real objects. This opens up completely new options for further processing. Compared to Bash, the syntax of PowerShell is much more logical (but still not always intuitive and in any case rather verbose and lengthy).

In this chapter, I will give you a first impression of the basic functions of PowerShell. Numerous examples will then follow in the other chapters.

Execution Policy

For security reasons, the execution of (unsigned) scripts is often prohibited on company computers. The reasons for this limitation and various setting options are described in Section 4.5.

4.1 Installation

PowerShell is preinstalled on current Windows versions, but rarely in its latest version. To find out the version of the installed PowerShell, you need to search for "Terminal" in the **Start** menu and run the program with the same name. (For older Windows versions, searching for *PowerShell* will get you there.)

In the terminal, type `$PSVersionTable` and press Enter. In response, you'll receive a table containing the key data of the PowerShell version:

```
> $PSVersionTable

  Name           Value
  ----           -----
  PSVersion      5.1.22000.1335
  PSEdition      Desktop
  ...
```

This result was created on a Windows 11 machine in winter 2023. What's slightly perplexing is the fact that PowerShell version 5.1 is used, which shipped in 2016. Is there really no later version available?

In fact, when I wrote this chapter, version 7.3 was the current version. However, with the jump from version 5.*n to* 7.*n*, more than just the version number has changed:

- PowerShell has had an open-source license since version 6. The program is also available free of charge for other operating systems.
- Accordingly, the program name is no longer "Windows PowerShell" but simply "PowerShell."

However, versions 5.*n* and 7.*n* are not fully compatible with each other. Even though further development of version 5.*n* has long since been discontinued, this version remains preinstalled for compatibility reasons.

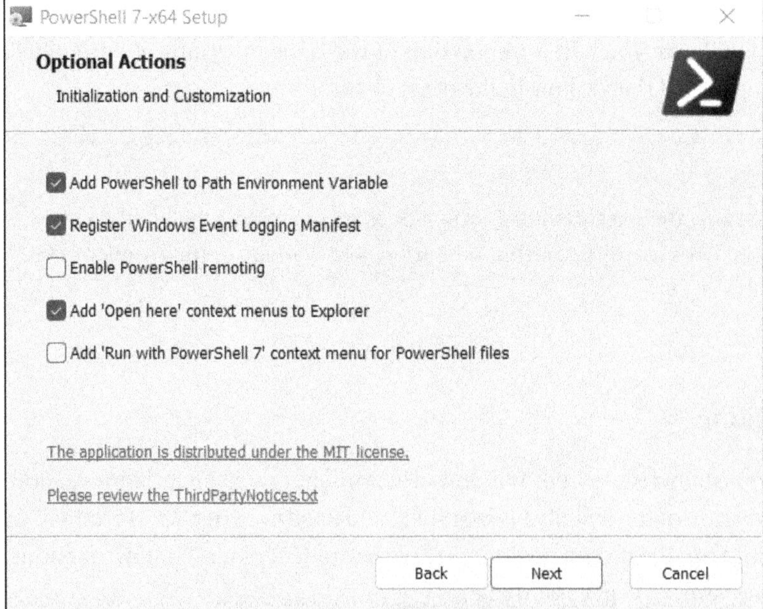

Figure 4.1 Installing the Current PowerShell Version

For this point onward, however, I assume that you use the current PowerShell version. Although most of the commands and scripts presented in this book also work with version 5.1, I tested my examples exclusively with version 7.3. All scripts should also run with PowerShell 7.4, which is on the horizon at the time of writing and will most likely be available as you're reading this book.

Several ways to install PowerShell exist, but I recommend you simply run the `winget install Microsoft.PowerShell` command in a terminal or `cmd.exe`. `winget` is a relatively new component of Windows 10 and 11 that simplifies package management.

As an alternative, you can download and run an MSI package from *https://aka.ms/PSWindows*. Make sure you install the 64-bit version (`PowerShell-7.n-win-x64.msi` file), not the 32-bit version (`PowerShell-7.n-win-x86.msi`)!

The installation of version 7.*n* is done parallel to the existing version 5.1. Subsequently, you can choose which version you want to use. After restarting the terminal, notice the new entry: **PowerShell** (not **Windows PowerShell**, which denotes version 5.1). The `$PSVersionTable` command, which simply displays the contents of the `PSVersion` variable (and some other variables containing information about the PowerShell version), should now return this result:

```
> $PSVersionTable

  Name          Value
  ----          -----
  PSVersion     7.3.1
  PSEdition     Core
  ...
```

4.1.1 Installation on Linux

Since PowerShell is subject to an open-source license, Microsoft also provides versions for other operating systems. The installation isn't complicated at all. I will focus in this section on the procedure on Ubuntu. The string at `wget` must be specified without the \ character and without spaces in a long line. `wget` downloads a small package that sets up a package source. From this package source, Ubuntu then obtains the `powershell` package. The advantage of this somewhat cumbersome procedure is that, in the future, you'll automatically receive the latest version of PowerShell as part of the usual updates.

```
$ sudo apt update
$ sudo apt install -y wget apt-transport-https \
                  software-properties-common

$ wget -q "https://packages.microsoft.com/config/ubuntu/\
         $(lsb_release -rs)/packages-microsoft-prod.deb"
```

```
$ sudo dpkg -i packages-microsoft-prod.deb
$ sudo apt update
$ sudo apt install -y powershell
```

After the installation, you can start PowerShell in a terminal window using the `pwsh` command. Instructions for installing PowerShell for other distributions can be found at *https://docs.microsoft.com/en-us/powershell/scripting/install/installing-powershell-on-linux*.

4.1.2 Installation on macOS

Many macOS machines used for software development have the *Homebrew* package management system installed (see also *https://brew.sh*). If Homebrew is installed, the PowerShell installation succeeds with the following simple command in the terminal:

```
$ brew install --cask powershell
```

Alternatively, you can download a `*.pkg` file with the latest PowerShell version from *https://docs.microsoft.com/en-us/powershell/scripting/install/installing-powershell-on-macos*.

Double-clicking this file starts the installation process; 30 seconds later everything is done. Now, you can start PowerShell in a terminal window using the `pwsh` command, just like on Linux.

4.1.3 Limitations of PowerShell on Windows versus Linux/macOS

Even though PowerShell realizes many good ideas, the longing of Linux or macOS users for yet another shell is limited. The choice has already been pretty large.

The main problem with using PowerShell outside of Windows is that a much smaller number of commands are available to choose from. Using `Get-Command`, you can get a list of all commands. (Strictly speaking, the commands are cmdlets, functions, etc., which I will describe in more detail later in Section 4.3.) `Measure-Object` enables you to count the number of commands. The following listing summarizes the results determined on Windows, Linux, and macOS:

```
> Get-Command | Measure-Object
  Count: 1953   (Windows 11 Pro)
  Count:  273   (Linux/macOS)
  ...
```

Notice how much smaller the number of commands is on Linux and macOS. This limitation has to do with the fact that many PowerShell commands perform Windows-specific tasks, such as setting up a new Windows user. Such commands would not make sense on Linux or macOS. In general, the infrastructure on Windows is quite different. On

Linux and macOS, there are no *scheduled jobs*, no *Common Information Model (CIM)*, no *Windows Management Instrumentation (WMI)*, and so on. (Linux and macOS have comparable functions, of course, but they are implemented quite differently.) For this reason, some of the examples presented in this book do *not* work on Linux or macOS.

But no reason to bury your head in the sand! PowerShell provides the option to install extension modules. Many modules have functions that are equally suitable on Windows, Linux, and macOS, for instance, for the administration of external services such as Amazon Web Services (AWS).

In conclusion, PowerShell scripts for Windows administration do not work on Linux and macOS because the commands and underlying software foundation are missing. However, scripts that perform general, non-Windows-focused tasks and access modules in the process can very well be developed for cross-platform scenarios.

4.1.4 Configuration

At first, rarely will you need to configure PowerShell. However, once you gain some experience using PowerShell, you may want certain functions or command shortcuts (called *aliases*) to be defined when PowerShell is started, modules to be loaded automatically, and so on. The right place for such customization is the *profile file*, whose path is stored in the `$PROFILE` variable (spread across two lines in this book only for space reasons):

```
> $PROFILE
  C:\Users\kofler\Documents\PowerShell\
    Microsoft.PowerShell_profile.ps1
```

To modify the file, a best practice is to launch the editor directly in PowerShell:

```
> notepad $PROFILE       (Notepad.exe)
> code $PROFILE          (Visual Studio Code, if installed)
```

4.2 Windows Terminal

In the introduction to this section, I asked you to run a terminal to find out the PowerShell version. This instruction may have seemed contradictory to you. So, what is the difference between PowerShell and Terminal, and how are the two programs related?

The terminal is a program that can run different shells. Windows-compatible shells include the deprecated command prompt (`cmd.exe`), Windows PowerShell 5.*n*, PowerShell 7.*n*, Azure Shell, and Git Bash as well as Linux's Bash via the *Windows Subsystem for Linux (WSL)*.

The terminal's job is simply to accept your keyboard input, pass it to the active shell, and then display the shell's result as text. Besides that, the terminal fulfills a few more functions that only play a minor role for us.

The terminal is a relatively new component of Windows and has only been around since 2019. In the past, `cmd.exe` or PowerShell simply handled the terminal functions themselves or delegated this task to the *Windows Console Host*. On Linux and macOS, the separation of tasks between shell and terminal has proven itself for decades, and so, Microsoft finally got around to developing a "real" terminal app.

In current Windows versions, the terminal should already be preinstalled. If that isn't the case, you should run `winget install Microsoft.WindowsTerminal` or install the program from the Microsoft Store.

Remember to update to the latest version every now and then. The terminal is currently under intensive development and receives new features almost every month!

```
> winget upgrade Microsoft.WindowsTerminal
```

What can the terminal do? Perhaps the most important innovation compared to the traditional execution of `cmd.exe` or PowerShell is that you can launch multiple shell instances and run them side by side in "tabs" (called *dialog sheets*). This view is often handy when you want to test different functions in parallel, work in different directories, or run PowerShell in one tab but Bash (Linux) in a second one.

Running the Terminal with Administrator Privileges

You can execute most PowerShell commands as an ordinary user. But if you want to perform administrative work, you'll need more rights.

For this purpose, you need to search for "Terminal" in the **Start** menu, right-click or touchpad-click the entry, and select **Run as administrator**.

4.2.1 Configuration

Microsoft is particularly proud that the terminal can now also keep up visually with corresponding Linux programs. If you want, you can change the foreground and background colors of the terminal, underlay the terminal with an image, or make it transparent so that you can see what's going on in the windows beneath the terminal. In the screenshots for this book, I have refrained from describing these gimmicks. However, I changed the terminal colors (light background, dark text colors) to make the illustrations easier to read in print.

You can change these and countless other options in the settings. The program distinguishes between global basic settings, which apply to the entire program, and profiles. Each profile is assigned to a shell.

In the **Startup Settings** dialog sheet, you can (and should) make PowerShell 7 the default shell (**Default profile** dropdown list). You should also make the terminal the default program for running shells (**Default terminal application** dropdown list) if these options are not already selected.

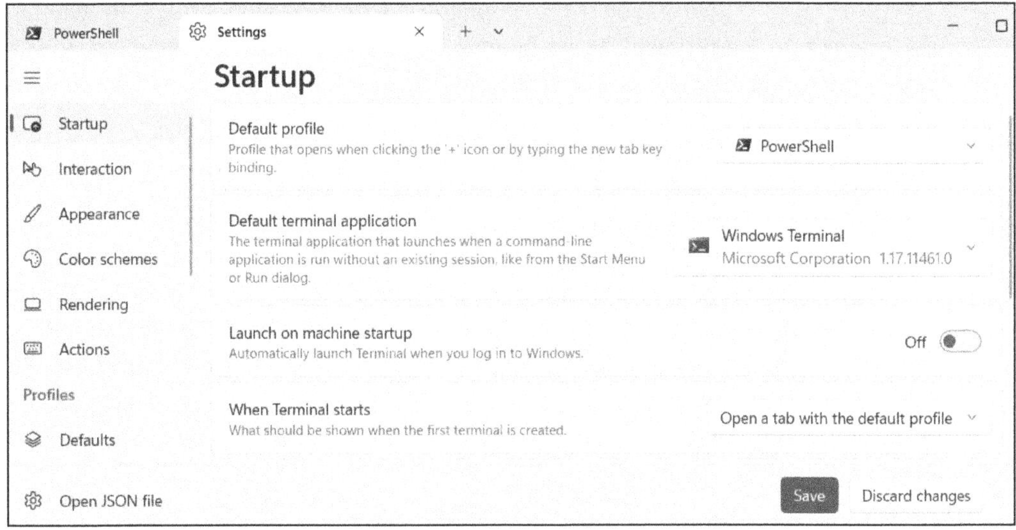

Figure 4.2 Countless Options for Influencing the Appearance and Function of the Terminal

> **Tip**
>
> If a strange file appears in an editor when you open the settings, you're using an outdated version of the terminal without a proper settings dialog. A solution to this issue is updating the terminal in the Microsoft Store.

4.2.2 Operation

If you have previously used `cmd.exe`, old PowerShell versions, or a terminal in another operating system, you already know that a mouse or touchpad is of little use in the terminal. In particular, you cannot change the cursor position. Inputs are only possible in the last line of the terminal. Within this line, you can move the cursor via the `←` and `→` keys. Pressing `↑` and `↓`, you can call commands entered earlier again and change them if necessary.

After all, you can select a text area using the mouse and then copy it to the clipboard by pressing `Ctrl` + `C`. (If a command is currently running, `Ctrl` + `C` has a different function: It cancels the execution.) `Ctrl` + `V` inserts the current clipboard content at the cursor position.

If you specify the first letters of a command, the most plausible continuation is displayed in gray font. Pressing `→` completes the input. Alternatively, by repeatedly pressing `Tab`, you can cycle through additional extension options. This feature works in an analogous way for command options as well as for filenames in the current directory. `Ctrl` + `C` displays all possible additions at once.

[Shift] + [Ctrl] + [P] takes you to the *command palette*, a long list of functions you can perform within the terminal. Many functions are related to tab management (open, close, switch, rename, etc.) and visual details (font size, color). Not only does the **Actions** dialog sheet list all the keyboard shortcuts, but you can also modify them.

4.3 Calling cmdlets and Functions

Before you start programming your first scripts, you should interactively familiarize yourself with the options provided by PowerShell. The following examples should be understandable without basic knowledge. You'll come across the commands used in this process again and again later. Details of individual commands (actually, they are cmdlets, but we'll deal with this term later) can be obtained from `Get-Help <command name>`.

In the following listing, `Get-Location` determines the current path. `Set-Location` changes to the `Downloads` subdirectory where `Get-ChildItem` determines all files that have the `*.exe` extension. Finally, `Remove-Item` deletes a setup program.

```
> Get-Location

  Path
  ----
  C:\Users\kofler

> Set-Location Downloads

> Get-ChildItem *.exe

  Directory: C:\Users\kofler\Downloads

  Mode         LastWriteTime      Length Name
  ----         -------------      ------ ----
  -a---    18.07.2022 17:24     1414600 ChromeSetup.exe
  -a---    19.07.2022 11:49    49381480 Git-2.37.1-64-bit.exe
  -a---    11.01.2023 18:49    25218984 python-3.11.1-amd64.exe

> Remove-Item ChromeSetup.exe
```

I mentioned at the beginning that PowerShell works with objects. However, this functionality is not always apparent at first glance. For example, `Get-Date` returns the current date and time. By default, PowerShell displays only one string that summarizes the most important data:

```
> Get-Date

  Wednesday, 5/3/2023 5:11:04 PM
```

Only when you pass the Get-Date result to Get-Member via the pipe operator (|) does it become clear that the result of Get-Date has the System.DateTime data type and knows innumerable properties and methods. (I have greatly abridged the issue here for space reasons.)

```
> Get-Date | Get-Member

  TypeName: System.DateTime
  Name              MemberType     Definition
  ----              ----------     ----------
  Add               Method         datetime Add(timespan value)
  AddDays           Method         datetime AddDays(double value)
  AddHours          Method         datetime AddHours(double ...)
  AddMilliseconds   Method         datetime AddMilliseconds(...)
  ...
  Ticks             Property       long Ticks {get;}
  TimeOfDay         Property       timespan TimeOfDay {get;}
  Year              Property       int Year {get;}
```

Tip

Get-Member often returns an almost endless list of methods and properties. On Windows, you can display the result in a separate window using Get-Member | Out-GridView. Various options for formatting (like Out-GridView) or exporting cmdlet results will be introduced in Chapter 7, Section 7.6.

If you don't need the entire date, but only the year, you should place Get-Date in parentheses to force an immediate evaluation. From the resulting object, you analyze only one property with .Year:

```
> (Get-Date).Year

  2023
```

You can use the AddHours(2) method to calculate the date and time in 2 hours:

```
> (Get-Date).AddHours(2)

  Wednesday, 5/3/2023 7:13:03 PM
```

4.3.1 cmdlets

Up until now, I have simply said that you can run "commands" in PowerShell. However, PowerShell actually distinguishes between different types of commands—specifically among cmdlets, functions, aliases, and conventional commands. By far the most important ones are cmdlets, which are commands specially optimized for PowerShell.

The term "cmdlet" comes from the fact that a cmdlet is not a program of its own, but rather, groups of cmdlets are collected in a library. In more technical terms, internally, each cmdlet is an instance of a .NET class. This particular way of organizing has many advantages. In particular, common functions, such as the processing of parameters, do not have to be implemented anew for each cmdlet. In addition, the processing of objects thus has a central foundation, which should also make it clear that cmdlets are not PowerShell scripts. Libraries with cmdlets are mostly programmed in C#.

4.3.2 The Verb-Noun Terminology

The names of cmdlets follow a scheme and are composed of a verb and a noun (*verb-noun pairs* in the original documentation). The verb describes what the command does, the noun which data it processes. Microsoft has even defined a clear set of verbs that you should use if you program commands yourself. For example, you should always use `Remove` for delete operations, but not `Delete`, `Eliminate`, or `Drop` (see *https://docs.microsoft.com/en-us/powershell/scripting/developer/cmdlet/approved-verbs-for-windows-powershell-commands*).

Case Sensitivity

PowerShell is not case-sensitive when recognizing commands and cmdlet options, methods, and properties. For this reason, `(Get-Date).Month` and `(get-date).month` both return the number of the current month.

4.3.3 Aliases

`Get-ChildItem` may be a generic name for a command that gets the contents of a directory, but the typing overhead compared to `dir` or `ls` is considerable. Thus, abbreviations ("aliases") for many cmdlets exist. `dir`, `ls`, and `gci` are also allowed instead of `Get-ChildItem`.

A list of all aliases can be displayed via `Get-Alias` or `gal`. Many predefined abbreviations are composed of the first letters of verb and noun, such as `fl` for `Format-List` or `rnp` for `Rename-ItemProperty`. Sometimes, however, names familiar from Linux or `cmd.exe` are used, such as `cp` for `Copy-Item`.

`Set-Alias` allows you to define your own abbreviations. The following statement enables you to execute the `New-Item` command for creating an empty file also via the `Linux-typical` name, `touch`:

```
Set-Alias touch New-Item
```

If necessary, you should store your Set-Alias statements in Documents/profile.ps1 so that they are automatically parsed each time PowerShell is started.

Which Command Denotes an Alias?

If you know an alias but you're not sure which command it represents, run Get-Command -Name <alias>. For example, Get-Command -Name sls (or Get-Alias sls, which does the same thing) reveals that sls is the abbreviation for Select-String.

4.3.4 Parameters and Options

You can pass parameters to most commands. You can also use options to control the behavior of a command. The following command searches C:\Users and all subdirectories for PNG files:

```
> Get-ChildItem -Path C:\Users\kofler -Recurse -Filter *.png

  Directory: C:\Users\kofler\OneDrive
  ... test.png

  Directory: C:\Users\kofler\Pictures
  ... img_1234.png
```

Get-Help <cmd> summarizes which parameters must be passed in which order and which options are provided by a cmdlet. Three options are passed to the sample command in this example: -Path, -Recurse, and -Filter. The options for cmdlets are always introduced with a hyphen. Options can also be abbreviated as far as a clear addition is possible. (For example, -p is not allowed instead of -pa because there is also the -PipelineVariable option.) The following is a direct translation of the first line in our previous code snippet:

```
gci -pa C:\Users -r -fi *.png
```

In script programming, abbreviations are not recommended because adding an option to a command later may cause your script to stop working.

4.3.5 Splatting

Sometimes, cmdlets must be called with a larger number of options, which often results in very extensive statements which are difficult to read. As an alternative, you can store desired options in advance in a hash table (Section 4.7) and then pass this information to the cmdlet. The keys in the hash table must match the option names of the command. The following example reuses the above `Get-ChildItem` statement and clarifies the syntax:

```
$opts = @{ Path = "C:\Users"; Recurse = $true; Filter = "*.png" }
Get-ChildItem @opts
```

Other splatting variants are documented at *https://learn.microsoft.com/en-us/powershell/module/microsoft.powershell.core/about/about_splatting*.

4.3.6 Functions

In script programming, you can easily combine multiple PowerShell commands into one function (Section 4.11). To pass functions, save the code as a module (file identifier `*.psm1`) in one of the designated directories (`$env:PSModulePath`).

If modules are installed correctly, the functions defined in them cannot be distinguished from “real” cmdlets. Microsoft also makes intensive use of this option: Of the approximately 1,900 commands available for selection in a standard installation of PowerShell on Windows 11, more than half are functions.

```
> (Get-Command -CommandType Function | Measure-Object).Count
  1028
> (Get-Command -CommandType cmdlet | Measure-Object).Count
  843
```

This concatenation of the `Get-Command` and `Measure-Object` commands is an example of using the pipe operator, which I will introduce in more detail in Section 4.4.

4.3.7 Running Conventional Commands

Finally, you can also run traditional commands in PowerShell. An example of such a command is `ping` (usually `C:\Windows\System32\PING.EXE`) for testing network connections. However, traditional commands have the disadvantage that they do not behave like cmdlets; for instance, they return text instead of objects.

Syntactically things get complicated with commands that are located at directories where PowerShell does not search (i.e., which are not known to the `$Path` environment variable). The attempt to simply specify the entire path then often fails due to the use of spaces:

```
> C:\Program Files\Git\usr\bin\nano.exe myfile.txt

  'C:\Program' is not recognized as a name of a cmdlet ...
```

The program must then be started using the `&` call operator, which is passed a string with the entire path in the first parameter. This operator can be followed by separate parameters and options.

```
> & "C:\Program Files\Git\usr\bin\nano.exe"  "myfile.txt"
```

4.3.8 Online Help

This book lacks the space for a comprehensive description of all cmdlets (but look at Chapter 7). For this reason, I will keep introducing you to new cmdlets through my examples.

Fortunately, PowerShell is equipped with excellent help features. `Get-Help <command>` (extended by the `-Examples`, `-Detailed`, or `-Full` options as required) returns comprehensive help texts for any command. If you additionally pass the `-Online` option, the help text will be displayed in the web browser.

The first time `Get-Help` is called, PowerShell may indicate that the local help files are incomplete. The solution to this problem is to run `Update-Help -UICulture en-US` once. The `-UICulture` option is necessary because most help texts are only available in English. However, download errors often occur despite this option because, for some (often smaller) modules, no help texts are available at all.

If you're looking for a command, `Get-Command` will always help. Without further options, it simply provides a list of all commands. Using `Select-String`, you can then filter the almost endless output. The following command generates a sorted list of all commands that contain the search term `VM`, which obviously control virtual machines:

```
> Get-Command | Select-String VM | Sort-Object

  Add-NetEventVmNetworkAdapter
  Add-NetEventVmSwitch
  ...
```

`Get-Command` offers a lot more search options. Check out `Get-Help Get-Command -Examples`!

Searching for Uninstalled Commands

`Get-Command` only considers cmdlets and functions that are already installed. However, countless PowerShell extension modules can be installed. The fastest way to discover a command hidden in an extension is to use `Find-Command`. More tips on using add-on modules are provided in Chapter 7, Section 7.8.

cmdlets return objects. The `Get-Member` method you apply to a result reveals which properties and methods such an object makes available for selection. The following example shows that `Get-ChildItem` usually returns `System.IO.FileInfo` objects, which can be further analyzed or processed with countless properties and methods. (Note that `Get-ChildItem` is also used for other tasks depending on the context, for example, for reading registry entries. The return data type then changes accordingly.)

```
> Get-ChildItem somefile.txt | Get-Member

  TypeName: System.IO.FileInfo
```

```
Name         MemberType      Definition
----         ----------      ----------
Target       AliasProperty   Target = LinkTarget
LinkType     CodeProperty    System.String LinkType{get=...;}
AppendText   Method          System.IO.StreamWriter AppendText()
...
```

4.4 Combining Commands

You now know how to run individual commands. But the great art of script programming is to combine multiple commands in a meaningful way. The `&&` and `||` operators are available only from PowerShell version 7 onwards.

Syntax	Function
`command1 | command2`	`command2` processes the results of `command1`.
`command1 ; command2`	First run `command1`, then `command2` (even if `command1` has triggered an error).
`command1 && command2`	First run `command1`, then `command2` (only if `command1` did not cause an error).
`command1 || command2`	First run `command1`; `command2` will be run only if `command1` has triggered an error.

Table 4.1 Combining Commands

In this section, I will focus on the pipe operator (`|`), which is most important in real-life scenarios. Further processing of intermediate results requires that the second command can cope with the result data type of the first command.

Note that cmdlets always return objects internally. These objects usually contain many more properties than are displayed on the screen. The screen output is optimized to provide a (reasonably) clear result for users. Many properties of the objects are omitted. If you want to view the result with all details, you need to pass the output to `Format-List` or to `Get-Member`. Try, for example, `Get-ChildItem | Format-List` or `Get-Process | Get-Member`!

In the following example, `Get-Process` determines all processes of the Microsoft Edge browser. The process objects are redirected to `Stop-Process`; this command terminates the web browser, if it is running.

```
> Get-Process msedge | Stop-Process
```

The following command determines the number of PNG files in a directory and all subdirectories:

```
> Get-ChildItem -Recurse *.png | Measure-Object

  Count          : 327
  Average        :
  Sum            :
  ...
```

`Measure-Object` returns all possible properties. In our example, however, only `Count` is of interest:

```
> (Get-ChildItem -Recurse *.png | Measure-Object).Count
  327
```

How much space do these files take up? `Measure-Object` can analyze and total a specific property from the `Get-ChildItem` results list. In this case, only `Sum` is relevant from the result properties:

```
> (Get-ChildItem -Recurse *.png |
   Measure-Object -Property Length -Sum).Sum

  97344806
```

4.4.1 Chains of Commands

The pipe operator can of course be used multiple times (i.e., `command1 | command2 | command3` etc.). This option opens up fascinating possibilities. The following command determines all files in the `Downloads` directory. Then, it sorts the results list by size (largest file first), extracts the first ten files, and determines their space requirements.

```
> (Get-ChildItem -Path Downloads |
   Sort-Object -Property Length -Descending |
   Select-Object -First 10 |
   Measure-Object -Property Length -Sum).Sum

  22737476
```

If you want to delete the ten largest files and use a query to double-check that this process is complete, you should proceed as follows:

```
> Get-ChildItem -Path Downloads |
  Sort-Object -Property Length -Descending |
  Select-Object -First 10 |
  Remove-Item -Confirm
```

4.4.2 Multiline Statements

In the terminal, you can enter statements of any length, but in this book, a maximum line length has been defined. In this book, I've often spread out complex commands across several lines.

When you enter multiline commands, PowerShell behaves quite intelligently: Provided that it is clear that the command is not yet complete, you can simply press Enter and continue typing on the next line. This incompleteness condition is always met if there are still open parentheses or if the last character in the line is an operator that requires a continuation, as was the case with our previous examples (| at the end of the line).

If, on the other hand, the continuation is not clearly recognizable to the shell but you still want to separate the input across several lines, the affected line must end with a space and a *backtick* (`). The space character before ` is mandatory, and ` must be immediately followed by Enter.

```
> Do-Something -LongOption 123 -OtherOption 456 `
    -YetAnotherOption "lorem ipsum"
```

4.4.3 Dealing with Special Characters

In PowerShell, many characters have a special meaning: # introduces a comment, { and } form code groups, > redirects output, etc. Sometimes, using such characters directly, that is, without the PowerShell-specific function, is required, for example, when calling external commands. In the next example, the > and # characters must not be interpreted. (I will introduce the `magick` command in more detail in Chapter 16, Section 16.1.)

In such cases, you must prefix the backtick (`) mentioned earlier. The backtick is thus the quotation mark of PowerShell and fulfills the same task as the backslash (\) in Bash and many other programming languages.

```
> magick in.png -resize 1024x1024`> -background `#733 out.jpg
```

In most cases, it is easier to enclose the relevant strings in quotes:

```
> magick in.png -resize '1024x1024>' -background '#733' out.jpg
```

If you need a line break in a string, you should use `` `n ``:

```
> Write-Output "line 1`nline 2"
  line 1
  line 2
```

4.5 The First Script

PowerShell already provides excellent options in interactive mode. With your own scripts, you can even go a step further and permanently save commands that have been tested interactively. Not only does this feature save future typing effort, but also avoids the need to memorize various commands, options, and so on.

To write scripts, you'll need an editor. For your first experiments, *Notepad* is sufficient, but the free *Notepad++* program provides significantly more functions. In the longer term, however, I recommend that you install Visual Studio Code (VS Code), described in detail in Chapter 13, if this program is not already available on your computer anyway. Whether you develop PowerShell, Bash, or Python scripts, VS Code provides excellent support. (What's not recommended, however, is the *PowerShell ISE* development environment described in many older manuals. The program is no longer developed by Microsoft and is only for PowerShell versions up to 5.1.)

4.5.1 Hello, World!

The first script is supposed to output the text "Hello, World!" (Don't worry, more serious examples will follow later in this section.) Open the editor of your choice, type the following line, and save the text file as `Hello.ps1` in an easy-to-find directory (e.g., in `Documents`). The `Write-Output` cmdlet outputs the passed string as a parameter to the screen.

```
Write-Output "Hello, World!"
```

The `*.ps1` file extension stands for PowerShell 1. When Microsoft released the second version of PowerShell, they did not want to change the then already established extension, and thus, it has absurdly remained `*.ps1` to this very day.

To run the script, you simply need to enter the filename including the prepended directory, for example:

```
> Documents\Hello.ps1

  Hello, World!
```

If the script is located in the current directory, you must prepend `.\` to explicitly name the directory, for example:

```
> .\Hello.ps1

  Hello, World!
```

In this context, "`.`" is a short notation for the directory you're currently in. For security reasons, scripts without a directory specification are only executed if the `*.ps1` files are located in a directory named in the `$PATH` environment variable. I will describe these concepts in more detail momentarily.

4.5.2 Trouble with the Execution Policy

Depending on the Windows version, your first attempt to run a custom script will fail with the following error message:

```
> .\Hello.ps1:

  File C:\Users\kofler\Documents\Hello.ps1 cannot be
  loaded because running scripts is disabled on this system.
  For more information, see about_Execution_Policies at
  https://go.microsoft.com/fwlink/?LinkID=135170
```

The cause of this error message is what's called the *execution policy*. This policy specifies the circumstances under which scripts are allowed to run on Windows. There are four possible settings:

- `Restricted`: No scripts can be executed at all.
- `AllSigned`: Only signed scripts can be executed.
- `RemoteSigned`: All custom scripts can be executed, but installed or downloaded scripts can be executed only if they have been signed.
- `Unrestricted`: All scripts can be executed.

Usually `RemoteSigned` applies on Windows Server, but `Restricted` applies for desktop versions:

```
> Get-ExecutionPolicy
  Restricted
```

For this reason, on many Windows installations, scripts cannot be run at all. For security reasons, this default setting makes sense, but it is of course unsuitable for learning scripting. The following command allows the execution of custom scripts as well as signed foreign scripts for the current user:

```
> Set-ExecutionPolicy -Scope CurrentUser RemoteSigned
```

You can also run the above command without the `-Scope CurrentUser` option—then, the setting will apply to all users of the computer. However, changing the execution policy at the system level is only allowed if you run PowerShell or Windows Terminal with admin privileges.

Even More Setting Options

The execution policy can be configured at different levels (machine, user, process). Details about the configuration options can be found at *https://docs.microsoft.com/en-us/powershell/module/microsoft.powershell.core/about/about_execution_policies*.

> **What Does Signed Mean?**
>
> A *signed script* contains a comment block with a digital signature (i.e., a cryptographic code). This code indicates who wrote the script. The code applies only to the state of the script at the time of the signature. Any subsequent change will invalidate the signature. You can sign your own scripts using `Set-AuthenticodeSignature`. This command requires that you have a certificate—either (for testing purposes) a self-created one or a real certificate from a certification authority. You can find more information on this topic at *https://docs.microsoft.com/en-us/powershell/module/microsoft.powershell.core/about/about_signing*.

4.5.3 Setting Up a Custom Script Directory

For your first script, where you save it doesn't matter. But before you write more and more scripts over the next few weeks, a good idea is to set up a directory for your scripts and add that directory to the `PATH` environment variable. In our examples, I assume that you name the directory `myscripts` and create it directly in your working directory. `Set-Location` makes the user directory the current directory if not already the case. `NewItem` creates the directory. (If you have used `cmd.exe` or Bash so far, `cd myscripts` or `mkdir myscripts` will also get you there with less typing and headaches. But I want to make an effort in this chapter to present you with the "right" PowerShell cmdlets.)

```
> Set-Location
> New-Item -ItemType Directory myscripts
```

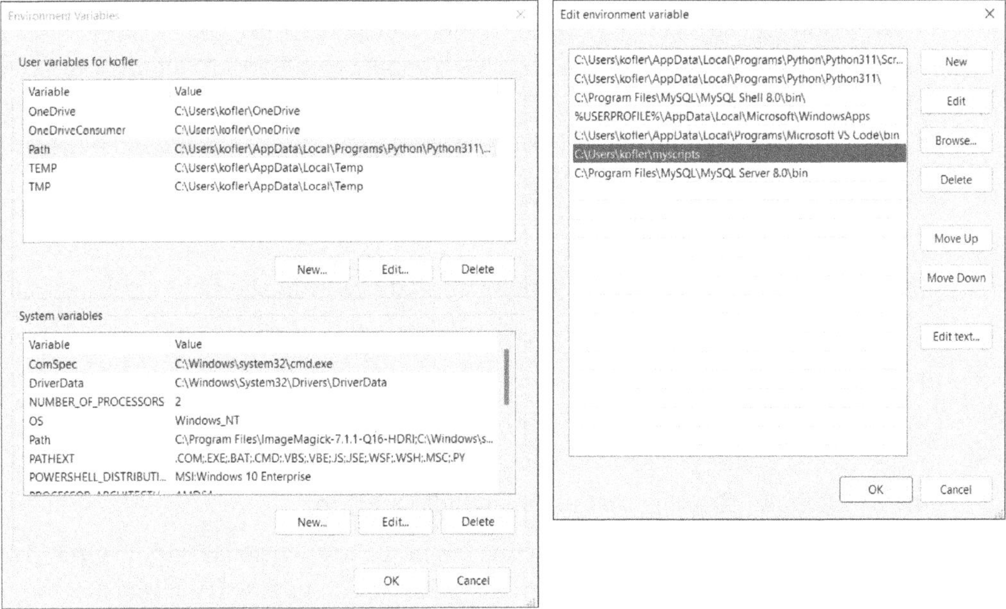

Figure 4.3 Adding a Custom Script Directory to the Path Variable

Now, we still need to set up the Path variable. This variable contains a list of all directories where PowerShell searches for executable programs and scripts. If you add the myscripts directory to this list, you can run scripts stored there without specifying the path. No matter which directory is currently active, it is now sufficient to enter Hello to start the Hello World script. Thanks to the Path variable, you don't need to specify the location or the .ps1 identifier.

To configure this variable, search for **Edit System Environment Variables** in the **Start** menu and then click the **Environment Variables** button in the **System Properties** dialog. In the dialog box of the same name, select Path from your user variables and add your script directory via **Edit • New • Browse**.

Note that changes to the Path variable take effect only after restarting the terminal or PowerShell.

4.5.4 Running Scripts on Linux and macOS

I generally assume in this chapter that you're using Windows. But of course, you can also run PowerShell scripts on Linux or macOS. Although no execution policy exists in Linux or macOS (Section 4.5.2), other rules must be observed, such as the following:

- First, the script file must start with the what's called the *shebang line* (see also Chapter 3, Section 3.5):

  ```
  #!/usr/bin/env pwsh
  ```

  This line specifies that the env command must search for the pwsh shell and execute the following code with it. For platform-independent scripts, you can also use this line on Windows, in which case this line is simply considered a comment with no effect.

- On the other hand, you must mark the script file, via chmod as *executable* (hence, x):

  ```
  $ chmod  +x Hello.ps1       (Linux)
  $ chmod a+x Hello.ps1       (macOS)
  ```

Once you have met these two requirements, you can run the script on Linux and macOS:

```
$ ./Hello.ps1
  Hello, World!
```

4.5.5 Example: Cleaning Up the Downloads Directory

After our minimalistic Hello World script, I want to return to an idea from Section 4.4, in the second example: The Tidy-Downloads.ps1 script is supposed to search the *n* largest files from the downloads directory and delete them after a query. In this way, you can quickly create space in a minimal amount of time. (After all, usually just a few huge files take up most of the space.)

Compared to Section 4.4, note two major new features:

- The script uses the `DownPath` variable, which contains the location of the downloads directory. The easiest way to determine this location would be `$DownPath = "$HOME\Downloads"`. However, this procedure does not work in every case (see *https://stackoverflow.com/questions/57947150*). For example, some users might have set different locations for their download directories. The approach taken in this case is a bit more cumbersome and uses the Known Folders API. However, this method also has a disadvantage: It works only on Windows, not on Linux or macOS.
- The number of files to be deleted can be passed to the script via an optional parameter. If the parameter is missing, the script searches for the ten largest files.

More details about the handling of variables and parameters will follow later in this chapter. But the basic concepts should be clear: In PowerShell, variables are prefixed with a dollar sign ($) character. All parameters of a script or function are declared using `param()`, where you can specify a data type, a default value, and a lot of other additional information. (Unless you use functions, `param` must be the first statement in the script!)

```
# Sample file Tidy-Downloads.ps1

# $NoOfFiles specifies how many files to delete
# (by default: 10)
param([int] $NoOfFiles = 10)

# $DownPath contains the location of the Downloads directory
$DownPath = (New-Object -ComObject Shell.Application).
               NameSpace('shell:Downloads').Self.Path
# delete the largest files in the downloads directory with
# query
Get-ChildItem -Path $DownPath |
     Sort-Object -Property Length -Descending |
     Select-Object -First $NoOfFiles |
     Remove-Item -Confirm
```

Comments

As with most scripting languages, comments in PowerShell scripts are introduced with the # character and then extend to the end of the line. Multiline comments are introduced with <# and end with #>. Such comments are especially intended to formulate help texts for `Get-Help`. The syntax is for comments is documented at *https://docs.microsoft.com/en-us/powershell/module/microsoft.powershell.core/about/about_comment_based_help*.

4.5.6 Differentiating Between PowerShell Versions

On many computers, PowerShell versions 5.*n* and 7.*n* are installed in parallel. Nevertheless, all scripts share the `*.ps1` file extension. If your code explicitly requires a specific PowerShell version or has other requirements, you must include one or more `# Requires` statements in the script:

- **`#Requires -Version <n>`**
  The script can be executed only with the specified or a newer version.
- **`#Requires -PSEdition Core`**
  The script can be executed only with the core variant (applies to all PowerShell versions from 6.0).
- **`#Requires -PSEdition Desktop`**
  The script can be executed only with the desktop variant (all Windows PowerShell versions up to and including 5.1).
- **`#Requires -Modules <name>`**
  The script requires the specified module.
- **`#Requires -RunAsAdministator`**
  The script can only be executed with admin rights.

`#Requires` statements can be placed anywhere in the script.

4.6 Variables, Strings, and Objects

You made your first acquaintance with PowerShell variables in the previous section. Basically, handling variables is quite simple: With `$Name = ...` you can assign content to a variable. Later, you can use this content again. To output the contents of a variable, you can use `Write-Output`; an even easier approach is to name the variable or a string as a standalone statement. Note that variables in strings that are between double quotation marks are replaced by their contents. More details about handling strings will follow later.

```
> $UserName = "Michael"

> Write-Output $UserName
  Michael

> $UserName
  Michael

> $UserId = 123

> Write-Output "$UserName has the ID $UserId."
  Michael has the ID 123.
```

```
> "$UserName has the ID $UserId."
  Michael has the ID 123.
```

If you accidentally use an uninitialized variable, PowerShell usually doesn't encounter any trouble: The variable is empty, but the analysis does not cause an error:


```
> "$UserName has the ID $UId."
  Michael has the ID .
```

However, uninitialized variables can cause logic errors. Therefore, including `Set-StrictMode -Version 1.0` at the start of a script makes sense. Using an uninitialized variable then leads to an error message. (However, the script continues to run anyway. More information about `Set-StrictMode` and how to handle errors in scripts will follow in Section 4.13.)

Variable Names

PowerShell allows almost any characters when naming variables, functions, etc. If you want to use spaces or special characters, the `${name}` notation is appropriate, for example `${this is a variable name too!}`. The curly brackets in this context clearly indicate where a variable's name begins and ends.

Despite this freedom in syntax, a useful practice is to compose variable names only from letters, digits, and a few special characters (_).

Typical for Windows, PowerShell does not differentiate between uppercase and lowercase. So, you could just as well parse `$userid` or `$USERID` in our earlier example as these names are equivalent for PowerShell.

You can also store the result of other commands in variables, as in the following example:

```
> $Images = Get-ChildItem *.jpg
```

`Read-Host` can be used to perform user input, as in the following example:

```
> $Name = Read-Host "Enter your name!"
  Enter your name!: Michael

> "Hello, $Name!"
  Hello, Michael!
```

4.6.1 Data Types

The attempt to perform calculations with a number entered via `Read-Host` fails because PowerShell differentiates between different data types:

```
> $N = Read-Host "A number, please".
  A number, please: 123

> $N * 7
  123123123123123123123
```

The result of Read-Host is considered as a string. For strings, however, * does not signify multiplication, but proliferation instead. The solution is to declare the variable with a suitable data type. For this task, you must prefix the desired type in square brackets. For our earlier example, [int] or [double] comes into play:

```
> [int] $N = Read-Host "A number, please".
  A number, please: 123

> $N * 7
  861
```

Note that an input like "abc" will now trigger an error.

Data Type	Meaning
bool	Boolean value ($true or $false)
int/long	32-bit or 64-bit signed integer
float/double	32-bit or 64-bit float
decimal	128-bit fixed point number
String	Character string

Table 4.2 The Most Important PowerShell Data Types

A type specification is optional. For variable assignments in code, PowerShell mostly chooses the correct data type, which you can verify later using Get-Member, as in the following example:

```
> $Price = 100.0

> $Price | Get-Member
  TypeName: System.Double
  ...
```

If you want to run through different branches of code in a script depending on the data type, the -is or -isnot operators provide help, as in the following example:

```
> $Price is [double]
  True
```

Typed variables, however, have an advantage in that the later assignment of data in the wrong type will trigger an error:

```
> [double] $Price = 100.0

> $Price = "abc"
  Error: Cannot convert value "abc" to type "System.Double".
```

4.6.2 Calculating and Comparing

As long as the data type is correct, all common basic arithmetic operations work in PowerShell. PowerShell also supports the increment and decrement operators ++ and -- as well as assignments combined with a calculation, as in the following example:

```
> $Price = 100.0
> $Price * 1.19 + 10
  129

> $Cnt = 27
> $Cnt++     # corresponds to $Cnt = $Cnt + 1
> $Cnt+=3    # corresponds to $Cnt = $Cnt + 3
> $Cnt
  31
```

However, PowerShell does not recognize the ^ character for exponents. For exponential numbers, you must use the Pow function:

```
> [Math]::Pow(2, 4)
  16
```

In this expression, [Math] refers to the class of the same name, and ::Pow refers to a function defined within[Math. (If you're familiar with the concepts of object-oriented programming, Pow is a static method.) In addition to Pow, the Math object provides countless other functions to choose from, such as Sin, Cos, or Sqrt.

Comparisons are much more cumbersome than calculations. PowerShell cannot analyze a condition like $Price > 140 because the < and > characters are used for output redirection (Section 4.8). Instead, you need to resort to various operators that look like options:

```
> $Price = 100.0
> $Price -gt 80
  True
> $Price -eq 80
  False
```

Operator	Meaning
-eq	Equal
-ne	Not equal
-gt	Greater than
-ge	Greater or equal
-lt	Less than
-le	Less than or equal

Table 4.3 Comparison Operators for Numbers and Strings

With `-not (condition)` or the short notation `!(condition)`, you can invert a condition. If you want to link multiple conditions, you should use `-and`, `-or`, or `-xor`:

```
> (100 -lt 110) -or (200 -lt 220)
  True
```

4.6.3 Strings

For many scripts, strings are more important than numbers. Like most other shells, PowerShell distinguishes between two ways of expressing strings. If you formulate strings in simple quotation marks, the content will be taken over unchanged. If, on the other hand, you use double quotation marks, then variables named within the string will be replaced by their contents. In other words, a *variable substitution* is performed. Consider the following examples:

```
> $A = "abc"
> $B = "efg $A"
> $C = 'efg $A'
> $A, $B, $C

  abc
  efg abc
  efg $A
```

If the variable name cannot be clearly delimited, you must enclose it in curly brackets:

```
> Write-Output "${A}${B}"
  abcefg abc
```

Multiline strings or strings that themselves contain the characters `"` and `'` are best assembled as *herestrings*. Such strings start with `@"` or `@'` and end with `"@` or `'@`, depending on whether you want to use variable substitution or not. The start codes and end codes must each be on separate lines:

```
$json = @"
{
  "first": "item",
  "second": "item"
}
"@
```

To compare strings, you can use the familiar operators, but keep in mind that PowerShell is not case sensitive:

```
> "abc" -eq "ABC"
  True
```

For all comparison operators, however, a *case sensitive* variant is available with a preceding `c`:

```
> "abc" -ceq "ABC"
  False
```

Using `-like` or `-notlike`, you can perform a simple pattern matching. In this context, `?` is used as a placeholder for any character, and `*` is a placeholder for several characters:

```
> "PowerShell" -like '*sh*'
  True
```

You can formulate much more complex comparison patterns based on regular expressions using `-match` and `-notmatch` (see Chapter 9).

Internally, strings are objects (see also the next subsection). As a result, strings can be processed via methods and properties. The following lines show some examples without any claim to completeness. You can get a complete list of all methods using `"" | Get-Member`.

```
> $UserName = "Michael Kofler"
> $UserName.Length
  14
> $UserName.ToUpper()
  MICHAEL KOFLER
> $UserName.StartsWith("Michael")
  True
> $UserName.Substring(8, 6)    # 6 characters from position 8
  Kofler
> $UserName.Split(" ")         # returns array
  Michael
  Kofler
```

Some processing steps can be performed with special operators instead of methods, as in the following examples:

```
> $UserName -split " "        # returns array
  Michael
  Kofler

> $UserName -replace "Michael", "Mike"
  Mike Kofler

> "Name: {0}  ID: {1}" -f "Kofler", 123
  Name: Kofler  ID: 123
```

Operator	Meaning
-eq, -ne, etc.	Comparison operators
-ceq, -cne, etc.	Case-sensitive comparison operators
-like and -notlike	Simple pattern matching
-match and -notmatch	Pattern matching with regular expressions
-f	Format
-replace	Search and replace
-split	Decompose string

Table 4.4 Important Operators for Strings

With the -f formatting operator, the placeholders {0}, {1}, etc. are replaced by the subsequent parameters. PowerShell provides countless formatting options, described further at *https://docs.microsoft.com/en-us/dotnet/standard/base-types/standard-numeric-format-strings.*

An example of using -f follows in Section 4.10.

4.6.4 Command Substitution

As mentioned earlier, thanks to variable substitution, you can include or output the contents of variables in strings:

```
> $account = "Maria"
> Write-Output "Account-Name: $account"

  Account-Name: Maria
```

However, substitution does not work if you want to apply a method to the variable:

```
> Write-Output "Account name: $account.ToLower()"  # Error
  Account name: Maria.ToLower()
```

Often, PowerShell variables contain objects (see also the following section). Intuitive access to their properties also fails. Instead, PowerShell outputs the contents of the variable and then the property name:

```
> $process = Get-Process |  Select-Object -First 1

> Write-Output "Process name: $process.ProcessName"  # Error
  Process name:
  System.Diagnostics.Process (AggregatorHost).ProcessName
```

The solution in this case is what's called *command substitution* with the `$( expr )` syntax. The `expr` expression is analyzed, and its result is inserted into the string. The expression does not have to reference existing variables—any cmdlet can be executed: The spaces before and after the parentheses are optional but can improve readability. The following listing shows some examples of command substitution:

```
> Write-Output "Account name: $( $account.ToLower() )"
  Account name: maria

> Write-Output "Process name: $( $process.ProcessName )"
  Process name: AggregatorHost

> Write-Output "Date and time: $(Get-Date)"
  Date and time: 02/12/2023 10:08:34

> $now = Get-Date
> "Time in two hours: $($now.AddHours(2).ToShortTimeString())"
  Time in two hours: 12:08
```

4.6.5 Objects

Most cmdlets do not return strings like commands in conventional shells but return full-fledged objects. For example, `Get-Process` returns an array of `Process` objects. You can use `Select-Object` to pick one object and then use `Get-Member` to view its properties and methods:

```
> Get-Process | Select-Object -First 1 | Get-Member

  TypeName: System.Diagnostics.Process

  Name                  MemberType     Definition
  ----                  ----------     ----------
  Handles               AliasProperty  Handles = Handlecount
  Name                  AliasProperty  Name = ProcessName
  NPM                   AliasProperty  NPM = NonpagedSystemMem...
  ...
```

```
Disposed              Event          System.EventHandler Dis...
Exited                Event          System.EventHandler Exi...
...
BeginOutputReadLine   Method         void BeginOutputReadLine()
CancelErrorRead       Method         void CancelErrorRead()
```

The following command sorts processes by their start times and then returns the five most recently started processes:

```
> Get-Process | Sort-Object -Property StartTime -Descending |
  Select-Object -First 5
```

You cannot directly access the properties that a cmdlet returns as a result via `cmdlet.property`. Instead, you must enclose the cmdlet in parentheses.

```
> Get-Date.Year         # error, term not recognized
> (Get-Date).Year       # OK
  2023
```

`(cmdlet).prop` is a short notation for `cmdlet | ForEach-Object { $_.prop }`. Thus, PowerShell processes all objects returned by the cmdlet and then analyzes the desired property. `(Get-ChildItem *.txt).FullName` accordingly returns the full filenames of the text files in the current directory.

4.6.6 Assembling Custom Objects

Not only can you process objects from given classes in your scripts, but you can also return results yourself in the form of your own ad hoc assembled objects. The easiest way to do this is to use a `PSCustomObject` as a basis, as in the following example:

```
$MyObject = [PSCustomObject]@{
                UserName = "Michael"
                UserId   = 123
}
```

Often a hash table (i.e., a simple key-value store) serves the same purpose. The main advantage is that the typing effort is somewhat lower:

```
$Data = @{
  UserName = "Michael"
  UserId = 123
}
```

If you want to save lines, you can separate the key-value pairs by semicolons:

```
$Data = @{ UserName = "Michael"; UserId = 123 }
```

4

4.6.7 Predefined Variables

Normally, you must take care of the initialization of your variables yourself. However, a number of predefined variables, called *automatic variables*, are available in the PowerShell terminology. These variables contain information about PowerShell, the state of the current script, and so on.

Variable	Contents
`$?`	Status of the last executed command (`$false` if an error occurred)
`$_`	The current object being processed by a pipe (`$PSITEM`)
`$args`	Array with the parameters passed to a script or function
`$Error`	Object, describes the last error that occurred
`$Event`	Object, describes the currently processed event
`$false`	Boolean state "false"
`$HOME`	String with the home directory of the current user
`$input`	Data passed to a function via standard input (pipe)
`$IsLinux`	`$true` if PowerShell is running on Linux
`$IsMacOS`	`$true` if PowerShell is running on macOS
`$IsWindows`	`$true` if PowerShell is running on Windows
`$null`	Null (uninitialized state)
`$PID`	Current process ID
`$PROFILE`	String with the path to the profile file for initialization/configuration of PowerShell
`$PWD`	Object with the path of the current directory
`$true`	Boolean state "true"

Table 4.5 The Most Important Predefined Variables of PowerShell

I have only compiled the most important variables in this table. As always, a complete description of all variables (there are about 50!) can be found in the online documentation at *https://docs.microsoft.com/en-us/powershell/module/microsoft.powershell.core/about/about_automatic_variables*.

No Globbing!

When you run a Bash script such as `script.sh *.txt`, the names of all text files in the current directory are passed to the script. On the other hand, if you pass `*.txt` as a parameter to a PowerShell script, then exactly this string gets passed.

You must take care in the script itself to use the corresponding filenames. If only one parameter is involved, `Get-Item $args` will work. If multiple parameters may be passed to your script (e.g., `script.ps1 file1 file2` or `script.ps1 *.jpg *.png`), then you must create *two* loops.

The first loop processes the parameters and executes `Get-Item`; the second processes the results returned by `Get-Item`. For a code example involving sorting photos by date taken, see Chapter 16, Section 16.2.

4.6.8 Environment Variables

Environment variables are also predefined variables. However, they are defined at the operating system level and are available not only to PowerShell, but to all processes. Many environment variables contain the locations of important directories.

Variable	Contents
`$Env:APPDATA`	Directory for program settings
`$Env:HOME`	Home directory
`$Env:HOMEDRIVE`	Drive of the home directory
`$Env:LOCALAPPDATA`	Directory for program settings
`$Env:Path`	Directory list for executable programs
`$Env:PROCESSOR_ARCHITECTURE`	CPU architecture (e.g., `AMD64`)
`$Env:PSModulePath`	Directory list for PowerShell modules
`$Env:SHELL`	Path to the active shell
`$Env:TEMP`, `$Env:TMP`	Temporary directory
`$Env:USER`	Current account name
`$Env:windir`	Path to the Windows directory (e.g., `C:\Windows`)

Table 4.6 The Most Important Environment Variables

Access to environment variables through PowerShell occurs in the somewhat unusual form, `$Env:[<varname>]`, such as `$Env:Path`. All environment variables return strings instead of objects. I have specified only a few particularly important predefined environment variables, which are rather inconsistent in terms of uppercase and lowercase names.

4.7 Arrays and Hash Tables

An array is a data structure to store multiple objects. PowerShell makes extensive use of arrays, and many commands return arrays. For example, `Get-ChildItem` usually returns an array of `FileInfo` and `DirectoryInfo` objects (unless `Get-ChildItem` is used to process registry entries).


```
> $Files = Get-ChildItem
> $Files.Length
  4

> $Files.Count    # equivalent, Count is an alias for Length
  4

> $Files.GetType()

  IsPublic  IsSerial  Name      BaseType
  --------  --------  ----      --------
  True      True      Object[]  System.Array
```

The pipe operator can perfectly handle arrays and processes the elements of an array one after the other—many examples of this processing have been shown already in this chapter. You can use `ForEach-Object` to explicitly loop and output details about each array element. Inside the loop, `$_` (short notation for `$PSItem`) provides access to the current item. More details on loops will follow in Section 4.9.

```
> $Files | ForEach-Object {  "$($_.GetType()) $($_.FullName)" }

  System.IO.DirectoryInfo C:\Users\kofler\myscripts\mydir
  System.IO.FileInfo      C:\Users\kofler\myscripts\Hello.ps1
  System.IO.FileInfo      C:\Users\kofler\myscripts\MyTest.ps1
  System.IO.FileInfo      C:\Users\kofler\myscripts\Loop.ps
```

4.7.1 Creating and Processing Custom Arrays

You can easily create arrays in your own scripts, as in the following examples:

```
> $Data = 1, 17, 39, 45
> $Data = @(1, 17, 39, 45)   # equivalent
```

Once created, the size of an array cannot be changed. Nevertheless, you can easily add more elements using the += operator. Behind the scenes, however, this operation creates a new, slightly larger array. For arrays with a large number of elements, this operation can thus be quite inefficient!

```
> $Data += 23, 27
> $Data
  1
  17
  39
  45
  23
  27
```

Array elements are accessed via an index in square brackets. As in most programming languages, the allowed index values range from 0 to the element count minus 1:

```
> $Data[0]
  1
> $Data[5]
  27
```

When an invalid index is specified, the behavior of PowerShell depends on the mode. By default, PowerShell simply returns null, but does not raise an error. If, on the other hand, you have activated strict mode (which is highly recommended in your own scripts!), an error will occur:

```
> $Data[6]
> Set-StrictMode -Version Latest
> $Data[6]
  OperationStopped: Index was outside the bounds of the array.
```

You can also specify multiple index entries. Then, the result is a new array with the selected entries:

```
> $Data[1, 2, 5]
  17
  39
  27
```

The `start..end` notation returns all elements in the specified range. If `start` is greater than `end`, the elements will be returned in reverse order. (Be sure you don't type three periods by mistake! Then, the third period would be interpreted as a decimal point, and the index value that follows, as a floating point number.)

```
> $Data[3..5]
  45
  23
  27
> $Data[5..3]
  27
  23
  45
```

4.7.2 Hash Tables

Like arrays, hash tables allow data to be stored but with a significant difference: The access to the elements is not provided through a numbered index, but by self-selected keys. For this reason, hash tables are often referred to as *key-value stores*. You can use this feature to create clear data structures. Using hash tables is just as easy as using arrays. Consider the following examples:

```
> $Data = @{ OS = "Windows"; Version = 11; ReleaseYear = 2021 }

> $Data.MinimumRamGB = 4      # Add element

> $Data                       # Read all elements

  Name            Value
  ----            -----
  MinimumRamGB    4
  ReleaseYear     2021
  OS              Windows
  Version         11

> $Data.ReleaseYear           # Read an element
  2021
```

Normally, a hash table does not care about the order of the elements. So, you must not rely on a loop to return the elements in the order in which you inserted them. If the order is important for you, you must create the hash table with the `[ordered]` keyword:

```
> $Data = [ordered]@{ Key1 = Value1; Key2 = Value2 ... }
```

4.8 Output Redirection

By default, the result of each command is displayed in the terminal. If you run `Get-ChildItem`, the terminal will contain a list of found files afterwards. You can output variables or strings either with the `Write-Output` cmdlet or simply by naming them. The following two statements are therefore equivalent, and each results in the output of "Hello, World!":

```
> Write-Output "Hello, World!"
  "Hello, World!"
```

4.8.1 Streams

What looks trivially simple at first glance is more complex behind the scenes: PowerShell differentiates between several "streams" (channels) that are intended for different purposes.

Number	Description	Cmdlet
1	Success stream	Write-Output as well as direct output
2	Error stream	Write-Error
3	Warning stream	Write-Warning
4	Verbose stream	Write-Verbose
5	Debug stream	Write-Debug
6	Information stream	Write-Information
*	All streams	–

Table 4.7 Streams

While you use Write-Output for "normal" output, you should process error messages using Write-Error, warnings using Write-Warning, and so on. Note that you can also combine these commands via the pipe operator. The following command writes the current process list to the debug stream:

```
> Get-Process | Write-Debug
```

By default, only streams 1 to 3 are displayed in the terminal. Streams 4 to 6 remain invisible to avoid bothering users with debugging information. You can control which streams are displayed (for streams 3 through 6) via Preference variables:

```
> $WarningPreference, $VerbosePreference, $DebugPreference,
   $InformationPreference

  Continue
  SilentlyContinue
  SilentlyContinue
  SilentlyContinue
```

This listing shows the default settings. Other allowed settings are the Inquire and Stop strings (see also Table 4.9 at the end of this chapter). Thus, any output in the corresponding stream results in a script interruption. With Inquire, the script can be continued after a query; with Stop, it cannot.

4.8.2 Output Redirection

The big advantage of streams is that they can be redirected to files. The classic redirection operator for the success stream is > file. Thus, all outputs of the success stream are no longer displayed on the screen but instead saved in a text file. If the file already exists, it will be overwritten. Within PowerShell, you can view the contents of the file using `Get-Content`:

```
> Get-ChildItem > files.txt
> Get-Content files.txt
  ...
```


Instead of overwriting an existing file, you can add the text outputs at the end. For this task, you must use the >> operator instead of the > operator.

The > and >> operators only affect the success stream. All other streams can be redirected with `2>` to `6>` if necessary. (When you redirect streams 3 through 6, the `Preference` variables remain valid. If `SilentlyContinue` is set, nothing will be saved in the specified file because the output will be suppressed.)

Instead of redirecting the streams to separate files, you can merge streams 2 through 6 with the success stream and then redirect that stream to one file. The following command first adds the error stream to the success stream. The outputs of both streams are then stored in the `out.txt` file.

```
> Do-Something 2>&1 > out.txt
```

Finally, using *>, you can redirect all streams to a common file.

Operator	Function
>	Redirect success stream to a file
>>	Add success stream to a file
2> through 6>	Redirect streams 2 through 6 to a file
2>> through 6>>	Add streams 2 through 6 to a file
2>&1 through 6>&1	Merge streams 2 through 6 with success stream
*>	Redirect all streams to one file
2>&1 >>	Merge streams 1 and 2 and then add them to a file

Table 4.8 Operators for Input and Output Redirection

Write-Host versus Write-Output

The `Write-Host` command executes output directly in the terminal (on the "host"). At first glance, the result looks like the result of `Write-Output`.

The crucial difference is that no redirection is possible for these outputs. With `Write-Host`, your scripts lose flexibility. The users of your scripts cannot simply redirect their output to a file. Use `Write-Output`!

4.8.3 Duplicating Output (Tee-Object)

Sometimes, you want to see the output of a cmdlet or script on the screen *and* save it to a file. To do this, `Tee-Object` can help you: This command is used with the pipe operator. It takes the success stream, displays it, and redirects it to the specified file at the same time. If you run the following command, you'll see the files of the current directory in the terminal; at the same time the file list will be saved in `files.txt`.

```
> Get-ChildItem | Tee-Object files.txt
```

`Tee-Object` only considers the success stream. However, you can use `n>&1` to add another stream to the success stream first:

```
> Get-ChildItem 2&>1 | Tee-Object files-and-errors.txt
```

4.8.4 (Not) Formatting the Output

By default, PowerShell formats every output. For example, `Get-ChildItem` returns an array of `FileInfo` and `DirectoryInfo` objects as a result. However, PowerShell does not display these objects with all their properties but instead creates a text representation from these objects that is reasonably readable for humans. Alternative representations with more or less details can be obtained by passing the outputs to various `Format` commands:

```
> Get-ChildItem | Format-List
> Get-ChildItem | Format-Table
> Get-ChildItem | Format-Custom Name,Length
```

When you redirect the result of a PowerShell command to a text file, an often appropriate task is to eliminate any formatting. With the sample command `Get-ChildItem`, you're probably only interested in the filenames, not in a table with multiple columns, or color codes for a nicer representation of the column labels, etc. Unfortunately, this common task can only be realized in a rather awkward way in PowerShell.

The following example shows a possible approach: The result of `Get-ChildItem` is passed to `ForEach-Object`, and `$_.Name` extracts the filename from each object. (Details about `ForEach-Object` and the `$_` notation follow in Section 4.9.) `Out-String` outputs the resulting names without further formatting. Finally, `>` redirects all output to the `files.txt` file. This file then contains a file or directory name on each line.

```
> Get-ChildItem |
  ForEach-Object {$_.Name} |
  Out-String > files.txt
```

4.8.5 No Input Redirection

Many shells also provide the option of input redirection via `<`. On Linux, `command1 | command2` is therefore equivalent to the following command sequence (apart from the fact that the detour via a file costs storage space and time):

```
$ command1 > file.txt
$ command2 < file.txt
```

Unfortunately, PowerShell does not support < because PowerShell commands expect objects most of the time. But if you first write the result of a PowerShell command into a text file via `command1 > file.txt`, the object information will be lost. The text file contains only formatted text and subsequently cannot serve as a basis for processing the data in another command.

The lack of input redirection becomes problematic when you use commands from the Linux world that require just input redirection. For example, you can make a backup of a database using `mysqldump` and restore it later via `mysql`. On Linux and macOS, the following code would work:

```
$ mysqldump dbname > backup.sql   # Create backup
$ mysql dbname  < backup.sql      # Restore database
```

In PowerShell, only the first command works, not the second. However, a workaround exists for this problem. For this purpose, run `Get-Content` to output the contents of the `backup.sql` file. Then, redirect this output to `mysql` by using `|`, as in the following example:

```
> Get-Content backup.sql | mysql dbname
```

4.9 Loops

Often, you need to process several elements one after the other in a script, such as each line of a text file, each file of a directory, and so on. Loops, which are available in several syntax variants in PowerShell, can help you with this process. In practice, the most important loop is `foreach($item in $data)`. This loop inserts all elements from `$data` (i.e., a variable with an array or other enumeration) in sequence into the `$item` loop variable and processes them. In the following example, the string in `$Text` is split into words by using `Split`. These words are then output in a loop on the screen.

```
> $Text = "I love PowerShell!"

> foreach ($Word in $Text.Split(" ")) {
      $Word
  }

  I
  love
  PowerShell!
```

4.9.1 ForEach-Object

With `ForEach-Object`, PowerShell provides an alternative approach. The main difference is that `ForEach-Object` expects the objects to be processed as input. This expectation makes the command particularly suitable for pipes. Within the loop construct, you can access the currently active object via `$_`. The following loop is equivalent to the previous example:

```
$Text.Split(" ") | ForEach-Object { $_ }
```

If you want to output the length of all words, you should use the following code:

```
> $Text.Split(" ") | % { Write-Host $_.Length }
  1
  4
  11
```

For this relatively common case (i.e., the application of a property or a method to the loop variable), there is a short notation available:

```
> $Text.Split(" ") | ForEach-Object Length
  1
  4
  11
```

Finally, because the `ForEach-Object` keyword is needed so often, it can be shortened even further using `%`:

```
> $Text.Split(" ") | % ToUpper()
  I
  LOVE
  POWERSHELL!
```

When you combine `ForEach-Object` with the `-Parallel` option, it runs the statements in the loop (that is, the code between the curly brackets) in parallel threads. This approach can save a lot of time on powerful computers with many CPU cores. This parallel processing is the case in the following example: `Get-ChildItem` determines all `*.bmp` files in the current directory. `Compress-Archive` compresses each image into a file named `<filename.bmp>.zip`.

```
> Get-ChildItem *.bmp | ForEach-Object -Parallel {
      Compress-Archive -DestinationPath "$_.zip" $_
  }
```

4.9.2 for, while, do-while, and do-until

PowerShell also uses the loop constructs known from other programming languages, namely, `for`, `while`, `do-while`, and `do-until`. This kind of looping is rather uncommon in shell scripts, which is why I only provide a short example of each without further explanation. If necessary, you can refer to the documentation.

```
> for ($i=0; $i -lt 5; $i++) { $i }

  # Output: 0, 1, ..., 4

> $i=0
> while ($i -lt 5) {
      Write-Host $i
      $i++
  }
  # Output again: 0, 1, ..., 4

> $i=0
> do {
      Write-Host $i
      $i++
  } while ($i -lt 5)
  # Output again: 0, 1, ..., 4

> $i=0
> do {
      Write-Host $i
      $i++
  } until ($i -eq 5)
  # Output yet again: 0, 1, ..., 4
```

4.10 Branches

A common scenario is that you want to execute code only when a certain condition is met. Depending on the state of a variable, different branches of your code should be executed. The easiest way to create branches is to use an `if-elseif-else` statement. Any number of `elseif` blocks are allowed. Both `elseif` and `else` are optional.

```
if (condition1) {
    statements
} elseif (condition2) {
    statements
} else {
    statements
}
```

Blank Character

The notations `if(condition)` and `if (condition)` are both syntactically valid. The more common and more readable version is the one that uses a space before the parentheses. This advice also applies to `for`, `foreach`, `while`, `until`, and so on.

Note, however, that for functions and methods you cannot have a space between the names and the opening parenthesis!

The following sample script first uses `Get-CimInstance` to create an array of `Win32_LogicalDisk` objects that describe the file systems of the current computer. The CIM standard helps you manage IT resources and is supported by Microsoft through the WMI API. In our example, we are only interested in type 3 disks (*local disks*). For each file system on a hard disk or SSD, the script calculates the free space as a percent and in gigabytes.

```
# Sample file Get-DiskFree.ps1
$Drives = Get-CimInstance -ClassName Win32_LogicalDisk
foreach ($Drive in $Drives) {
    if ($Drive.DriveType -eq 3) {
        $PercentageFree = 1.0 * $Drive.FreeSpace / $Drive.Size
        $GBFree = $Drive.FreeSpace / 1000000000
        "{0:S} {1:P1}  / {2,5:F0} GB free" -f `
            $Drive.DeviceId, $PercentageFree, $GBFree
    }
}
```

To format the output, the script uses the `-f` format operator, in the following structure:

```
"format code" -f value1, value2, value3, ...
```

The string with the formatting statements is followed by the `-f` operator and then an array of values to be processed. Within the formatting string, `{0}` is replaced by the first value, `{1}` by the second value, and so on. The number can be followed by other formatting codes. In this example, I have used the following codes:

- `{0:S}`: Output the first value of the following array unchanged as a string
- `{1:P1}`: Format the second value as a percentage with one decimal place
- `{2,5:F0}`: Output third value as a float without decimal places (`F0`) right-aligned with five digits

You can find good documentation on the allowed format codes, which PowerShell inherits from the .NET framework like so much else, at *https://docs.microsoft.com/en-us/dotnet/standard/base-types/standard-numeric-format-strings*.

The script then returns the following output, for example:

```
> .\Get-DiskFree.ps1

  C: 84.2 %  /   180 GB free
  F: 98.3 %  /    15 GB free
```


This script was supposed to illustrate the use of `if`. However, I will not hide from you that this code can also be formulated quite differently. In the following lines, `Where-Object` filters out the desired file systems from the array. `ForEach` processes the remaining results, accessing the current element through `$_` instead of the loop variable `$Drive`. If you are familiar with functional programming—no matter which language—this solution will probably look more elegant to you:

```
$Drives = Get-CimInstance -ClassName Win32_LogicalDisk
$Drives | Where-Object -Property DriveType -eq 3 | ForEach {
    $PercentageFree = 1.0 * $_.FreeSpace / $_.Size
    $GBFree = $_.FreeSpace / 1000000000
    "{0:S} {1:P1}  /  {2,5:F0} GB free" -f `
         $_.DeviceId, $PercentageFree, $GBFree
}
```

4.10.1 Case Distinctions Using switch

`switch` can replace multiple `if` statements if different cases are to be processed for an expression. The following syntax is used in the simplest case:

```
$option = "b"
switch ($option) {
    "A"      { Write-Output "Option A" }
    "B"      { Write-Output "Option B" }
    "C"      { Write-Output "Option C" }
    default { Write-Output "Invalid" }
}
```

Note that string comparisons in this context are not case sensitive, as usual.

4.11 Functions and Parameters

Functions provide the option to bundle multiple PowerShell commands, which facilitates organizing extensive scripts. In its simplest form, a function has the following structure:

```
function Do-Something {
    command1
    command2
    ...
}
```

Within a script, functions can only be used *after* they have been defined. Thus, a script file first contains all the functions, while the code that is ultimately to be executed is located at the end.

Naming Rules

The PowerShell documentation recommends naming custom functions, such as cmdlets, according to the *verb-noun* pattern. The hyphen required in the name, like almost any other character, can be used without special marking.

4.11.1 Function Results

What is unusual compared to "real" programming languages is the structure of the return value of a function in PowerShell: The result is obtained from all the outputs created in the function! All partial results caused by the commands within the function are returned collectively. Statements whose results end up in variables are not taken into account.

For example, when the following three statements are run within the function, the function result is an array formed by the result of `command1`, the `"lorem ipsum"` string, and the result of `command2`:

```
command1
command2
Write-Output "lorem ipsum"
# Result: Array with the partial results from command1 and
# command2 and a string
```

In the second example, only `$a + $b`, which is a number, causes output to the success stream:

```
$a = 123
$b = command    # command returns 456 as the result
$a + $b
# Result: integer number 579
```

Additionally, three statements are executed in the third example. But because the results of `command1` and `command2` are stored in variables, and because `Write-Debug` does not write to the success stream, no result is produced!

```
$a = command1
Write-Debug "lorem ipsum"
$b = command2
# no result (therefore $null)
```

The structure of the result outlined in this context naturally also applies to commands that are executed in loops. Each output within the loop expands the function result that is returned at the end.

Be Careful with Write-Output!

For debugging purposes, you might be tempted to include `Write-Output` in a function to output intermediate results. *Don't do this!* `Write-Output` produces an output that becomes part of the function result. A better approach is to use `Write-Debug` and enable debugging outputs via `$DebugPreference = "Continue"`!

As an alternative, you can also use `Write-Host`. But this approach has a disadvantage in that you must remove these statements later. Output from `Write-Host` cannot be redirected or otherwise disabled. Compared to `Write-Output`, using `Write-Host` has an advantage in that it does not change the function result.

4.11.2 return

A function typically ends with the execution of the last command. However, you can also terminate a function prematurely using `return` (e.g., within a loop as soon as a condition is fulfilled). If you use `return` without parameters, the function result is composed of all previous outputs as before:

```
command1
command2
return
# Result: Array with the partial results of command1 and command2
```

Alternatively, you can pass a variable, expression, or command to `return`. In this case, the result of this expression is added to the previous partial results. (As a matter of fact, one would assume that only the `return` expression determines the result. But this is not the case with PowerShell!)

```
command1
command2
return command3
# Result: Array with the partial results of command1, command2
# and command3
```

4.11.3 Parameters

Usually, parameters are supposed to be passed to functions. Declaring the position, name, data type, default value, and other properties in advance using `param` makes sense. PowerShell offers a wealth of syntactic options, of which I will only consider the most important ones in this book. In the simplest case, you simply specify a list of parameters that are mandatory to pass. Specifying the data type in square brackets is optional; if you choose to do so, the data type will be checked when a parameter is passed.

```
function Do-Something {
    param(
        [type1] $Parameter1
        [type2] $Parameter2
        [type3] $Parameter3
    )
}
```

Alternatively, the following short notation is allowed:

```
function Do-Something ([type1]$Para1, [t2]$P2, [t3]$P3) { ... }
```

If you specify a default value for parameters, as in the following example, the parameter becomes optional, and thus does not need to be specified when called:

```
function Do-It ([int]$A, [int]$B = 2, [String]C = "abc") { ... }
```

Functions without an Explicit Parameter List

The use of `param` is optional. All data that does not correspond to the predefined parameter list is accessible within the function in the predefined `$args` variable. If you do not declare a parameter list, then `$args` applies to all parameters. The PowerShell documentation speaks of *positional parameters* in this context because the parameters have no name and can only be analyzed based on their position.

However, the analysis of `$args` is prone to errors. Internally, `$args` is an array, so `$args(0)` is the first parameter, `$args(1)` is the second one, etc. `$args.Length` specifies how many parameters not declared via `param` were passed.

4.11.4 Calling Functions

Remember to pass parameters when calling functions *without* naming parentheses! This behavior is equivalent to calling cmdlets but, of course, differs from the behavior of almost all other programming languages.

```
Do-It 1 2 "abc"
```

Parameters can be used like options. The associated values follow either separated by a space or in the `-Parameter name:Value` notation. The order then no longer plays a role. The following two calls of `Do-It` are equivalent to the previous line:

```
Do-It -C "abc" -A 1 -B 2
Do-It -B:2 -C:"abc" -A:1
```

4.11.5 Processing Standard Input

Sometimes, a function is to be programmed in such a way that it can process objects from the standard input; that is, it can be called via the pipe operator in the following form: `... | My-Function`. The easiest approach in such cases is to select the predefined `$input` variable. The following function calculates the total of the `Length` properties of all objects, divides the result by 1,000,000, and then displays the calculated result:

```
function Get-TotalSize {
    $TotalSize = 0
    foreach($item in $input) {
        $TotalSize += $Item.Length
    }
    $TotalSize /= 1000000
    "Total size: {0:F1} MB" -f $TotalSize
}
```

To calculate the space required by all files in the `Downloads` directory, the function can be called in the following way:

```
> Get-ChildItem -Recurse C:\Users\kofler\Downloads\ |
  Get-TotalSize

  Total size: 247.4 MB
```

This script has a flaw: It relies on the fact that any object passed via standard input actually has a `Length` property. `Set-StrictMode` also interferes with this script if you pass a version number greater than 1. The simplest solution is to check the data type within the loop and then make an assignment into a typed variable, as in the following example:

```
foreach($Item in $input) {
    if ($Item.GetType().Name -eq "System.IO.FileInfo") {
        [System.IO.FileInfo] $FInfo = $Item
        $TotalSize += $FInfo.Length
    }
}
```

If the data type does not match, the script will trigger an error.

4.11.6 Syntax Variants

For functions that are supposed to process standard input, PowerShell provides two syntax variants. One version involves organizing the function into the three blocks, `begin`, `process`, and `end`:

```
function Process-Data {
    begin   { initialization ... }
    process { process data ...  }
    end     { output, cleanup ... }
}
```

The `process` block is run for each element of the standard input, where `$_` provides access to the currently active element. All three blocks are optional. If you define *one* of these blocks in a function, the entire code of the function must be specified in `begin`, `process`, and `end`. The function `Get-TotalSize` can then be programmed in the following way:

```
function Get-TotalSize {
    begin {
        $TotalSize = 0
    }
    process {
        $TotalSize += $_.Length
    }
    end {
      $TotalSize /= 1000000
      "Total size: {0:F1} MB" -f $TotalSize
    }
}
```

With `Set-StrictMode -Version 2`, PowerShell complains again that it is not sure if `$_` has a `Length` property. If necessary, you need to rebuild the code, as explained earlier.

`filter` is a short notation for a function where the `begin` and `end` blocks are empty:

```
filter Process-Data {
    code
}
# equivalent
function Process-Data {
    begin   { }
    process { code }
    end     { }
}
```

In practice, `filter` is only useful in exceptional cases. Without the initialization performed in `begin` or without final commands in `end`, programming a meaningful function can be difficult.

4.12 Modules

Functions stored in a *.ps1 file are only accessible within this script, not outside the script. If you want to call your functions interactively in the shell (like cmdlets) or use them in another script, you must save the code of the functions in a module (file identifier *.psm1):


```
# File MyModule.psm1
Function F1 { ... }
Function F2 { ... }
Function F3 { ... }
```

Before you can call any of the functions stored in the module, you must import the module once:

```
> Import-Module .\MyModule.psm1
```

Until the end of the current PowerShell session, you can then call functions F1, F2, and F3 like cmdlets:

```
> F1
```

When you make changes or corrections in the module, running Import-Module again is not sufficient, however. You must first explicitly delete the module from the internal PowerShell memory using Remove-Module and then load it again!

```
> Remove-Module MyModule
> Import-Module .\MyModule.psm1
```

You can list the functions defined in a loaded module via Get-Command, as in the following example:

```
> Get-Command -Module MyModule

  CommandType     Name   Version    Source
  -----------     ----   -------    ------
  Function        F1     0.0        MyModule
  Function        F2     0.0        MyModule
  Function        F3     0.0        MyModule
```

4.12.1 Module Directories

For Import-Module, you must always specify the path of the directory where you saved the module file. You can avoid this step if you save the module in a directory that PowerShell provides for module files. A list of these directories that are separated by semicolons is contained in the $Env:PSModulePath environment variable. In the following command, I used -split to output the content of the variable in a more readable way:

```
> $Env:PSModulePath -split ';'

  C:\Users\kofler\Documents\PowerShell\Modules
  C:\Program Files\PowerShell\Modules
  C:\program files\powershell\7\Modules
  C:\Program Files\WindowsPowerShell\Modules
  C:\Windows\system32\WindowsPowerShell\v1.0\Modules
```

Notice how the `Documents\PowerShell\Modules` directory in your home directory is a good place to store your own modules. (This directory is provided for by default in `$PSModulePath`, but it does not exist yet. You must create the directory using `mkdir` before you can use the directory for the first time.)

Note that you must not store your module directly in one of the `PSModulePath` directories; instead, you must first set up a subdirectory that has the same name as the module file (in this example, `MyModule`)!

```
> mkdir C:\Users\kofler\Documents\PowerShell\Modules\MyModule
> Copy-Item MyModule.psm1 `
  C:\Users\kofler\Documents\PowerShell\Modules\MyModule
```

If required, you can also extend `PSModulePath` with additional directories in the system settings.

mkdir or New-Item?

The `mkdir` command we used earlier does not correspond to the typical appearance of cmdlets. In fact, the quasi-official way to create a directory is `New-Item -ItemType "directory" -Name mydir`. But even Microsoft has realized that this is going too far. For this reason, the `mkdir` function is available, which calls `New-Item` and passes the necessary options.

Loading Modules Automatically

If the functions you program are so important that you want to use them in every PowerShell session, you should include `Import-Module` into your profile file. The easiest way to open this PowerShell initialization file is to use `<editor> $PROFILE` in your favorite editor. If you have VS Code installed, the command is `code $PROFILE`.

4.12.2 Modules for Experts

To make your modules behave like full-fledged cmdlets as much as possible, many optimization options are available, but I will only hint at them briefly here:

- **Export-ModuleMember**
  By default, all functions and aliases declared in a module file are available after Import-Module. You can use the Export-ModuleMember statement to make selected functions public:

  ```
  # Export only the F2 function
  Export-ModuleMember -Function F2
  ```

  Note that Export-ModuleMember must be specified *after* the declaration of the functions, not at the start of the module file! You can find more details at *https://docs.microsoft.com/en-us/powershell/module/microsoft.powershell.core/about/about_modules*.
- **Manifest file**
  If you want to make your module publicly available for download, you must also set up a manifest file (*.psd1 identifier). This file contains an exact description of your module's metadata (i.e., your name, the module's version number, the assumed PowerShell version, etc.). You can find more details at *https://docs.microsoft.com/en-us/powershell/module/microsoft.powershell.core/about/about_module_manifests*.
- **CmdletBinding**
  You can use the CmdletBinding keyword to describe attributes of your function in more detail: Where is a help text located? Should users of your function be given the option to confirm each action beforehand? (This option is appropriate if your function modifies or even deletes data.) Should the outputs of the function be displayed page by page? You can find more details at *https://docs.microsoft.com/en-us/powershell/module/microsoft.powershell.core/about/about_functions_cmdletbindingattribute*.

Installing Additional Modules

Instead of programming modules yourself, you can access a wide range of free modules in the PowerShell Gallery. I will tell you how to install such modules in Chapter 7, Section 7.8.

4.13 Error Protection

Prior to executing a script, PowerShell performs a cursory syntax check. Only in the case of serious syntax errors, such as unclosed parentheses or quotation marks, will a script not be executed at all.

Also, as a consequence, PowerShell, like many other scripting languages, is quite tolerant of errors. If a command does not exist, a file to be accessed does not exist, or some other error is thrown, PowerShell displays an error message but then continues the script with the next statement. In this section, I'll describe how you can make your PowerShell scripts as error proof as possible.

4.13.1 Set-StrictMode

The `Set-StrictMode` command, mentioned several times earlier in this chapter, sets how picky PowerShell should be about detecting errors. `Set-StrictMode` currently supports three versions:

- `Set-StrictMode -Version 1.0` causes an error message when using an uninitialized variable. Variables in strings (i.e., `"text $UnknownVariable"`) are excluded.
- `Set-StrictMode -Version 2.0` triggers an error for each uninitialized variable as well as when using non-existent properties.
- `Set-StrictMode -Version 3.0` also throws an error when accessing non-existent array elements.

The inaccuracies detected by `Set-StrictMode` will result in an error message, but the script will still continue! You can also specify `Latest` instead of a version number. However, the results of these tests should be taken with a grain of salt: If more validity tests are added in a future PowerShell version, your script may report an error even though nothing has changed in the code.

4.13.2 Aborting Scripts on Errors

The way PowerShell behaves when it detects an error depends on the contents of the `$ErrorActionPreference` variable. You can change the desired behavior simply by assigning a string to the variable. This change is allowed everywhere in a script. You can cause a different response to errors in different parts of the program.

Setting	Effect
`"Continue"`	Display error message, continue script (applies by default)
`"Inquire"`	Display error message and ask if script should be continued
`"SilentlyContinue"`	Continue script without error message
`"Stop"`	Display error message, end script

Table 4.9 The Most Important Settings for the $ErrorActionPreference Variable

4.13.3 Separating Error Messages from Other Output

When you run a script interactively in PowerShell, ordinary outputs and errors alike appear in the terminal. However, if you redirect the output of a script to a file using `> outfile.txt`, then that file will contain only the regular output. The error messages are still visible on the screen. This behavior has to do with the fact that PowerShell differentiates between multiple "streams" that are intended for different purposes. For background information on this topic, see Section 4.8.

4.13.4 Error Protection Using try/catch

As with most higher-level programming languages (like C#, Java, etc.), PowerShell provides the option to wrap multiple statements of critical (error-prone) code into a `try` block. If an error occurs in that block during execution, the code continues in the `catch` block. The `Error` variable provides information about the error there.

```
try {
    command1
    command2
    ...
} catch {
    # Here code will be executed only if a
    # an error has occurred
    Write-Host "An error occurred: $_"
}
```

The decisive advantage of `try-catch` constructs is that you can continue your script even if errors occur without an error message and, if necessary, respond specifically to an error.

Outputting Error Messages

PowerShell does not make outputting error messages easy. In our earlier example, I used `Write-Host`. The error message thus appears in the terminal but cannot be redirected.

`Write-Output` is usually not recommended because it makes the error message part of the result of the script or function.

`Write-Error` is only useful in exceptional cases, because—depending on the setting of `$ErrorActionPreference`—this output then triggers another error.

Two important syntax variants to the `try-catch` syntax are worth exploring:

- You can define multiple `catch` blocks for different error types. PowerShell then only considers the `catch` code that matches the error which occurred.
- Following the `catch` blocks, there may be a `finally` block, which is for cleanup. Code formulated in this block is *always* executed, regardless of whether an error occurs or not, and regardless of whether the script or function is exited in a `try` or `catch` block via `return`.

For more details about these syntax variants, refer to *https://docs.microsoft.com/en-us/powershell/module/microsoft.powershell.core/about/about_try_catch_finally*.

4.13.5 Terminating the Script Execution Prematurely (Exit)

You can use `Exit` to terminate a script prematurely. Optionally, you can return an error code in the process: 0 means no error arose; any other number is an error code whose meaning you can freely choose.

```
Exit 1   # Terminate script with error code
```

After executing a script, you can retrieve its exit code from the `$LASTEXITCODE` variable. Note that exit codes exist only for conventional commands and for scripts. (cmdlets do not have exit codes.)

Chapter 5
Python

Python is currently one of the most popular programming languages, and surprisingly for a wide variety of purposes: as a *first language* for learning programming; for scientific tasks including statistics and visualization; and also for AI research (neural networks, image recognition, etc.).

In this book, I focus on using Python as a scripting language. The focus is thus on the development of often tiny programs to perform or automate administrative tasks. For example, Python is great for converting data from one format to another (e.g., comma-separated values [CSV] to JSON); extracting data from or storing data in databases; or processing data from the network (e.g., web scraping, requests for REST APIs).

As I explained in Chapter 1, Python is more accessible compared to Bash and PowerShell: The syntax is clear and consistent, and the documentation available on the web is outstanding. In Python, you can reproduce relatively easily a complicated logic through functions. Python manages the balancing act across all common operating systems and is not strongly anchored to a particular operating system like Bash or PowerShell are, while Bash and PowerShell have by no means lost their reason for existence. These languages excel in calling operating system-related commands or cmdlets. A backup script that primarily combines a few external commands into a meaningful whole is easiest to implement in Bash. Similarly, this advice applies to PowerShell if you want to administer a Microsoft Active Directory system.

This chapter provides a brief introduction to Python. It focuses on the language features that are particularly important for scripting. Should you "fall in love" with Python and want to write more than just short scripts, you'll find a large volume of literature on the internet and on the book market for more in-depth study.

5.1 Installing Python

Python is installed by default on almost all Linux distributions. All you need to do is determine which version you have by opening a terminal window and running the following command:

```
python --version
  Python 3.11.1
```

If the version number 2.7 is displayed, your distribution has the outdated version 2 and the current version 3 installed in parallel. You must then run Python 3 using the `python3` command.

5.1.1 Windows

For Windows, for links to the latest Python releases for Windows, refer to *https://python.org/downloads/windows*.

Once you have selected the desired version number, you still need to decide on the right installer. Usually, you would select the *Windows installer (64-bit)*.

Make sure you enable the **Add python.exe to PATH** option in the installer before clicking **Install Now**! This option ensures that you can easily launch Python from `cmd.exe` or PowerShell later.

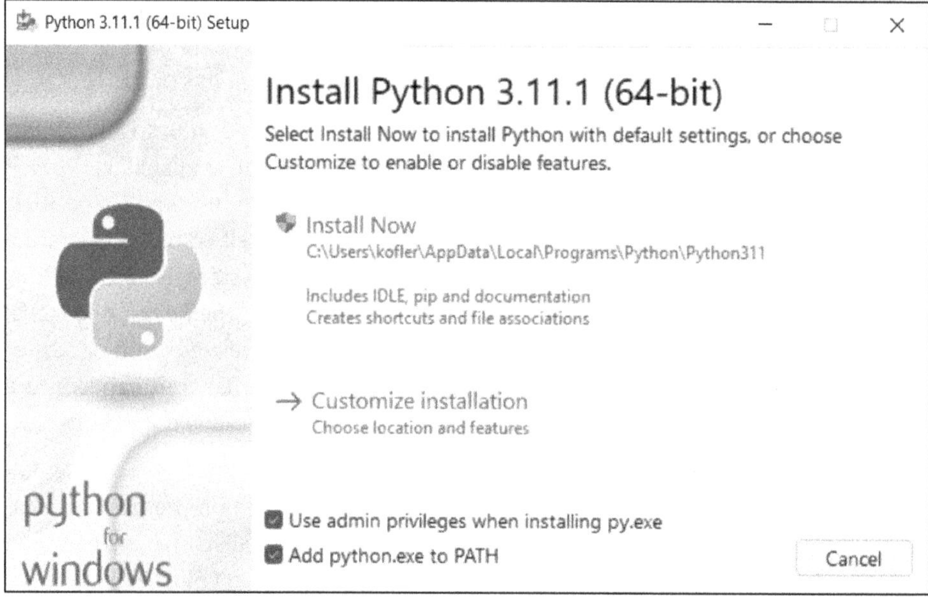

Figure 5.1 Python Installer for Windows

Once the actual installation is complete, you have the option of overriding the typical Windows limit of 260 characters for starting commands. If a Python program is called with a large number of parameters, this limit may cause errors. For this reason, you should click **Disable path length limit**. (The button will not be displayed if the limit has already been disabled during a previous installation or by some other way.)

After the installation, start `cmd.exe` or PowerShell and verify that Python and its module manager *pip* can be started with the following commands:

```
> python --version
  Python 3.11.1

> pip --version
  pip 22.3.1 from C:\Users\kofler\AppData\Local\Programs\Python\
                  Python311\Lib\site-packages\pip (python 3.11)
```


Avoid Multiple Installations!

Installing Python on Windows is quite easy—and that's where the problem lies: The Microsoft Store, development environments, editors, and so on are always happy to help you install the latest Python version, which can easily result in two or three versions installed in parallel. At first glance, everything seems to work until you try to install an extension module using pip. Although pip won't report any error, Python won't be able to find the module. The cause is trivial: The pip version you're calling is from a different Python version than the one you're currently using—most likely because the older version is preferred in the PATH environment variable.

Trying to solve the resulting problems has already driven me (and more often my students) to despair. The best solution is to systematically search for all Python versions on the computer and uninstall each of them. After that, you must remove all PATH directories related to Python in the **System Properties** preference pane. A Windows restart certainly won't hurt either. Finally, you need to download the installer from the website mentioned earlier and install the latest Python version. Avoid the Microsoft Store or any other installation methods!

5.1.2 macOS

The easiest way to install Python 3 on macOS is to use the graphical installer (**.pkg* file). You can find it on the Python download page at *https://python.org/downloads*.

During installation, a Finder window opens where you must double-click the `Install Certificates.command` script to run it. This script installs various SSL certificates and thus allows you to install root certificates that Python programs can use to verify HTTPS encryption. (Python does not use macOS certificates. This step is therefore absolutely necessary!)

After the installation, you should launch a new terminal window and double-check that everything has worked out fine, just like on Linux. Note that the commands are `python3` and `pip3`, not `python` and `pip`, as on Windows and with current Linux distributions.

```
$ python3 --version
  Python 3.11.1
$ pip3 --version
  pip 22.3.1 from /Library/Frameworks/Python.framework/Versions/
              3.11/lib/python3.11/site-packages/pip (python 3.11)
```

5.2 Getting to Know Python in a Terminal Window

Unlike most other programming languages, you can try out Python *without* writing code to a file. Simply open a terminal window and run the python or python3 command in it. This will start an interactive Python environment. In it, the three >>> characters (the "Python prompt") indicate the place where you can perform input yourself. [Enter] terminates the input, and Python then displays the result:

```
$ python
>>> 1+2
    3
```

When trying out Python interactively, you can mostly do without print, because results are displayed automatically anyway:

```
>>> x=5
>>> print(x + 7)
    12
>>> x + 7
    12
```

You can even enter multiline statements, such as for loops. There are two things to keep in mind: On the one hand, the statements within the loop must be indented by spaces, and on the other hand, you must terminate the entire input by pressing [Enter] *twice*. The Python interpreter prepends >>> to the first line, and three dots appear on all subsequent lines:

```
>>> for i in range(3):
...     print(i)
...
    0
    1
    2
```

To exit Python, press [Ctrl] + [D].

Interactive Outputs versus Script Outputs

In the following sections, you'll see numerous Python commands that are meant for interactive experimentation and are marked with the >>> prompt. Even though these examples look trivial, you should make the effort to follow them yourself and maybe conduct a few more experiments.

Note that, when using Python interactively, the result of an expression always gets displayed. x and [Enter] shows the content of x, entering x + 3 calculates the total and shows the result.

In scripts, things are different: There you need to use print for creating outputs. This means you must include print(x) or print(x + 3) in your script to output x or the total.

5.3 Programming Custom Scripts

Of course, you don't want to use Python primarily interactively; you want to program scripts to do a particular task over and over again. Countless editors and development environments are available to help you do this.

A good choice is Visual Studio Code (VS Code). As soon as you edit a Python script in it, VS Code asks if you want to install the recommended Python extensions. You should definitely do that! In addition to various additional functions, VS Code then provides the option to start your script directly from the editor.

Once you have created a new, still empty file in VS Code, you need to enter the following line and save the file as `HelloWorld.py`:

```
print('Hello, World!')
```

Provided that you have installed the Python extension, you can start the program by clicking the **Run** button. On Windows, the actual output is unfortunately somewhat lost in the status information used behind the scenes in VS Code and PowerShell.

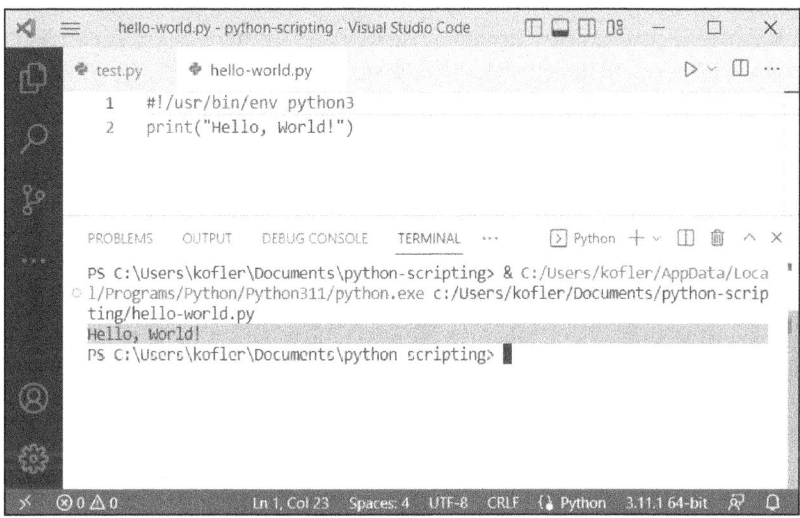

Figure 5.2 The Hello World Script in the VS Code Editor on Windows

5.3.1 Shebang

To run Python scripts on Linux and macOS without VS Code or another development environment, you must preface the script with the following shebang line. On current Linux distributions, you can simply specify `python` instead of `python3`, but on older distributions and on macOS, only `python3` provides clarity as to which Python version you're referring to.

```
#!/usr/bin/env python3
```

You already know the shebang syntax from Bash: The line specifies which program (which interpreter) should execute the following code. But what is new in this case is env: Python is installed in different directories depending on the operating system or distribution. env searches in the common directories and therefore works more reliably than specifying a rigid path.

Now, you need to mark your script as executable using chmod before starting it in the terminal:

```
$ chmod  +x hello-world.py          (Linux)
$ chmod a+x hello-world.py          (macOS)

$ ./hello-world.py

  Hello, World!
```

On Windows, the shebang line is not relevant; the *.py identifier is sufficient. However, the shebang line does not cause any trouble either and increases compatibility with other operating systems.

Python Scripts Are Executed in Separate Windows

On Windows, a new terminal window may open each time a Python script is started from a terminal running PowerShell. The script will run there, then the window will close without giving you a chance to see the result.

The reason for this misbehavior is that the .py identifier is not listed in the PATHEXT system variable. Actually, this omission should not happen (at least not after a Python reinstallation), but I can confirm from painful experience that it does happen sometimes. Well, that's Windows!

The solution is to search for "Edit System Environment Variables" in the **Start** menu. Then, the **Control Panel** dialog appears, in which you must click **Environment Variables**. Next, look for PATHEXT (not Path) in the system variables (lower half of the dialog), edit it, and add a semicolon and the extension .py. After restarting the terminal, your Python scripts should run *within* the terminal.

5.4 Elementary Syntax Rules

Python statements usually consist of a single line. Unlike many other programming languages, they do not end with a semicolon or any other character.

Multiline statements are allowed if their beginning and end are clearly indicated by parentheses, for example, in function calls. Alternatively, multiline statements can also be formulated using the \ separator:

```
print("abc",
      "efg")
a = 1 + 2 + \
    3 + 4
```

Statements may end with a semicolon. Normally, this semicolon is optional and has no effect on the program execution. Semicolons, however, allow multiple statements to be formulated on a single line:


```
a = 1; b = 2; c = 3
```

You can also perform this triple assignment in another way, by specifying both the variables and the values in groups whose components are each separated by commas. Tuples are created internally in Python. Both variants are *correct*, but the following second variant corresponds more to the language concepts of Python:

```
a, b, c = 1, 2, 3
```

5.4.1 Block Elements

In Python, as in any other programming language, some language elements can introduce an entire block of additional statements, such as branches with `if`, loops with `for` and `while`, or function definitions with `function`. In Python, such language elements always end with a colon. All other instructions pertaining to the corresponding block must be indented. For block elements, you don't need any parentheses as you would in other languages, as in the following syntax:

```
if xxx:
    statement1a
    statement1b
else:
    statement2a
    statement2b
    statement2c
```

If condition `xxx` is met, statements 1a and 1b will be executed; if the condition is not met, statements 2a, 2b, and 2c will be executed instead. More details about `if` and `else` will follow in Section 5.11.

The indentation of code is not optional in Python like in other programming languages, but part of the syntax! No rigid rules govern the extent of the indentation: 1 character is enough, but 4 characters are commonly used. You should be careful when you use editors that use tab characters for indentation. Python assumes that the tab position is at multiples of 8 characters. If you have set a different tab width in your editor and mix tab and space characters, then Python may get confused when interpreting the indentations. A best practice is to set your editor to use only spaces and no tabs.

You can also specify code directly after a block element. In simple cases, single-line conditions or loops can be formulated in this way:

```
if xxx: statement
```

If necessary, you can run several statements in one line in this way:

```
if xxx: statement1; statement2; statement3
```

5.4.2 Comments

Simple comments are introduced with the # character and extend to the end of line (EOL):

```
# a comment
print("abc")  # another comment
```

You can use """ to create multiline comments, as in the following example:

```
""" a long
    comment """
```

5.5 Numbers

In the following section, I will explain how to use basic Python data types and data structures based on examples. I want to start with integers and floats. Basic arithmetic operations function in Python as they would in any other programming language:

```
>>> 7+12
    19
>>> 3*6
    18
>>> 100-3*5
    85
```

Interestingly, Python knows no boundaries for integers. For instance, 2**100 calculates 2^{100}. However, the result is not a float with only 16 significant digits, but still an integer without any loss of precision. (You can also calculate 2^{10000}. The result has more than 3,000 digits, which is no problem for Python!)

```
>>> 2 ** 100    # corresponds to 2^100
    1267650600228229401496703205376
```

In Python, divisions are always performed in floating point arithmetic. If you explicitly want an integer division, you should use the // operator. The percentage sign returns the remainder of an integer division.

```
>>> 17 / 4      # Python always performs floating point divisions
    4.25
>>> 17 // 4     # Use // for integer divisions
    4
>>> 17 % 4      # % returns the remainder of an integer division
    1
```


You can write numbers in hexadecimal notation (0xnnn) or convert them to a string in hexadecimal notation using the hex method:

```
>>> 0xff
    255
>>> hex(240)
    '0xf0'
```

5.5.1 Floats

If only one number of the expression is a float, Python performs the entire calculation in floating point arithmetic. The accuracy is 16 digits.

```
>>> 12.0 - 2*3
    6.0
>>> 100 / 7
    14.285714285714286
```

Many mathematical functions and constants are located in the math module, which must be imported before its first use:

```
>>> import math             # load math module
>>> math.sqrt(2)
    1.4142135623730951
>>> math.sin(math.pi / 8)
    0.3826834323650898
```

Modules

Python consists of a relatively compact language core and countless extension modules that must be loaded via import before they can be used for the first time. import math is the first example of this, with numerous more to come. Details about this concept, including a description of the different import syntax variants, will follow in Section 5.17.

5.5.2 Random Numbers

Random numbers can be generated using the functions of the random module. randrange(n) returns a random integer from 0 to n-1. For example, randrange(10, 20) returns a random number from 10 to 19. For randint, however, the boundaries are inclusive; that is, randint(10, 20) returns a random number from 10 to 20. random() returns a random float between 0 and 1.

```
>>> import random          # load random module
>>> random.randrange(100)  # random number between 0 and 99
    58
>>> random.random()        # float between 0 and 1
    0.26011495295431664
```

5.6 Strings

In Python, strings can be optionally placed in single or double quotation marks. Both spellings are equivalent and differ only in that the other quotation marks can be integrated into the character string in an uncomplicated way. Three strings are defined in the following example, stored in the s, t, and u variables:

```
>>> s = 'Python is fun!'
>>> t = "Rheinwerk"
>>> u = '<img src="https://xxx">'
```

Regardless of the quotation mark type, quotation marks with \' or \" can be included in the string. Other \ character combinations, referred to as *escape sequences*, exist in Python. In Python's interactive application, strings containing such special characters behave differently depending on whether they are output directly or via print:

```
>>> v='abc\nefg'
>>> v
    'abc\nefg'
>>> print(v)
    abc
    efg
```

To create multiline strings, you need to triple the quotation marks:

```
>>> sql = """INSERT INTO mytable (name, date)
             VALUES ('Maria Miller',
                     '1988-12-31')"""
>>> print(sql)

INSERT INTO mytable (name, date)
             VALUES ('Maria Miller',
                     '1988-12-31')
```

You can also choose between the two quotation mark types for multiline strings. Spaces at the beginning of the line (in the most recent example, before INSERT) are part of the string. If necessary, you can remove unwanted indentations using `inspect.cleandoc`. In this case, indentations relative to the first indented line are preserved:

```
>>> import inspect
>>> print(inspect.cleandoc(sql))

INSERT INTO mytable (name, date)
VALUES ('Maria Miller',
        '1988-12-31')
```


Character Sequence	Meaning
\a	Bell (acoustic signal)
\f	Form feed (new page)
\n	Line break
\r	Carriage return (for Windows text files)
\t	Tab character
\unnnn	Unicode characters with hex code &xnnnn
\'	The ' character
\"	The " character
\\	The \ character

Table 5.1 Selected Escape Sequences

5.6.1 Raw Strings

Some strings contain the \ character without being evaluated as an escape sequence, for example, Windows directory names or LaTeX commands. To formulate such strings without a constant doubling of \, you need to prefix the entire string with the letter `r` (*raw*):

```
windir = r'C:\Windows\System'
latex = r'\index{raw strings}'
```

5.6.2 Processing Strings

The + and * operators are used to concatenate or duplicate strings, respectively:

```
>>> 'abc' + 'efg'
    'abcefg'
>>> 'abc' * 3
    'abcabcabc'
```

Once a string is available, it can be analyzed and processed in a variety of ways:

```
>>> len(s)              # number of characters
   18
>>> s.lower()           # convert to lowercase letters
   'python is fun!'
>>> s.find('is')      # gets the position where the
                        # string 'is' occurs in s
   7
>>> s.count('n')        # counts the occurrences of 'n'
   2
>>> s.replace('n', 'N') # replaces 'n' with 'N'
   'PythoN is fuN!'
>>> s.split(' ')        # splits s into a list
   ['Python', 'is', 'fun!']
```

Method	Function
`len(s)`	Determines the number of characters
`str(x)`	Converts x to a string
`sub in s`	Tests whether sub occurs in s
`s.count(sub)`	Determines how often sub occurs in s
`s.endswith(sub)`	Tests if s ends with sub
`s.expandtabs()`	Replaces tab characters with spaces
`s.find(sub)`	Searches sub in s and returns the start position or -1
`s.isxxx()`	Tests properties of s; examples include `islower()` and `isupper()`
`s.join(x)`	Connects the strings in x (list, set, tuple)
`s.lower()`	Returns s with all lowercase letters
`s.partition(sub)`	Splits s and returns three parts as a tuple
`s.replace(old, new)`	Returns s, where old is replaced by new in each case
`s.rfind(sub)`	Like find but starts the search at the end of the string
`s.split(sub)`	Decomposes s at each occurrence of sub and returns a list
`s.startswith(sub)`	Tests if s starts with sub
`s.upper()`	Returns s with all uppercase letters

Table 5.2 Selected String Methods and Functions

5.6.3 Slicing

The s(n) notation allows you to extract a single character from a string. n specifies the position of the character, where 0 stands for the first character. (This rule applies generally in Python: In any kind of enumeration 0 denotes the first element!) For negative numbers, the calculation starts from the end of the string.

```
>>> s[0], s[1], s[2]      # returns the first, the second
                          # and the third character
    ('P', 'y', 't')
>>> s[-1], s[-2]          # returns the last and the penultimate
                          # character
    ('!', 'n')
```

To read multiple characters at once, Python uses s[start:end], where start indicates the beginning and end indicates the end of the substring. Both specifications are optional. The start position is specified as inclusive, but the end position is exclusive! Thus, s[:5] returns all characters up to and including the fifth character. The official name for this type of character access is *slicing*.

```
>>> s[:]                   # all
    'Python is fun!'
>>> s[:5]                  # everything up to the fifth character
    'Pytho'
>>> s[5:]                  # everything starting from the sixth character
    'n is fun!'
>>> s[5:10]                # from the sixth to the tenth character
    'n is fu'
```

You can also specify the start and end positions by negative numbers—then Python starts counting from the end of the string:

```
>>> s[:-3]                # everything except the last three characters
    'Python is f'
>>> s[-3:]                # everything starting from the third last character
    'un!'
```

An optional third parameter enables you to specify a kind of step size. In practice, the -1 value is most commonly used in this context to reverse the order of a string:

```
>>> s[::2]                # every second character
    'Pto s u'
>>> s[::-1]               # everything in reverse order
    '!nuf si nohtyP'
```

5.6.4 print and input

When you learn Python, the print function is ubiquitous. You can pass one or more parameters to the function. print converts the parameters into strings and outputs them. A space is placed between each parameter, and a newline character, at the end. print is easy to use and works with any kind of Python object (e.g., also works with lists):

```
>>> print(1, 2, 3/4, 'abc', 2==3)
    1 2 0.75 abc False
>>> print('1/7 ist', 1/7)
    1/7 ist 0.14285714285714285
>>> lst = ['a', 'list']
>>> print(lst)
    ['a', 'list']
```

print allows three optional parameters:

- sep sets the string that will be output between the parameters—by default, that's ' '.
- end defines the string that will be output after the last parameter—by default, that's '\n'.
- file determines where the output will occur. Usually, the outputs are redirected to the standard output. file enables you to write the outputs to a text file.

```
>>> print(1, 2, 3, sep='---')
    1---2---3
>>> print(1, 2, 3, sep=';', end='.\nEOF\n')
    1;2;3.
    EOF
>>> f = open('out.txt', 'w')
>>> print(1, 2, 3, file=f)
>>> f.close()
```

Just as you can use print to perform output in a terminal window, input processes text input. input first outputs the text specified in the optional parameter and then expects input, which must be completed via Enter. Empty input—that is, pressing Enter without text—is acknowledged by input with an error.

```
name = input('Specify your name:')
print('Your name is:', name)
```

input always returns a string. If you want to interpret the string as a number (for example, to perform a calculation afterwards), you must insert int:

```
number = input('Enter a number:')
print(int(number) * 2)
```

5.6.5 Formatting Outputs

Often, you need to create strings from numbers, dates, times, etc. In the simplest case, you can use the `str(x)` or `repr(x)` functions, which represent any object as a string. The `repr` function proceeds in such a way that the resulting string can be read again using `eval`. `str`, on the other hand, strives to format the strings so that they are easily readable by humans. Both functions do not influence the formatting. If you want to format numbers as right justified or with a thousands separator, then you need special formatting functions. In Python, you can choose between several procedures. The most commonly used ones are the `%` operator and the `format` method:

- **format string % (data, data, data)**
  In this case, the format string is formulated in the syntax of the `printf` function of the C programming language. Within this string, `%` characters indicate the positions where data is to be inserted.
- **formatstring.format(data, data, data)**
  The structure of the string has great similarities with the structure of the method of the same name in Microsoft's .NET framework. Within this string, `{}` bracket pairs indicate the position of the parameters.

Let's first look at two examples of the `%` method:

```
>>>'1/7 with three decimal places: %.3f' % (1/7)
    '1/7 with three decimal places: 0.143'

>>> '<img src="%s" alt="%s" width="%d">' % ('foto.jpg',
         'Portrait', 200)
    '<img src="foto.jpg" alt="Portrait" width="200">'
```

The biggest advantage of the newer `format` method is that you can freely choose the placeholder order via `{n}` or `{parameter name}`. The following examples illustrate the resulting options:

```
>>> '{} is {} years old.'.format('Peter', 9)
    'Peter is 9 years old.'

>>> '{1} is {0} years old.'.format(9, 'Peter')
    'Peter is 9 years old.'

>>> '{name} is {age} years old.'.format(age=9, name='Peter')
    'Peter is 9 years old.'

>>> '1/7 with three decimal places: {:.3f}'.format(1/7)
    '1/7 with three decimal places: 0.143'

>>> 'SELECT * FROM table WHERE id={:d}'.format(324)
    'SELECT * FROM table WHERE id=324'
```

Countless codes can be used for building strings in the two formatting systems. Unfortunately, not enough space in this book is available for a complete reference. But you can find numerous resources on the internet that describe all permissible codes in all conceivable variants. For example, refer to the official Python documentation at *https://docs.python.org/3/library/stdtypes.html#printf-style-string-formatting* or *https://docs.python.org/3/library/string.html#format-string-syntax*.

Code	Meaning
%d	Integer (decimal)
%5d	Integer with 5 digits, right justified
%-5d	Integer with 5 digits, left justified
%f	Float
%.2f	Float with two decimal places
%r	String; Python uses repr
%s	String; Python uses str
%10s	String with 10 characters, right justified
%-10s	String with 10 characters, left justified
%x	Output integer as hexadecimal

Table 5.3 Selected Codes for % Formatting (printf Syntax)

Code	Meaning
{}	Parameter, any data type
{0}, {1}, ...	Numbered parameters
{one}, {two}, ...	Named parameters
{:d}	Integer
{:<7d}	Integer with 7 digits, left justified
{:>7d}	Integer with 7 digits, right justified
{:^7d}	Integer with 7 digits, centered
{:f}	Float
{:.5f}	Float with 5 decimal places
{:s}	Character string

Table 5.4 Selected Codes for the Format Method

The Agony of Choice

Which method is better—using % or using format? You can reach your goal with both methods. If you're familiar with the printf syntax, you can stick with the % procedure. Otherwise, you should prefer format for new code since the resulting code is generally more readable.

5.7 Lists

With *lists*, Python offers an immensely flexible language construct for managing larger volumes of data. Lists are formulated in square brackets. Lists can hold elements of any data type. The elements in a list can be accessed in the same way as the characters of a string by "slicing," that is, with list[start:end]. In addition, Python provides countless functions and methods for processing lists.

```
>>> lst = [1, 2.3, 'abc', 'efg', 12]
>>> lst[2]                # the third element
  'abc'
>>> lst[2:4]              # from the third to the fourth element
  ['abc', 'efg']
>>> lst[::-1]             # reverse order
  [12, 'efg', 'abc', 2.3, 1]
>>> lst[0] = 3            # changes the first list element
>>> lst
  [3, 2.3, 'abc', 'efg', 12]
```

Since any Python object is allowed as a list element, nested lists are also allowed:

```
>>> lst = [[1, 2],
           [3, 4]]
>>> lst
  [[1, 2], [3, 4]]
```

The characters of a string can be converted to a list via list:

```
>>> characters = list('Hello World!')
>>> characters
  ['H', 'e', 'l', 'l', 'o', ' ', 'W', 'o', 'r', 'l', 'd', '!']
```

Function/Method	Meaning
del l[start:end]	Removes the specified list items
n = len(l)	Returns the number of elements

Table 5.5 Important Functions and Methods for Editing Lists

Function/Method	Meaning
`l.append(x)`	Adds element x to the end of the list
`l.clear()`	Deletes the list (corresponds to `l=[]`)
`n = l.count(x)`	Determines how often element x occurs in the list
`l1.extend(l2)`	Adds list `l2` at the end of `l1` (thus: `l1 += l2`)
`iterator = filter(f, l)`	Returns the elements to which `f(element)==true` applies
`n = l.index(x)`	Determines the first position of x in the list
`l.insert(n, x)`	Inserts element x at position n into the list
`iterator = map(f, l)`	Applies function f to all elements
`x = l.pop(n)`	Reads the element at position n and removes it
`l.remove(x)`	Removes element x from the list
`l.reverse()`	Reverses the list (the first element comes last, etc.)
`l.sort()`	Sorts the list
`iterator = zip(l1, l2)`	Connects the list elements in pairs to tuples

Table 5.5 Important Functions and Methods for Editing Lists (Cont.)

5.7.1 List Comprehension

With *list comprehension*, a statement is created in the format: `[expression for x in list]`. Python then puts each element of the list in turn into variable `x` and parses the expression. The results represent a new list. In the second example, each result is itself a list consisting of two elements, so the resulting list is nested.

```
>>> lst = [x for x in range(10, 101, 10)]
>>> lst
   [10, 20, 30, 40, 50, 60, 70, 80, 90, 100]
>>> [x * 2 + 1 for x in lst]
   [21, 41, 61, 81, 101, 121, 141, 181, 201]
>>> [ [x, x * x] for x in lst]
   [[10, 100], [20, 400], [30, 900], [40, 1600], [50, 2500],
    [60, 3600], [70, 4900], [90, 8100], [100, 10000]]
```

5.7.2 map and filter

`map` applies a function to all elements of a list. For efficiency reasons, `map` does not immediately return a result list, but an *iterator*. This object can be parsed in a loop or converted to a list via `list`, for example. The following example first breaks down a sentence into a word list and then uses `map` to determine the length of all words:

```
>>> lst = 'Python is fun!'.split(' ')
    # lst contains ['Python', 'is', 'fun!']
>>> map(map(len, lst)
    <map object at 0x7f17bfbd1090>
>>> list(map(len, lst))
    [6, 5, 5]
```


`filter` applies a function to each list item similar to `map`. However, the goal this time is not to return the function results, but rather to return all list items for which the filter function returns `true`. So, we need to filter out all elements from a list that meet a condition. As with `map`, the result is an iterator that can be analyzed into a list via `list` if required.

The following example filters out all even numbers from a list. The lambda expression returns `true` if no remainder remains when dividing by 2. In this case, `lambda` defines the filter function ad hoc. An explanation of `lambda` follows in Section 5.13.

```
>>> lst = list(range(1,11)); lst
    [1, 2, 3, 4, 5, 6, 7, 8, 9, 10]
>>> even = filter(lambda x: x % 2 == 0, lst)
>>> list(even)
    [2, 4, 6, 8, 10]
```

You can achieve the same result by using *list comprehension* if you formulate the condition after the list:

```
>>> [ x for x in lst if x % 2 == 0 ]
    [2, 4, 6, 8, 10]
```

5.8 Tuples, Sets, and Dictionaries

Lists represent the dominant data structure in many Python scripts. Nevertheless, you should also know three other basic Python data structures, namely, *tuples* (sequences), *sets*, and *dictionaries*.

A *tuple* is a special form of an immutable list. In a sense, tuples are the *more primitive* data structure. Their internal administration is associated with low overhead. Tuples are formulated in parentheses. If no syntactic ambiguities can occur, it is permissible to omit the parentheses.

```
>>> t = (12, 73, 3)
>>> t
    (12, 73, 3)
```

```
>>> t = 12, 73, 3
>>> t
    (12, 73, 3)
```

A useful way to apply tuples are functions that do not return *one* result, but a pair of values or a combination of several data. Thus, the following example returns a pair of coordinates. (You'll learn how functions work in Section 5.13.)

```
def myfunc():          # Define function
  x = 27
  y = 42
  return (x, y)

print(myfunc())        # Call function, output: (27, 42)
```

5.8.1 Sets

A *set* is an unordered set of elements without duplicates. It is impossible for a set to contain the same object more than once. Unlike lists, Python does not remember the order of the elements. You must not assume that the elements will be processed in the same order in which you inserted them.

Sets are formulated in curly brackets. Strings can be converted to a character set by using set; in this process, duplicates are automatically eliminated.

```
>>> s = {1, 2, 3}
>>> s
    {1, 2, 3}
>>> s = set('Hello World!')
>>> s
    {'r', 'W', '!', ' ', 'e', 'd', 'H', 'l', 'o'}
```

You can use sets to perform set operations, for example, to find out which objects from set 1 are also contained in set 2. I have presented the outputs in the next example in order only for better readability; if you try the tests yourself, the letters will be output in random order.

```
>>> x = set('abcdef')
>>> y = set('efgh')
>>> x | y     # join
    {'a', 'c', 'b', 'e', 'd', 'g', 'f', 'h'}
>>> x - y     # difference
    {'a', 'c', 'b', 'd'}
>>> x & y     # intersection (common elements)
    {'e', 'f'}
```

5.8.2 Dictionaries

For lists and tuples, access to individual elements occurs via a numeric index, that is, via list(n) or tuple(n). Dictionaries, on the other hand, allow element lists to be managed with an arbitrary key. In some programming languages (such as Bash), such data structures are called *associative arrays*.

Dictionaries are formulated like sets in curly brackets. In contrast to sets, however, dictionaries always store key-value pairs. The following example stores some HTML color codes, using the name of the color as the key:

```
>>> colors = {'red' : 0xff0000, 'green' : 0xff00, 'blue' : 0xff,
              'white' : 0xffffff}
```

Not only are dictionaries syntactically related to sets, but also in terms of their function: They do not preserve the order of the elements. To access the elements of the dictionary you can use the key. hex converts the numbers stored as decimals to hexadecimal notation:

```
>>> colors['red']          # Access to an element
    16711680
>>> hex(colors['red'])
    '0xff0000'
```

Attempting to access an element that does not exist will result in a KeyError. To avoid this error, you can use key in dict to test in advance whether the dictionary contains an element for a certain key:

```
>>> colors['yellow']
    KeyError: 'yellow'
>>> 'yellow' in colors
    False
```

len returns the number of elements as for lists, sets, and tuples. The dict[key]=value statement enables you to extend the dictionary:

```
>>> len(colors)            # determines the number of elements
    4
>>> colors['black'] = 0   # adds an element
```

del dict[key] removes an element:

```
>>> del colors['red']      # deletes an element
>>> colors                 # output all key-value pairs
    {'black': 0, 'blue': 255, 'white': 16777215, 'green': 65280}
```

The keys and values methods return all keys and all values of the dictionary, respectively. If necessary, you can convert this data to lists or sets by using list or set:

```
>>> colors.values()
    dict_values([0, 255, 16777215, 65280])
>>> colors.keys()
    dict_keys(['black', 'blue', 'white', 'green'])
>>> set(colors.keys())
    {'black', 'blue', 'white', 'green'}
>>> list(colors.keys())
    ['black', 'blue', 'white', 'green']
```

When you create a `for` loop through a dictionary, Python puts all the keys in the loop variable:

```
>>> for c in colors:
      print("The color", c, " has color code", hex(colors[c]))

The color black has color code 0x0
The color blue has color code 0xff
The color white has color code 0xffffff
The color green has color code 0xff00
```

These examples used strings as keys. Basically, however, any Python object is suitable as a key. The only requirement is that the keys are unique.

"Real" Examples

On the preceding pages, I have tried to illustrate the operation of basic data structures with examples that are as simple as possible. If this has given you the mistaken impression that lists, sets, and the like are just a mathematical gimmick, you can skip ahead to Section 5.14 or take a look at the examples in Chapter 10.

5.9 Variables

In Python, simple rules apply to the handling of variables:

- **Assignment prior to use**
  Each variable must be assigned an initial value before the variable can be parsed in an expression. For example, you cannot execute `x=x+1` if you have not done a first-time assignment like `x=0`, `x=1`, `x=n` beforehand.
- **No type declaration**
  Python variables can store objects of any type. Python remembers the type and thus knows what kind of data a variable refers to.

  Unlike many other programming languages, however, the type of variable cannot be specified or restricted. You can easily store data of different types in the same variable, for example, first a number (`x=1`), later a string (`x='abc'`), and finally a list (`x=[3,2,1]`).

- **Names**
  Variable names must start with letters or an underscore. However, the underscore at the beginning of variable names is intended for internal Python data, so you should avoid using it in your own scripts if possible. The other characters can also contain digits.


```
a = 1
b = 'abc'
a = a + 1
a = c + 1                # Error: Nothing was ever assigned to c.
longName = 3             # OK
another_long_name = 4  # also OK
long name = 5            # Error: Spaces are not allowed.
long-name = 6            # Error: - is not allowed.
```

Python Does Not Know Constants

Python does not provide a way to define constants. A common practice is to use a variable as constant, but with only capital letters in its name, such as `MAXNO=10`. However, you cannot prevent this variable from being assigned a different value later.

5.9.1 Assignments

Ordinary assignments of the `variable = expression` type exist in every programming language. Python also knows some unusual variants. For example, you can assign the same content to multiple variables at once. Python proceeds from right to left. Thus, in the next example, the following assignments are made: `c=16`, then `b=c`, and finally `a=b`. Thus, all three variables reference the same object in the memory, which represents the number `16`.

```
a = b = c = 16          # assign the same value to three variables
```

If you want to assign different values to multiple variables in a compact notation, you can use lists or tuples for this purpose. For example, the following assignments will work:

```
a, b = 2, 3
[e, f, g] = [7, 8, 9]
e, f, g = [7, 8, 9]     # equivalent
```

You can also use this type of assignment to swap the contents of two variables. With most other programming languages, you would need a third, temporary variable to do this swap.

```
x, y = y, x              # swap x and y
```

A special variant of list and tuple assignments arises when there are fewer variables on the left than list items on the right. In this case, you can prefix *a* variable with an asterisk. All surplus elements are then assigned to this variable as a list.

```
>>> a, *b, c = [1, 2, 3, 4, 5]
>>> a
   1
>>> b
   [2, 3, 4]
>>> c
   5
```

5.9.2 Data Types

Python knows several predefined data types.

Data Type	Function	Example	Mutable
`int`	Integers	`x = 3`	No
`float`	Floats	`x = 3.0`	No
`bool`	Boolean values	`x = bool(1)`	No
`str`	Strings	`x = 'abc'`	No
`tuple`	Tuples	`x = (1, 2, 3)`	No
`list`	Lists	`x = [1, 2, 3]`	Yes
`set`	Sets	`x = {1, 2, 3}`	Yes
`dict`	Dictionaries	`x = {1:'red', 2:'blue'}`	Yes
`bytearray`	Byte arrays	`x = bytearray(...)`	Yes
`io.TextIOWrapper`	Files	`x = open('readme.txt')`	Yes
...	Other classes	...	Yes

Table 5.6 Important Python Data Types and Classes

Only in a few cases does Python take care of data type conversion on its own. For example, if you multiply an integer by a float, the integer is automatically converted to a float so that floating point multiplication is possible afterwards.

Apart from such exceptions, you must take care of the type conversion yourself. For this task, you need to use functions whose names match the respective data types. For example, to combine a string and a number into a new, longer string, you would use the `str` function:

```
s = 'abc'
x = 3
s = s + str(x)  # Result 'abc3'
```

In the opposite direction, int and float convert a string into a number. Note that the *invalid literal* error may occur when you do this, for example, when you try to convert the string 'abc' into a number.

```
n = int('123')
f = float('123.3')
```

5.9.3 Mutable or Immutable?

What happens when b=a, that is, when one variable is assigned to another? The question is not as trivial as it may seem. Let's start with an example that contains integers. In the following code, the value 3 is stored first in a. For the assignment b=a, a is replaced by 3. So, the number 3 is also stored in b. To put it more precisely: a and b are now two variables that both reference an object with the integer 3. Via a=4, a is assigned a new value. This has no influence on b. Thus, a and b are independent of each other: a now contains the value 4; b, the value 3.

```
a = 3
b = a          # b
a = 4
print(a, b)  # Output 4, 3
```

The code for the second example is quite similar. However, in this case, in a and b, no simple numbers are stored, but lists. After the assignment b=a, both variables refer to the same list. The use of a(0)=4 changes one element of the list. As the print call proves, this change applies to both a and b! So, a and b are not independent of each other as in the previous example!

```
a = [1, 2, 3]
b = a          # b references the same list as a
a[0] = 4       # changes the first list element
print(a, b)  # Output [4, 2, 3] [4, 2, 3]
```

Why does Python behave so differently in two seemingly similar programs? The reason is that Python distinguishes between mutable and immutable data types—technically speaking, it distinguishes between mutable and immutable types. Numbers, strings, and tuples are *immutable*; that is, it is impossible to change them. Instead, every time an expression results in new data, a new object is created as well!

If you first execute x=10 and then x=x+1, Python first creates an object with the number 10, and then, x references this object. The x+1 calculation yields the number 11. For this purpose, another object is created in the memory. The x variable is now changed so that it points to the new object 11. Creating another object also happened in the first code example in line a=4: Python has created an object for the number 4. a references this object, which has no effect on b as b still references the object for the number 3.

Other data types, however, are mutable. Because of this mutability, you *can* change the elements of a list without creating a new object right away. The a(0) assignment does not change the list in its entirety, but only one element of the list. In the second example, a and b continue to reference the same object whose *content* has changed.

How do you proceed if, for example, you need an independent copy of a list so that two initially similar lists can be modified independently of each other via two variables? In such cases, you should use the copy or deepcopy methods from the copy module:

```
import copy
a=[1, 2, 3]
b=copy.copy(a)  # b references an independent copy of a.
a[0] = 4        # changes the first list element of a,
                # b remains unchanged.
print(a, b)     # Output [4, 2, 3] [1, 2, 3]
```

The copy method creates a copy of the specified object, whereas deepcopy goes one step further: It also creates copies of all mutable objects referenced by the source object. In this latest example, deepcopy is superfluous because the list contains only three integers, which are immutable objects. However, if the list itself contains mutable objects, deepcopy duplicates the entire object tree.

5.10 Operators

Python uses essentially the same operators as most other programming languages. However, I would like to point out a few special features:

- **Division**
  The / operator always performs floating point division, even if both operands are integers. To perform an integer division, you must use the // operator.
- **Associating assignments with calculations**
  Assignments can be associated with basic arithmetic operations. In other words, a=a+1 can also be formulated as a+=1. Not only is this short notation allowed for basic arithmetic operations, but for almost all Python operators as well. In contrast to other programming languages, however, a++ and a-- in the sense of a=a+1 and a=a-1 are *not* allowed.
- **Multiple comparisons**
  Multiple comparisons are also possible using the comparison operators <, >, and so on. For example, 10 <= x <= 20 tests whether the value of x is between 10 and 20.

Internally, all comparisons are linked with a logical AND, i.e., `10 <= x <= 20` corresponds to `10<=x and x<=20`.

- **Comparing contents**
  `==` tests whether two expressions have the same content, for example, whether the value of the `x` variable is 3 (`if x==3: ...`) or whether the `s` string matches `'abc'` (`if s=='abc': ...`).
- **Comparing objects**
  In contrast, the `a is b` operator checks whether the variables `a` and `b` reference the same object. Even if `a==b` holds true, it may well be that `a` and `b` reference different objects with the same content. `a is b` thus corresponds to a deeper equality than `a==b`.

Operator	Function
`+ -`	Sign
`+ - * /`	Basic arithmetic operations
`//`	Integer division (20 // 6 results in 3.)
`%`	Remainder of integer division (20 % 6 results in 2.)
`**`	Exponential function or superscript (2**8 results in 256.)
`+ *`	Join or multiply strings (`'ab'*2` results in `'abab'`.)
`%`	Format string (`printf` syntax)
`=`	Assignment (`var = 3`)
`:=`	Assignment and evaluation (`if x:=func() == value ...`)
`+=`	Assignment and addition (`var+=3` corresponds to `var = var + 3`.)
`-=`	Assignment and subtraction
`*=`	Assignment and multiplication
`/=`	Assignment and division
`==`	Test equality (`if a==3: ...`)
`!=`	Test inequality
`< > <= >=`	Smaller than, larger than, smaller than/equal to, larger than/equal to
`is`	Test whether two variables reference the same object
`is not`	Test whether two variables reference different objects

Table 5.7 Arithmetic, String, and Comparison Operators

Operator	Function
& |	Binary AND and binary OR
^	Binary exclusive OR
~	Binary NOT
<<	Shift binary to the left (2<<4 results in 32.)
>>	Shift binary to the right (768>>2 results in 192.)
or	Logical OR
and	Logical AND
not	Logical NOT

Table 5.8 Binary and Logical Operators

5.10.1 Combining Assignment and Evaluation

Available since Python 3.8, the := operator allows you to perform a variable assignment in one statement at the same time and to compare the result with a value (*assignment expression*). In the following example, this comparison is not visible explicitly at all in a while loop. The loop is executed as long as line is not empty (i.e., the end of file [EOF] has been reached).

```
with open('readme.txt') as txtfile:
    # Read one line of the text file, continue loop,
    # if not equal to False
    while line := txtfile.readline():
        print(line, end='')
```

5.11 Branches (if)

The syntax of if branches is simple. Do not forget the colons you need to place after the conditions and after else! Unlike other programming languages, Python does not understand switch or case constructs.

```
if condition1:
    block1
elif condition2:
    block2
elif condition3:
    block3
else:
    block4
```

5.11.1 Conditions

Conditions are usually formed with comparison operators (e.g., x == 3 or a is b). Multiple conditions can be logically linked with and or or.

```
if x > 0 and (y > 0 or z == 1):
  ...
```

Like almost all other programming languages, Python optimizes and and or expressions (in what is called a *short-circuit evaluation*):

- If the first partial expression of an and operation is False, the second partial expression will no longer be evaluated because the result will be False in any case.
- In an or operation, if the first partial expression returns True, the second partial expression will no longer be evaluated because the result will be True in any case.

Instead of a < x and x < b, the short notation a < x < b is allowed. Conditions can also be formulated without a relational operator, for example, in the following form:

```
if x:
  ...
```

This condition is met if the following is true:

- x is a number not equal to 0.
- x is a non-empty string.
- x is the Boolean value 1 (True).
- x is a list, a tuple, or a set with at least one element.
- x is an initialized object (not None).

5.11.2 Short Notation with if

Sometimes, you need if constructs only to assign a variable:

```
if condition:
    x = value1
else
    x = value2
```

You can use a space-saving short notation for such constructs:

```
x = value1 if condition else value2
```

5.12 Loops (for and while)

In Python, loops are primarily formed using for var in elements. The loop variable accepts each of the specified elements in sequence.

```
for var in mylst:
    statements
```

The var loop variable remains available after the end of the loop and then contains the last assigned value:

```
for i in [7, 12, 3]:
    statements
print(i)    # Output 3
```

Alternatively, loops can be formulated using while. The indented statements are then executed as long as the condition is met.

```
while condition:
    statements
```

5.12.1 break, continue, and else

break terminates for and while loops prematurely:

```
for var in elements:
    statement1
    if condition: break        # abort the loop
    statement2
```

continue skips the remaining statements for the current loop pass but then continues the loop:

```
for var in elements:
    statement1
    if condition: continue     # skip statement2
    statement2
```

Python also provides an else block for loops and thus differs from most other programming languages. The else block is run after all elements have been passed through in a for loop or in a while loop if the loop condition is no longer fulfilled.

```
for var in elements:
    statement1
    statement2
else:
    statement3
```

Tip: Break and Continue in Nested Loops

For nested loops, break and continue apply only to the innermost loop. To easily break a nested loop, you need to wrap it in a function and exit it using return. Another option is to secure all loops using try and to throw an exception to abort the loops.

5.12.2 Loops over Number Ranges (range)

For loops over a given number range, the elements are usually generated by `range(start, end)`, where the end value is exclusive. The following loop therefore runs through the values from 1 to 9 (not 10!). The `end=' '` option in `print` causes each output to be followed by a space (no line break).

```
for i in range(1, 10):
    print(i, end=' ')
# Output: 1 2 3 4 5 6 7 8 9
```

For `range`, the step size can be specified in the optional third parameter:

```
for i in range(0, 20, 3): print(i, end=' ')
# Output: 0 3 6 9 12 15 18

for i in range(100, 0, -10):  print(i, end=' ')
# Output: 100 90 80 70 60 50 40 30 20 10
```

`range` can only be used for integers, but not for floats. If you want to form a loop from 0 to 1 with a step size of 0.1, you can proceed as follows, for example:

```
for i in range(0, 11):
    x = i / 10.0
    print(x, end=' ')
# Output 0.0 0.1 0.2 0.3 0.4 0.5 0.6 0.7 0.8 0.9 1.0
```

Of course, you can also form loops over number ranges using `while`. This approach is especially advantageous if the numbers are expected to have irregular differences.

```
i = 1
while i < 100000:
    print(i, end=' ')
    i += i*i
# Output: 1 2 6 42 1806
```

5.12.3 Loops over the Characters of a String

You can process a string character by character in the following way:

```
for c in 'abc': print(c)
# Output: a
#         b
#         c
```

A more convenient approach may be to use `list` to convert the string into a list whose elements each contain one character. Then, you can process the elements with list functions.

5.12.4 Loops over Lists, Tuples, and Sets

You can easily process the elements of lists, tuples, and sets using for:

```
for i in (17, 87, 4):
    print(i, end=' ')
# Output: 17 87 4

for s in ['Python', 'is', 'fun!']:
    print(s)
# Output: Python
#         is
#         fun!
```

Often, the goal of such loops is to form a new list, tuple, or set. Then, it is mostly more elegant and efficient to use the list/tuple/set comprehension mentioned earlier in Section 5.7. In this case, the for loop is executed *in* square brackets, parentheses, or curly brackets and returns a list, tuple, or set as the result. The following examples all refer to lists.

In its simplest form, the syntax is [expression for var in list]. All list elements are inserted into the variable. The evaluated expressions result in a new list. Optionally, a condition for the loop variable can be appended using if: Then, only the list elements for which the condition applies will be considered.

```
>>> l = [1, 2, 3, 10]
>>> [ x*x for x in l ]            # Form the square of all list
                                  # elements
    [1, 4, 9, 100]
>>> [ x*x for x in l if x%2==0 ]  # include only even
                                  # numbers
    [4, 100]
```

The expression may of course itself be a list, a set, or a tuple—then the result is a nested expression:

```
>>> [ [x, x*x] for x in l ]
    [[1, 1], [2, 4], [3, 9], [10, 100]]
```

To build a dictionary from a list, tuple, or set, you should use the { k:v for x in list } notation, where k and v are expressions for the key and value of each dictionary element.

```
>>> { x:x*x for x in l }
    {1: 1, 2: 4, 3: 9, 10: 100}
```

5.12.5 Loops over Dictionaries

The comprehension syntax described earlier in Section 5.7 can also be used for dictionaries. In the simplest form, a loop is formed over the keys of the dictionary elements. Depending on whether you enclose the expression in square brackets or curly brackets, the result is a list or a set.


```
>>> d = {'a':12, 'c':78, 'b':3, 'd':43}
>>> { x for x in d }
    {'a', 'c', 'b', 'd'}
>>> [ x for x in d ]
    ['a', 'c', 'b', 'd']
```

If you need two variables in the loop for the key-value pair, then you need to use the items method:

```
>>> { k for k,v in d.items() }
    {'a', 'c', 'b', 'd'}
>>> { v for k,v in d.items() }
    {43, 3, 12, 78}
```

To make the result of the expression itself a dictionary again, you should form the result expression in the key:value format:

```
>>> { k:v*2 for k,v in d.items() }
    {'a': 24, 'c': 156, 'b': 6, 'd': 86}
```

5.12.6 Loops over the Parameters of a Script

When you pass parameters to a Python script, you can evaluate them in the script using the sys.argv statement. sys is a module; it must be read first via import. argv is a list whose first element is the filename of the script. The other list elements contain the passed parameters. Since the script name is rarely needed, it is eliminated using the [1:] expression.

```
# Sample file script-parameters.py
import sys
if(len(sys.argv) <= 1):
    print("No parameters were passed.")
else:
    for x in sys.argv[1:]:
        print("Parameter:", x)
```

A possible call of the script could look as follows:

```
./script-parameters.py a b
Parameter: a
Parameter: b
```

The terminal window normally runs Bash. It immediately evaluates expressions like *.txt and then passes the list of found files to the called command. So, if the current directory contains the readme.txt, copyright.txt and gpl.txt files, then ./script-parameters.py *.txt will pass the names of all three files:

```
./script-parameters.py *.txt
Parameter: copyright.txt
Parameter: gpl.txt
Parameter: readme.txt
```

5.12.7 Globbing on Windows

If you run myscript.py *.txt on macOS or Linux, the names of all text files in the current directory are passed to the script and can be evaluated via sys.argv[:1]. This task does not work on Windows. The script receives *.txt as the only parameter and must take care of finding the text files itself. The glob function from the module of the same name provides help in this respect:

```
import glob from glob
filenames = glob('*.txt')
```

If you want to analyze all parameters passed to a script in this way, you need to formulate the glob call in the following way:

```
filenames = []
for arg in sys.argv[1:]:
    filenames.extend(glob(arg))
```

This procedure works on all operating systems even if multiple file patterns are passed (e.g., myscript.py *.jpg *.png). For an application example of this technique, see Chapter 16, Section 16.3.

5.12.8 Loops over the Lines of a Text File

Quite often, you need to process a text file line by line. For this purpose, Python accepts file objects in for loops and passes one line at a time to the loop variable. (I will introduce the open function in more detail in Section 5.14.)

In the print statement, end='' prevents a blank line from appearing after each output line. The strings inserted into the loop variable already contain the newline codes from the text file.

```
f = open('readme.txt', 'r')
cnt = 0
for line in f:
```

```
    cnt+=1
    print("line ", cnt, ": ", line, sep='', end='')
f.close()
```

5.12.9 Loops over All Files in a Directory

The `os.listdir` function returns an unordered list of all files and subdirectories in a directory. You can easily loop through it using `for`.

When processing the files, however, note that `listdir` returns the filenames without path information, for example, `readme.txt` instead of `/home/kofler/readme.txt`. For further processing, you must therefore often form the complete filename via `os.path.join`, for example, in the following listing:

```
# Sample file list-directory.py
import os
startdir = os.path.expanduser('~')
print('All files and directories in', startdir)

for filename in os.listdir(startdir):
    fullname = os.path.join(startdir, filename)

    if os.path.isfile(fullname):
        print("File: ", fullname)
    elif os.path.isdir(fullname):
        print('Directory: ', fullname)
```

In this example, `os.path.expanduser('~')` returns the full path of the home directory. If instead you're only interested in `*.pdf` files in this directory, you can proceed with the following code:

```
for filename in os.listdir(startdir):
    if not filename.lower().endswith('.pdf'): continue
    fullname = os.path.join(startdir, filename)
    if os.path.isfile(fullname):
        print('PDF file: ', fullname)
```

5.13 Functions

Python provides two options for defining your own functions: You can introduce ordinary functions using the `def` keyword. Alternatively, you can define and immediately apply what are called *lambda functions* with little overhead. Let's start with ordinary functions.

The definition of functions starts with the def keyword. This keyword is followed by the function name, for which the same rules apply as for variable names. The parameters must be enclosed in parentheses.

```
def myfunc(para1, para2, para3):
    code
```

Some rules for programming and using functions include the following:

- Functions must be defined before they can be used. As a result, a common practice is to define all functions first and then specify the rest of the code. The execution of the code thus begins in the first line that does *not* belong to a function definition.
- Functions can be exited prematurely using return. The use of return is optional.

  If you use return, the function can return a result, even in the form of lists, tuples, and so on. In this way a function can easily return *multiple* values.

In the following mini program, two functions are first defined and then called to demonstrate the basic handling of functions:

```
def f1(x, y):                # function without result
  print('Parameter 1:', x)
  print('Parameter 2:', y)

def f2(x, y):                # function with result
  return x + y

# here begins the actual code execution
f1(2, 3)       # outputs the parameters
# Output: Parameter 1: 2
#          Parameter 2: 3

n = f2(4, 5)
print("Result:", n)
# Output: Result: 9
```

5.13.1 Global and Local Variables

Functions can read (but not modify) variables that are defined outside the function:

```
def f1():
  print(x)

x = 3
f1()  # Output 3
```

Conversely, variables that are initialized in a function—that is, functions that are on the left side of an assignment—are considered *local*: They can only be used within the function. This rule also applies if a variable within a function has the same name as a variable outside the function.


```
def f1():
  y = 5
  print(y)     # Output 5

f1()
print(y)       # Error, y is not defined!
```

If you want to change a variable in a function that was initialized outside the function, then you must mark this variable as `global` inside the function. Strictly speaking, you're saying that the function should not consider `z` as a local variable, but as a variable from the *global scope* of the program.

```
def f1():
  global z
  z = z + 3

z = 3
f1()
print(z)       # Output 6
```

In practice, you should avoid the `global` keyword as it leads to cluttered code. A better approach is to return the function result via `return` and then save it:

```
def f1(x):
  return x + 3

z = 3
z = f1(z)
print(z)    # Output 6
```

5.13.2 Parameters

Parameters are used to pass data to a function. Internally, the parameters behave like local variables. A parameter named `x` is thus completely independent of a variable of the same name defined outside the function.

The same rules apply for passing data in the parameters of a function as for variable assignments (Section 5.9.3). Thus, for immutable data types, a change of the data through the function is excluded (see the previous example).

With mutable data types, changes to the *contents* of an object, list, set, etc. are possible. In the following example, the function adds an element to the list:

```
def f1(x):
  x.append(3)

x = [1, 2]
f1(x)
print(x)   # Output [1, 2, 3]
```

5.13.3 Optional Parameters

You can use `para=default` to define a default value for a parameter. At the same time, this parameter will then be optional. All optional parameters must be specified at the end of the parameter list.

To make the call of functions with many optional parameters more manageable, the function parameters can also be passed in the `name=value` notation. Creating a function call with named parameters also has an advantage in that you don't need to adhere to the order of the parameters, and the code can thus be more readable.

```
def f(a, b, c=-1, d=0):
  print(a, b, c, d)

f(6, 7, 8, 9)      # Output 6 7  8 9
f(6, 7, 8)         # Output 6 7  8 0
f(a=6, b=7, d=9)   # Output 6 7 -1 9
f(d=9, b=7, a=6)   # Output 6 7 -1 9
f(6, 7)            # Output 6 7 -1 0
f(6, 7, d=3)       # Output 6 7 -1 3
f(6)               # Error, b is missing
f(b=6, c=7)        # Error, a is missing
```

5.13.4 Variable Number of Parameters

If you define a parameter in the `*para` or `**para` format, then this parameter will take any number of values. With `*para`, these parameters are subsequently available as tuples, with `**para` as a dictionary. `**para` arguments *must* be passed as named parameters.

```
def f(a, b, *c):
  print(a, b, c)

f(1, 2, 3)            # Output 1 2 (3)
f(1, 2, 3, 4)         # Output 1 2 (3, 4)
f(1, 2, 3, 4, 5, 6)   # Output 1 2 (3, 4, 5, 6)
```

If the data you want to pass to a function is in a list, tuple, or other enumerable data structure, the `function(*list)` notation is also allowed when calling the function. In this way, the elements of the list will be automatically distributed among the parameters:

```
l = [1, 2, 3, 4, 5, 6]
f(*l)                  # Output 1 2 (3, 4, 5, 6)
```


5.13.5 Lambda Functions

You can use custom functions for two reasons: on the one hand, to break complex code into manageable chunks or, on the other hand, because you want to perform a particular task in different places in the code and thus avoid redundant code. Sometimes, however, you need a third variant.

At *one* point in the code—for example, in a `map` statement, in a `filter` statement, or for formulating a callback function—you need a function that is often quite simple. The conventional way to create temporary functions is then cumbersome: You must first define the function using `def`, then use that function only once.

In such cases, lambda functions represent an alternative that saves space and that, above all, is much clearer: The function can be defined ad hoc and at the same time used immediately at this point in the code. As these functions are not assigned any name at all, lambda functions are also referred to as *anonymous functions*.

The following line contains the syntax for defining a lambda function. The `lambda` keyword is first followed by the parameters of the function and, after a colon, by the function expression. A major limitation compared to other functions is that lambda functions can only consist of a single expression.

```
lambda var1, var2, var3, ...: expression
```

The following mini program demonstrates the use of two lambda functions: The first lambda expression recognizes numbers that are divisible by 3 and uses this criterion to include elements in `lst2`. The second lambda expression is applied to all elements of `lst2` to divide integers by 3. The resulting list ends up in `lst3`.

```
lst1 = [1, 2, 3, 9, 345, 36, 33]
# lst2 contains all elements of lst1 divisible by 3
lst2 = list(filter(lambda x: x % 3 == 0, lst1))
print(lst2)    # Output [3, 9, 345, 36, 33]
# divide all elements of lst2 by 3
lst3 = list(map(lambda x: x // 3, lst2))
print(lst3)    # Output [1, 3, 115, 12, 11]
```

5.14 Processing Text Files

Before you can read or write a text file, you must open the file via open. Then, you can pass the filename in the first parameter and the access mode in the second. With the additional letter b, you can also process binary files, but we won't cover this topic here.

Mode	Meaning
'r'	Read file (applies by default)
'w'	Write file (existing files will be overwritten!)
'a'	Write to the end of an existing file (*append*)
'r+'	Read and write file

Table 5.9 Access Modes of the Open Method

open returns a file object, which can then be processed with various methods. close() terminates access to the file and releases it again for other programs. In short scripts, you can do without close() because, at the end of the program, all open files will be closed anyway.

Method	Meaning
s = f.read()	Reads the entire file
s = f.read(n)	Reads n bytes and returns them as a string
s = f.readline()	Reads one line of the file
f.write(s)	Writes the string s to the file
n = f.tell()	Indicates the current read/write position
f.seek(n, offset)	Changes the read/write position
close()	Closes the file

Table 5.10 Important Methods for File Objects

readline() always returns the EOL character of each line (i.e., \n on macOS and Linux). However, often, this EOL character is undesirable. If necessary, line.rstrip() eliminates the whitespace (i.e., any blank, tab, and newline) at the EOL.

When the EOF is reached, readline() returns an empty string. Since empty lines *within* a file consist at least of \n, no ambiguity can arise about when the EOF is reached.

If the structure of your code allows it, you should formulate the entire code for processing a file using with open() as f. This approach ensures that the file will automatically be closed when an error occurs or when the current code block (e.g., a function) is exited. Thus, you don't need to worry about close at all. (with also works for other Python objects that should be closed after they are used, for instance, for network and database connections.)

```
# Read and output text file line by line
with open('readme.txt') as f:
    for line in f:
        print(line, end='')
```

When writing text files, don't forget to include \n in the strings you want to output because write() doesn't care about line endings! Note also that, unlike print, write expects only one parameter, and this parameter must really be a string. If you want to save numbers or other data in the text file, you must first convert them into strings.

```
# writes 'line 1' to 'line 10' into a text file
with open('result.txt', 'w') as out:
    for i in range(1, 11):
        out.write('Line %d\n' % i)
```

5.14.1 Example: Analyzing a CSV File

The starting point for our next example is the *employees.csv* file, which contains fictitious company data:

```
emp_no,first_name,last_name,birth_date,salary,hire_date
87461,Moni,Decaestecker,1952-02-01,67914,1989-05-31
237571,Ronghao,Schaad,1952-02-01,59355,1994-06-14
406121,Supot,Remmele,1952-02-01,76470,1989-01-27
91374,Eishiro,Kuzuoka,1952-02-01,42250,1999-07-08
...
```

The first goal of our script is to display the first name, last name, and date of birth for each employee neatly formatted on the screen:

```
first_name          last_name           birth_date
Moni                Decaestecker        1952-02-01
Ronghao             Schaad              1952-02-01
Supot               Remmele             1952-02-01
```

Four lines of code are sufficient for this goal:

```
# Sample file employees.py
with open('employees.csv', 'r') as f:
    for line in f:
        columns = line.split(',')
        print('%-20s %-20s %s' % tuple(columns[1:4]))
```

The loop reads each line of the file. split divides the line into its columns (it returns a list, with each element representing one column). Note that the last column contains \n because the for loop includes the newline characters. columns[1:4] extracts the columns 2 to 4. (Remember, the count starts at 0!) tuple turns the list into a tuple, as is expected by the % format operator.

5.14.2 Example: Creating SQL Commands

The second task is a bit more demanding: The employees must be stored in the employees table. The following script is supposed to create the required SQL commands and save them in a new file named *employees.sql*, where the column names of the CSV file match those of the table:

```
INSERT INTO employees (emp_no, first_name, last_name,
                       birth_date, salary, hire_date)
VALUES ('87461', 'Moni', 'Decaestecker', '1952-02-01',
        '67914', '1989-05-31');
INSERT INTO ...
```

The code is not much longer, but a bit more complex. with opens two files in this case: one for reading and one for writing. The first line contains the column names and could be copied unchanged. Only for cosmetic reasons will a space be inserted after each comma (replace), and also the newline character is removed at the EOL.

In the for loop, all further lines are read and split into columns. Each element of the list in data will then be enclosed in quotes and reassembled into the values string. The output to the SQL file is performed using write.

```
# Sample file employees.py
sqlcmd = 'INSERT INTO employees (%s)\nVALUES (%s);\n'
with open('employees.csv', 'r') as csv,\
     open('employees.sql', 'w') as sql:

    # Read column names from the first line
    columnnames = csv.readline().rstrip().replace(',', ', ')

    # loop through all other lines
    for line in csv:
        columns = line.rstrip().split(',')
        # Put columns in quotes
        data = ["'" + c + "'" for c in columns]
        # join the list in data to a string
        values = ', '.join(data)
        # Output in the SQL file
        sql.write(sqlcmd % (columnnames, values))
```

5.15 Error Protection

When errors occur, like many modern programming languages, Python throws an *exception*. If your program does not provide protection against such exceptions, you'll end up with a nasty error message. You can avoid this if you secure your code by using try/except.

5.15.1 try/except

The syntax for try/except is simple:

```
try:
    # error prone code
except someError:
    # response to a specific error
except:
    # response to all other errors
finally:
    # is always executed
```

Note that try must be followed by at least one except or finally block. All other parts of the try construct are optional. When an error occurs, Python looks for the first except statement that applies to the error. Using except without an error name is considered the default statement that applies to any type of error.

If an applicable except block exists, the code specified there will be executed. Then, the error is considered to be resolved. The program continues below the try construct.

Code within the finally block is *always* executed, even if the try construct is in a loop or function that you terminate prematurely using break or return. finally is the right place for cleaning up.

If you formulate the except statement as except xxxError as e, then e contains an exception object. In its evaluation, e.args is of particular interest as it will give you a tuple with all the parameters that were passed when the error was triggered. When an exception object is converted to a string—either explicitly via str(e) or implicitly in the print function—the contents of args are automatically converted to a string.

```
try:
    n = 1 / 0
except ZeroDivisionError as e:
    print(e)  # Output: 'division by zero'
```

5.16 System Functions

This section focuses on some basic system functions, many of which are located in the sys module, which must be included via import. Simply enter the following command:

```
import sys
```

5.16.1 Access to the Program Parameters

sys.argv contains the list of all parameters passed to a Python script. You must note that the first list element contains the program name, which you usually do not want to evaluate. The easiest way to access the remaining elements is then via sys.argv[1:].

5.16.2 Access to Standard Input and Standard Output

sys.stdin and sys.stdout contain file objects that you can use to output data to standard output or read data from standard input. The same functions are available as for ordinary files (Section 5.14). Error and logging messages are best sent to sys.stderr.

5.16.3 Exiting a Program

Usually, a Python program ends with the execution of the last statement or when an unhandled error occurs. If you want to terminate a program prematurely, you must run sys.exit(). With sys.exit(n), you can also return an error code, the meaning of which is the same as in Bash scripts. Alternatively, you can pass a string to the exit method, which is then displayed as an error message. In this case, 1 is automatically applied as the error code.

exit Produces an Exception!

Note that, internally, the exit method throws a SystemExit exception. The end of the program can therefore be prevented by try/except.

5.16.4 Calling Linux Commands

By using subprocess.run, you can execute another program or command from within a Python script. In the simplest case, you can pass a list with the command name and its options to run. The following lines call the ls command with the -l option, which displays details about the files in the current directory. run returns an object of the CompletedProcess class as a result (see Table 5.11).

```
import subprocess
result = subprocess.run(['ls', '-l'])
```

Property	Meaning
args	The executed command as a string or list
returncode	The return code (0 = OK; otherwise, error)
stdout	Standard output of the command
stderr	Error messages of the command

Table 5.11 Properties of an Object of the CompletedProcess Type

5.16.5 Processing Results

When run is executed as in the previous listing, the output of the command occurs directly in the terminal where the Python script is executed. stdout and stderr of the result object remain empty.

If you want to process the output yourself, you must pass the capture_output=True parameter to run. After running the command, the stdout and stderr properties return the output and error messages of the command as byte strings, respectively. You turn this string into an ordinary Unicode string using decode('utf-8'). If you want to process the string line by line, the easiest approach is to use splitlines:

```
import subprocess
result   = subprocess.run(["ls", "-l"], capture_output=True)
output   = result.stdout
errormsg = result.stderr
for line in output.decode('utf-8').splitlines():
    print('Result:', line)
```

5.16.6 Running Commands through the Shell

Instead of running a command directly through Python, you can redirect it through the standard shell. For many Linux distributions, this standard shell is Bash. For this task, you must pass the additional shell=True parameter to run. There are two advantages to this approach: First, you can specify the command or commands to be executed in a simple string, where the pipe character (|) also works. Thus, for example:

```
import subprocess
result = subprocess.run('dmesg | grep -i eth', capture_output=True, shell=True)
print('Shell:\n', result.stdout.decode('utf-8'))
```

Second, the shell evaluates the * and ? wildcard characters, which allows you to easily process files that match a certain pattern:

```
result = subprocess.run('ls -l *.py', capture_output=True, shell=True)
```

However, using the shell causes increased overhead. If you're concerned with executing many commands as quickly as possible, you should avoid using shell=True if possible. For tips on how to succeed with common tasks without shell=True, see *https://docs.python.org/3/library/subprocess.html.*

5.16.7 Error during a Command Call

The way in which run responds to errors depends on whether you run the command directly or through the shell and what type of error occurs. For example, if you make a typo in the command name, then without shell=True, you'll get an OSError exception. With shell=True, you'll only get a return value not equal to 0.

The additional `check=True` parameter is recommended. In this way, you can ensure that an exception is thrown on every error where the exception type is `CalledProcessError`. You must import this error class from the `subprocess` module.

5.16.8 Waiting (sleep)

The `sleep` function from the `time` module waits for the specified time in seconds without blocking the CPU for other tasks:

```
import time
print("wait 200 ms")
time.sleep(0.2)
print("End of program")
```

5.17 Modules

For beginners, the Python language often seems more extensive than it actually is. In fact, the number of functions implemented directly in Python is quite manageable. For this purpose, all conceivable additional functions are implemented as add-on modules. These modules must be imported before they can be used.

5.17.1 import

Several syntax variants are available for the `import` command, with the following three main ones:

- **`import modulename`**
  This statement reads the module. After this step, you can use all functions defined in the module in the `modulname.functionname()` notation. Using `import m1, m2, m3`, you can also import multiple modules at once.
- **`import modulename as m`**
  With this variant, the functions defined in the module can be used as `m.functionname()`. For long module names, this approach minimizes the typing effort and makes the code more clear.
- **`from modulename import f1, f2`**
  In this variant, you can use the functions `f1` and `f2` without prefixing the module name.

Internally in Python, `import` causes the `modulename.py` file to be read and executed. Many modules simply contain the definition of various functions; thus, these functions are now known to Python and can be used. However, modules can also contain code that is executed immediately, for example, to perform initialization work.

A common practice is to always place `import` statements at the beginning of a Python script. Modules can import other modules themselves. Python remembers which modules it has already read and thus avoids further import attempts for already activated modules.

More details about handling modules are available in the Python documentation at *https://docs.python.org/3/reference/simple_stmts.html#import*.

5.17.2 Distributing Custom Scripts across Multiple Files

You can also use the module mechanism to distribute large scripts across multiple files. To do this, you simply import the relevant files into your main script using `import myname`. This loads the `myname.py` file from the local directory. The functions defined there are then available in the main script.

It is convenient to define only functions (or classes, but I won't go into that in this book) in your own module files. Code that is immediately executable should be located only in the main file of your script.

Name Conflicts with Standard Modules

This useful mechanism can cause errors that are difficult to understand. For example, you want to use the Python module `csv` in your script. If your own *csv.py* file exists in the local directory, then it will be loaded instead of the Python module.

You should therefore avoid naming your own script files the same as Python modules! This recommendation is easier said than done, because you can't possibly know the names of all Python modules. In any case, keep this possibility of an error in mind.

5.18 Installing Additional Modules Using pip

In Python, you can choose from a selection of several hundred modules by default. These modules can be activated via `import` without any further preparatory work. But wait, there's more! On the *Python Package Index* platform at the *https://pypi.org*, files from more than 400,000 projects are also available for download.

To install external modules, Python provides the `pip` command (for Windows and current Linux distributions) or `pip3` (for macOS and older Linux distributions). Just convince yourself of the existence of this command in a terminal window!

```
> pip --version
  pip 22.3.1 from C:\Users\kofler\AppData\Local\Programs\Python\
                  Python311\Lib\site-packages\pip (python 3.11)
```

5.18.1 Installing pip

On Windows and macOS, pip or pip3 is an integral part of Python. In most Linux distributions, pip is located in a separate package that must be installed separately—on Ubuntu, for example, with the following commands:

```
$ sudo apt update
$ sudo apt install python3-pip
```

5.18.2 Applying pip

Once the installation obstacles have been overcome, using pip is child's play: For example, to install *Matplotlib*, which allows you to create diagrams, you can just run one of the following two commands in the terminal (`pip` on Windows and on new Linux distributions, `pip3` on macOS or on older Linux distributions):

```
> pip install --user matploblib
$ pip3 install --user matplotlib

  Collecting matplotlib
  Downloading matplotlib-3.6.3-cp311-cp311-win_amd64.whl
  Downloading contourpy-1.0.7-cp311-cp311-win_amd64.whl
  ...
  Successfully installed contourpy-1.0.7 ... matplotlib-3.6.3
```

With some packages (like in this example with `matplotlib`), pip installs not only the actual package but also some additional packages with functions that the main package needs.

On Linux and macOS, run pip or pip3 without `root` privileges and without `sudo`. The `--user` option, which mostly applies by default, ensures that the relevant package is installed locally in the relevant user directory (usually in `.local/lib/python<n>/site-packages`) and is only available to that user.

If you want to upgrade an installed module at a later time, you should run `pip install` with the `--upgrade` option, as in the following example:

```
> pip install --upgrade <name>
```

Surprisingly, no simple command exists to update all modules. Stack Overflow provides some tips on how you can work around this limitation if needed at *https://stackoverflow.com/questions/2720014*.

5.18.3 pip Problems with Windows

Unfortunately, pip often causes trouble even when installed correctly. This warning is especially true on Windows, where two causes of errors dominate:

- pip is installed, but not in PATH: To run pip in cmd.exe or in the terminal, its location (e.g., C:\Users\<name>\AppData\Local\Programs\Python\Python<nnn>\Scripts) must be included in the PATH environment variable.

  The Python setup program provides an option to adjust PATH automatically. If you have overlooked this option, you must either repeat the installation or add the path to pip.exe to PATH by yourself. Search for "Edit system environment variables" in the Windows menu!

- You have several Python versions installed in parallel: If Python is installed multiple times, pip may work but won't install the modules for the Python version you're currently using.

  From my experience, the safest solution is to first uninstall all Python versions and also clean up the PATH settings accordingly. After that, reinstall Python, following exactly the instructions in Section 5.1.

5.18.4 pip Problems with Linux

pip is also increasingly causing problems under Linux because many distributors offer a huge collection of packages with Python extensions. The parallel installation of a module, once with apt or dnf and a second time with pip, can then lead to conflicts, especially if not exactly the same versions are used. Python developers have therefore stipulated in *Python Enhancement Proposal (PEP) 668* that packages from Linux repositories are preferable in such cases. PEP 668 has been valid since Python 3.11. Attempting to install a module with pip leads to the following error message with current versions of Debian, Ubuntu, Raspberry Pi OS, and Arch Linux:

```
$ pip install matplotlib

error: externally managed environment
This environment is externally managed
    To install Python packages system-wide, try apt install
    python3-xyz, where xyz is the package you're trying to
    install.

    If you wish to install a non-Debian-packaged Python package,
    create a virtual environment using python3 -m venv path/to/venv.
    Then use path/to/venv/bin/python and path/to/venv/bin/pip. Make
    sure you have python3-full installed.

    If you wish to install a non-Debian packaged Python application,
    it may be easiest to use pipx install xyz, which will manage a
    virtual environment for you. Make sure you have pipx installed.

    See /usr/share/doc/python3.11/README.venv for more information.
```

```
note: If you believe this is a mistake, please contact your Python
installation or OS distribution provider. You can override this,
at the risk of breaking your Python installation or OS, by
passing --break-system-packages. Hint: See PEP 668 for the
detailed specification.
```

The error message points directly to the best solution, namely, the installation of the corresponding Linux package with apt python3-xxx (where xxx is the package name). For matplotlib, run the following command under Debian, Ubuntu, and Raspberry Pi OS:

sudo apt install python3-matplotlib

This recommendation has two restrictions: It requires that you have root or sudo privileges, and it assumes that the desired module is actually available in the repository of your Linux distribution. The latter is often the case, but not always. Almost 500,000 projects are available at *https://pypi.org*, whereas Debian standard repositories "only" contain about 4,000 projects (apt list | grep python3- | wc -l).

An alternative is to use a *virtual environment*. In the context of Python, a virtual environment is simply a project directory in which the modules required for the project are installed locally and project-specifically. This approach has several advantages:

- You can clearly see which modules a particular project requires. The project can thus be transferred more easily to another computer later.
- No conflicts arise between different projects that require different modules.
- You aren't restricted to the Python modules offered by your Linux distribution and do not need administrator rights to install Linux packages.

Virtual environments are supported by Python through the venv module. This module must be installed in advance, either with apt install python3-venv or with apt install python3-full. Then, set up your project with the following command:

```
$ python3 -m venv my-project
```

Python creates the directory *my-project*, if it does not already exist, and sets up a minimal Python environment there. ("Minimal" means approximately 1,500 files, with a space requirement of approximately 25 MB.) Now, execute the shell script activate in your terminal window with source to activate the environment:

```
$ cd my-project
$ source bin/activate
(my-project)$
```

In this environment, pip works as usual. You can then execute your script, which uses the locally installed modules:

```
(my-project)$ pip install requests beautifulsoup4
(my-project)$ ./my-webscraping-script.py
```

5.18.5 requirements.txt

To document the modules required by your script, you can create the `requirements.txt` file in the project directory. This file records which module is used in which version. The following lines illustrate the simple syntax of this file:

```
beautifulsoup4==4.12.0
requests==2.28.2
requests_html==0.10.0
```

Instead of maintaining the file manually, you can also use the `pipreqs` command. This command evaluates the `import` statements of all Python files in a directory, determines which versions of the modules are currently installed, and then creates the appropriate file. `pipreqs` is itself a module that must be installed via `pip install pipreqs` before its first use.

```
$ pipreqs code/directory
```

Once `requirements.txt` exists, you can easily install all the modules listed within it with the following command:

```
$ pip install -r requirements.txt
```

5.18.6 pipenv

If you develop various Python projects on your computer, which need different add-on modules, pip can lead you directly into chaos, if you're unlucky. Quickly, which modules are required for which scripts becomes unclear. You'll notice this problem easily whenever you try to run your scripts on another computer. In rare cases, installing modules in parallel or performing module updates for multiple projects can lead to conflict: A script that was working fine before may suddenly report strange errors.

You can avoid such trouble by using a virtual environment (Section 5.18.4). Manually managing such environments is difficult, however. Instead, you can use `pipenv` to organize your project in a separate directory and manage the required modules. First, install this tool:

```
$ pip install --user pipenv       (Windows, macOS)
$ sudo apt install pipenv         (Debian, Ubuntu)
```

In the directory of your project, you should use `pipenv`, instead of `pip`, to install the required modules:

```
$ cd my-project
$ pipenv install requests beautifulsoup4

  Creating a virtualenv for this project...
  Pipfile: /home/kofler/my-project/Pipfile
  Creating virtual environment, virtualenv location:
```

```
/home/kofler/.local/share/virtualenvs/py-project-6zwWqRDz
...
To activate this project's virtualenv, run 'pipenv shell'.
Alternatively, run a command inside the virtualenv with
'pipenv run'.
```

I will introduce the `requests` and `beautifulsoup4` modules mentioned in the example in more detail in Chapter 17. Now, to run a script that uses these two modules, you must use `pipenv run`:

```
$ pipenv run ./myscript.py
```

Alternatively, you can start a new shell using `pipenv shell`. Inside this shell, you can run your script as usual via `./myscript.py`. At the same time, you can also start Python interactively there and use all modules that have been installed using `pipenv`. If you don't need the shell anymore, you can exit it via `Ctrl` + `D` or `exit`.

The biggest advantage using of `pipenv` is that it sets up a `pipfile` in your project directory. This file summarizes which modules are used by your project:

```
# File Pipfile (shortened)
...
[packages]
beautifulsoup4 = "*"
requests = "*"

[requires]
python_version = "3.10"
```

Now, to port your script to another computer, you can copy the code and the `pipfile` there and run `pipenv install` once without any further parameters. This step will install all the required modules. Done!

`pipenv` uses `virtualenv`, a Python tool for setting up several separate Python environments on one computer. `virtualenv` provides more features than `pipenv` but is a bit more difficult to use (see *https://virtualenv.pypa.io*). For our tasks, `pipenv` is usually sufficient. Other alternatives to Python project management are the built-in Python functions of the `venv` module (a minimal version of `virtualenv`) and `pip-tools`.

Disadvantages and Limitations

`pipenv` is not without controversy. One problem is that modules are installed separately for each project. With extensive modules like Matplotlib or Pandas, this separation costs space, which is unnecessary. Also, the execution of scripts via `pipenv run` is a bit more cumbersome.

Chris Warrick lists other shortcomings in his blog at *https://chriswarrick.com/blog/2018/07/17/pipenv-promises-a-lot-delivers-very-little*. His fundamental critique is well founded, but no longer up to date on all points. In particular, the speed problems of `pipenv` have now been fixed.

PART II

Work Techniques and Tools

Chapter 6
Linux Toolbox

6

Before you develop your own Bash scripts using Bash, you need a basic vocabulary of elementary commands. You can then use these commands to create files, copy or delete directories, create compressed archives, install additional commands, switch to root mode, and so on. The commands can be used both interactively in a terminal and automatically in scripts.

This chapter is a kind of crash course for Linux newbies. If you have already worked frequently in the Linux terminal, you can safely skip this chapter.

Most of this chapter also applies to macOS. Although macOS is not based on Linux, but on BSD (another Unix derivative), basic commands like `cp` or `mkdir` work in the same way as on Linux. Unfortunately, there are occasional functional deviations in the individual options, which can result in compatibility issues if you want your scripts to run on both platforms.

Many of the commands presented in this chapter even work on Windows! However, this functionality requires you to use Git Bash. This shell is usually installed together with Git; see also Chapter 14.

Prerequisites for This Chapter

You can use Linux commands even without prior knowledge of Bash. But before you can call these commands in your own scripts, you must have some basic knowledge of Bash programming (see Chapter 3).

A Little Advertising

An even remotely complete reference of all important Linux commands is impossible at this point. However, as a small self-promotion, you can find most everything you need to know in my book *Linux: The Comprehensive Guide* (Rheinwerk Computing, May 2024) at *https://rheinwerk-computing.com/5779*.

6.1 Directories and Files

Dealing with directories is simple: You can change directories using the `cd` command. If you do not pass a parameter to `cd`, you'll be taken to your home directory. The `cd ..`

command takes you to the *parent directory*, while `cd -` allows you to go to the last active directory.

`pwd` displays the path of the current directory, and `mkdir` creates a new directory. A particularly useful option for `mkdir` is `-p` which allows you to create an entire chain of directories, for example, `mkdir -p dir/subdir/subsubdir`. The option also avoids error messages if directories already exist.

`rmdir` deletes a directory, but only if the directory is empty. You can delete directories including their contents via `rm -r`, but you should be careful with it! This command works recursively and also deletes all subdirectories. In general, the deletion of files and directories cannot be undone!

```
$ cd                    # change to the home directory
$ pwd
/home/kofler
$ mkdir subdir          # create new directory
$ cd subdir             # change there
$ cd ..                 # back to the home directory
$ rmdir subdir          # delete subdir again
```

Linux beginners must first learn to orient themselves in the branched directory tree. Note that you need root privileges to modify system files (for example, in the */etc* directory). See Section 6.4 for more information on this topic.

Directory	Contents
/boot	System files for the boot process
/dev	Device files for hardware components
/etc	System settings
/home	User directories
/mnt	External file systems and data carriers
/proc	Process information (virtual file system)
/usr	Programs and libraries
/tmp	Temporary files (lost on reboot)
/var	Variable data (web files, databases, mail server log files)

Table 6.1 Important Linux Directories

6.1.1 Listing, Copying, Moving, and Deleting Files

`ls` lists files. When you add the `-l` option, the command displays a lot of additional information besides the filename, such as the size in bytes and the time of the last change. With the -a option, ls also takes into account so-called "hidden" directories and files whose name simply starts with a dot (for example .ssh with the configuration files of the ssh command).

touch creates a new empty file. If the file already exists, only the time of the last change will be updated.

The cp old new command copies one file. cp file1 file2 file3 dir copies multiple files to another directory. When used as in cp -r olddir newdir, the command copies an entire directory tree (r as in *recursive*). cp -a olddir newdir serves the same purpose but leaves the access rights and the time of the last change unchanged.

mv works similar to cp: mv old new renames the file. mv file1 file2 dir moves the files to a new location.

rm irrevocably deletes the specified files. With the already mentioned -r option, the command works recursively, so it also deletes subdirectories and their contents. Proceed with caution!

```
$ mkdir tst                # creates a new directory
$ cd tst                   # changes there
$ date > now.txt           # saves date and time in now.txt
$ cp now.txt copy.txt      # creates a copy of now.txt
$ mv copy.txt backup.txt # gives the copy a different name
$ ls *.txt                 # lists all *.txt files
  backup.txt now.txt
$ rm *.txt                 # deletes all *.txt files
```

6.2 Finding Files

You can use find to search a directory including all subdirectories for files that have certain characteristics. Possible search criteria include the name, the file size or the date of the last modification. However, find never includes the content of the file.

You need to pass the initial directory for the search to the command (or . for the current directory). The search criteria are formulated with countless options, whereby all criteria must apply simultaneously (logical AND operation). The following examples are merely a small indication of the capabilities of find. You can get much more information via man find. Some find commands are preceded by sudo, which will run the search in root mode (Section 6.4). This addition is necessary because, as an ordinary user, you're not even allowed to read a large number of files in the */var* and */etc* directories.

```
# files in /var/log that are larger than 250 KB
$ sudo find /var/log -size +250k
```

```
# files in /etc that have been modified in the last 28 days
# mtime = modify time
$ sudo find /etc -mtime -28

# all subdirectories in /etc (-type d = directory)
$ sudo find /etc -type d

# PDF files in downloads that are larger than 1 MB
# and have not been read for at least 60 days
# (atime = access time)
$ find Downloads -name '*.pdf' -size +1M -atime +60
```

6.2.1 Text Search Using grep

The command `grep pattern file.txt` filters out all lines from a text file that match the search pattern `pattern`. In the following example, all lines containing a specific IP address are to be filtered out of a logging file from the Apache web server. Because the search pattern is processed as a regular expression (see Chapter 9), the period (.) character must be marked by a backslash. (In regular expressions, a period is a placeholder for any character.)

```
$ sudo grep '175\.55\.93\.123' /var/log/apache2/access.log
```

Text Evaluation and Analysis

I will discuss `grep` in much more detail in this book with regard to its function as a filter command (see Chapter 8, Section 8.1). In this chapter, I want to introduce you to other commands for text evaluation, including `wc` (*word count*), `head` and `tail` (display the first/last lines of a text), `sort` (sort text), and `uniq` (remove doubles).

With a few options, the `grep` filter command becomes a powerful search tool. The following command searches the `/etc` directory recursively (`-r`) for files that contain the search term `password` in uppercase or lowercase (`-i`). The resulting files will be output in a list (`-l`).

```
$ sudo grep -r -i -l password /etc
```

6.3 Compressing and Archiving Files

To compress a single file, the easiest approach is to use `gzip`. This command renames the file immediately (i.e., `name` becomes `name.gz`). To unpack the file again, you must use `gunzip`. The extension `.gz` will be removed again.

```
$ gzip somefile        # compresses the file -> somefile.gz
$ gunzip somefile.gz  # decompresses the file -> somefile
```

A number of alternatives to the standard gzip and gunzip commands are available. xz compresses much better, but also requires much more CPU power. Conversely, lz4 works much more efficiently than gzip but does not provide as small files.

6.3.1 Archiving Files Using tar

The tar command actually stands for *tape archive*, so it comes from a time when tape drives were still used. Today, tar is mostly used to create compressed file archives. tar files play a similarly important role on Linux as zip files on Windows.

For tar, the first option (-c, -r, -x, or -t) specifies the action that tar is supposed to perform. All other options affect the operation.

Option	Meaning
-c	Create new archive (*create*)
-r	Extend existing archive (*replace*)
-x	Unpack archive (*extract*)
-t	List contents (*list*)
-v	Show visual feedback (*verbose*)
-z	Compress/decompress using gzip
-j	Compress/decompress using bzip2
-J	Compress/decompress using xz
-f file.tar	Filename of the archive (*file*)
-f -	Use standard input/standard output
-C directory	Work in this directory

Table 6.2 tar Options

A particularly important option is -f filename: This option defines the filename of the archive file. If you forget this option, tar will try to access a tape drive. Since tape drives don't exist on most computers, an error will occur.

When you use -f -, tar writes the archive to the standard output or reads it from there. This approach is useful if you want to combine tar with another command, for example, to immediately encrypt an archive using tar cf - | gpg ....

A common tactic is to combine the options passed to tar into a block of letters without a minus sign. Thus, -c -z -f or the short notation -czf simply becomes czf.

The first of the following commands creates the compressed backup.tar.gz file, which contains all files within the images directory. (tar works recursively by default, so it also takes subdirectories into account.)

The other commands display the table of contents of the archive and finally unpack it. Instead of .tar.gz, the shortened identifier .tgz is also common.

```
$ tar czf backup.tar.gz images    # create archive

$ tar tzf backup.tar.gz           # show contents

$ cd other-directory              # unpack archive
$ tar xzf backup.tar.gz
```

Backups

More use cases for tar will follow in Chapter 15, where I will discuss various techniques for automating backups.

6.3.2 ZIP Files

Maybe your archives need to be compatible with the Windows world, or you want to unpack a ZIP file. In such situations you can use the zip, zipinfo, and unzip commands, whose syntax I will explain in this section based on only three examples.

These examples again refer to the images directory that is to be backed up. Note that zip does not work recursively (i.e., subfolders are not included) by default. If necessary, the -r option can provide help in this context.

```
$ zip backup.zip -r images        # create archive
$ zipinfo backup.zip              # show archive
$ unzip backup.zip                # unpack archive
```

6.4 Using Root Privileges

On Linux and macOS, you can modify only your own files and read only selected files of other users. Working within this limitation may be sufficient for your everyday work, but not for scripts that are supposed to perform admin tasks.

The solution in such cases is sudo which allows you to execute a single command or an entire script with admin rights (or, as it is called in Linux, with "root privileges"). The first of the following two commands performs a software installation (Section 6.5), while the second command runs a script in the local directory:

```
$ sudo apt install somepackage
  [sudo] Password for <accountname>: ********
$ sudo ./myscript.sh
```


6.4.1 sudo Privileges for Selected Accounts Only

sudo can only be used by selected users—usually, the person who performed the Linux installation and whose account was created first.

sudo users must authenticate using their own password. The authentication will then remain valid for a few minutes. For additional sudo calls within this period of time, it is therefore not necessary to enter the password again.

The /etc/sudoers file controls who has which privileges in sudo. Fortunately, changes to this relatively complex file are rarely necessary. If you want to assign sudo privileges to another account, you should run the following command (which of course assumes that you have sudo privileges yourself):

```
$ sudo usermod -a -G sudo <account>     # Debian, Ubuntu ...
$ sudo usermod -a -G wheel <account>    # Fedora, RHEL ...
```

These usermod commands add the <account> user to the sudo group (for Debian, Ubuntu, and compatible distributions) or to the wheel group (for Fedora and Red Hat Enterprise Linux [RHEL] compatible distributions). All members of these two groups will automatically have sudo privileges.

6.4.2 Issues with Output Redirection

The following two commands each attempt to modify a file in the */etc* directory. The first command works, the second one triggers an error. Why's that?

```
$ sudo touch /etc/new-file            # works
$ sudo echo "hello" > /etc/new-file  # Error: no permission
```

The problem is the output redirection. While sudo runs echo "hello" with root privileges, the rest of the command (i.e., the redirection of the output to the /etc/new-file file) is handled by Bash—and Bash runs with normal privileges. That's where the error occurs.

Once the cause is clear (I stumble into this trap myself at regular intervals), the solution is not difficult. Instead of just running echo (or whatever command) via sudo, you pass a new Bash process to sudo, which in turn executes the rest of the command, including the redirection. The -c option signifying *command* allows you to pass the command to be run to the Bash process:

```
$ sudo bash -c 'echo "bla" > /etc/new-file'
```

6.4.3 Access Rights

There is a three-tier system that controls who is allowed to read, write, and execute which files on Linux or macOS. Along with each file, nine access bits are stored, namely r (*read*), w (*write*), and x (*execute*) for the owner of the file, for all members of the group to which this file is assigned and finally for all other accounts.

For example, the */etc/shadow* system file, which contains hash codes for passwords on Linux, belongs to the root user and is assigned to the shadow group. root can read and modify the file, members of the shadow group can read it, and all other users have no rights. You can determine all this information using ls -l:

```
$ ls -l /etc/shadow

-rw-r-----  root shadow  ... shadow

 ^^^                              rights for owners
    ^^^                           rights for group members
       ^^^                        rights for other users
            ^^^^                  assigned owner
                 ^^^^^^           assigned group
                         ^^^      time (not shown)
                             ^^^^^^ filename
```

The chown (*change owner*), chgrp (*change group*), and chmod (*change mode*) commands allow you to change the assignment of a file to its owner, the assigned group as well as the access rights. All this data can also be changed for directories, although the execute bit x has a different meaning for directories: It allows the use of this directory (i.e., cd directory).

The following three lines show simple examples of how to use chown, chgrp, and chmod: The first command makes the peter account the owner of the /var/www/html/index.html file. The second command assigns the www-data group to this file. The third command sets the read and write bits for the owner (u for *user*) and the group but disables these bits for all others (o for *other*). As a result, the index.html file can be read and modified by peter and by all members of the www-data group, but by no one else. (www-data is the group assigned to the web server on Debian and Ubuntu.)

```
$ sudo chown peter        /var/www/html/index.html
$ sudo chgrp www-data     /var/www/html/index.html
$ sudo chmod ug+rw o-rw   /var/www/html/index.html
```

The execution of all three commands requires root privileges in most cases. Exceptions include changes for your own files, which only affect your own user account or groups assigned to you. Such modifications—for example, chmod +x myscript.sh to make a script executable—can take effect without sudo. (The macOS variant of chmod differs minimally from the Linux variant; you must run chmod a+x instead.)

We lack space for further details, such as the many syntax variants of chmod or the octal representation of access rights. A more detailed description of Linux/Unix access rights can be found in any good Linux book as well as on numerous websites, for example, at *https://kb.iu.edu/d/abdb*.

6.4.4 Managing Processes

The ps command without options lists the processes that have been started from the terminal. The result of ps ax is already impressive: It will provide you with a list of all processes running on the computer or in the virtual machine along with detailed information (process number, parameters, etc.). More information is provided by ps axu: This command also shows who started which process.

The result of ps can be further processed with other commands. In the following examples, wc -l (*word count, lines*) counts the output lines and thus the active processes. grep filters the lines from the result that contain the ssh search term.

```
$ ps ax | wc -l       # count number of processes
$ ps ax | grep ssh    # show only SSH processes
```

top shows the running processes sorted by their CPU usage. The display is refreshed every 3 seconds until you end the command via Q.

Alternatives to top

Some useful alternatives to top exist. While htop has a clear display, iotop, iftop, or powertop use other sorting criteria—I/O load, network performance, or (estimated) power consumption, respectively. These commands usually must be installed separately.

6.4.5 Terminating Processes

To terminate an out-of-control or infinite loop script that you started in the terminal, you can simply press Ctrl + C. You can stop other processes associated with your account via kill pid. Instead of pid, you must specify the process number, which you can determine either via ps ax or top.

Despite its dramatic name, kill actually only sends signals to other processes. Without any additional options, it sends the SIGTERM signal, which is effectively a polite request that the process be terminated. However, the process can ignore this signal. In such cases, kill -9 pid usually provides the desired result. In this context, -9 indicates the signal number. Signal 9 is called SIGKILL and terminates every process immediately unless a longer lasting system function is being executed. If that's the case, even SIGKILL won't help.

As you may have guessed already, you can only terminate your own processes using kill. Only root is allowed to stop external processes. For this purpose, you can combine kill with sudo (e.g., sudo kill -9 pid).

A bit annoying that you must find out the process number first before you can run kill. A more convenient command in this context is killall n, where n is the name of the process to be terminated. Watch out, though: sudo killall n can have far-reaching consequences because it kills *all* processes with the same name, no matter who started them.

6.4.6 Background Processes and System Services

When you boot a Linux system, numerous background processes are started automatically. These processes are responsible for various system tasks and server services. You can use the systemctl command to stop such system services, restart them, start them automatically in the future, and so on.

```
$ sudo systemctl                # list all services
$ sudo systemctl stop name      # stop 'name' service
$ sudo systemctl start name     # start the service
$ sudo systemctl restart name   # restart the service
$ sudo systemctl reload name    # read configuration files
$ sudo systemctl enable name    # start the service automatically
                                # in the future
$ sudo systemctl disable name   # no longer start the service
                                # in the future
```

systemctl is especially important if you have installed a new server service on Linux. Depending on the distribution (e.g., Fedora or Red Hat), services do *not* get started automatically once the installation process has completed. You must take care of the configuration first and then start the service manually using systemctl start. If everything works, you can enable the service permanently via systemctl enable.

In other distributions, newly installed services are started immediately with a default configuration (e.g., Debian, Ubuntu), but even in this case, changes to the configuration are usually required. For your changes to take effect, you must run systemctl reload. (For very fundamental changes, even systemctl restart is required.)

6.4.7 Logging Files

The services running on Linux log a large amount of data. Some programs store log files as text files in the /var/log directory, such as most mail and web servers. The following command lists all logging messages of the mail server that concern a specific email address:

```
$ sudo grep customer@somecompany.com /var/log/mail.log
```

Smaller server processes mostly use the central syslog. You can read the messages using `journalctl`, as in the following examples:

```
$ journalctl                # read all syslog messages
$ journalctl -u sshd        # read only messages from the SSH server
```


6.4.8 Determining Free Memory

`free -h` determines the free memory. The `-h` option stands for *human readable*. The numerical data is therefore provided with suitable units, such as M for megabyte (MB), G for gigabyte (GB), and so on. However, the result is not easy to interpret. The free memory is indicated in the final *available* column and is around 15 GBs on the test computer. According to the *free* column, it would seem to be less than 1 GB, but the system takes into account a lot of buffer memory that Linux can make available at any time.

```
$ free -h

         total      used      free     shared  buff/cache  available
Mem:      30Gi      14Gi     938Mi      478Mi        15Gi       15Gi
Swap:       0B        0B        0B
```

You can determine the free space on the hard disk or SSD using `df -h` (*disk free*). By default, the command lists all Linux file systems, including various internal file systems. Using `-x tmpfs`, you can at least eliminate the temporary file systems and this way reduce the information overload a little. In the following example, the second and third lines are the most interesting ones. There are still 159 GBs free in the root file system and 195 GBs in the `/home` file system for the user directories.

```
$ df -h -x tmpfs

Filesystem                 Size  Used Avail Use% Mounted on
dev                         16G     0   16G   0% /dev
/dev/mapper/vgcrypt-root   196G   28G  159G  15% /
/dev/mapper/vgcrypt-home   590G  366G  195G  66% /home
/dev/nvme0n1p1             2.0G   80M  1.9G   4% /boot
/dev/sdb1                  1.7T  1.1T  570G  66% /run/media/kofler/p1-backup2
```

A great alternative to `df` is the `duf` command, but it needs to be installed separately. Basically, the command provides the same information, but it formats the result much more clearly.

6.4.9 Determining Other System Information

Do you want to know which distribution is running in a virtual machine or on a server? Take a look at the /etc/os-release file:

```
$ cat /etc/os-release

  NAME="Arch Linux"
  BUILD_ID=rolling
  ...
```

You can determine the version of the running kernel by using uname:

```
$ uname -r

  6.1.1-arch1-1
```

You can read error, warning, debug, and status messages from the kernel with dmesg. The best approach is to redirect the result of dmesg to less so that you can scroll through the information, which can extend over several pages. In most current distributions, the kernel messages can only be read with root privileges.

```
$ sudo dmesg |  less
```

6.5 Software Installation

Linux distributions contain a good basic set of commands by default. However, depending on the direction in which your scripts develop, it can happen that exactly one specific command is missing. This case occurs particularly often when you use containers, for example, with Docker. In containers, the basic equipment is reduced to a minimum for reasons of space.

A missing command is rarely an insurmountable problem: Most Linux distributions are associated with a huge archive of software packages. All you need to do is install the correct package from these package sources that contains the commands you need.

Differences among apt, dnf, zypper, and brew

Fundamental differences exist between Linux distributions when it comes to package management. In this section, I focus on the apt command, which is used on Debian, Ubuntu, and related distributions.

In the Red Hat world, for example, on Fedora or AlmaLinux, you would use dnf instead, which works quite similarly to apt. For SUSE Linux Enterprise Server (SLES) distributions in turn, zypper is used.

By default, no package management exists at all on macOS. However, external tools like `brew` (see *https://brew.sh*) can take care of this task and make a rich selection of open-source tools accessible for macOS. Once installed, the `brew` command also works similarly to `apt` or `dnf`.

6.5.1 Updating Software

You can update all packages installed on Debian or Ubuntu with only two commands:

```
$ sudo apt update
$ sudo apt full-upgrade
```

You'll probably ask yourself why two (similar sounding) commands are necessary; why isn't one sufficient? `apt update` only updates the information as to which packages are available in the external package sources. So, the program updates the directory of available software, but without touching the existing packages. Only `apt full-upgrade` downloads the updated packages after a query and installs them. If the update affects basic functions such as the Linux kernel, a reboot must be performed afterwards for the update to take effect.

6.5.2 Installing Additional Packages

The installation of new software also starts with `apt` update (unless you have just run this command as part of an update). `apt install` then downloads the desired software package, in the following example various encryption tools collected in the `openssl` package:

```
$ sudo apt update
$ sudo apt install openssl
```

In Linux, software is often distributed across multiple packages. Relatively often, to execute the commands from package A, libraries are required that are located in package B. `apt` recognizes such dependencies and installs all the required additional packages after a query. So, don't be surprised if `apt install xy` reports that it installs not just one package, but five or ten!

Finding Packages

If you need a certain command for your script, guessing in which package the command is located can often be difficult. Package and command names do not always match, especially if a package contains multiple commands. Sometimes (but unfortunately not always!), the `apt search xy` command, which searches for search term `xy` in the package description, delivers the desired result. Package search engines available on the internet work better; for Ubuntu, you can use visit, for example, *https://packages.ubuntu.com*.

6.6 Other Commands

To conclude this chapter, I want to briefly introduce you to a few more frequently used commands:

- **alias**
  `alias` defines shortcuts. `alias ll='ls -lh'` allows you to run the frequently used `ls -l -h` command (to list files with detailed information and present the file size as *human readable*) in the `ll` short notation. Shortcuts are best specified in the *.bashrc* file so that they are permanently available.

- **cat file**
  `cat file` outputs a text file. The command is often combined with input or output redirection. For example, `cat text1 text2 text3 > result` joins three text files and saves the result in a new file.

  `Cat > newfile` is also particularly useful. This construct allows you to create a short new text file without launching an editor. Because no file was passed to the command for reading, it expects the input in the terminal (i.e., from standard input). Pressing Ctrl + D terminates the input:

  ```
  $ cat > newfile
  Line 1
  Line 2
  <Ctrl>+<D>
  ```

- **date**
  `date` returns the current date and time. A string starting with + optionally controls the output format. For example, `date "+%Y-%m-%d"` generates a string with the date in International Organization for Standardization (ISO) format (for example, 2023-12-31).

- **history**
  `history` lists all recently executed commands.

- **ip**
  `ip` determines or changes the network configuration. The following examples contain commands that are used particularly often:

  ```
  $ ip addr       # lists all IP addresses of the computer
  $ ip link       # lists the network adapters
  $ ip route      # displays the routing table
  ```

- **less file**
  `less file` displays a text file just like `cat`. This command is suitable for longer files because you can scroll through the text at your leisure using the cursor keys. Q terminates the program.

- **ln file link**
  ln file link creates a link to an existing file. The -s option creates a symbolic link instead of a *hard link*.

  If you're unsure about the order in which you need to specify the parameters: All important Linux commands expect the source first, then the target. This rule applies to cp, mv, ln, and so on.
- **man command**
  man command displays the help text for a command. As with less, you can use the cursor keys to scroll through the often several pages of text. / allows you to specify a search term. [Q] terminates the help.
- **ping hostname/ipaddress**
  ping hostname/ipaddress sends Internet Control Message Protocol (ICMP) packets to another host and shows how long the response takes. This command typically runs endlessly until it is terminated via [Ctrl] + [C]. ping -c <n> sends only *n* packets and then terminates by itself.
- **wc file**
  wc file counts the number of lines, words, and characters in a text file. By using the -c (*count bytes*), -w (*words*), or -l (*lines*) options, you can reduce the output to one number.
- **which command**
  which command determines the location where the command is stored. For example, which cp returns the following result: /usr/bin/cp.

Chapter 7
cmdlets for PowerShell

This chapter presents a compact compilation of the most important cmdlets—a kind of basic PowerShell vocabulary for interactive operation and for script programming. If you have had years of experience in PowerShell, you can safely skip this chapter.

Besides the preinstalled cmdlets, countless PowerShell extensions are available on the internet. The NuGet package manager, which I will introduce to you in Section 7.8, helps with the installation of these additional modules.

The chapter ends with a reference of the main aliases. These shortcuts save a lot of typing when using PowerShell interactively and allow for efficiency similar to what is available on Linux.

Prerequisites for This Chapter

By its nature, reading this chapter makes sense only if you're familiar with the basic PowerShell concepts presented in Chapter 4, Section 4.4, such as chaining cmdlets using the pipe operator (|).

7.1 Directories and Files

You can use the following commands to set your home directory (*My Documents*) as the working directory, create a new directory there, and change it. Later, you can leave the new directory and then delete it.

```
> Set-Location                # set the home directory as working directory
> Get-Location                # show its location

  Path
  ----
  C:\Users\kofler
> New-Item -ItemType "directory" subdir   # create new directory
> Set-Location subdir        # now subdir is the working directory
> Set-Location ..            # get back into your home directory
> Remove-Item subdir         # delete subdir
```

For all cmdlets used in this listing, aliases or functions are available that allow for the completion of these actions with less typing. Since I recommend avoiding these shorthand notations in your own scripts, I always use the original cmdlet name in all further examples in this chapter.

```
> cd                # cd is an alias for Set-Location
> pwd               # pwd is an alias for Get-Location
> md subdir         # md is an alias for the mkdir function
> cd subdir
> cd ..
> rmdir subdir      # rmdir is an alias for Remove-Item
```

`New-Item` also enables you to create a group of nested directories. Although directories are separated by \ in Windows, cmdlets also accept / as the directory separator.

```
> New-Item -ItemType "directory" images\2023\12
> New-Item -ItemType "directory" images/2023/12  # equivalent
```

7.1.1 Listing, Copying, Moving, and Deleting Files

In the following listing, the `tst` directory is created first. In that directory, the current time is stored in the `now.txt` file. This file is copied first, then the copy is renamed. `Get-ChildItem` lists the text files that now exist. `Remove-Item` cleans up again at the end.

```
                               # creates the tst directory
> New-Item -ItemType "directory" tst
> Set-Location tst             # changes there
> Get-Date > now.txt           # saves date and time
                               # to now.txt
> Copy-Item now.txt copy.txt   # creates a copy of now.txt
> Move-Item copy.txt backup.txt # renames the copy
> Get-ChildItem *.txt          # lists all *.txt files

  Mode         LastWriteTime   Length  Name
  ----         -------------   ------  ----
  -a---     24.01.2023 12:29       40  backup.txt
  -a---     24.01.2023 12:29       40  now.txt

> Remove-Item *.txt            # deletes all *.txt files
```

Note that files or directories that are deleted using `Remove-Item` do not go to the recycle bin but are instead irrevocably deleted!

To test whether a file exists, you can use `Test-Path`. The cmdlet returns `True` or `False`.

```
> Test-Path file1.txt
  False
```

You can use Copy-Item or Move-Item to process multiple files at once. However, keep in mind that the source files must either be specified as a pattern or be separated by commas. Note that it is not allowed to list multiple files without commas! You can use -Recurse to copy entire directory trees. If the target directory does not exist yet (for example, dir2 in the previous example), it will be created automatically.

```
> Copy-Item *.txt another-directory    # OK
> Copy-Item file1.txt, file2.txt a-d   # also OK
> Copy-Item file1.txt file2.txt a-d    # Error!
> Copy-Item -Recurse dir1 dir2         # OK
```


Get-ChildItem or its short versions dir, gci, and ls (only on Windows) lists files and directories in the specified or current directory. With the -Recurse option, the cmdlet also takes all subdirectories into account. With the -File option, Get-ChildItem determines only files; with -Directory, only directories.

By default, in addition to the filename, the Get-ChildItem displays the mode, the time of the last modification, and the file size. Behind the scenes, however, Get-ChildItem returns objects with much richer data. It is up to you to evaluate this data. In the following example, Where-Object only considers *.exe files in the *Downloads* directory that are larger than 1 MB. Select-Object selects the filename, size, and time of the last access from the result objects. The -gt option stands for *greater than*.

```
> Get-ChildItem Downloads\*.exe |
  Where-Object {$_.Length -gt 1000000} |
  Select-Object Name, Length, LastAccessTime

  Name                              Length   LastAccessTime
  ----                              ------   --------------
  emacs-28.1-installer.exe        47972467   22.01.2023 08:09:58
  npp.8.4.4.Installer.x64.exe      4533912   24.01.2023 08:44:01
  VSCodeUserSetup-x64-1.69.2.exe  81424833    2.02.2023 12:47:04
  ...
```

Universal Items

In this section, I have presented New-Item, Copy-Item, and so on as commands for manipulating files and directories. In fact, these cmdlets are much more flexible and, depending on the context or options you choose, can also process completely different objects, such as registry entries or certificates.

7.1.2 Reading and Writing Text

Get-Content (alias cat) outputs the specified file completely in the terminal:

```
> Get-Content todo.md
```

For longer files, scrolling through the text using the cursor keys is convenient. On Linux, less is certainly one of the most frequently called commands—all the more surprising then that PowerShell offers only rudimentary functions in this regard: Out-Host -Paging allows you to scroll one line further with [Enter] and one page further with [Space], but there is no way back, let alone a search function.

```
> Get-Content tst.csv | Out-Host -Paging
```

Using Out-Host (alias oh). you can also study extensive cmdlet results page by page:

```
> Get-Process | Out-Host -Paging
```

Ultimately, it is quite easy to look only at the first or last result objects of a cmdlet:

```
# view the first five / the last ten processes
> Get-Process | Select-Object -First 5
> Get-Process | Select-Object -Last 10
```

To save the results of a cmdlet in a text file, you can simply use output redirection. Note that the underlying objects will not be saved—only the text that you usually see in the terminal.

```
> Get-Process > processes.txt
```

Set-Content enables you to write a string into a text file. If the file already exists, it will be overwritten. You should pay attention to the correct order of the parameters; alternatively, you can use options.

```
> Set-Content out.txt "some text"
> Set-Content -Value "some text 2" out.txt  # equivalent
```

To add text to an existing file, you can use Add-Content, as in the following example:

```
> Add-Content out.txt 'second line'
```

Clear-Content deletes the content of a file. However, the file itself remains intact (file size: 0 bytes). Clear-Content raises an error if the specified file does not exist.

```
> Clear-Content out.txt
```

7.1.3 Inputting and Outputting Text

To input text in a script, you must use Read-Host. Note that the cmdlet automatically adds a colon to the passed text. To output a string again (with or without variables), you can use Write-Output (alias echo):

```
> $firstname = Read-Host "First name"

  First name: Michael

> Write-Output $firstname

  Michael

> Write-Output "Hello, $firstname!"

  Hello, Michael!
```

7.2 Finding Files

To search for files that have certain properties, you can proceed as in the previous example: Create a result list via `Get-ChildItem` and then use `Where-Object` to select the objects that match your expectations. The condition must be formulated in curly brackets. Within this formulation, `$_` refers to the object currently being processed.

In the following listing, we first create a variable that contains the date from 60 days ago. `Get-ChildItem` searches the current directory and all subdirectories for all `*.pdf` files. `Where-Object`, which can be abbreviated quite elegantly with `?`, filters out the PDF documents that were created or modified in the last 2 months. (`-ge` stands for *greater than or equal to*.)

```
> $twoMonthsAgo = (Get-Date).AddDays(-60)
> Get-ChildItem -Recurse *.pdf |
  ? {$_.LastWriteTime -ge $twoMonthsAgo}
```

You can also combine multiple conditions. The next command searches the *Downloads* directory for files larger than 1 MB that have not been read for about 2 months:

```
> Get-ChildItem -Recurse Downloads |
  ? {$_.Length -gt 100000 -and
     $_.LastAccessTime -lt $twoMonthsAgo}
```

If you want to include multiple file identifiers, a best practice is to use the `-Include` option and pass the desired file types, separated by commas:

```
> Get-ChildItem -Recurse -Include *.png, *.jpg, *.jpeg, *.tif ...
```

Alternatively, you can use `-Exclude` to exclude from the result files that match the specified pattern. Note that `-Include` and `-Exclude` only work in combination with `-Recurse`.

7.2.1 Searching Text Files

Get-ChildItem, combined with Where-Object, only considers the metadata of files (i.e., name, type, size, etc.) but not the content. Select-String allows you to search text files. In the simplest case, you can apply Select-String directly to files. The following command finds all logging files in the current directory that contain the error text in uppercase and lowercase:

```
> Select-String error *.log
```

However, unlike Get-ChildItem, Select-String does not provide any recursive file search options. Thus, the two commands are often combined. In the following example, Get-ChildItem searches for *.txt files in the current directory and in all subdirectories. Select-String looks at the contents of these files and lists all occurrences.

```
> Get-ChildItem -Recurse -Include *.txt | Select-String license

  init/readme.txt:6:This work is licensed under ..., see
  init/readme.txt:7:https://creativecommons.org/licenses/by/4.0/
```

Usually, you're not interested in the match details, but just want to see a list of files that have been found. Each Select-String result is a MatchInfo object. Its Path property contains the filename. By forming groups of such MatchInfo objects and then displaying the name of each group, you can get only the filenames:

```
> Get-ChildItem -recurse *.txt | Select-String license |
  Group-Object Path | Select-Object Name

  init/readme.txt
  other/gpl.txt
  ...
```

The behavior of Select-String can be influenced by various options. I want to mention only the most important four here:

- -CaseSensitive makes the search pattern case sensitive.
- -List shows only the first match of the search pattern. This option provides clearer results when a large number of matches is found. This option also speeds up the evaluation if, as in the previous example, only the files that contain a hit are to be listed.
- -NotMatch returns matches (without -List, for each line) that do *not* contain the search pattern.
- -Quiet returns only True or False, depending on whether the pattern was recognized.

Select-String cannot count the number of matches. For a single file, you can evaluate the Matches property of the resulting object. The following statement counts how many times an error occurs in the access.log file:

```
> (Select-String error access.log).Matches.Count
```

A more difficult task is to list the number of hits for multiple files. The perhaps obvious way to apply Select-String with Matches.Count in a pipeline is not allowed and leads to an error message:

```
> Get-ChildItem *.log | (Select-String error).Matches.Count

  ParseError:
  Expressions are only allowed as the first element of a pipeline
```


ForEach-Object leads the way to this goal: It allows you to perform an action for each file found. In the following example, Write-Host outputs the name of the file. Then, Select-String determines the number of error texts:

```
> Get-ChildItem *.log | ForEach-Object -Process {
    Write-Host -NoNewline $_.Name " -> "
    (Select-String error $_).Matches.Count
  }

  error.log  -> 231
  ...
```

The search pattern passed to Select-String is evaluated as a regular expression (see Chapter 9, Section 9.4.2).

7.2.2 Text versus Objects

Unlike the grep command in Linux, you cannot use Select-String to filter the results of any cmdlets in general. The reason is simple: cmdlets return objects, not text. (Text is displayed in the terminal but only because PowerShell automatically converts the objects to text beforehand.)

Thus, for example, if you want to know what alias the Start-Process cmdlet has, the following command will have no effect. It does not recognize any text in the Get-Alias result.

```
> Get-Alias | Select-String Start-Process
```

Now, you can use Out-String to convert the Get-Alias result into a string and search it. Basically, this approach works because Select-String also finds the match. However, Out-String turns the result into *one* string. Instead of displaying only the alias definition of Start-Process, the command returns the complete list of all aliases, which ultimately is the original result of Get-Alias. But nothing is gained by this exercise.

```
> Get-Alias | Out-String | Select-String Start-Process

  CommandType     Name
  -----------     ----
  Alias           ? -> Where-Object
  Alias           % -> ForEach-Object
  Alias           cd -> Set-Location
  ...
```

Only Out-String -Stream provides the desired result. With this additional option, the cmdlet returns each line as a single string. Finally, the searched aliases saps and start are displayed.

```
> Get-Alias | Out-String -Stream | Select-String Start-Process

  Alias           saps -> Start-Process
  Alias           start -> Start-Process
```

But command | Out-String -Stream | Select-String ... is rarely a good idea because cmdlets return objects. You can find out the result data type using Get-Member or Format-List and then formulate an appropriate condition for evaluation:

```
> Get-Alias | ? {$_.Definition -eq 'Start-Process'}

  Alias           saps -> Start-Process
  Alias           start -> Start-Process
```

What is even more expedient is to consult Get-Help every now and then. With the -Definition option, Get-Alias directly determines the alias for the desired command:

```
> Get-Alias -Definition Start-Process

  Alias           saps -> Start-Process
  Alias           start -> Start-Process
```

7.3 Compressing and Archiving Files

The Compress-Archive command allows you to pack a directory or individual files into a compressed archive file. Basically, the application of the command is simple:

```
> Compress-Archive mypictures\ mypictures.zip
> Compress-Archive *.txt archive.zip
```

With -Update, you can extend or change an existing archive, and with -Force, you can overwrite a possibly existing ZIP file. -CompressionLevel enables you to influence the compression algorithm. Permitted settings are Optimal (applies by default), Fastest, and NoCompression (for example, for already compressed image or PDF files).

To unpack an archive, you can use Expand-Archive:

```
> Expand-Archive my.zip      # unpack in the current directory
> Expand-Archive my.zip -DestinationPath dir   # unpack in dir
```

Amazingly, there is no way to view or list the contents of an archive file. If necessary, you may have to use commands from one of the numerous ZIP extension modules available on the internet.

7.3.1 Compressing Search Results

Basically, Compress-Archive can also process results of Get-ChildItem, as long as you specify the filename of the archive with the -DestinationPath option. However, the behavior of Compress-Archive takes some getting used to. Let's assume we have the following directory structure:

```
dirA\
  file1
  file2
  dirB\
     file3
```

Get-ChildItem will now recursively traverse the contents of dirA and pass it to Compress-Archive:

```
> Get-ChildItem -Recurse dirA |
  Compress-Archive -DestinationPath my.zip
> Expand-Archive my.zip -DestinationPath dirC
```

The dirC directory now contains the following files and directories:

```
dirC\
  file1
  file2
  file3 (!)
  dirB\
     file3
```

This result occurs because Compress-Archive received the dirB directory once and the file3 file once from Get-ChildItem. dirB was processed correctly. However, file3 was processed without considering the directory. The file was therefore inserted into the archive twice. The documentation points out this special case, so the behavior is apparently not considered an error. In this respect, you should use Compress-Archive for further processing of files only if all files are located in the same directory.

7.4 Process Management

`Start-Process` allows you to start a new process, such as the Notepad editor for first tests:

```
> Start-Process notepad
```

`Start-Process` starts the process in the background. If you do not want it to start, you can pass the `-Wait` option to it. Then, the terminal or your script will be blocked until the process ends.

Usually, the new process has the same rights as the terminal or your script. To run a new process with admin rights, you must use `-Verb RunAs`. However, a warning dialog will then display in which the user of the computer must confirm that the app can make changes to the computer.

`Get-Process` returns a list of all processes running on the computer. If you specify a process name as a parameter, only processes with the same name will be determined. With `-IncludeUserName`, the cmdlet also shows the assigned user:

```
# all processes
> Get-Process

  NPM(K)  PM(M)  WS(M)  CPU(s)    Id  SI ProcessName
  ------  -----  -----  ------    --  -- -----------
       6   1.09   6.14    0.05  3888   0 AggregatorHost
      24   9.11  34.42    0.52  7492   1 ApplicationFrameHost
      10   1.79   8.25    0.00  2916   0 blnsvr
                                         ...
# show only notepad processes, with user names
> Get-Process -IncludeUserName notepad

     WS(M)   CPU(s)      Id UserName        ProcessName
     -----   ------      -- --------        -----------
     60.01     0.50    1212 KVMWIN\kofler   Notepad
     59.88     0.47    8640 KVMWIN\kofler   Notepad
```

Provided you have a suitable process object and have started the process yourself, you can also stop processes via `Stop-Process`. Watch out, though: The following command terminates not only the process started earlier, but *all* running Notepad instances! (Only with admin rights can you also terminate foreign processes.)

```
> Get-Process notepad | Stop-Process
```

7.4.1 Launching Other PowerShell Scripts

If you want to run another PowerShell script—starting from an already running script—the best approach is to proceed as follows:

```
> Start-Process powershell.exe `
  -ArgumentList "-file C:\directory\myscript.ps1", "arg1", "arg2"
```

Start-Process thus starts a new PowerShell process to which you can pass the location of your script and any necessary parameters.

If you do not want to start a second script as a new process, but only want to read (import) its code at the current position, you can do this by using the . source operator:

```
. other-file.ps1
```

For complex tasks that require a lot of code, you should divide your script into modules and import them using Import-Module.

7.4.2 Running Commands in the Background

Sometimes, you don't want to run an entire script in the background; often, a few commands are sufficient. You can pass these commands to Start-Job. In the following example, the contents of a directory are stored in a ZIP file. If the statement is in a script, the script will continue in the meantime.

```
> Start-Job { Compress-Archiv mydir\ archive.zip }
```

If you need to rely on the completion of the ZIP file later in the script, you must remember the job ID. This allows you to later read the output of the operation using Receive-Job or wait for completion by using Wait-Job:

```
$myjob = Start-Job { Compress-Archive mydir\ archive.zip }
# first do something else ...
# then wait for Compress-Archive to finish
Wait-Job $myjob
```

7.4.3 Managing Services

Services (also referred to as system services) are background processes required for the operation of Windows and its functions. You can find out which services are running on your system by using the program of the same name or via the Get-Service command which lists all the services. You can also pass a pattern to the cmdlet to search specifically for services:

```
> Get-Service  wl*

  Status   Name     DisplayName
  ------   ----     -----------
  Stopped  WlanSvc  automatic WLAN configuration
  Running  wlidsvc  login wizard for Microsoft accounts
  Stopped  wlpasvc  service wizard for local profiles
```

Like many cmdlets, Get-Service displays less data than is actually available internally. If you want to know which of these services starts automatically, you can use Select-Object to also display the StartType property:

```
> Get-Service  wl* | Select-Object Name, StartType
  Name      StartType
  ----      ---------
  WlanSvc     Manual
  wlidsvc     Manual
  wlpasvc     Manual
```

You can start or stop the specified service using Start-Service, Restart-Service, and Stop-Service. Suspend-Service temporarily disables the service; it remains in the memory but stops responding. Resume-Service reactivates the service. (Note, however, that not all services support Suspend and Resume).

```
> Start-Service winrm
```

All the commands just listed have an immediate effect. To set the startup behavior for the future, on the other hand, you must use Set-Service with the -StartupType option, as in the following example:

```
> Set-Service -StartupType Automatic winrm
```

If necessary, you can set up your own services via New-Service and remove them again with Remove-Service.

7.4.4 Working on Other Computers

Basically, cmdlets are always executed on the local computer. Invoke-Command allows you to execute commands on other computers. Among other things, this requires that Windows Remote Management is active on this computer (the winrm service). The following two examples first run the Get-Process command and then run myscript.ps1 on the otherhost computer:

```
> Invoke-Command otherhost { Get-Process }
> Invoke-Command otherhost -FilePath C:\myscript.ps1
```

Instead of just running individual commands, you can use `Enter-PSSession hostname` to connect to another computer and open a PowerShell session there. If necessary, you can use `-Credential name` to specify the desired login name if different from your own. Of course, you must authenticate yourself with a password. You can end an active session using `Exit-PSSession`.

```
> Enter-PSSession otherhost
[otherhost]: PS C:\Users\username> Get-Process

  ...

[otherhost]: PS C:\Users\username> Exit-PSSession
```

An alternative to `Enter-PSSession` is the `New-PSSession` cmdlet. This approach also creates a connection to another computer. You can subsequently pass the session object as a parameter to other cmdlets, for example, to `Copy-Item` to copy files to another computer. However, `New-PSSession` is not intended for interactive use.

Remoting Does Not Work

`Enter-PSSession` and `InvokeCommand` often fail with uninformative error messages (such as "Access denied") without further explanation. The solution is usually the `Enable-PSRemoting` command, which is executed on the target computer. For the causes of various errors and tips on how to fix them, refer to *https://learn.microsoft.com/en-us/powershell/module/microsoft.powershell.core/about/about_remote_troubleshooting*.

SSH instead of Remoting

SSH provides a functionality that's comparable to `Invoke-Command` and `Enter-PSSession` but works across different platforms. However, SSH requires a running SSH server on the target computer, which is rather unusual on Windows.

Since version 6, PowerShell even supports *SSH remoting*, that is, the use of the `Enter-PSSession` or `New-PSSession` commands via an SSH connection. In my tests, however, the configuration proved to be as error prone as for Windows Remote Management. More details on using SSH directly and on SSH remoting will follow in Chapter 12.

7.5 Registration Database and System Information

Many important settings are located in the registration database. To read its entries, you can use the `Get-ChildItem` command you're already familiar with from Section 7.1. The following command returns a list of your own entries (`HKEY_CURRENT_USER`) on the first level. With the additional `-Recurse` option, the cmdlet runs through all levels of the registry.

```
> Get-ChildItem HKCU:\

  Name           Property
  ----           --------
  Console        ColorTable00                 : 789516
                 ...
  Environment    OneDrive         : C:\Users\kofler\OneDrive
                 OneDriveConsumer : C:\Users\kofler\OneDrive
                 ...
```

Get-ItemProperty and Get-ItemPropertyValue allow you to view specifically the contents of a registry directory and a single entry, respectively:

```
# alle Einträge von HKEY_CURRENT_USER\Show environment
> Get-ItemProperty HKCU:\Environment\

  OneDrive         : C:\Users\kofler\OneDrive
  OneDriveConsumer : C:\Users\kofler\OneDrive
  Path             : C:\Users\kofler\AppData\Local\Programs\...
  ...

# show only the Path entry
> Get-ItemProperty HKCU:\Environment\ | Select-Object Path

  C:\Users\kofler\AppData\Local\Programs\Python\Python311\...

# same result
> Get-ItemPropertyValue "HKCU:\Environment" -Name Path

  C:\Users\kofler\AppData\Local\Programs\Python\Python311\...
```

Of course, you can also modify the registry. New-Item creates a new key, while Set-ItemProperty stores an entry. But be careful to avoid changing any important settings!

```
# creates the \michael\mykey directory in two steps
> New-Item HKCU:\michael
> New-Item HKCU:\michael\mykey

# saves version=1.0 there
> Set-ItemProperty HKCU:\michael\mykey -Name version -Value 1.0

# reads the data again
> Get-ChildItem HKCU:\michael\

  Hive: HKEY_CURRENT_USER\michael
```

```
Name    Property
----    --------
mykey   version : 1
```

```
> Get-ItemPropertyValue "HKCU:\michael\mykey" -Name version
  1
```

`Remove-Item` deletes all registry directories and entries created in this example. Make sure you specify the correct path when you run this command. You can do a lot of damage with `Remove-Item -Recurse`, regardless of whether you're deleting files or registry entries.

```
> Remove-Item -Recurse HKCU:\michael\
```

7.5.1 Determining System Information

`Get-ComputerInfo` returns a long list of version numbers and strings to identify the Windows version. You can use `Select-Object` to filter out the information relevant to it:

```
> Get-ComputerInfo | Select-Object OsName, OSType, OsProductType

  OsName                      OsType   OsProductType
  ------                      ------   -------------
  Microsoft Windows 11 Pro     WINNT     WorkStation

> Get-ComputerInfo | Select-Object OsVersion, WindowsVersion

  OsVersion  WindowsVersion
  ---------  --------------
  10.0.22621 2009
```

However, the what's called the *display version* for installed function updates can only be found in the registry:

```
> $key = "HKLM:\SOFTWARE\Microsoft\Windows NT\CurrentVersion"
> (Get-ItemProperty $key).DisplayVersion
  22H2
```

Often the language, time zone and installation location are also of interest:

```
> Get-ComputerInfo | select OsLocale,TimeZone,OsWindowsDirectory

  OsLocale TimeZone                              OsWindowsDirectory
  -------- --------                              ------------------
  de-DE    (UTC+01:00) Amsterdam, Berlin, ...    C:\Windows
```

`Get-ComputerInfo` also reveals the name of the CPU, the number of cores, the RAM size, and so on, if required. `Get-PSDrive` determines the free space on the drives (in our example, only for the *C:* drive, with information displayed in bytes):

```
> Get-ComputerInfo | Select-Object CsProcessors

  {Intel(R) Core(TM) i7-8750H CPU @ 2.20GHz, ...}
> Get-PSDrive C | Select-Object Used, Free

         Used         Free
         ----         ----
  40943972352 173030539264
```

7.5.2 Evaluating the Logging System

Windows logs all conceivable events in a logging system. `Get-EventLog -List` reveals the names of the logs. Using `Get-EventLog <name> -Newest n`, you can read the most recent *n* entries.

```
> Get-EventLog Security -Newest 5 |
  Select-Object TimeGenerated, Message

  TimeGenerated          Message
  -------------          -------
  01/30/2023 03:47:30 PM  A new login has been ...
  01/30/2023 03:47:30 PM  An account has been successfully registered.
  01/30/2023 03:41:52 PM  A new login has been ...
  01/30/2023 03:41:52 PM  An account has been successfully registered.
  01/30/2023 03:13:48 PM  A new login has been ...
```

7.6 Processing cmdlet Results

cmdlets return objects, not just text. The text displayed in the terminal is created because PowerShell converts the objects into text by default. To achieve better readability, many details are removed in the process.

One of the most basic PowerShell tasks is to pass results to a second cmdlet using the pipe operator. This allows you to filter, process, or format the data in a variety of ways. You have already seen some cmdlets for this purpose, such as `Select-Object` or `ForEach-Item`. This section summarizes the basic functions of these frequently needed cmdlets.

7.6.1 Select-Object and Sort-Object

You can use Select-Object (alias select) to reduce the output to single properties or select only the first/last results. This function is especially useful if you previously sorted the results according to a criterion using Sort-Object (alias sort). The -Descending option sorts in descending order. The following examples illustrate the most important application variants. Take the trouble and try the commands in a directory with many files.

```
> Get-ChildItem    # show all files/default properties
> Get-ChildItem | Select-Object Name         # show name only
> Get-ChildItem | Select-Object Name, Size   # name and size

# show the three smallest/largest files
> Get-ChildItem | Sort-Object Size | Select-Object -First 3
> Get-ChildItem | Sort-Object Size | Select-Object -Last 3

# for the alphabetically first ten files, name and size only
> Get-ChildItem | Sort-Object Name |
  Select-Object -First 10 Name, Size

# last modified/created, name, size and modification time
> Get-ChildItem | Sort-Object LastWriteTime |
  Select-Object -Last 10 Name, Size, LastWriteTime
```

Select-Object and Sort-Object can also be applied to properties that are not displayed at all by default, for example, to LastAccessTime for Get-ChildItem results. If you do not know the properties, you should apply Get-Member to the first result object, as in the following example:

```
# Show properties of the first result of cmdlet
> cmdlet | Select -First 1 | Get-Member -MemberType Properties
```

Select-Object can also skip the first *n* objects (-Skip n); skip the last objects (-SkipLast n); eliminate duplicates (-Unique); or select specific objects (-Index 2, 3, 7 for the 3rd, 4th, and 8th element; counting begins at 0).

7.6.2 Where-Object

Where-Object (alias ?) allows you to select the objects that meet a certain criterion. The condition is formulated in curly brackets. The respective object is addressed using $_.

```
# Show files > 1 MByte, only name and size
> Get-ChildItem | ? {$_.Size -gt 1000000} | Select Name, Size
```

7.6.3 Group-Object

Group-Object (alias group) forms groups of elements that have one property in common. The result contains the number of objects for each group, the value of the group property, and an enumeration of the elements.

```
> Get-ChildItem | Group-Object -Property Extension

  Count  Name   Group
  -----  ----   -----
     73  .jpg   {C:\Users\kofler\img_2234.jpg, ...}
      5  .jpeg  {C:\Users\kofler\tree.jpeg, ...}
    334  .png   {C:\Users\kofler\screenshot.jpeg, ...}
      3  .tif   {C:\Users\kofler\figure-23.tif, ...}

# the largest groups first, only three groups
> Get-ChildItem | Group-Object -Property Extension |
  Sort-Object -Property Count -Descending |
  Select-Object -First 3

# Processes with more than 5 subprocesses (threads)
> Get-Process | Group-Object -Property ProcessName |
  Where-Object { $_.Count -gt 5 }
```

7.6.4 ForEach-Item

ForEach-Item (alias %) enables you to further process any of the determined objects. Which type of further processing is possible depends strongly on the type of objects. For example, you can copy or delete files, terminate processes, close open database connections, and update installed packages. The action to be executed is formulated in curly brackets, and access to the object is again created via $_. The following command sequence moves all files from the current directory that are older than one year (-lt for *less than*) to the old subdirectory:

```
> $oneYear = (Get-Date).AddDays(-365)
> mkdir old
> Get-ChildItem | ? {$_.LastWriteTime -lt $oneYear} |
  ForEach-Object { Move-Item $_ old\ }
```

7.6.5 Measure-Object

Measure-Object (alias measure) applies aggregate functions to the specified objects. Without any further parameters, it simply counts the objects (Count result property). Depending on the option, the total, average, and minimum or maximum of a property can also be determined.

```
# number of files, size of the smallest and largest file
> Get-ChildItem | Measure-Object  -Property Size -Min -Max |
  Select-Object Count, Minimum, Maximum
  Count    Minimum       Maximum
  -----    -------       -------
    431   4096,000   3263035,000

# lines, words and characters in the todo file
> Get-Content todo.md | Measure-Object -Line -Word -Character

  Lines  Words  Characters
  -----  -----  ----------
    195    899        6396
```

If you just want to count the number of objects, you can simply apply the Count property to the result. The following command determines the number of PDF files in the current directory and all subdirectories:

```
> (Get-ChildItem *.pdf -Recurse).Count
```

7.6.6 Formatting and Exporting cmdlet Results

What you see when you run a command in the terminal is mostly a short version of the available data. The Out-Default cmdlet is responsible for the default formatting. Among other things, the cmdlet takes into account XML files that specify for important classes (e.g., for System.IO.DirectoryInfo); which properties are to be output; and how.

If you're not happy with the default formatting, you can influence it in the following ways:

- The cmdlet | Select-Object prop1, prop2, prop3 construct, which you already know, allows you to define which properties you want to see.
- Use cmdlet | Format-List to specify the most important properties of each object in list form. If you really want to see all properties, you can use Format-List -Property *. But be careful not to get overwhelmed by all the data since Get-Process | Format-List -Property * can return a thousand lines of output. In my work environment, there were about 11,000 lines that could be measured this way:

  ```
  > Get-Process | Format-List -Property * | Out-String |
    Measure-Object -Line
  ```

- cmdlet | Format-Table performs table-based output, as is the default for many classes. But you can influence the output via options. If you have a wide monitor, you can try, for example, Get-Process | Format-Table -Property * -AutoSize. The -AutoSize option takes the data into account to determine the ideal column width.

- `cmdlet | Format-Wide` tries to spread the most important property (such as the filename) across multiple columns. `Get-ChildItem | Format-Wide -AutoSize` returns, for example, a multi-column list of the names of all files in the current directory.
- `cmdlet | Out-Gridview` displays the result in a separate graphical window. The data can be re-sorted and filtered in that window, which is extremely helpful especially for extensive results.

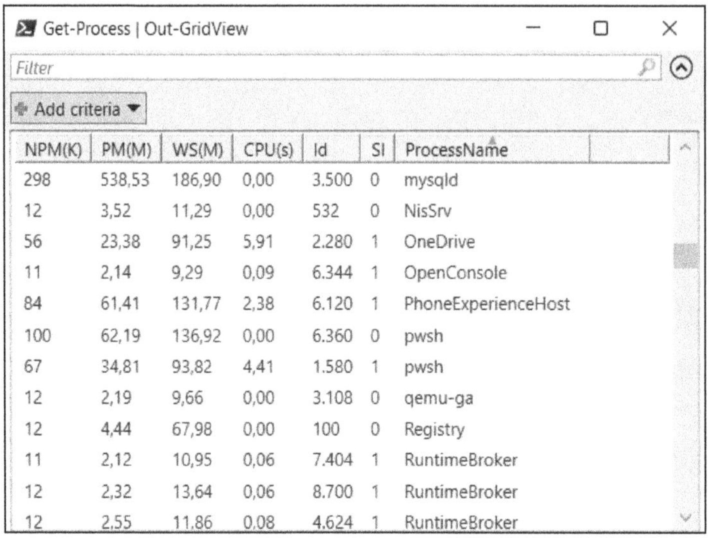

Get-Process | Out-GridView

Filter

Add criteria

NPM(K)	PM(M)	WS(M)	CPU(s)	Id	SI	ProcessName
298	538,53	186,90	0,00	3.500	0	mysqld
12	3,52	11,29	0,00	532	0	NisSrv
56	23,38	91,25	5,91	2.280	1	OneDrive
11	2,14	9,29	0,09	6.344	1	OpenConsole
84	61,41	131,77	2,38	6.120	1	PhoneExperienceHost
100	62,19	136,92	0,00	6.360	0	pwsh
67	34,81	93,82	4,41	1.580	1	pwsh
12	2,19	9,66	0,00	3.108	0	qemu-ga
12	4,44	67,98	0,00	100	0	Registry
11	2,12	10,95	0,06	7.404	1	RuntimeBroker
12	2,32	13,64	0,06	8.700	1	RuntimeBroker
12	2,55	11,86	0,08	4.624	1	RuntimeBroker

Figure 7.1 Graphical Output of cmdlet Results

- `cmdlet | Export-Csv` saves the cmdlet result to a comma-separated values (CSV) file. By default, the first row contains the names of all properties as column labels. In the other rows, all texts are enclosed in quotation marks and separated by commas. You can manipulate the formatting details of the file via various options. The counterpart to `Export-Csv` is `Import-Csv`. I will introduce you to this command in Chapter 8, Section 8.1.
- Using `Test-NetConnection`, you can check a network connection. Basically, the cmdlet is a modern ping alternative, but you can also pass a port number:

```
> Test-NetConnection kofler.info

  ComputerName           : kofler.info
  RemoteAddress          : 168.119.33.110
  InterfaceAlias         : Ethernet Instance 0
  SourceAddress          : 192.168.122.162
  PingSucceeded          : True
  PingReplyDetails (RTT) : 29 ms
```

7.7 Other cmdlets

In this section, I'll briefly introduce you to some other cmdlets that are often needed but don't fit the content of any of the previous sections:

- **Get-Command <name>**
  Get-Command <name> returns information about a cmdlet or command. For cmdlets, the Source property reveals the underlying module. With conventional commands, on the other hand, you can evaluate the Path property—then, you'll know where the command is installed (comparable to which on Linux):

```
> (Get-Command Get-ChildItem).Source
  Microsoft.PowerShell.Management
> (Get-Command ping.exe).Path
  C:\Windows\system32\PING.EXE
```

- **Get-History**
  Get-History returns a list of all recently executed commands.
- **Get-Random**
  Get-Random returns a random number between 0 and 2,147,483,647. Using -Minimum and -Maximum you can limit the number range. When you apply Get-Random to an array, the cmdlet returns a random element.
- **Measure-Command { expr }**
  Measure-Command { expr } determines how long it takes to execute the specified expression.
- **Start-Sleep n**
  Start-Sleep n (alias sleep) stops the running process or script for *n* seconds.
- **Get-Clipboard**
  Get-Clipboard reads the contents of the clipboard. Although no comparable cmdlet can fill the clipboard with data, you can use the clip.exe command for this purpose. For example, Get-Date | clip copies the current date as text to the clipboard.

7.8 Installing Additional Modules

By default, Windows has quite a few PowerShell modules with cmdlets installed, and countless extension modules are available on the internet. The *PowerShell Gallery* has established itself as a central source for such extensions. More than 10,000 modules are offered for download at *https://powershellgallery.com*.

To install modules from the PowerShell Gallery, the PowerShellGet module is available by default. This module contains cmdlets like Install-Module and Find-Module.

PowerShellGet Update for PowerShell 5.1

Along with PowerShell 7.n, an up-to-date version of PowerShellGet is shipped. But if you use PowerShell 5.1, you must update the `PowerShellGet` module first. The prerequisites (i.e., the installation of a current .NET framework, activation of TLS 1.2, etc.) are summarized at *https://learn.microsoft.com/en-us/powershell/scripting/gallery/installing-psget*.

To install a module from the PowerShell Gallery, you can simply run `Install-Module`:

```
> Install-Module PSReadExif

  Untrusted repository
  You're installing the modules from an untrusted repository.
  Are you sure you want to install the modules from 'PSGallery'?
  [Y] Yes  [A] Yes to All  [N] No  [L] No to All  ...: y
```

You can update previously installed modules using `Update-Module`, for example:

```
> Update-Module SQLServer
```

7.8.1 Listing Modules, Commands, and Package Sources

In PowerShell, you have two commands to list modules:

- **`Get-Module`**
  `Get-Module` lists the modules loaded in the current PowerShell instance. If you have the terminal window freshly opened, only a few modules will be loaded. Since modules are loaded automatically as soon as a command they contain is executed, the list increases depending on which commands you use.

  `Get-Module -ListAvailable` lists all the modules that are available on your computer.

- **`Get-InstalledModule`**
  `Get-InstalledModule` is part of the `PowerShellGet` module and lists only those modules that you have set up previously via `Install-Module`. If you have never used `Install-Module`, the result will be empty.

```
> Get-InstalledModule

  Version   Name        Repository   Description
  -------   ----        ----------   -----------
  1.0.2     PSReadExif  PSGallery    Read EXIF metadata ...
```

To learn what commands a particular module provides, you should run `Get-Command` with the `-Module` option:

```
> Get-Command -Module PSReadExif
  CommandType    Name            Version     Source
  -----------    ----            -------     ------
  Function       Add-ExifData    1.0.2       PSReadExif
  Function       Get-ExifData    1.0.2       PSReadExif
  Function       Get-ExifTag     1.0.2       PSReadExif
```

To find out which package sources are currently set up, you can run Get-PackageProvider. Usually, PowerShellGet and NuGet are preconfigured, even if you use PowerShell on Linux or macOS.


```
> Get-PackageProvider

  Name           Version  DynamicOptions
  ----           -------  --------------
  NuGet          3.0.0.1  Destination, ExcludeVersion, ...
  PowerShellGet  2.2.5.0  PackageManagementProvider, ...
```

7.8.2 NuGet and winget

PowerShellGet is the package manager for PowerShell. On Windows, however, various other package managers are available, such as *NuGet*, *winget*, and *Chocolatey*. At this point, I will only discuss the NuGet and winget tools developed by Microsoft. These tools have a completely different objective than PowerShellGet:

- **NuGet**

  NuGet is a package manager for software developers. You can use NuGet to manage all conceivable software components, .NET libraries, and tools. More than 300,000 packages can be downloaded for free at *https://nuget.org*. NuGet has been shipped with the Visual Studio development environment for many years.

  From a PowerShell perspective, NuGet is useful in two ways: On the one hand, you can control NuGet through PowerShell commands such as Find-Package, Install-Package, and Uninstall-Package. On the other hand, sometimes, a PowerShell module relies on other tools or libraries, which you can easily install using NuGet.

- **winget**

  winget is a new package management tool. Unlike NuGet, which is only aimed at developers, winget helps install user software. winget provides the same functions and also uses the same sources as the Microsoft Store, but can be operated efficiently in text mode:

  ```
  > winget install Mozilla.Firefox
  ```

  The winget command is available by default in Windows 11 as well as in current versions of Windows 10. You can use winget in PowerShell scripts to install or update programs.

However, winget is currently implemented only as a traditional command. A PowerShell module with cmdlets like `Install-WinGetPackage` is already being developed at *https://github.com/microsoft/winget-cli/tree/master/src/PowerShell/Microsoft.WinGet.Client*.

7.9 Standard Aliases

Compared to Linux, where the names of important commands are rarely longer than 4 characters, the names of frequently needed cmdlets are often rather verbose. However, shortcuts for frequently used commands are available for PowerShell professionals.

Alias	cmdlet	Alias	cmdlet
?	Where-Object	measure	Measure-Object
%	ForEach-Object	mv	Move-Item
cat	Get-Content	ni	New-Item
cd	Set-Location	oh	Out-Host
cpi	Copy-Item	ps	Get-Process
curl	Invoke-WebRequest	pwd	Get-Location
del	Remove-Item	rm	Remove-Item
dir	Get-ChildItem	select	Select-Object
echo	Write-Output	sleep	Start-Sleep
ft	Format-Table	sls	Select-String
gci	Get-ChildItem	sort	Sort-Object
gm	Get-Member	tee	Tee-Object
ls	Get-ChildItem	write	Write-Output
md	mkdir		

Table 7.1 Aliases of the Most Important cmdlets and Functions

Many aliases are simply derived from the first letters of the verb and the noun of the cmdlet, such as `mi` for `Move-Item`. Other aliases like `cat`, `dir`, or `ls` correspond to common DOS and Linux commands.

You can define your own aliases using `Set-Alias` and save these custom aliases permanently in *Documents/profile.ps1*. A complete reference of all currently defined aliases is provided by the `Get-Alias` command.

Avoid Using Aliases in Scripts!

Once you get used to the most important aliases in interactive mode, you may be tempted to use them in scripts as well, but doing so is not a good idea. Depending on the configuration or operating system, different abbreviations may be active. For example, on Windows, `ls` is an alias for `Get-ChildItem`; on Linux and macOS, however, `ls` calls the Unix-style `ls` command!

The aliases specified in this book always apply to Windows.

Aliases versus Functions

At first glance, you may find it difficult to determine whether a short name is an alias or a function. If you're curious, you can call `Get-Command`. This cmdlet reveals, for example, that `mkdir` is a function, while `rmdir` is an alias.

Chapter 8
Analyzing Texts with Filters and Pipes

Part of the daily routine of system admins is the analysis of logging files. However, extracting relevant data from files that are often millions of lines long is like the proverbial search for a needle in a haystack. By cleverly combining commands like `grep`, `sort`, `cut`, or `uniq`, you can make your life easier. With a little practice, one-line commands can work miracles.

But how does this topic involve the terms "filter" and "pipe"?

- In the shell context, a filter is a command that expects text as input and returns new text as output. In Section 8.1, I will introduce the most important filter commands that Linux and macOS provide by default.
- You should be familiar with the `|` pipe operator from Chapter 3, Section 3.7. This operator redirects the output of a command to a second command for further processing. For example, `sort my.txt | uniq` causes the lines of `my.txt` to be sorted first and then eliminates all duplicates in the second step.

By its very nature, the use of filters and pipes is by no means limited to logging files. You can also use them to analyze address data, user directories, comma-separated values (CSV) files, and so on.

Prerequisites for This Chapter

This chapter is very much based on Bash. Bash is the ideal environment to apply commands like `sort` or `grep`. Accordingly, I assume that readers of this chapter have basic knowledge of Bash. Only in Section 8.5 will I briefly use Python and PowerShell as well.

PowerShell also has a pipe operator `|`. However, this operator redirects objects instead of text, which results in greater processing capabilities compared to Bash—but only if the underlying data is *not* text. For this reason, PowerShell plays only a minor role in this chapter—sorry about that!

8.1 grep, sort, cut, and uniq

This section introduces four commands mentioned in this heading, plus a few more. All presented commands are part of the standard repertoire on macOS and Linux, so they do not need to be installed separately.

To make this section as useful as possible, I will show you how to use all these commands using the *employees.txt* text file. This file contains fictitious data about 500 employees in the US. The following listing shows the first three lines, each of which has been wrapped:

```
FirstName;LastName;DateOfBirth;Street;Zip;City;
  State;Gender;Email;Job;Salary

Ruthanne;Summers;1977-06-04;4 Dewy Turnpike;27698;Clifton Hill;
  NJ;F;ruthanne_ferguson5693@fastmail.cn;Engineer;5201.45

Lorie;Warner;1972-04-27;59 Hickory Way;78509;Simsbury Center;
  MA;F;lorie7961@mailforce.net;Climatologist;3794.34
```

You can find the *employees.txt* file in the sample files for this book.

Trying Out the Examples on Windows

On Windows, some commands exist with the same names (some of them originating from DOS times!) or PowerShell aliases, but their functionalities and options differ from Linux/macOS. If you want to reproduce the examples presented in this chapter on Windows, the best approach is to use Windows Subsystem for Linux (WSL) or Git Bash.

8.1.1 grep

After `ls`, `grep` is probably the command I run most often in the terminal. In its most basic form, from a text file, it filters the lines that contain the specified search term. The first example filters all error messages from `log.txt`, and the second filters all employees from California (abbreviation `CA`):

```
$ grep error log.txt
$ grep CA employees.txt

  Elissa;David;...;CA;...
  Sammie;van Luyn;...;CA;...
  Dinorah;Mcgee;...;CA;...
```

The behavior of `grep` can be influenced by various options. I want to mention only the most important behaviors:

- `-i` does not distinguish between uppercase and lowercase during the search (*ignore* case).
- `-r` searches all files in the current or specified directory and in all subdirectories (*recursive*).
- `-c` does not display the lines found, but only their number (*count*).

- `-l` lists only the files that contain hits (*list*). The `-l` and `-c` options are especially useful when you process multiple files at once, for example, `grep -l myfunction *java`.
- `-v` inverts the search (i.e., it only considers lines that *do not* contain the search term).

`grep` always applies the search pattern to the entire line, not to columns. For this reason, you should make sure that your search pattern is unique. Let's suppose you want to list all people born in 1985:

```
$ grep 1985 employees.txt

  Dorthea;Mckinney;1985-06-02;915 Field Divide;...
  Kandi;Meester;1985-01-27;424 Smith Vale;...
  ...
  Kanesha;Matthews;1968-06-24;P.O. Box 19858;...
```

The first hits are correct, but the last line is wrong. *Kanesha* was born in 1986. However, her address unfortunately contains the P.O. Box number 19858. By formulating the search pattern more precisely, you can eliminate the error in this case:

```
$ grep ';1985-' employees.txt
```

Regular Expressions

The search term passed in the first parameter is evaluated as a regular expression. As long as you're looking for ordinary text, it doesn't matter. However, if your search term contains special characters, you must pay attention and prefix the special characters with `\`. For example, you would use `help\.com` to search for `help.com`. You'll learn what regular expressions are and their applications in general and specifically for `grep` in Chapter 9.

8.1.2 wc

`wc` (*word count*) counts the lines, words, and characters of a file, for example:

```
$ wc employees.txt

  501  2628 61102 employees.txt
```

`wc` can be excellently linked with other commands. For instance, how many female employees live in the state of Colorado (abbreviation CO)?

```
$ grep ';CO;' employees.txt | grep ';F;' | wc -l
  4
```

The first `grep` command returns all Colorado lines. Instead of outputting them, they are passed to the second `grep` using the pipe operator. The second `grep` filters out women from the intermediate result (gender `F`). `wc -l` then only needs to count the resulting lines.

8.1.3 cut

`cut` (not to be confused with `cat`!) cuts columns from a text. For most applications, knowing the following three options is usually sufficient:

- `-d` specifies the separator character. The default setting is the tab character. Special characters often must be "quoted" by \ or put in quotation marks—for example, `-d\;` or `-d ';'`.
- `-f` selects the desired columns. For example, `-f 1,4` extracts the first and fourth columns, and `-f 4-7` extracts columns four through seven.
- `-s` ignores lines in which the separator does not occur.

If you want to see only the names and email addresses of the employees, you could use the following command:

```
$ cut -d ';' -f 1,2,9 employees.txt

  FirstName;LastName;Email
  Ruthanne;Ferguson;ruthanne_ferguson5693@fastmail.cn
  Lorie;Warner;lorie7961@mailforce.net
  Kerri;Tsioupra;kerri2377@emailuser.net
  ...
```

The next two commands identify the email addresses of employees in New York State. First, the addresses are displayed in the terminal, and thanks to `less`, you can browse through the result at your leisure using the cursor keys; then the results are saved in *emails.txt*.

```
$ grep ';NY;' employees.txt | cut -d ';' -f 9 | less

  nakesha_lambrinou6390@speedymail.org
  vancapelle1740@fastmailbox.net
  noble7595@internetemails.net
  ...

$ grep ';NY;' employees.txt | cut -d ';' -f 9 > emails.txt
```

8.1.4 sort

In the simplest case, `sort my.txt` causes the lines to be output to the screen in alphabetical order. Instead of processing a file, however, you can use the pipe operator to sort the results of another command. As usual, a few options are available to control the sorting behavior:

- `-n` sorts numerically, for instance, 1, 2, 3, 10, and so on (not 1, 10, 2, 3, etc.).
- `-r` sorts in descending order instead of ascending order (*reverse*).

- -k <n> specifies from which column onwards sorting should occur. The option is mostly used in combination with -t.
- -t specifies the separator for columns, for instance, -t ';'. Without this option, sort considers the transition from a space to a text character as the start of a new column.

The following command creates two lists of employees sorted by name:

```
# Sort by first name (i.e., from the beginning of the line)
$ sort employees.txt

# Sort by last name (second column)
$ sort -t ';' -k 2 employees.txt
```


Use sort with Caution!

Sorting 500 lines should not challenge a modern computer. However, you should proceed with caution when using sort with larger volumes of data. When you sort a logging file with millions of lines, a lot of time and memory may be required. Furthermore, with cmd | sort, sort cannot start working until cmd is complete.

If possible, you should first filter large text files using grep and perhaps reduce the number of columns via cut before applying sort.

8.1.5 head and tail

Especially with regard to sort, a common scenario is that you only want to see the first or last *n* results. In this case, head and tail come to the rescue:

```
# the three employees with the lowest salary (column 11)
$ sort -t ';' -k 11 -n employees.txt | cut -d ';' -f 1,2,11 | \
  head -n 3

  Mohamed;Mcbride;1804.67
  Gabrielle;Melendez;1807.37
  Benedict;Oconnor;1812.30
# the three employees with the highest salary (erroneous)
$ sort -t ';' -k 11 -n employees.txt | cut -d ';' -f 1,2,11 | \
  tail -n 3

  Estella;Guerra;5586.85
  Dolly;Leonard;5600.00
  FirstName;LastName;Salary
```

Note, however, that the second result is incorrect and also contains the label line! From *employees.txt*, actually only the lines 1 to 501 should be sorted, but not line 1 with the column label. To skip the first line, use `tail -n +2`. This unusual wording means that all lines from the second line to the end of the file should be output.

```
# the three employees with the highest salary (correct)
$ tail -n +2 employees.txt | sort -t ';' -k 11 -n | \
  cut -d ';' -f 1,2,11 | tail -n 3

  Arden;Lit;5584.95
  Estella;Guerra;5586.85
  Dolly;Leonard;5600.00
```

8.1.6 uniq

`uniq my.txt` eliminates consecutive identical lines of the text file and prints the result in the terminal. However, `uniq` does not recognize duplicates if they are not immediately consecutive. You can avoid this limitation by sorting the text beforehand.

In the following listing, the first command determines an alphabetical list of all states in which employees reside. `tail` eliminates the column labels, and `cut` cuts out the seventh column containing the state. The second command proves that employees appear to reside in all 50 states of the United States.

```
$ tail -n +2 employees.txt | cut -d ';' -f 7 | sort | uniq
  AK
  AL
  AR
  ...

$ tail -n +2 employees.txt | cut -d ';' -f 7 | sort | \
  uniq | wc -l

  50
```

Now, we are still interested in the following question: How many employees are there in each state? This question can also be answered by `uniq` if you pass the option `-c` (*count*) to it:

```
$ tail -n +2 employees.txt | cut -d ';' -f 7 | sort | uniq -c
     11 AK
     12 AL
      8 AR
    ...
```

If we want to see the five states with the most employees now, we need to sort the `uniq` result again. The `-n` option ensures that `sort` sorts numerically correctly. `-r` reverses the sort order, so that the largest results are shown first. head shows only the first five lines of the result:

```
$ tail -n +2 employees.txt | cut -d ';' -f 7 | sort | uniq -c | \
  sort -n -r | head -n 5

     21 OH
     19 MN
     16 MS
     14 OK
     14 NV
```


8.1.7 tr

tr (for *translate*) replaces individual characters in a text with others. tr works purely based on characters, and so cannot replace words. The -d (*delete*) option eliminates the characters in question. The following three examples illustrate how tr works:

```
# replace . with ,
$ tr '.' ',' < in.txt > out.txt

# replace lowercase letters with uppercase letters
$ tr "a-zäöü" "A-ZÄÖÜ" < in.txt > out.txt

# eliminate German special characters without replacement
$ tr -d "äöüßÄÖÜ" < in.txt > out.txt
```

Of course, tr can also be used as a filter. The following command returns the first and last names and email addresses of all Texas-based employees, with the columns separated by the : character. Previously, the columns were separated by a ;:

```
$ grep ';TX;' employees.txt |  cut -d ';' -f 1,2,9 | tr ';' ':'

  Mae:van Diedenhoven:mae5561@emailgroups.net
  Nancee:Coleman:nancee_coleman4689@150ml.com
  Mitch:Matse:matse2138@theinternetemail.com
  ...
```

8.1.8 awk and sed

In addition to the commands presented so far, each of which is easy enough to use on its own and which only enhance their versatility in combination, the Unix ecosystem also provides much more complex commands to choose from. The awk tool developed by developers Alfred V. Aho, Peter J. Weinberger, and Brian W. Kernighan is a custom scripting language for editing and analyzing text. The sed stream editor is at least as versatile.

Although there is not enough space in this book for a detailed treatment of these programs, I would like to introduce awk and sed briefly, at least through an example.

Remember our earlier grep example from Section 8.1.1, grep 1985 employees.txt? It filters all lines from the text file that contain the 1985 string at any position. However, we actually wanted only those hits where the date of birth was 1985, that is, those hits which contain 1985 in the third column. It is difficult to formulate such a search condition using grep. For awk, on the other hand, this scenario is no problem. In this case, the -F option specifies the column separator. $3 refers to the third column. This column must contain the search term specified between //:

```
$ awk -F ';' '$3 ~/1985/' employees.txt

  Dorthea;Mckinney;1985-06-02;915 Field Divide;...
  Kandi;Meester;1985-01-27;424 Smith Vale;...
  ...
```

If you need to perform this kind of task frequently, learning the awk syntax is worthwhile. Various tutorials on the internet, but we recommend the example-oriented tutorial at *https://linuxhandbook.com/awk-command-tutorial*.

sed also provides similar functions as awk. An example of using sed is provided in Chapter 9, Section 9.3, where I will show you how to use sed to search for patterns in a text file using regular expressions and to replace found text with other expressions.

8.2 Example: Statistical Data Analysis

You probably thought to yourself, looking at the examples in the previous section, "If I just need to sort some contact data, I'll use Excel to do it. That's easier." Of course, that's how I do it, although I prefer it even more if the data is stored in a database and I can use SQL. The examples had the sole purpose to show you the application options of grep, cut, sort, uniq, and so on with easy-to-understand data.

From now on, it's all about examples that are closer to everyday scripting. I will start with the evaluation of a CSV file from *https://ourworldindata.org/energy* with public data on energy production and consumption. The following lines show the basic structure of the file:

```
country,year,iso_code,population,...,energy_per_capita,...
...
China,2020,CHN,1424929792,...,29133.936,...
China,2021,CHN,1425893504,...,30768.826,...
China,2022,CHN,1425887360,...,31051.480,...
Germany,2022,DEU,83369840,...,40977.492...
United States,2022,USA,338289856,...,78754.273...
...
```

The file is approximately 8 MB in size and contains 22,000 lines of data from 125 years and from 222 countries or regions. More than 120 columns provide information about every conceivable aspect of energy use and production. Let's concentrate on the first three columns and column 32 (`energy_per_capita`) with the primary energy consumption per capita and year in kilowatt hours. According to the example rows shown earlier, this consumption amounted in 2022 to approximately 31,000 kWh in China, approximately 41,000 kWh in Germany, and almost 79,000 kWh in the United States.

8.2.1 Data Extraction via Script

The task of the following script is to download a CSV file from the internet, save it locally, and then extract the per capita energy consumption for a specific country for 1 year:

```
./get-energy-consumption.sh GBR 1999
  Primary energy consumption per person
  for United Kingdom in 1999: 45017.871 kWh/a
```

If too few or too many parameters are passed or if the script does not find a suitable data set, an error message is displayed, such as the following:

```
./get-energy-consumption.sh GBR
  Usage:   get-energy-consumption <countrycode> <year>
  Example: get-energy-consumption FRA 2021
./get-energy-consumption.sh GBR 2040
  Sorry, no data found for GBR 2040.
```

The full code looks as follows:

```
#!/bin/bash
# sample file get-energy-consumption.sh
# script expects two parameters
if [ $# -ne 2 ]; then
  echo "Usage:   get-energy-consumption <countrycode> <year>"
  echo "Example: get-energy-consumption FRA 2021"
  exit 2
fi
# download file if not yet locally saved
if [ ! -f owid-energy-data.csv ]; then
  wget https://nyc3.digitaloceanspaces.com/owid-public/data/energy/owid-energy-
data.csv
fi
# remove not needed columns, filter lines,
# use last line if result has more than one line
data=$(cut -d ',' -f 1,2,3,32 owid-energy-data.csv | \
       grep $1 | grep $2 | tail -n 1)
```

```
# extract items from result
country=$(echo $data | cut -d ',' -f 1)
year=$(echo $data | cut -d ',' -f 2)
energy=$(echo $data | cut  -d ',' -f 4)
# output result
if [ "$country" ] && [ "$energy" ]; then
  echo "Primary energy consumption per person for $country in $year: "
  echo "$energy kWh/a"
else
  echo "Sorry, no data found for $1 $2."
fi
```

8.3 Example: ping Analysis

You can use the ping command to check the network connection to another computer. The -c option specifies how many Internet Control Message Protocol (ICMP) packets are to be sent in the process (i.e., after how many attempts ping will terminate). Without the option, ping runs on Linux and macOS until you terminate the command via Ctrl + C. The following listing shows a typical ping result:

```
$ ping -c 4 google.com

  PING google.com(bud02s41-in-x0e.1e100.net
     (2a00:1450:400d:802::200e)) 56 data bytes
  64 bytes from bud02s41-...: icmp_seq=1 ttl=117 time=15.4 ms
  64 bytes from bud02s41-...: icmp_seq=2 ttl=117 time=17.4 ms
  64 bytes from bud02s41-...: icmp_seq=3 ttl=117 time=17.3 ms
  64 bytes from bud02s41-...: icmp_seq=4 ttl=117 time=15.6 ms

  --- google.com ping statistics ---
  4 packets transmitted, 4 received, 0% packet loss, time 3006ms
  rtt min/avg/max/mdev = 15.434/16.431/17.382/0.914 ms
```

Note that some servers are configured to send no response at all to ping requests (supposedly for security reasons). A prominent example is Microsoft (i.e., microsoft.com).

Imagine you want to extract only the average response time from this result; in the previous listing, the value is 16,431 milliseconds. For this task, you first must filter the last line from the result using grep. Then, you can use cut to filter the fifth column from the result, using / as the separator:

```
$ ping -c 4 google.com | grep avg | cut -d '/' -f 5

  16.431
```

If you specify the additional -s option for cut, you can even omit grep. The -s option causes cut to consider only those result lines in which the column separator (in this case, /) occurs.

```
$ ping -c 4 google.com | cut -s -d '/' -f 5
```

8.3.1 ping Call via Script

Now, you can include the ping call in a script and pass the hostname of the computer. The script checks that exactly one parameter is passed and outputs the result properly formatted:


```
# Sample file ping-avg.sh
if [ $# -ne 1 ]; then
  echo "usage: ./ping-avg.sh <hostname>"
  exit 2
else
  hostname=$1
fi
avg=$(ping -c 4 $hostname | cut -s -d '/' -f 5)
echo "Average ping time for $hostname is $avg ms"
```

In my test call, the server of python.org responded slightly more quickly than Google's server:

```
$ ./ping-avg.sh python.org

  Average ping time for python.org is 12.796 ms
```

A conceivable extension of the script would be the processing of multiple hostnames. The script then expects any number of parameters (at least one), as in the following example:

```
#!/bin/bash
# Sample file ping-avg.sh
if [ $# -lt 1 ]; then
  echo "usage: ./ping-avg.sh <hostnames>"
  exit 2
fi
for hostname in $*; do
  avg=$(ping -c 4 $hostname | cut -s -d '/' -f 5)
  echo "Average ping time for $hostname is $avg ms"
done
```

A test call looks like the following:

```
$ ./ping-avg.sh apple.com dell.com lenovo.com

  Average ping time for apple.com is 22.675 ms
  Average ping time for dell.com is 259.528 ms
  Average ping time for lenovo.com is 12.251 ms
```

8.4 Example: Apache Log Analysis

The starting point for this example is a log file from an Apache web server in what is called the *combined logging* format. The first lines of this file look as follows (wrapped here for reasons of space):

```
65d3:f5b9:e9e5:4b1c:331b:29f3:97c1:c18f - - [05/Feb/2023:00:00:22
    +0100]
  "POST /consumer/technology HTTP/1.1" 200 5166
  "https://example.com/land/raise/authority/him"
  "WordPress/6.1.1; https://example.com"

221.245.9.91 - - [05/Feb/2023:00:00:21 +0100] "GET /explain/out
    HTTP/1.1"
  200 31222 "https://example.com/add/maybe/person"
  "FreshRSS/1.20.2 (Linux; https://freshrss.org)"

37e3:498f:44d8:c471:3ba3:9902:17e7:2be8 - -
  [05/Feb/2023:00:00:24 +0100]
  "GET /by/financial/within/benefit HTTP/1.1" 200 97598
  "https://example.com/defense/friend/race/protect"
  "Mozilla/5.0 (iPhone; CPU iPhone OS 16_3 like Mac OS X)
   AppleWebKit/605.1.15 (KHTML, like Gecko) Version/16.3
   Mobile/15E148 Safari/604.1"
```

The columns of this file indicate the IP address from which the request was made, the user (if known) who made the request, the type of request (GET, POST, etc.), the address of the web server requested, the HTTP code returned (e.g., 200 "OK"), the data volumes transferred, from which page the request was triggered (referrer address), and which client it is.

To reproduce the following examples, you'll need to use the *access.log* file from the sample files. wc shows that the file contains more than 170,000 lines.

```
$ wc -l access.log

  172607 access.log
```

Anonymized Data

access.log.gz is a real logging file that has been anonymized for privacy reasons. All IP addresses, URLs and usernames were replaced with random data. This anonymization was of course also done by a script. If you're interested in the code, look at *anonymize-log.py*, which makes extensive use of regular expressions. If you have access to "real" logging files from your own web server, you should use those.

8.4.1 Extracting IP Addresses

You can use `cut` to extract the IP addresses from the logging file:

```
$ cut -d ' ' -f 1 access.log | less

  65d3:f5b9:e9e5:4b1c:331b:29f3:97c1:c18f
  221.245.9.91
  37e3:498f:44d8:c471:3ba3:9902:17e7:2be8
  135.84.251.52
  ...
```

`grep` enables you to determine how many access events to the web server have been made via IPv4 or IPv6:

```
$ cut -d ' ' -f 1 access.log | grep ':' | wc -l      # IPv6
  65405
$ cut -d ' ' -f 1 access.log | grep -v ':' | wc -l  # IPv4
  107202
```

An ordered list of all IPv4 addresses is provided by `sort` and `uniq`:

```
$ cut -d ' ' -f 1 access.log | grep -v ':' | sort  |  uniq

  0.117.133.93
  0.125.223.169
  0.164.206.211
  ...
```

While some IP addresses appear only once in the log, others appear quite frequently. `sort` sorts all IP addresses, `uniq -c` counts the addresses, `sort -n -r` sorts their frequency in decreasing order, and `head -n 5` finally extracts the top 5 results:

```
$ cut -d ' ' -f 1 access.log | sort | uniq -c | sort -n -r | \
  head -n 5

  6166 65d3:f5b9:e9e5:4b1c:331b:29f3:97c1:c18f
  6048 3547:0b26:4c84:4411:0f66:945e:7741:d887
```

```
  5136 186.107.89.128
  4620 d741:a4ea:f6e1:6a17:78b1:1694:f518:c480
  2362 168.81.233.22
```

8.4.2 Identifying Popular Pages

In the combined format, the request data is enclosed in quotation marks. Using `cut -d '"'`, you can separate the requests from the rest of the data:

```
$ cut -d '"' -f 2 access.log | less

  POST /consumer/technology HTTP/1.1
  GET /explain/out HTTP/1.1
  GET /by/financial/within/benefit HTTP/1.1
  GET /action/but HTTP/1.1
  ...
```

We are only interested in the `GET` requests and only in the address:

```
$ cut -d '"' -f 2 access.log | grep GET | cut -d ' ' -f 2 | less

  /explain/out
  /by/financial/within/benefit
  /action/but
  /place/paper
  ...
```

The proven combination of `sort`, `uniq -c`, and again `sort` determines the most popular URLs:

```
$ cut -d '"' -f 2 access.log | grep GET | cut -d ' ' -f 2 | \
  sort | uniq -c | sort -n -r | head

  25423 /explain/out
   5822 /international/hundred/can
   4979 /goal/Congress/short/peace
   4874 /rate/victim/detail
    ...
```

If you apply this command to the original logging file (which I unfortunately can't share), you'll get the following result:

```
$ cut -d '"' -f 2 access.log.orig | grep GET | \
  cut -d ' ' -f 2 | sort | uniq -c | sort -n -r | head

  25424 /feed/
```

```
   5822 /
   4979 /wp-content/plugins/wp-spamshield/js/jscripts-ftr2-min.js
   4874 /favicon.ico
   4347 /blog/feed/
   3352 /wp-content/uploads/fonts/49ff7721659f0bc7d77a59e1de422e07/font.css?v=
1664309579
   3328 /wp-content/themes/twentyfourteen/genericons/genericons.css?ver=3.0.3
    ...
```

Thus, the web server hosts a WordPress website. The most frequent access concerns the feed page, the home page (/), the spam protection plugin, the website icon, and another feed page.

8.5 CSV Files

CSV is a text format where the columns are separated by commas. Other country-specific separators are also used, for instance, the semicolon in German-speaking countries. This separator helps to clearly differentiate between columns and the decimal part of numbers. Basically, any separator is allowed, including the colon or tab character (\t).

The analysis of CSV files becomes much more complicated if the separator character can also occur *within* the columns. The column contents are then enclosed in quotes, usually with ' or ".

The starting point for the following examples is the *2023_population.csv* file from *https://www.kaggle.com/datasets/rsrishav/world-population*. This file contains data on the population of various countries of the world and has the following structure:

```
iso_code,country,2023_last_updated,2022_population,area_sq_km,
  land_area_sq_km,density_/sq_km,growth_rate,world_%,rank,un_member

IND,India,"1,433,381,860","1,417,173,173",3.3M,3M,481,0.81%,17.85%,1,IND

CHN,China,"1,425,542,952","1,425,887,337",9.7M,9.4M,151,-0.02%,17.81%,2,CHN

...
```

The cut command for column extraction is overwhelmed with this data. If you want to use Bash, you can install the csvkit. This collection of commands helps with processing CSV files (see *https://csvkit.readthedocs.io*). In this section, however, I will instead briefly describe the CSV features of Python and PowerShell.

8.5.1 Processing CSV Files Using Python

In a Python script, you can read CSV data line by line from a text file (in the simplest cases) and then split the lines into its columns using `split`. The following script analyzes the *access.log* file from Section 8.4 and determines the most frequent IP addresses. Unlike the equivalent Bash commands, the Python script is more efficient, especially with large log files, because there is no need to sort all the IP addresses.

```
# Sample file analyze-access-log.py
counters = {}   # dictionary with counters for all IP addresses

# loop through all lines of access.log
with open('access.log') as f:
    for line in f:
        # the IP address is in the first column
        ip = line.split()[0]
        if ip in counters:
            counters[ip] += 1
        else:
            counters[ip] = 1

# create ordered list of dictionary elements;
# each list element is itself a list: [ip, cnt]
sortedIps = sorted(counters.items(),
                   key = lambda x: x[1], reverse = True)

# show top 5 IP addresses
for i in range(5):
    print('%6d: %s' % (sortedIps[i][1], sortedIps[i][0]))
```

However, the `split` method used in this case to extract the columns fails with complex CSV files like *2023_population.csv*. To read such complex files, the best approach is to use the `csv` module. The following listing shows a simple application of this module:

```
# Sample file analyze-population.py
import csv
total = 0
with open('2022_population.csv', newline = '') as f:
    reader = csv.reader(f, delimiter = ',', quotechar = '"')
    next(reader)              # skip column labels
    for columns in reader:    # read line by line, columns contains
        print(columns)        # list with columns
        total += int(columns[2].replace(',', ''))

print("Earth population:", total)
```

The documentation for the csv module recommends opening the CSV file with the newline='' option to avoid possible problems with the end of line (EOL) characters on Windows (i.e., \r\n). When opening the CSV reader, you can use the delimiter and quotechar options to specify which characters identify columns and strings, respectively. Then, you can use the reader to read the CSV file line by line in a loop. In each case, the loop variable contains a list with the columns of this line. The first line with the column label is skipped due to next.

To calculate the total population of the earth, the population values in the third column are converted to numbers and then totaled. replace eliminates the commas used to separate thousands.

8.5.2 Processing CSV Files in PowerShell

In PowerShell, you can use Import-Csv to read CSV files. By default, Import-Csv expects that columns are separated by commas. You can use -Delimiter to set another character if required. Strings that are enclosed in double quotes are processed correctly. However, you cannot set another character to identify strings.

As a result, the cmdlet returns PSCustomObject objects whose properties are taken from the column labels of the CSV file. If the CSV file does not have a column label row, you must specify the names of the columns using the -Header option, for example, in the following way:

```
> Import-Csv -Header colA, colB, colC file.csv
```

Make sure that you don't name too few columns with -Header: Only as many columns will be processed as you specify names!

To determine the earth population from 2023_population.csv as in the previous example, you can proceed with the following code:

```
# Sample file analyze-population.ps1
$population = Import-CSV "2023_population.csv"
$total = 0
$population | ForEach-Object {
    $total += [long]($_.'2023_last_updated'.Replace(',', ''))
}
Write-Output "World population: $total"
```

Within the loop, the commas are removed in the string of the 2023_last_updated property. [long] converts the string into a number.

Instead of performing the totaling yourself, you can also calculate the result via Measure-Object. However, because of the required conversion of the 2023_last_updated column to a number, the resulting code is not shorter or more efficient:

```
$total = $population | ForEach-Object {
     [long]($_.'2022_last_updated'.Replace(',', ''))
} | Measure-Object -Sum
Write-Output "World population: $($total.Sum)"
```

With `Export-Csv`, PowerShell provides a great way to save cmdlet results to a CSV file. The resulting CSV file enumerates all properties of the result objects in the first row for column labeling. The values of the relevant properties follow in the other lines, with all output separated by commas and enclosed in quotation marks:

```
> Get-Process | Export-Csv processes.csv

> Get-Content processes.csv

  "Name","SI","Handles","VM","WS","PM","NPM","Path",...
  "AggregatorHost","0","92","2203375112192","2568192",...
  "ApplicationFrameHost","1","378","2203582570496",...
  ...
```

Performance Issues

In my tests, the execution of `Get-Process | Export-Csv` took an incomprehensibly long time—about 10 seconds on an idle Windows 11 desktop installation. `Get-Process` alone is executed in a few milliseconds, so `Get-Process` can't really be the problem. The resulting file is tiny (only 130 KB). Even in PowerShell running on Linux, the command took several seconds to execute.

Chapter 9
Regular Expressions

A *regular expression* (*regex*) is a character string that describes a search pattern for searching through text. In this context, specific rules must be followed that are not very intuitive. Let's start right away with an example. The following pattern recognizes a date in US format (i.e., mm/dd/yyyy):

```
(0[1-9]|1[0-2])\/(0[1-9]|1\d|2\d|3[01])\/(19|20)\d{2}
```

The pattern accepts months between 01 and 12, days between 01 and 31, and years between 1900 and 2099. However, you still cannot verify whether a date is really correct, for example, because the pattern also accepts the date 02/30/2023, although February can never have 30 days.

Regular expressions have a relatively high barrier to entry as you must first learn and practice the syntax, which will cost at least a few hours of your time. But once you're familiar with regular expressions, there's an almost infinite number of possible ways to apply them—and in all common programming languages. Some tasks can also be solved without regular expressions. But if you're familiar with the syntax, regular expressions will lead you more reliably and more quickly to your goal while avoiding spaghetti code!

This chapter starts with the syntax rules, where I consider the most important syntax variants—Portable Operating System Interface for Unix (POSIX) Regular Expressions, POSIX Extended Regular Expressions (ERE), and Perl Compatible Regular Expressions (PCRE). You didn't expect the same rules to apply to every tool or programming language, did you? Don't worry, the basic rules are always the same, and the variations between the regex variants are manageable. In the following sections, I will show you how to use regular expressions in Bash scripts (especially in the `grep` and `sed` commands), in Python, and in PowerShell through various examples.

Prerequisites for This Chapter

Large parts of this chapter apply regardless of your favorite scripting language. Only in the language-specific sections will you need basic knowledge of Bash, PowerShell, or Python. A logical follow-up after reading this chapter is thus Chapter 17 where you'll again find some application examples as well as some hints on the limitations of regular expressions.

9.1 Syntax Rules for Regular Expressions

The first concepts for regular expressions were formulated as early as the 1950s. Over time, several dialects or syntax variants developed:

- **POSIX**
  Regular expressions were first standardized in the Unix environment as *POSIX Regular Expressions*.
- **ERE**
  In this extension, references to already processed patterns (called *back references*) as well as codes for character classes (e.g., digits and letters) were defined, among other things.
- **PCRE**
  The script language Perl has already passed its zenith, but the syntax for regular expressions valid in Perl has established itself as a benchmark. Most popular programming languages (like Python and .NET languages including PowerShell, JavaScript, etc.) are PCRE-compatible except for a few details.

  Taken to the extreme, *two* PCRE variants exist: simply "PCRE" (since 1997) and "PCRE 2" (since 2015).

In this chapter, I will present regular expressions in an abbreviated way, so I won't discuss some advanced features. Unless I explicitly refer to other dialects, I will always refer to PCRE or the great common denominator of all regex variants.

Don't be put off by the various regex dialects: The comparatively few differences among them mainly concern advanced features. In many cases, you can adapt a pattern formulated for a particular regex dialect to another dialect.

Comparison Table

For most use cases, the basic knowledge provided in this section should be sufficient. However, when you want to use additional special functions, language-specific functions, or framework-specific functions, you probably won't be able to avoid looking into the respective documentation. If you're interested in the specific differences, you should search the internet for the "Regular Expression Engine Comparison Chart." The address of this excellent comparison site is just as daunting as its content, which is, however, excellently researched: *https://gist.github.com/CMCDragonkai/6c933f4a7d713ef712145c5eb94a1816*.

The differences between PCRE and PCRE 2 are very well summarized on Stack Overflow at *https://stackoverflow.com/questions/70273084*.

9.1.1 Characters

In regular expressions, various ways exist to express a single character or a character within an entire group. Basically, regular expressions differentiate between uppercase and lowercase, although this behavior can often be disabled by options depending on the tool or programming language. Thus, the `[Hh][ae]llo` expressions corresponds to the strings "Hallo," "Hello," "hallo," or "hello," but not to "HALLO." The `[0-9a-fA-F]` expression recognizes a hexadecimal digit.

Note that `a-z` covers all lowercase letters of the ASCII character set, but not special characters such as ä, ö, ü, or ß. You may have to add these letters separately, for example, as in `[a-zA-ZäöüßÄÖÜ]`. If the hyphen itself is to be an allowed character, you must specify it at the end, such as `[a-zA-Z-]` (ASCII lowercase and uppercase plus hyphen).

Expression	Meaning
`.`	Any character
`[aeiou]`	a, e, i, o, or u
`[^aeiou]`	Not a, e, i, o, or u
`[a-g]`	a to g
`[0-9]`	0 to 9
`\.`	A period (in general, \ must precede various regex special characters so that they lose their special meanings)

Table 9.1 Codes for Characters

PCRE uses various abbreviations for character classes.

Expression	Meaning
`\d`	Digit, equivalent to `[0-9]`
`\D`	No digit, equivalent to `[^0-9]`
`\s`	Whitespace (space, tab, etc.)
`\S`	No whitespace
`\w`	Letter or digit, corresponds to `[a-zA-Z0-9_]`
`\W`	Not letter/number

Table 9.2 PCRE Codes for Character Classes

In POSIX Regular Expressions, different codes apply to character classes. Note that these codes themselves are again used in square brackets, such as `[[:upper:]]`. In this context, you can save space by simply writing `[a-z]`. The `[[:lower:]äöüß]` expression recognizes lowercase letters including the German letters ä, ö, ü, and ß.

Expression	Meaning
[:upper:]	Uppercase letters, corresponds to [A-Z]
[:lower:]	Lowercase letters, corresponds to [a-z]
[:alpha:]	Letters, corresponds to [A-Za-z]
[:alnum:]	Letters and digits, corresponds to [A-Za-z0-9]
[:word:]	Letters, digits, and underscore, like \w
[:digit:]	Digits, corresponds to [0-9] or \d
[:xdigit:]	Hexadecimal digits, corresponds to [0-9a-fA-F]
[:punct:]	Punctuation marks (".,:;" etc.)
[:blank:]	Space and tab
[:space:]	Space, tab, and newline character
[:cntrl:]	Control characters such as Ctrl-C
[:graph:]	Character with graphical equivalent (corresponds to [^[:cntrl:]])

Table 9.3 POSIX Codes for Character Classes, Must Be Used within "[...]"

9.2 Groups and Alternatives

You can use () to create a group within an expression. Then, within the expression, you can use | to formulate alternative patterns, one of which optionally applies. In addition, you can access the contents of recognized groups using \1, \2, etc. or using $1, $2, etc., depending on the regex dialect. Various applications exist for this feature, such as detecting repetitions or performing search-and-replace operations.

The following three examples illustrate the use of groups. However, I must use + and {1,2} to anticipate the next section, which is about quantifiers. + means that the preceding expression must occur once or more often. {1,2} means that the preceding expression must occur exactly once or twice.

- **Regular expression: ([1-9]|10|11|12)**
  This expression applies to the numbers 1 through 12, but not to 0, not to 01, and not to 13.
- **Regular expression (for PCRE 2): ([0-9]+) \1** or **([0-9]+) $1**
  The first part of this expression applies to any integer, such as 0, 1, 34, or 789123. In the second part of the pattern, this group is referenced again; that is, the same number must be specified again after a space.

The expression applies to the following strings: 123 123, 7 7, 456 456, and abc1 1abc, where in the latter case only the 1 1 substring is recognized.

However, the expression does not match 123123 (no space) or 123   123 (too many spaces).

- **Regular expression: #([0-9a-fA-F]{1,2})\1\1**
  This expression recognizes CSS color codes for gray values. Such color codes must be introduced using the # character and may contain three or six hexadecimal digits. For the target color to be a gray value, the red, green, and blue components must each be equal. The twofold repetition of the first group serves this purpose.

  For example, the expression applies to the following color codes: #000, #222222, #ababab, #777 and #777777. The expression does not apply to #aabbcc, #abc, #0000 (the wrong number of digits), or 000 (the introductory # character is missing).

  The expression unfortunately fails with #aAa. This value is a correct gray value, but a (recognized group) and A (first repetition) do not match in terms of uppercase and lowercase.

Expression	Meaning
(...)	Everything between (and) forms a group
(abc)	The abc expression as a group
(abc|efg)	Alternatives are the abc or efg expressions
\1, \2	Reference to the contents of the 1st or 2nd group (POSIX, PCRE)
$1, $2	Reference to the contents of the 1st or 2nd group (PCRE 2)

Table 9.4 Regular Expression Groups

9.2.1 Quantifiers

Quantifiers allow you to express how often an expression may or must occur. You can apply quantifiers to character ranges or groups. Caution: abc+ first means ab, then any number of times c (but at least once). If, on the other hand, abc may occur any number of times, you must express this using (abc)+.

Expression	Meaning
x?	Zero or one time the characters described by x
x*	Zero times or more (any number of times)
x+	Once or more (but not zero times!)
x{3}	Exactly three times

Table 9.5 Regular Expression Pattern Quantifiers

Expression	Meaning
x{3,5}	Three to five times
x{3,}	At least three times

Table 9.5 Regular Expression Pattern Quantifiers (Cont.)

The following examples show quantifiers are easy to use:

- [a-f]
  Without a quantifier, this expression requires exactly one character a through f.
- [a-f]?
  With ?, one of the characters or none at all is expected.
- [a-f]+
  With +, any number of characters between a and f are allowed, but at least one character must be specified. Thus, a, aaa, and abcdef are fine. abcx also applies, but the expression includes only the first three letters, not the letter x.
- .*
  This open pattern allows any number of (even zero) arbitrary characters.
- (abc|efg){4}
  In this pattern, abc or efg must be specified exactly four times. abcabcefgabc would be appropriate, but abcefg would not.

9.2.2 On Greed (Greedy versus Lazy)

No, this section does not describe human morality or the characteristics of economic systems. Rather, greed in this context is a matter of how large the string captured by an expression should be. By default, the evaluation of regular expressions is *greedy*; that is, the regex function returns the largest possible matching strings.

Let's assume that the expression is <.+>. This expression means an HTML tag that starts with < and ends with > is to be recognized. There may be any number of characters in between (at least one).

If you apply this expression to the string <html><body><p>lorem ipsum<p>dolores est, the result is <html><body><p>lorem ipsum<p>. In most cases, this match will not meet your expectations.

You're lucky if the regex functions of your tools are PCRE-compliant. Then, you can simply enter a question mark after the quantifier. The expression is then analyzed as *lazy* or *non-greedy*, that is, as minimalistic as possible. The following listing illustrates this:

```
Expression:          <.+?>

Text:          <html><body><p>lorem ipsum<p>dolores est
```

```
First hit:  <html>
Second hit:        <body>
Third hit:              <p>
Fourth hit:                            <p>
```

Unfortunately, in the Bash environment, the PCRE syntax is rarely an option. Many Unix tools are only POSIX compliant. In such cases, you must formulate the expression more precisely. In our example, you describe the inside of the HTML tag using `[^>]+` instead of `.+?`. Thus, all characters except > are allowed inside. The entire expression then reads `<[^>]+>`.

Lazy Is Efficient

You may have always suspected it, but overeagerness rarely pays off. This cannot be said in such a general way for regular expressions, but in practice *lazy* expressions are often more efficient. This is especially true when a complex pattern is to be applied to a long string because then the number of possible cases and the volume of the text to be evaluated will decrease.

Regular Expressions and HTML: A Bad Combination!

You should resist the temptation to analyze HTML code using regular expressions. This usually goes wrong because HTML is not a "regular" language (in the scientific sense). To analyze HTML documents, you should use parsers that understand HTML code and ideally make a Document Object Model (DOM) from HTML. In Python, for example, the `BeautifulSoup` module performs this task. Examples are provided in Chapter 17.

9.2.3 Alpha and Omega

Until now, we have ignored the place where an expression is detected in the text. You can use the ^ and $ characters to express that the pattern is recognized at the beginning or end of the text.

Expression	Meaning
x	The x expression may occur anywhere in the text.
^x	The expression must occur at the beginning of the text.
x$	The expression must occur at the end of the text.
^x$	The expression must correspond to the entire text.

Table 9.6 Position of Regular Expressions

> **Multiline Text**
>
> When regular expressions are applied to longer texts or text files, then usually each line is considered separately. Some regex tools or functions provide options to perform expression recognition across multiple lines. However, you should make sure to carry out performance tests before using such an option indiscriminately!

9.2.4 Exercise Pages and Cheat Sheets

Before you can use regular expressions with any degree of confidence, you need to practice! Several great websites exist where you can solve a series of exercises of increasing complexity—complete with solutions and explanations. Just invest an hour on one of these sites—I promise it will be worth it!

- *https://regexone.com*
- *http://regextutorials.com*

For those of you who already have some routine with regular expressions, there are web pages where you can enter regular expressions and apply them immediately to test data. When I need to develop complicated patterns, I *always* use a page like this before incorporating the now working code into my script! Note, however, that both sites support only PCRE dialects:

- *https://regex101.com*
- *https://regexr.com*

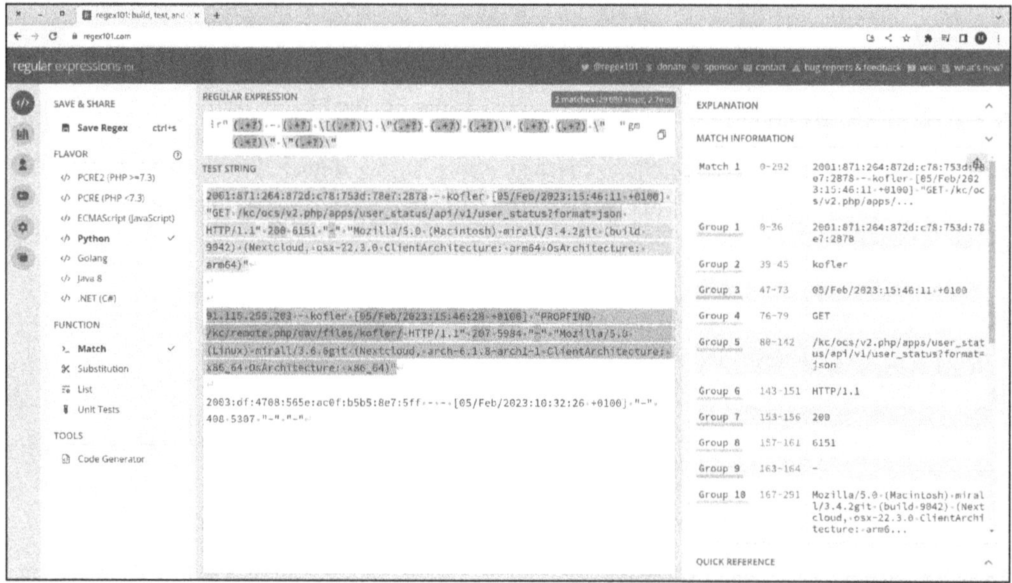

Figure 9.1 Testing a Regular Expression for Processing Apache Log Files

I have internalized the most important regex characters over the years, but for the details, I must read again and again. A useful tool in this context are "cheat sheets" that summarize the most important codes on a single page that you can print out, such as the following:

- *https://github.com/shadowbq/Cheat-Sheets/raw/master/regex/regular-expressions-cheat-sheet-v2.pdf*
- *https://jamesbachini.com/resources/REGEXCheatSheet.pdf*

Composing Regular Expressions Using Artificial Intelligence (AI)

AI tools like ChatGPT also understand regular expressions. The input "Can you show me a regular expression for recognizing email addresses?" immediately returns a result along with explanations of what the individual characters of the expression mean. However, especially with complex tasks, you should check whether the result really meets your requirements! ChatGPT likes to present solutions with great confidence but may not cover all matches or may filter out too much.

9.2.5 Example: Recognizing a Date

Let's assume your script is supposed to process a date in International Organization for Standardization (ISO) format (yyyy-mm-dd), either as input or from a file. A simple regular expression that basically works looks like `\d{4}-\d{2}-\d{2}`.

The date consists of eight digits separated by two hyphens. However, the pattern also accepts completely insane data, such as `4375-52-68`. With only a little effort, you can delimit the permissible value ranges quite easily, in this case, to the years between 0000 and 2999, the months between 01 and 12, and the days between 0 and 31. The following expression is not perfect but at least prevents complete input errors:

```
[012]\d{3}-(0[1-9]|10|11|12)-([012]\d|30|31)
```

9.2.6 Example: Recognizing IPv4 Addresses

You can also be more or less exact with IPv4 addresses. To extract IP addresses from a logging file, which will contain only correct addresses anyway, the following expression is sufficient:

```
(\d{1,3}\.){3}\d{1,3}
```

- `\d{1,3}` requires a 1- to 3-digit number.
- `\.` requires a dot. Do not forget the preceding \ character. Just `.` allows any character!
- `(...){3}` causes a tripling of this expression, so that it would capture "1.2.3." for IP address 1.2.3.4. Note that `{4}` would be wrong because the IP address would have to end with a dot.
- Now, `\d{1,3}` is still missing for the last digit.

More exact expressions, which accept only the number range from 0 to 255 for each digit, can be found at *https://stackoverflow.com/questions/5284147.*

9.2.7 Example: Recognizing Email Addresses

For a rough check if an email address is correct, you can use the following expression:

```
[a-zA-Z0-9+_.-]+@[a-zA-Z0-9.-]+
```

In this case, too, perfectionists will find completely unreadable patterns on Stack Overflow, which, however, take into account all conceivable rules and special cases.

9.3 Regular Expressions in Bash (grep, sed)

You should now understand the basic principles of regular expressions. Let me point out again that, in the previous section, I only outlined the most important syntax rules. Whole books of hundreds of pages are available that focus exclusively on this subject, covering every conceivable variation.

In this and the following sections, we want to look at the application of regular expressions. At this point, I'll start with Bash, focusing mostly on the `grep` and `sed` commands.

9.3.1 Bash Comparison Operator for Regular Expressions

In an elementary way, Bash and Zsh can process regular patterns without external tools. For this purpose, you can use the `=~` comparison operator, which you must apply in double square brackets.

```
if [[ string =~ pattern ]] then;
  echo "string matches pattern"
fi
```

In this case, ERE patterns are used. You must therefore use POSIX-compliant expressions such as `[:digit:]` or `[:alnum:]` instead of the short notations `\d` for *digit* or `\w` for *word*. Alternatively, you can formulate character ranges directly with `[0-9]`.

For example, the `=~` operator can be used to validate an input. In the following example, the script expects the input of a date `yyyy-mm-dd` in the format. If even the format of the string does not correspond to the specified format, the input must be repeated.

The expression expects year numbers in the range between 1900 and 2099, months between 01 and 12, and days between 00 and 31. Note that the expression does accept some invalid data, such as `2000-01-00` or `2023-04-31`.

```
# Sample file input-date.sh
pattern='^(19|20)[0-9]{2}-(0[1-9]|10|11|12)-([012][0-9]|30|31)$'
while true; do
    read -p "Enter a date in ISO format (yyyy-mm-dd): " date
    if [[  $date =~ $pattern ]]; then
        break
    else
        echo "Invalid date, please try again."
    fi
done
echo "Valid date: $date"
```


9.3.2 Filtering Text Using grep

You already learned about the grep command in Chapter 6 and Chapter 8. So far, we have used this command as a simple text filter. In fact, however, the first parameter passed to grep is analyzed as a regular pattern, by default in simple POSIX syntax. However, the command can also handle the ERE and PCRE regex dialects:

- -e: Enable ERE
- -P: Enable PCRE
- -o or --only-matching: Output only the expression that matches the pattern (i.e., do not display the entire line)

To avoid the various regex special characters being analyzed by Bash, you should pass the pattern in quotes.

The following command filters all IPv4 addresses from the access.log logging file and displays only the addresses. (You can find the file in the sample files for the previous chapter.)

```
$ grep -o -P '(\d{1,3}\.){3}\d{1,3}' access.log

  221.245.9.91
  135.84.251.52
  160.85.252.207
  ...
```

If you want to extract all IPv6 addresses in an analogous manner, you can call grep using the following expression:

```
$ grep -o -P '([\da-f]*:){1,7}\d{1,4}' access.log
```

The search pattern works for most "common" IPv6 addresses. However, the IPv6 syntax allows for various special cases, whose correct processing requires much more complex (and slower!) patterns. If necessary, you should look at the following Stack Overflow webpage: *https://stackoverflow.com/questions/53497.*

9.3.3 The "sed" Stream Editor

The `sed` *Stream Editor* is a universal command for text processing. You pass a command in the first parameter that `sed` applies to the standard input or to the file specified in the next parameter. The processed text is written to the standard output.

In the GNU variant of `sed` that's common on Linux, the `-i` (*in place*) option causes the source file to be modified directly. `-i.bak` creates a backup of the source file with the `.bak` identifier.

GNU versus BSD

In the BSD variant of `sed`, which is installed on macOS, for example, the `-i` option has a different meaning. In general, some other small differences exist between GNU `sed` and BDS `sed`. If necessary, you can install the GNU variant of `sed` using `brew`!

The following introductory example shows the delete command `d`. This example reads the `myfile.txt` file, deletes lines 3 to 5, and writes all other lines to the `out.txt` file.

```
$ sed 3,5d myfile.txt > out.txt
```

If you want to pass multiple commands to `sed`, you can use `-e`:

```
$ sed -e 'cmd1' -e 'cmd2' in.txt > out.txt
```

Alternatively, you can save the commands in a separate file and process that file using `-f`:

```
$ sed -f sedcmds.txt in.txt > out.txt
```

`sed` can also process regular expressions. In that case, POSIX Regular Expressions are used by default. With the equivalent `-E` or `-r` options, `sed` also supports ERE. Unlike `grep`, there is unfortunately no option for PCRE.

In the following command, `sed` searches for lines that start with an IPv4 address. These lines will be deleted. All other lines are stored in `ipv6.log`. The search pattern is usually formulated between two slashes. However, if you need to use the slash itself in the expression, you can use any other character that does not appear in it. But the entire expression must then start with a backslash. The following two commands are therefore equivalent:

```
$ sed -E  '/^([0-9]{1,3}\.){3}[0-9]{1,3}/d' access.log > ipv6.log
$ sed -E '\@^([0-9]{1,3}\.){3}[0-9]{1,3}@d' access.log > ipv6.log
```

9.3.4 Searching and Replacing Using sed

One of the most important sed commands is s/pattern/replace/. This command replaces the expressions recognized by pattern with the replace string in each line. Within \replace, you can access the groups detected by pattern using \1, \2.

In addition, other separators instead of / are allowed with this command, which do not occur in the pattern, such as s:pattern:replace:. However, the separator is not specially marked by a backslash. The third separator can be followed by two letters (also in combination):

- s/ptrn/rpl/g means that multiple search-and-replace operations are performed per line if necessary (g as in *global replace*).
- s/ptrn/rpl/i means that the analysis of the expression is *case insensitive*.

To test an expression or sed command, the best approach is to combine echo and sed:

```
$ echo "abc ABC" | sed 's/abc/efg/gi'
  efg efg
```

9.3.5 sed Example: Manipulating Paths of Image Files

Personally, I am intensely *committed* to the typesetting of my books. I write most of the texts in a Markdown syntax. Various scripts turn them into LaTeX, HTML, and PDF files. Among other things, when creating the print files, I must replace my screenshots and photos (**.png* and **.jpg* identifiers) with PostScript files optimized by the publisher (**.eps* identifier), which are also located in a different directory. So, for example, the original Markdown file contains image references in the following format:

```
![Relaisboard \label{b-rb}](images-chris/relayboard.png)
![Audioplayer \label{b-mpd}](images-michael/mpd.png)
![L298N-Pins \label{b-l298}](images-charly/L298_Pins.png)
```

Before I create the print file, the Markdown code must be rebuilt:

```
![Relaisboard \label{b-rb}](images-final/relayboard.eps)
![Audioplayer \label{b-mpd}](images-final/mpd.eps)
![L298N-Pins \label{b-l298}](images-final/L298_Pins.eps)
```

This tedious work is of course taken care of by a script that contains the following sed command, among other things:

```
# Sample file preprocess-markdown.sh
cmd="s,\(images-.*\/(.*)\.(jpg|png)\),(images-final/\1.eps),"
sed -E "$cmd" text.md > text-final.md
```

Because the / character occurs within the sed command, I have structured the command in the s,pattern,replace, format. The regular pattern recognizes expressions structured as (images-<aname>/<iname>.jpg|png), where aname is the author name and iname is the image name. This pattern is replaced by (images-final/<iname>.eps).

9.4 Regular Expressions in PowerShell

Because of the object-oriented approach of PowerShell, analyzing text is less often required than in Bash scripts. Often the simple reading of properties leads to the goal. On Windows, text files for configuration or with logging data are the exception rather than the rule. Nevertheless, PowerShell also provides various regex features to help process text. In PowerShell, the regex syntax of the .NET framework applies, which is largely compatible with PCRE. Refer to *https://learn.microsoft.com/en-us/dotnet/standard/base-types/regular-expression-language-quick-reference*.

9.4.1 The match and replace Operators

The easiest way to use regular expressions is with the various match operators: txt -match pattern tests whether the specified pattern can be recognized in the text. The result is True or False.

As is specific to PowerShell (or should we rather say, as is typical of Microsoft), uppercase and lowercase is ignored—unless you use -cmatch (*case sensitive match*). -notmatch or -cnotmatch simply have the inverse meaning of -match, so you can test if the pattern is *not* included. These match operators can be tried out interactively in a simple way, which is also useful if for quickly testing whether the syntax of your regular expression is correct and works the way you want it to.

```
> "I love PowerShell" -match "p.*l"
  True

> "I love PowerShell" -cmatch "p.*l"
  False

> "connection from 127.0.0.1" -match "(\d{1,3}\.){3}\d{1,3}"
  True
```

You can also apply -match to filenames or directory names. The following command searches C:\Windows recursively for directories of the xx-xx format, where x is a letter or a digit. This will return numerous directories with names like de-DE or en-US with localization files (i.e., files containing strings in a specific language).

```
> Get-ChildItem C:\windows -Recurse -Directory |
  Where-Object { $_.name -match "^\w\w-\w\w$" }
```

You can use the replace operator to perform search and replace operations for strings, as in the following example:

```
> $txt = "connection from 127.0.0.1 to 192.168.74.104"
> $txt -replace "(\d{1,3}\.){3}\d{1,3}", "-hidden-"
  connection from -hidden- to -hidden-
```

9.4.2 Select-String

Like grep, Select-String analyzes the search text as a regular expression. I already described this cmdlet in detail in Chapter 7, Section 7.2. In this respect, an example in the regex context should suffice for this chapter.

In this example, I want to take a look at the C:\Windows\diagnostics\system directory. This directory contains various PowerShell scripts that are called from the **Troubleshooting Wizard** of **System Preferences** (i.e., **System • Troubleshoot • Other Troubleshooters**). The goal of the following command is to retrieve a reference of all the functions defined in these files. This task is relatively easy, but the result is confusing:

```
> Set-Location C:\Windows\diagnostics\system
> Get-ChildItem -Filter *.ps1 -Recurse |
  Select-String '^function '
  Apps\RC_WSReset.ps1:7:function Get-FaultyAppsFromEventLogs([...
  Apps\Utils_Apps.ps1:17:Function Write-ExceptionTelemetry($Fu...
  Apps\VF_WSReset.ps1:14:function Get-AppContainerEvents([Syst...
  ...
```

In my second attempt, I developed a more complicated regular expression that captures function <name> and, subsequently, the parameters of that function in a group. However, this time, I don't want to see the entire result line, but only function <name>. For this purpose, the match objects returned by Select-String must be analyzed. Groups(0) then returns the entire line, while Groups(1) returns the content of the first regex group:

```
> Get-ChildItem -Filter *.ps1 -Recurse |
  Select-String '^(function [^(]*)\(.*\)$' |
  ForEach-Object { $_.Matches.Groups[0].Value }
  function Get-FaultyAppsFromEventLogs
  function Get-CompletedTroubleshooterSessions
  Function Write-ExceptionTelemetry
  ...
```

9.4.3 Example: Input Validation

The following mini script expects the input of a color code in the #ccc or #cccc format, where c represents a hexadecimal digit. For example, the correct input for red would be #ff0000. If the input is incorrect, the user must try again.

```
# Sample file input-css-color.ps1
do {
    $color = Read-Host "Enter a CSS color (#ccc or #cccccc)"
} until ($color -match "^#([0-9a-fA-F]{3}){1,2}$")
Write-Host "Valid color code: $color"
```

9.4.4 Example: List of Figures

In a Markdown file, figures are included as follows:

```
![Image caption ...](images-michael/filename.png)
```

The images have PNG and JPEG formats. The script is supposed to extract the filenames of all images:

```
.\extract-images.ps1 text.md

  images-chris/relayboard.png
  images-michael/mpd.png
  images-charly/L298_Pins.jpg
```

If you want, you can also redirect the output to a text file:

```
.\extract-images.ps1 text.md > out.txt
```

The script is short:

```
# Sample file extract-images.ps1
# the script expects file names as parameters
Param( [string[]] $markdownfiles)

$pattern = '\]\((images-\w+[\/\\][\w-]+\.(png|jpg|jpeg))\)'

# loop through all files
foreach ($file in $markdownfiles) {
    # Recognize pattern, output the content of the pattern group
    Select-String $pattern $file |
      ForEach-Object { $_.Matches.Groups[1].Value }
}
```

The regular pattern searches for `](images-<aname>/<iname>.png|jpg|jpeg)`, where `<aname>` is the author name and `<iname>` is the image name.

Let's look at some parts of this expression in detail:

- `[\/\\]` allows both / and \ as directory separators. To comply with the regex syntax, both characters must be preceded by backslashes.

- [\w-]+ accepts all letters, digits, the underscore _, and the hyphen - in the filename. Note that the hyphen is not included in the character set of \w!
- As usual in PowerShell, Select-String is not case sensitive, which in this case is an advantage because identifiers in capital letters (such as *.PNG) are thus also accepted.

Our first variant of the script provides text output. You may wonder where the output is performed: The expression $_.Matches.Groups[1].Value returns a string that gets output directly. The following expression within the ForEach-Object construct would be equivalent:

```
Write-Output $_.Matches.Groups[1].Value
```


Scripts that output text conform to the Bash way of thinking, but do not make proper use of the object-oriented approach in PowerShell. In this example, it would be more obvious if the script returned FileInfo objects.

Exactly this task is performed by the extract-images2.ps1 variant. Again, I only changed the line in the ForEach-Object construct. The resulting string is then passed to Get-ChildItem. This cmdlet reads the file and returns a FileInfo object.

```
Get-ChildItem $_.Matches.Groups[1].Value
```

However, if you run a test using the sample text.md file, the script will return only error messages:

```
.\extract-images2.ps1 text.md

  Cannot find path '...\images-michael\mpd.png' because
  it does not exist.
  ...
```

This result is because the sample files only include the Markdown file, but not the associated image files.

9.5 Regular Expressions in Python (re Module)

To use regular expressions in Python, the default module re must be imported. This module provides various functions, of which I will briefly present the most important ones in this section:

- re.search(pattern, str) returns either a Match object with the location of the first hit or None. The groups defined in the pattern can be analyzed using the group property (see the sample code following this list).
- re.match(pattern, str) works like search; it considers the pattern only at the beginning of the string.

- re.fullmatch(pattern, str) also works like search, but now, the pattern must describe the entire string, from the beginning to the end.
- re.findall(pattern, str) returns a list of *all* matches found. Unlike search, match, and fullmatch, findall returns simple strings of matches, not match objects.

  If the pattern contains *one* group, then the result string specifies the contents of that group. On the other hand, if the pattern contains multiple groups, you'll receive a tuple with strings for each group.
- re.sub(pattern, replace, str) replaces all matching patterns with new text.

You can read the full documentation for the re module at *https://docs.python.org/3/library/re.html*.

In Python, a best practice is to express the search pattern as a raw string in the following format: r'pattern'. In this way, you can avoid issues caused by backslashes. The following script shows the application of search, first for a search pattern without groups and then for a search pattern with groups:

```
# Sample file hello-re.py, search pattern without groups
import re
pattern = r'\d{4}-\d{2}-\d{2}'
txt = 'Easter 2024 is on 2024-03-31.'
if result := re.search(pattern, txt):
    print(result.group())        # 2024-03-31
```

In the second variant, the group method without parameters returns the entire recognized pattern. Using len(result.groups()) allows you to determine how many pattern groups exist. These groups can then be analyzed using group(n). Note that group(0) is equivalent to group() and returns the overall result.

```
# Sample file hello-re.py, search pattern with groups
pattern = r'(\d{4})-(\d{2})-(\d{2})'
if result := re.search(pattern, txt):
    print(result.group())        # 2024-03-31
    print(len(result.groups()))  # 3
    year = result.group(1)
    month = result.group(2)
    day = result.group(3)
    print(year, month, day)      # 2024 12 31
```

9.5.1 Example: Verifying a MAC Address

In the following script, you'll be prompted to enter a Media Access Control (MAC) address for identifying network devices. A MAC address is a 12-digit hexadecimal number. The script accepts input in the 00-80-41-ae-fd-7e and 00:80:41:ae:fd:7e formats (i.e., with hyphens or colons between the groups of two). a through f are also accepted as uppercase letters.

Here is a brief explanation of the pattern: Exactly two hexadecimal digits must be followed by either the - or : character. This group must appear five times in the pattern and must be followed by two hexadecimal digits.

```
# Sample file input-mac.py
import re
ok = False
pattern = r'^([a-fA-F0-9]{2}[:-]){5}[a-fA-F0-9]{2}$'
while not ok:
    mac = input('Enter a MAC address: ')
    ok = re.match(pattern, mac)
    if not ok:
        print('Not valid, please try again:')

print('Valid address:', mac)
```


9.5.2 Example: Anonymizing a Logging File

In the previous chapter, I presented multiple usage examples for grep, sort, and uniq. The sample file access.log used there is a real Apache logging file of a web server, but I have anonymized it for privacy reasons. The logging file uses the Apache Combined Log format, described at *https://httpd.apache.org/docs/2.4/logs.html.*

The following listing contains excerpts from the anonymize-log.py script, which you can find in the sample files within the directory for the previous chapter. The regular expression consists of ten groups for recognizing the components of a line in the Apache Combined Log format. Although only one match per line is expected (result(0)), I used findall in this case, which simplifies the further analysis of the results. findall provides a tuple, which is converted into a list. Then, some components are replaced, and finally, the logging line is output again.

```
# Sample file anonymize-log.py
# (in the directory for the previous chapter)
# usage: ./anonymize-log.py in.log > out.log
import random, re, string, sys

def randomIPv4(): ...      # Functions for generating random IP addresses
def randomIPv6(): ...      # URLs and names
def randomUrl(): ...
def randomUsername(): ...

# Dictionary, assigns random addresses to real IP addresses
ips = {}
```

```
# Pattern with 10 groups for the Apache Combined Log Format
pattern = r'(.+?) - (.+?) \[(.+?)\] \"(.+?) (.+?) (.+?)\"
            (.+?) (.+?) \"(.+?)\" \"(.+?)\"'

# open file passed in the first parameter
with open(sys.argv[1], 'r') as f:
    # loop through all lines
    for line in f:
        result = re.findall(pattern, line)
        if len(result):
            groups = list(result[0])  # list -> tupel
            # replace IP address with random address
            # and save in ips dictionary
            ip = groups[0]
            if ip not in ips:
                if ':' in ip:
                    ips[ip] = randomIPv6()
                else:
                    ips[ip] = randomIPv4()
            groups[0] = ips[ip]

            # analogous code for names, URLs etc. ...

            # output of the line (stdout)
            print('%s - %s [%s] "%s %s %s" %s %s "%s" "%s"' %
                  tuple(groups))
```

Chapter 10
JSON, XML, and INI

JavaScript Object Notation (JSON) has established itself over the last decade as the dominant format when programs or web services such as REST APIs are supposed to exchange data.

The hype of the 2000s surrounding the *Extensible Markup Language (XML)* has now faded: Not only is the comparatively complex syntax, with its many special cases, difficult for humans to read, but also tedious to analyze through code. But even as XML is used less and less in new projects, you may still encounter its huge legacy of programs and web services based on XML. But we are not limited to only JSON or XML: To save a few configuration settings, the INI format is also completely sufficient.

10

In this chapter, I want to present some functions that PowerShell and Python provide for creating and processing such files. If necessary, these tasks can also be performed in Bash, but you would have to use external commands, such as `jq` or `xmllint`.

Prerequisites for This Chapter

This chapter takes all three scripting languages described in this book into account, this time with a focus on PowerShell and Python: These two languages provide excellent support for the JSON and XML formats. A good logical follow-up to this chapter is Chapter 18.

10.1 JSON in PowerShell

In PowerShell, two cmdlets that are as simple as they are powerful make processing JSON data a breeze:

- **`ConvertTo-Json`**
  `ConvertTo-Json` is mostly used in the `cmdlet | ConvertTo-Json` format and converts the result objects provided by the cmdlet into a string in JSON format. The properties of the objects serve as keys for the key-value pairs in the JSON document. The document can be saved to a file via output redirection.
- **`ConvertFrom-Json`**
  `ConvertFrom-Json` works exactly the opposite way: The cmdlet transforms the JSON string passed as parameters or via pipe back into `PSObjects` or `hash tables`, which can then be further processed using `Select-Object`, `ForEach-Object`, and so on.

The following examples show some applications of the two cmdlets.

10.1.1 Example: Saving Event Log Entries in JSON Format

The following command reads the last ten security-specific entries from the event log and stores them in a JSON file:

```
> Get-EventLog Security -Newest 10 |
  ConvertTo-Json > security-events.json
```

The resulting *security-events.json* file looks as follows:

```
[
  {
    "EventID": 4799,
    "PSComputerName": "localhost",
    "Index": 308255,
    "Message": "A security-enabled local
                group membership was ...",
    "Source": "Microsoft-Windows-Security-Auditing",
    ...
  },
  {
    "EventID": 4799,
    "PSComputerName": "localhost",
    "Index": 308254,
     ...
  }
]
```

10.1.2 Example: Analyzing Domain Queries

The second example involves the analysis of a web request. The *https://domainsdb.info* website makes accessible a rather large (but by no means complete!) database with public information about registered domains. PowerShell provides a straightforward way to perform GET requests by means of Invoke-WebRequest. (Invoke-WebRequest is roughly comparable to the Linux commands curl or wget.) To find domains containing the *rheinwerk* string, you would use the following commands:

```
> $url =
  "https://api.domainsdb.info/v1/domains/search?domain=rheinwerk"
> Invoke-WebRequest $url
  StatusCode        : 200
  StatusDescription : OK
  Content           : {"domains": [{"domain": "rheinwerk-
                        office.com", "create_date": ...
  ...
```

The exciting part of the result is accessible via the Content property and is in JSON format. When formatted, the document looks as follows (heavily shortened):

```
{
  "domains": [
    {
      "domain": "rheinwerk-office.com",
      "create_date": "2022-12-29T13:21:38.809015",
      "A": [
        "87.106.63.234"
      ],
      ...
    },
    {
      "domain": "rheinwerk-publishing.com",
      ...
    }, ... ]
}
```

The goal of this example is to filter out only the domain and A properties (i.e., the A record entry) from the rather large JSON document. After converting the JSON data into PowerShell objects, this filter step can be done pretty easily:

```
> (Invoke-WebRequest $url | ConvertFrom-Json).domains |
  Select-Object domain, A

  domain                   A
  ------                   -----------
  rheinwerk-office.com     {87.106.63.234}
  rheinwerk-publishing.com {46.235.24.150}
  rheinwerk-verlag.com     {46.235.24.168}
  ...
```

REST APIs

An alternative to the Invoke-WebRequest and ConvertFrom-Json combination is the Invoke-RestMethod command, which I will introduce in Chapter 18. This command converts JSON documents directly into PowerShell objects.

10.1.3 Example: Converting between CSV and JSON

Converting a comma-separated values (CSV) file to JSON format is a piece of cake. The only requirement is that the CSV file contains column labels in the first row. The starting point for this example is the *employees.csv* file, which contains the following information:

```
FirstName;LastName;DateOfBirth;Street;Zip;City;...
Ruthanne;Summers;1977-06-04;4 Dewy Turnpike;27698;Clifton ...
...
```

`Import-Csv` converts the file into PowerShell objects; `ConvertTo-Json` turns it into a JSON document:

```
> Import-Csv -Delimiter ';' employees.csv |
  ConvertTo-Json > employees.json
```

By default, `ConvertTo-Json` takes care of reader-friendly indentation of the JSON document. If the readability of the resulting file is not an issue, you can pass the additional `-Compress` option. The subsequent `Get-ChildItem` proves that the amount of space saved is quite noticeable.

```
> Import-Csv -Delimiter ';' employees.csv |
  ConvertTo-Json -Compress > employees-compressed.json

> Get-ChildItem *.json | Select-Object Name, Length

  Name                     Length
  ----                     ------
  employees-compressed.json 122528
  employees.json           165030
```

The conversion back from JSON to CSV is equally simple, as in the following example:

```
> Get-Content .\employees-compressed.json | ConvertFrom-Json |
  Export-Csv employees2.csv
```

10.2 JSON and Python

Python and JSON together form a dream team. To process JSON documents, you must import the `json` module. This module comes with Python by default and does not need to be installed separately. The module provides the following functions:

- **`load(filehandle)`**
  This function reads a text file previously opened via `open` and returns the JSON data it contains as Python dictionaries and lists.
- **`loads(str)`**
  In the sense of *load string*, this function expects the JSON document in the string passed as parameter.

- **dump(obj, filehandle)**
  This function stores the Python object passed in the first parameter as a JSON string in the specified file. Some additional parameters allow you to influence the resulting JSON document. `indent=2` specifies the desired indentation depth per nesting level. `ensure_ascii=False` ensures the correct processing of UTF-8 characters.
- **dumps(obj)**
  This function works like `dump` but returns the JSON document as a string.

The following listing shows the application of these four methods:

```
# Sample file hello-json.py
import json

# read JSON file
with open('employees.json', 'r') as f:
    employees = json.load(f)

# process JSON string
txt = '{"key1": "value1", "key2": "value2"}'
data = json.loads(txt)

# analysis of the data
print(data['key2'])   # Ausgabe: value2

# save Python object (list, dictionary) as JSON file
with open('otherfile.json', 'w') as f:
    json.dump(data, f, indent=2, ensure_ascii=False)

# output JSON string
print(json.dumps(data, indent=2, ensure_ascii=False))
```

10.2.1 Example: Collecting Birthdays

The starting point for the *birthdays.py* script is the *employees.json* file, which has the following structure:

```
[
  {
    "FirstName": "Ruthanne",
    "LastName": "Ferguson",
    "DateOfBirth": "1977-06-04",
    ...
  }, ...
]
```

The *birthdays.py* script reads the JSON file and processes the employees in a loop. In this process, a dictionary is created. The key is the day and month of the birthday (e.g., 06-24). The actual entry contains a list of employee names whose birthday is on that day.

```
# Sample file birthdays.py
import json
with open('employees.json') as f:
    employees = json.load(f)

birthdates = {}   # birthday dictionary
for employee in employees:
    # [5:] skips the first five characters, only month and day
    birthdate = employee['DateOfBirth'][5:]
    name = employee['FirstName'] + ' ' + employee['LastName']
    if birthdate in birthdates:
        # add name to existing list
        birthdates[birthdate].append(name)
    else:
        # create new dictionary entry with list
        birthdates[birthdate] = [name]

# test: all birthday children on 1/24
# output: ['Nannette Ramsey', 'Allena Hoorenman',
#          'Arden Lit', 'Duncan Noel']
print(birthdates['01-24'])
```

10.2.2 Example: Determining Holidays

After free user registration on the *https://calendarific.com* website, you'll receive an API key that allows you to determine the holidays and any other commemorative days imaginable for a given country and year, for example, with the following command:

```
$ curl 'https://calendarific.com/api/v2/holidays\?
            api_key=1234&country=DE&year=2023'
```

The result is a JSON document that is structured in the following way:

```
{
    "meta": {
        "code": 200
    },
    "response": {
        "holidays": [
            {
```

```
                "name": "Name of holiday,
                "description": "Description of holiday,
                "date": {
                    "iso": "2023-12-31",
                    "datetime": { ... }
                },
                "type": [ ... ]
            }, ...
        ]
    }
}
```


Our sample *holidays.py* script expects two optional parameters: a country code and a year. If this information is missing, the script uses 'US' and the current year by default. The script then performs a request, analyzes the result, and returns the result in the following format:

```
$ ./holidays.py DE 2023
  Holidays for DE in 2023
  2023-01-01: New Year's Day
    New Year's Day, which is on January 1, ...
  2023-01-06: Epiphany
    Epiphany on January 6 is a public holiday in 3 German states
    and commemorates the Bible story of the Magi's visit to
    baby Jesus.
  ...
```

Limitations

The use of *https://calendarific.com* is free of charge after a simple registration form but is subject to various restrictions. Commercial use is allowed only upon payment of a monthly fee.

The script starts with the import of various modules and the initialization of the api_key, country, and year variables. A loop analyzes all parameters passed to the script and overwrites year or country if necessary.

```
# Sample file holidays.py
import datetime, json, sys, urllib.request

# Please use your own key that you
# can obtain free of charge at https://calendarific.com.
api_key = "xxx"
```

```
# default settings
country = 'US'
year = datetime.datetime.now().year

# analyze script parameters, set year and country
for arg in sys.argv[1:]:
    if arg.isdigit():
        year = arg
    else:
        country = arg

print("Holidays for", country, "in", year)
```

For the web request, I used the `urllib` Python module, which is available by default, so it doesn't need to be installed using `pip`. The application of this module is rather cumbersome: First, you must create a `Request` object. Then, you'll pass this object to the `urlopen` method and get a `Response` object. The `read` method of that object gives you the data returned by the server in binary format, which you finally convert to a UTF-8 string by using `decode`.

In my tests, I discovered that *https://calendarific.com* denies requests from Python. (A request executed using `curl` with the same URL, on the other hand, works.) Presumably the operators of Calendarific want you to use the `python-calendarific` module, but I wanted to avoid that for didactic reasons. Instead, I used the `headers` parameter to override the default header and thus outsmart Calendarific.

From the point of view of this chapter, the last few lines of the script are the most exciting ones. `json.loads(txt)` turns the JSON document into a Python object tree. `data['response']['holidays']` returns a list of `holiday` dictionaries, which are then evaluated in a loop. As you can see, once the hurdles of downloading are overcome, the JSON analysis is rather easy to perform.

```
# Sample file holidays.py
# perform web request
query = "https://calendarific.com/api/v2/
         holidays?api_key=%s&country=%s&year=%s"
url = query % (api_key, country, year)
req = urllib.request.Request(url,
                             headers={"User-Agent": "curl"})
response = urllib.request.urlopen(req)
txt = response.read().decode("utf-8")

# analysis of JSON data
data = json.loads(txt)
```

```
for holiday in data['response']['holidays']:
    name = holiday['name']
    date = holiday['date']['iso']
    descr = holiday['description']
    print('%s: %s' % (date, name))
    print('  %s' % (descr))
```

requests instead of request

Instead of the `request` module, Python also has the `requests` module (with plural S). This module must be installed separately, but it is much more convenient to use. For examples of its use, refer to Chapter 17 and Chapter 18.

10.3 JSON in Bash

Bash does not contain any built-in JSON functions. However, the `jq` command (`jq` for *JSON query*) is available in most Linux distributions. If the execution of the command ends with the *command not found* error message, you must install the `jq` command. On Ubuntu, this step can be performed using `sudo apt install jq`.

`jq` reads a JSON document from the standard input or from files passed as parameters. This command then applies a filter expression to the document and writes the result to standard output. The simplest application is to format JSON documents in a readable way. For this task, you simply need to specify a dot (`.`) as the filter expression:

```
$ echo '{"key1":"123","key2":"456"}' | jq .

  {
    "key1": "123",
    "key2": "456"
  }
```

The basis for the following examples is the *commits.json* file which contains approximately 1,400 lines. This data is from the GitHub event log, which is publicly available in the JSON format. I used a repository from *Docker: Practical Guide for Developers and DevOps Teams* (Rheinwerk Computing, 2023), coauthored by myself and Bernd Öggl, as the database:

```
$ curl 'https://api.github.com/repos/docker-compendium/\
        samples/commits' > commits.json
```

The JSON file simply consists of an array of commit data. In `jq`, you can use `.[]` to access the entire array and use `.(0)` to access the first element (the latest commit).

```
$ jq '.[0]' commits.json

  {
    "sha": "8b17e24e278cd594456db77abbbefe4190ac1d88",
    "node_id": "C_kwD",
    "commit": {
      "author": {
        "name": "Michael Kofler",
  ...
```

You can use .keyname to access individual data elements:

```
$ jq '.[0].commit.author.name' commits.json
  "Michael Kofler"
```

Who performed how many commits?

```
$ jq '.[].commit.author.name' commits.json | sort | uniq -c

  11 "Bernd Oeggl"
   7 "Michael Kofler"
```

The next command lists all commit messages:

```
$ jq '.[].commit.message' commits.json

  "Update README.md"
  "add k8s sample code files"
  "add swarm sample code"
  ...
```

Using a pipe operator (|) within a filter expression is allowed. In the following expression, we'll extract two properties from each list item, give them new names, and make them new JSON elements:

```
$ jq '.[] | {date: .commit.author.date,
             msg: .commit.message}' commits.json

  {
    "date": "2023-01-22T06:40:14Z",
    "msg": "Update README.md"
  }
  {
    "date": "2023-01-21T20:50:32Z",
    "msg": "add k8s sample code files"
  }
  ...
```

However, the result itself is not a valid JSON document. To make it valid, you must wrap it in an array using square brackets:

```
$ jq '[ .[] | {date: .commit.author.date,
               msg: .commit.message} ]' commits.json

  [
    {
      "date": "2023-01-22T06:40:14Z",
      "msg": "Update README.md"
    },
    ...
```

By using `select`, you can formulate conditions. The following command creates a new JSON document with the commits of Bernd Öggl:

```
$ jq '[ .[] | select (.commit.author.name=="Bernd Oeggl") ]' >
  bernds-commits.json
```

For more examples of using the `jq` syntax, see the tutorial, and for a comprehensive reference of the many functions, refer to the following manuals:

- *https://stedolan.github.io/jq/tutorial*
- *https://stedolan.github.io/jq/manual*

10.3.1 Viewing JSON Files Interactively Using fx

Of course, you can browse through JSON files using `less`. But a much more comfortable approach is to use the `fx` command, which must be installed first, however, by visiting *https://github.com/antonmedv/fx*.

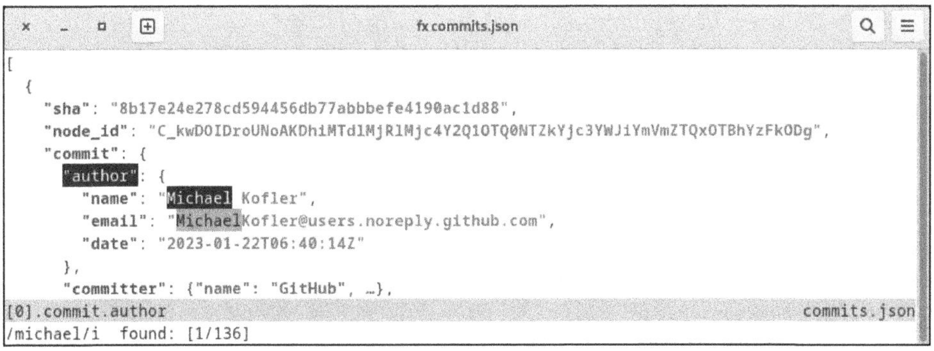

```
fx commits.json
[
  {
    "sha": "8b17e24e278cd594456db77abbbefe4190ac1d88",
    "node_id": "C_kwDOIDroUNoAKDhiMTdlMjRlMjc4Y2Q1OTQ0NTZkYjc3YWJiYmVmZTQxOTBhYzFkODg",
    "commit": {
      "author": {
        "name": "Michael Kofler",
        "email": "MichaelKofler@users.noreply.github.com",
        "date": "2023-01-22T06:40:14Z"
      },
      "committer": {"name": "GitHub", …},
[0].commit.author                                    commits.json
/michael/i  found: [1/136]
```

Figure 10.1 Reading JSON Files in the Terminal Using fx

Once installed, you can open a JSON document via `fx myfile.json` or `cmd | fx`, open and close JSON groups using [←] and [→], search for texts using /, and so on. The JSON document is neatly formatted; keys and entries are highlighted. In a nutshell, reading or analyzing large JSON files in the terminal becomes a pleasure when you use fx. Pressing [Q] terminates the program.

10.4 XML in PowerShell

Microsoft has gone all-in on XML for Windows, which is why numerous XML files exist in a Windows system. On my Windows 11 test machine, I encountered about 1,500 files with the **.xml* identifier in *C:\Windows* alone. Even quite "normal" Microsoft Office files (such as **.docx*) use XML content. (Strictly speaking, Microsoft Office files are ZIP archives, which in turn contain XML files.) In summary, XML is an ubiquitous format on Windows.

10.4.1 XML Data Type

PowerShell supports XML through its own data type. When reading an XML file, you must prefix the variable with the data type in square brackets so that PowerShell can clearly see that you don't want to view the file as ordinary text, but in XML format instead.

```
> [xml]$tmz = Get-Content `
    "C:\Windows\Globalization\Time Zone\timezoneMapping.xml"
```

The file used in this example contains information about time zones. (If you do not run Windows, you can find this file in the sample files for this book.) This file has the following structure:

```
<?xml version="1.0" encoding="UTF-8"?>
<TimeZoneMapping GeneratedAt="2022-11-08T09:34:04.6992291+05:30">
  <MapTZ TZID="Etc/GMT+12" WinID="Dateline Standard Time"
         Region="001" Default="true" StdPath="GMT+12/standard"
         DltPath="GMT+12/daylight" />
  <MapTZ TZID="Etc/GMT+12" WinID="Dateline Standard Time"
         Region="ZZ" ... />
  ...
```

You can access the elements of the XML structure via properties:

```
> $tmz.TimeZoneMapping.MapTZ[0]

  TZID    : Etc/GMT+12
  WinID   : Dateline Standard Time
  Region  : 001
  Default : true
```

```
StdPath : GMT+12/standard
DltPath : GMT+12/daylight

> $tmz.TimeZoneMapping.MapTZ[57].WinID
Mountain Standard Time
```

The following command loops through the first five time zones and returns objects whose properties correspond to the TZID and StdPath attributes:

```
> $tmz.TimeZoneMapping.MapTZ | Select-Object -First 5 |
  ForEach-Object {
    [PSCustomObject]@{ 'id' = $_.WinID; 'stdpath'=$_.StdPath}
  }

  id                      stdpath
  --                      -------
  Dateline Standard Time GMT+12/standard
  Dateline Standard Time GMT+12/standard
  UTC-11                  GMT+11/standard
  UTC-11                  Samoa/standard
  UTC-11                  Niue/standard
```

You can use GetElementsByTagName to access all XML elements with a specific name, regardless of the level of the XML document at which the elements are located.

```
> $tmz.GetElementsByTagName("MapTZ")
```

10.4.2 Select-Xml

Select-Xml applies XPath expressions to XML documents. XPath is a standardized query language for XML, which I won't discuss any further in this book. If necessary, you can find a good summary of the syntax in Wikipedia and countless examples of its use on the internet.

XML documents can be optionally read from a file (-Path option), passed within a string (-Content), or as an XML object (-Xml). For this reason, the following three Select-Xml examples are equivalent and each results in the number of MapTZ tags in the file. Note that, when reading the XML file into a string, Get-Content must be used with the -Raw option. This option causes the entire file to be processed as one object rather than as an array of lines.

```
> [xml]$tmz = Get-Content `
    "C:\Windows\Globalization\Time Zone\timezoneMapping.xml"

> $str = Get-Content -Raw `
    "C:\Windows\Globalization\Time Zone\timezoneMapping.xml"
```

```
> $xpath = "/TimeZoneMapping/MapTZ"

> (Select-xml -XPath $xpath -Path .\timezone-mapping.xml).Count
> (Select-Xml -XPath $xpath -Content $tmz ).Count
> (Select-Xml -XPath $xpath -Xml $tmz).Count
  616
```

The second example determines the text of the `WinID` attribute from the 58th `MapTZ` tag. The count begins at 0. `Select-Xml` returns `SelectXmlInfo` objects whose default representation is not particularly helpful in the output. Only `Select-Object -ExpandProperty Node` returns the actual text of the attribute.

```
> Select-Xml "/*/MapTZ[57]/@WinID" -Xml $tmz

  Node  Path        Pattern
  ----  ----        -------
  WinID InputStream /TimeZoneMapping/MapTZ[57]/@WinID

> Select-Xml -Xml $tmz -XPath $xpath |
  Select-Object -ExpandProperty Node

  #text
  -----
  Mountain Standard Time
```

The third example refers to **.vbox* files that describe virtual machines from *Oracle VM VirtualBox*. Despite the **.vbox* identifier, these files are ordinary XML files.

```
<?xml version="1.0"?>
<VirtualBox xmlns="http://www.virtualbox.org/" version="...">
  <Machine uuid="{c197c895-7b0c-4fa3-a05b-165377b33232}" ...>
    <MediaRegistry>
      <HardDisks>
        <HardDisk uuid="..." location="kali-english.vdi"
            format="VDI" type="Normal"/>
            ...
```

However, your first attempts to analyze the files may fail miserably. `Select-Xml` simply returns an empty result without any warning or error message:

```
> Select-Xml  './/HardDisk/@location' kali.vbox
```

The reason for this failure is that the XML file refers to a namespace. In this case, there is only one default namespace (`xmlns`), but some XML files even use multiple namespaces (`xmlns:name`). To process such files, you must pass a hash table to `Select-Xml` that assigns a prefix to each namespace. For the default namespace, `ns` is usually used, but any string is allowed with the exception of `xmlns`. You must subsequently specify the prefix in the XPath expression as well. The following command extracts the name of the image file of a virtual machine:

```
> $vbnamespace = @{ns = "http://www.virtualbox.org/"}

> Select-Xml './/ns:HardDisk/@location' -Namespace $vbnamespace `
  kali.vbox | Select-Object -ExpandProperty Node

  kali-install.vdi
```

The second example scans all virtual machines for active network adapters and returns objects with the **.vbox* filename and the MAC address used. The `Split-Path` cmdlet is used here with the `-Leaf` option to extract the filename from the path.


```
> Select-Xml './/ns:Network/ns:Adapter' `
     -Namespace $vbnamespace *.vbox |
  Where-Object { $_.Node.enabled -eq 'true' } |
  ForEach-Object {
    [PSCustomObject]@{path = Split-Path $_.Path -Leaf;
                      mac = $_.Node.MACAddress}
  }
  path                mac
  ----                ---
  kali-2022.vbox      080027DB966A
  kali.vbox           0800278EB571
  metasplaitable2.vbox 080027E770F0
  ubuntu.vbox         0800278556EA
```

10.4.3 ConvertTo-Xml, Export-Clixml, and Import-Clixml

Finally, I want to briefly introduce three cmdlets for conversions between PowerShell objects and XML documents:

- **`ConvertTo-Xml`**
  `ConvertTo-Xml` converts a PowerShell object into the XML data type:

  ```
  $myxmlvar = Get-Date | ConvertTo-Xml
  ```

  Note that no *official* `ConvertFrom-Xml` cmdlet exists with the reverse function. However, if you search the internet for `ConvertFrom-Xml`, you'll come across various cmdlets from the community that assemble a `PSCustomObject` from an XML document to which it corresponds as much as possible.

- **`Export-Clixml`**
  `Export-Clixml` saves a PowerShell object in an XML file that conforms to the Common Language Infrastructure (CLI) standard:

  ```
  Get-Date | Export-Clixml 'date.xml'
  ```

- **`Import-Clixml`**
  The counterpart reads a file again and creates the corresponding PowerShell object out of it:

  ```
  $olddate = Import-Clixml 'date.xml'
  ```

10.5 XML and Python

Various official (and even more external) XML libraries are available for Python. These modules are optimized for different application purposes, for example, for the particularly efficient processing of large files, for the most secure analysis of XML files, or for creating your own XML documents. The following pages provide a good overview:

- *https://docs.python.org/3/library/xml.html*
- *https://realpython.com/python-xml-parser*

This section focuses on the `xml.etree.ElementTree` module, which ships with Python by default. This module is easy to use and well suited for analyzing XML documents. The following lines show how you can read an XML string or an XML file and access the root element of the XML document:

```
import xml.etree.ElementTree as ET
# read XML file ...
root = ET.parse('filename.xml').getroot()

# ... or process XML from string
s = '<?xml ...>...'
root = ET.fromString(s)
```

`root` is an object of the `Element` class that has the following features:

- `tag`: Name of the current XML tag
- `text`: Text in tag (but no subelements)
- `attrib`: Dictionary with keys of the XML tag

All subelements of an `Element` can be directly looped. The loop variable itself contains `Element` objects as well:

```
for sub in e:  # loop through all sub-elements
```

Alternatively, you can access the *n*th element directly:

```
sub = e[3]     # 4. Sub-element (the count starts with 0)
```

If you want to process all XML elements with a specific name on the current level, you can use the `findall` method:

```
# traverse all <tagname> elements on the current level
for sub in e.findall('tagname'):
```

If you only want to process the first matching subelement anyway, you can omit the loop via `findall` and use `find` instead. Note, however, that the following statement will throw an error if no matching element can be found:

```
# access the first <tagname> element
sub = e.find('tagname')
```

On the other hand, if you want to search for elements on all levels of the XML document, you should use the `iter` method, as in the following example:

```
# traverse all <tagname> elements on all levels
for sub in e.iter('tagname'):
```


If the XML file uses namespaces, you must pass a dictionary with abbreviations for all namespaces used to `find` or `findall`. These tag names must be prefixed with the same abbreviations. Take a look at the third of the following examples, which demonstrates the procedure.

10.5.1 Example: Creating a Dictionary for Country Codes

This crash course is already sufficient for most use cases. The starting point for our first example is the *countries.xml* file, which is structured in the following way:

```
<countries>
  <country code="AF" iso="4">Afghanistan</country>
  <country code="AL" iso="8">Albania</country>
  <country code="DZ" iso="12">Algeria</country>
  ...
</countries>
```

The goal of the following script is to create a dictionary and, in doing so, to use the country codes as keys:

```
# Sample file read-countries.py
import xml.etree.ElementTree as ET
root = ET.parse('countries.xml').getroot()
countries = {}  # empty dictionary
for country in root:
    countries[country.attrib['code']] = country.text

print(countries['CH'])   # output: Switzerland
```

10.5.2 Example: Analyzing an RSS Feed

Many websites provide the option to quickly access the latest articles via a *Rich Site Summary Feed (RSS feed)*. For example, the RSS feed for the BBC World News website can be found at *http://feeds.bbci.co.uk/news/world/rss.xml*.

The resulting file has the following structure (strongly shortened):

```
<?xml-stylesheet ... ?>
<rss xmlns:dc="http://purl.org/dc/elements/1.1/"
     xmlns:content="http://purl.org/rss/1.0/modules/...">
  <channel>
    <title><![CDATA[BBC News - World]]></title>
    <lastBuildDate>Thu, 23 Feb 2023 11:02:41 GMT</lastBuildDate>
    <copyright>....</copyright>
    <item>
      <title><![CDATA[Gaza-Israel exchange of fire ...]]></title>
      <link>https://www.bbc.co.uk/news/world-...</link>
      <pubDate>Thu, 23 Feb 2023 09:22:38 GMT</pubDate>
    </item>
    <item>
    ...
```

The goal of the script is to display the headlines and links of the 10 latest articles, as in the following example:

```
$ ./read-bbc-news.py

  * Gaza-Israel exchange of fire follows deadly West Bank raid
    https://www.bbc.co.uk/news/world-middle-east-64742259
  * Selfie image shows US pilot flying over Chinese 'spy balloon'
    https://www.bbc.co.uk/news/world-us-canada-64735538
  ...
```

The required code looks as follows:

```
# Sample file bbc-world-news.py
import xml.etree.ElementTree as ET
import urllib.request

url = 'http://feeds.bbci.co.uk/news/world/rss.xml'
response = urllib.request.urlopen(url)
binary = response.read()       # binary data
txt = binary.decode('utf-8')   # convert to UTF-8 text
root = ET.fromstring(txt)      # RSS root tag
cnt = 0
for item in root.iter('item'): # loop through all items
```

```
    print('*', item.find('title').text)
    print(' ', item.find('link').text)
    cnt += 1
    if cnt >= 10:
        break
```

10.5.3 Example: Extracting MAC Addresses from Virtual Machine Files

As described earlier in Section 10.4, the following Python script also extracts MAC addresses from the **.vbox* files that have been passed as parameters:

```
$ ./vbox-mac.py vbox/*.vbox

      kali-2022.vbox: MAC=080027DB966A
   kali-english.vbox: MAC=080027B8A33A
                 ...
```


Since the **.vbox* file uses a namespace, the `iter` method cannot be used. Instead, the `find` and `findall` methods are used, each passing a dictionary with the namespace prefix as an additional parameter:

```
# Sample file vbox-mac.py
import os, sys
import xml.etree.ElementTree as ET
namesp = { 'ns': 'http://www.virtualbox.org/'}
for xmlfile in sys.argv[1:]:
    basename = os.path.basename(xmlfile)
    root = ET.parse(xmlfile).getroot()
    machine = root.find('ns:Machine', namesp)
    hardware = machine.find('ns:Hardware', namesp)
    network = hardware.find('ns:Network', namesp)
    for adapter in network.findall('ns:Adapter', namesp):
        if 'MACAddress' in adapter.attrib:
            print('%30s: MAC=%s' %
              (basename, adapter.attrib['MACAddress']))
```

10.6 XML in Bash

Bash can't handle XML documents any more than it can handle JSON files. A possible workaround in this context is external commands, but these commands must be installed separately. On Linux, you can use the package management tools for your distribution, while on macOS the best choice is to use Homebrew.

10.6.1 xmllint

The `xmllint` command displays XML documents with indentations in a readable way and verifies their compliance with XML syntax rules. If an XML file cannot be edited at all, a short test using `xmllint` is appropriate. On macOS, the command is installed by default, but on Linux, the command is hidden in different packages, depending on the distribution:

```
$ sudo apt install libxml2-utils    (Debian, Ubuntu)
$ sudo dnf install libxml2          (Fedora, RHEL)
$ yay -yS libxml2                   (Arch Linux)
```

In the simplest case, you pass the filename of an XML file to `xmllint`. The command verifies the XML syntax and either returns an error message or outputs the file unchanged.

```
$ xmllint countries-malformed.xml

  countries-malformed.xml:6: parser error: Opening and ending tag
    mismatch: country line 4 and countries </countries>
  countries-malformed.xml:7: parser error : Premature end of data
    in tag country line 4
```

Optionally, you can also validate an XML file against a *document type definition (DTD)* or *XML schema definition (XSD)*. You can correctly indent syntactically correct XML files with `--format` to improve readability:

```
$ xmllint --format countries-unformatted.xml

  <?xml version="1.0"?>
  <countries>
    <country code="AF" iso="4">Afghanistan</country>
    ...
```

Finally, you can also process XPath expressions using `xmllint`, as in the following example:

```
$ xmllint --xpath '/*/MapTZ[57]/@WinID' timezone-mapping.xml

  WinID="Mountain Standard Time"
```

To use `xmllint` as a filter, you must pass a single minus sign as a parameter, for example, in the following code:

```
$ curl -s <url> | xmllint - --format
```

Not Namespace Compatible

XPath expressions in `xmllint` can only be analyzed correctly if the XML document does not use namespaces. Although you can find instructions on the internet on how to work around this limitation, using another tool is a better approach. One option is the `xmlstarlet`, which I'll describe next.

10.6.2 XMLStarlet

On Linux and macOS, the `xmlstarlet` package provides the `xmlstarlet` command or simply `xml` (e.g., on Arch Linux). This package provides significantly more editing options than `xmllint`, especially for modifying XML documents. However, the project died down, and the current version has not been updated since 2014.

At this point, I will only describe the `sel` subcommand for analyzing XPath expressions. The following command first defines the `ns` abbreviation for the default namespace in **.vbox* files. `-t -v 'xpath` applies the specified XPath expression to the XML file and outputs the resulting value (`-v` for *value*). `-n` adds a newline to the output.

```
$ xml|xmlstarlet sel -N ns='http://www.virtualbox.org/' \
         -t -v  './/ns:HardDisk/@location' -n vbox/*.vbox

  Kali-Linux-2022.2-virtualbox-amd64-disk001.vdi
  kali-english.vdi
  ...
```

You can find information on the rather unintuitive syntax of `xml sel` via `xml sel --help`. Further documentation can be found at *https://xmlstar.sourceforge.net/docs.php*.

10.7 INI Files

INI files are text files for storing key-value pairs. An INI file can be divided into various sections by using `[section]`:

```
; File config.ini
[server]
hostname = example.com
port = 8080

[data]
imagePath = /mnt/images
dbName = mydb
```

INI files are often used to store configuration data. Only semicolons are provided for marking comments. Especially in the Linux environment, however, `#` is also mostly accepted.

10.7.1 Python

The easiest way to read INI files in Python is to use the ConfigParser module. The following listing shows the intuitive application. Note that the parser always returns strings. If you want to use port number 8080 as a number, you must perform an appropriate conversion using int().

```
# Sample file read-config.py
from configparser import ConfigParser
config = ConfigParser()
config.read('config.ini')
print(config['server']['port'])    # output: 8080
```

10.7.2 PowerShell

Although INI files are quite commonly used on Windows, PowerShell lacks a cmdlet to easily read this type of file. In many cases, you can simple use the following commands:

```
> $config = Get-Content 'config.ini' |
            Select-String '^.*=.*[^=]*$' |
            ConvertFrom-StringData

> $config.port
  8080
```

Get-Content reads the file and delivers it line by line. Select-String uses a regular expression to filter out all lines that match the key = value pattern. ConvertFrom-StringData turns the key-value pairs into a hash table.

However, this simple approach reaches its limits when the same keys are used in different groups. If you want to analyze complex INI files without falling into syntactical traps, you're better off using the popular PsIni extension, available at *https://www.powershellgallery.com/packages/PsIni*.

10.7.3 Bash

Like PowerShell, Bash lacks functions to parse INI files. In many Linux distributions, you can use crudini for this purpose. However, you must install the package of the same name beforehand. However, note that this package is itself a Python script! crudini therefore only works if Python is also installed.

To read a single value, you can simply pass the INI file, the section name, and the key name. You can find various other types of applications in crudini --help.

```
$ crudini --get config.ini server port
  8080
```

Chapter 11
Running Scripts Automatically

Many scripts aim to automate admin tasks such as running backups, uploading changed/new files, monitoring, and logging servers. This chapter describes ways to run scripts automatically on a regular basis. I am going to focus primarily on two processes: *cron* for Linux and Microsoft Windows Task Scheduler. I will also briefly discuss mechanisms for tracking changes in the file system "live," so to speak, and responding immediately.

Prerequisites for This Chapter

The automation of scripts is detached from the choice of script language. In this respect, you can read this chapter largely independently from the rest of this book. Section 11.1 on cron is easier to understand if you have some prior knowledge of Linux system administration. In particular, you must be able to modify system files using a text editor.

The examples presented in this chapter draw on working techniques from the previous chapters, such as using the `curl` command (see Chapter 8) or analyzing XML files (see Chapter 10).

A good follow-up to this chapter would be Chapter 15, where you'll find further application examples for the methods presented in this chapter.

11.1 cron

cron is a background program that runs on almost every Linux server. Its task is to start commands or scripts at fixed times, for example, every day at 3:00 am or every Sunday at 11:00 pm. cron is controlled by the */etc/crontab* file, whose somewhat strange syntax I will explain in a moment.

cron is installed by default on many Linux distributions. If the */etc/crontab* file does not exist on your system, you can easily resolve the situation:

```
$ sudo apt update && sudo install cron      (Debian, Ubuntu)
$ sudo dnf install cronie && \              (Fedora, RHEL)
  sudo systemctl enable --now crond
```

11.1.1 /etc/crontab

The following lines show an excerpt from a *crontab* file:

```
# File /etc/crontab
# every day at 3:00 am: Backup
0 3 * * * root /etc/myscripts/backup.sh
# on the first day of each month at 0:00:
# statistical analysis of login data
0 0 1 * * root /etc/myscripts/statistics.py
```

`crontab` files describe the commands to be executed line by line, where each entry is composed of seven columns:

```
minutes hours day-of-month month weekday user cmd
```

- `minutes`: 0-59
- `hours`: 0-12
- `day-of-month`: 1-31
- `month`: 1-12
- `weekday`: 0-7 (0 = 7 = Sunday, 1 = Monday, etc.)
- `user`: Account under which the script should be executed (often `root`)
- `cmd`: The command to execute, often simply the path to a script

Lines beginning with # are comments. The last line of the *crontab* file must end with a newline character. The following syntax rules apply to the first five columns in the *crontab* file:

- Enumerations: `7,9,12` (without spaces!)
- Sections: `3-5`
- Always: `*`
- All `n`: `*/10` corresponds to `0,10,20,30...`

The columns are usually linked by a logical AND. An exception is if `day-of-month` and `weekday` are specified; then, a logical OR applies to these two columns. The command is executed both on the *n*th day of the month and on the specified day of the week.

The following listing contains some syntax examples. You can verify your own cron time compositions at *https://crontab.guru*.

```
# every 15 minutes
*/15 * * * * root cmd
# daily at 0:15, 1:15, 2:15, etc.
15 * * * * peter cmd
# daily at 1:30
30 1 * * * maria cmd
```

```
# every Saturday at 0:29
29 0 * * 6 root cmd
# on every 1st of the month at 6:25
25 6 1 * * www-data cmd
# on the 1st and 15th of the month and every Monday
# always at midnight
0 0 1,15 * 1 root cmd
```

Provided that cron jobs are executed on a machine where a mail server is configured, the output or error messages are sent to `root@localhost`. You can change this address by setting `MAILTO=...` within */etc/crontab*.

Trouble with PATH and LANG

A different `PATH` default setting applies to cron jobs than in interactive mode. Changes to `PATH` in *.bashrc* are not taken into account. For this reason, commands installed outside the usual directories like */usr/bin* or */usr/sbin* cannot be executed!

You should therefore make sure to test whether your script is also executed correctly when started by cron. If necessary, you must specify the full path in the script for manually installed commands, for example, */usr/local/bin/aws* to run the Amazon Web Services (AWS) client. Alternatively, for some cron implementations, you can redefine the `PATH` variable directly in */etc/crontab*. There you need to specify all directories in which commands are to be searched for, for example as follows:

```
PATH=/usr/local/sbin:/usr/local/bin:/sbin:/bin:/usr/sbin:/usr/bin
```

Another possible source of errors can be the `LANG` environment variable, which may have a different setting in cron jobs than when you run your scripts locally. A setting in */etc/crontab* like for `PATH` is not possible. However, you can set `LANG` at the beginning of your script.

11.1.2 Personal crontab Files

Modifying */etc/crontab* requires system administrator privileges. If these privileges are not available to you, you can modify your own *crontab* file. This file is located in */var/spool/cron/<user>* or in */var/spool/cron/crontabs/<user>*, depending on the Linux distribution.

You can open your personal crontab file using the `crontab -e` command. By default, the vi editor is used in this context, which is not user friendly. If you've started the program by mistake, you can exit it by pressing [Esc], typing ":q!," and pressing [Enter] without saving changes. If necessary, you can select a simpler editor via the `EDITOR` variable before running the `crontab` command:

```
$ export EDITOR=/usr/bin/nano
$ crontab -e
```

Note that the sixth column for the account is omitted in the private *crontab* file. The command or script is always executed with the rights of your account. This limitation is the biggest disadvantage of this method: Many admin tasks (such as system-wide backups) require root privileges and cannot be performed in "ordinary" accounts. `sudo` does not help in this case either because this command requires the interactive input of your password.

11.1.3 Hourly, Daily, Weekly, and Monthly Directories

If you don't care about the exact time when your cron tasks are performed, you can save the script to be called in one of the following directories:

- */etc/cron.hourly*
- */etc/cron.daily*
- */etc/cron.weekly*
- */etc/cron.monthly*

The benefit of this method is that you do not need to deal with the crontab syntax. Remember to mark your script file as executable by using `chmod +x`! Your scripts will be executed with root privileges.

11.1.4 Alternatives to cron

On Linux, *systemd-timer* is becoming more frequently used. The biggest advantage of systemd-timer compared to cron is that started jobs can be monitored more comprehensively. But this advantage is offset by a much higher degree of complexity. While setting up a cron job can be done in 30 seconds with a little experience, timer jobs require you create *two* relatively complex configuration files. A good description of the mechanism can be found on the Arch Linus wiki at *https://wiki.archlinux.org/title/Systemd/Timers*. This information also applies to other distributions.

11.1.5 Starting Jobs Automatically on macOS

cron is also available on macOS but is considered obsolete there. The */etc/crontab* file does not exist by default. However, you only need to create the file (for example, using `sudo nano /etc/crontab`) and insert one correct entry; then, the job will be executed without any further configuration work. In this respect, cron is the simplest solution for automating the script call for macOS until further notice.

Apple recommends using the macOS-specific *launchd* program instead of cron. The configuration is done by XML files, whose syntax is documented here:

- *https://bas-man.dev/post/launchd-instead-of-cron*
- *https://developer.apple.com/library/archive/documentation/MacOSX/Conceptual/BPSystemStartup/Chapters/ScheduledJobs.html*

11.2 Example: Web Server Monitoring

For this example, we want to use curl to measure the time it takes to download the home page of a website. The curl command is written in the following way:

```
time=$(curl --connect-timeout 2 -s -S -w '%{time_total}\n' \
       -o /dev/null  2> /tmp/curl.error \
       https://example.com)
```

The various components of this command have the following meanings:

- --connect-timeout 2 aborts the connection setup attempt after 2 seconds.
- -s suppresses status outputs about the download progress.
- -S allows error outputs in deviation from this option.
- -w writes the runtime of the command to the standard output. This information ends up in the time variable.
- -o redirects the downloaded HTML file to /dev/null. Nothing is stored in this Linux-specific pseudo file.
- 2> redirects error outputs to the specified file.

In the script, a similar command analyzes the TMPFILE and HOST variables. The LANG= setting ensures that curl and date format numbers and dates in an international way. (The command unsets the LANG variable.)

If the curl command terminates with an error code, cat writes the error message to standard output. If the script is executed by cron, this output is sent by email to root@localhost (or to another address specified by MAILTO in */etc/crontab*). So, if the configuration is correct, you'll be notified by email whenever the website stops working correctly.

If, on the other hand, curl was executed without error and without exceeding the timeout time, echo saves the required time and the current time into the file specified by LOGFILE.

```
# Sample file webserver-ping.sh
LANG=
HOST=example.com
LOGFILE=/var/log/$HOST-ping-time.log
TMPFILE=/tmp/curl.error

time=$(curl --connect-timeout 2 -s -S -w '%{time_total}\n' \
       -o /dev/null  2> $TMPFILE \
       https://$HOST)

if [ $? -ne 0 ]; then
  # output is sent per mail if script is
```

```
  # run by cron on a Linux system with mail server
  cat $TMPFILE
else
  now=$(date)
  echo "$time sec @ $now" >> $LOGFILE
fi
```

To run the script every 15 minutes, I added the following line to */etc/crontab*:

```
# in /etc/crontab
*/15 * * * * kofler /home/kofler/bin/webserver-ping.sh
```

Now, the script inside the home directory of `kofler` in the `bin` subdirectory should be executed every 15 minutes with the rights held by the `kofler` account. The resulting */var/log/example.com-ping-time.log* file has the following structure:

```
0.347425 sec @ Mon Feb 27 12:30:01 CET 2023
0.347546 sec @ Mon Feb 27 12:45:02 CET 2023
...
```

11.2.1 Testing and Troubleshooting

Unlike many other examples in this book, this script cannot be easily tried out on any computer. You would need a Linux system with cron, ideally together with a mail server.

You also must modify the configuration variables at the beginning of the script to suit your own needs. If you do not run the script with root privileges, you must ensure that the logging file was writable for the script. If the script is executed by `kofler` while `HOST` and `LOGFILE` remain unchanged, you must execute the following two commands once:

```
$ sudo touch /var/log/example.com-ping-time.log
$ sudo chown kofler:root /var/log/example.com-ping-time.log
```

Once the script can be run manually without errors, the next step is to set up */etc/crontab*. For initial tests, the recommended approach is to set the first five columns using `* * * * *`, which will execute the script once per minute.

Syntax errors in */etc/crontab* will prevent both your script and other cron jobs from running. To track down such errors, run `systemctl status cron` and `journalctl -u cron`, which will provide you with information about the current cron status as well as the last logging outputs.

11.2.2 Real Monitoring

Selling this mini script as a monitoring solution is a bit daring. "Real" monitoring software checks various server parameters, sends warning emails only on every status message (and not on every error, which leads to an abundance of monitoring mails), offers a graphical visualization of the monitored parameters, and more.

Of course, you could conceivably implement all these capabilities using custom scripts, but using dedicated monitoring tools, such as *Grafana*, *Prometheus*, *Nagios*, etc., make much more sense. Although the initial startup of these tools may require considerable work, they provide a wealth of functions combined with expedient user interfaces (UIs).

11.3 Microsoft Windows Task Scheduler

Microsoft Windows Task Scheduler allows Windows to run programs and scripts at specified times and is, therefore, the Windows counterpart to cron. The program is equipped with a UI, as you would expect in the Windows environment. However, Microsoft Windows Task Scheduler has all the charm of the 1990s, to put it nicely. Its nested dialogs are, at best, as intuitive as the `crontab` syntax. Also, the program is amazingly slow and sometimes it hangs completely. If the start of jobs does not work as intended, no clear error messages are displayed despite event logging. In a nutshell, using this program is a pain. Why Microsoft can't get its act together and reimplement this central Windows component remains a mystery. (The current version has not been significantly changed since 2006.)

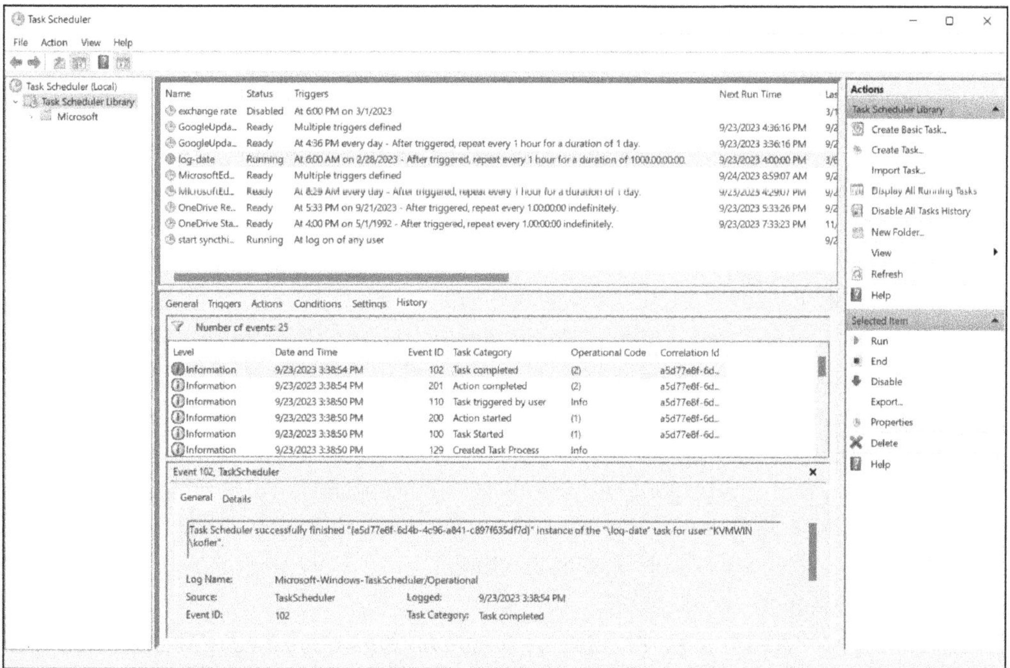

Figure 11.1 Microsoft Windows Task Scheduler's Antiquated UI

To become familiar with Microsoft Windows Task Scheduler, let's create a tiny script that logs the date and time to a logging file:

```
# File log-date.ps1
Get-Date >> date.log
```

This script is supposed to be executed every hour. For this purpose, open Microsoft Windows Task Scheduler and click the **Create Task** command in the **Actions** sidebar. This step will take you to a dialog box with several tabs:

- **General**

  In this tab, you can give the task a name, specify in which account your script should be run (usually your own), and specify whether it should be started only after a login or always when the computer is running.

  If you want to run a script with administrator privileges, you should not change the user or group, but just click the **Run with highest privileges** option.

- **Triggers**

  In this tab, you can add a new trigger to specify when and how often the action should take place. To run the script every hour, you must select **Daily** with the current time as the start time and **Repeat task every hour** as well as **For a duration of: 1 day**. (The more plausible setting **For the duration of: Indefinitely** did not work in my tests.)

  In contrast to cron, not only does Microsoft Windows Task Scheduler support time-based triggers, but it can also execute actions when various events occur, for example, when logging in or when the computer is currently in idle mode.

- **Actions**

  As a new action, you specify the script to be run. The procedure is more cumbersome than you would expect: The reason is that as a **program/script**, you must not simply specify the path of your PowerShell script file. Instead, you need to specify `pwsh` for PowerShell 7.*n* here. Only if your script is to be executed by the older Windows PowerShell 5.*n* is the program name `powershell`.

  In the **Add arguments** input field, specify the `-File` option and enter the full path to your script. When typing, you must not make any typos. Do not forget `-File`!

  By default, the `%Windir%\System32\` directory is active when the script is run. If you do not want to use this directory (e.g., because the script should read or write files in a different directory), you must specify the relevant directory in the **Start in** field. For the sample script to log the date and time in the same directory where the script file is located, you must specify this directory.

- **Conditions**

  This tab defaults to performing the action only when your computer is running in network mode. You can deactivate this option if you also want to run or test the task while using your notebook in battery mode.

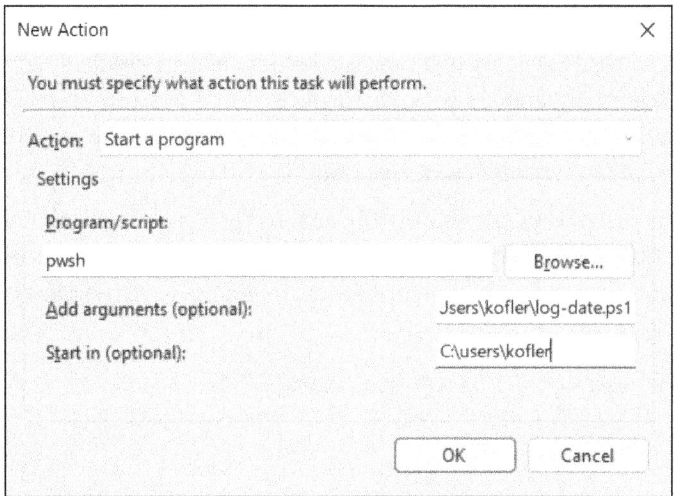

Figure 11.2 The log-date.ps1 Script to Be Run by PowerShell, with C:\Users\kofler as the Active Directory

- **Settings**
  Finally, you can adjust some settings, including whether your task should be completed exactly at the scheduled time; whether it can be run at a later time; whether the process should be terminated automatically after a certain runtime (by default, an absurd 3 days is used here!); and more. For our initial tests, you can leave all the options in their default settings.

With a little luck, the script should run right away. You can check whether the script has run by looking at the *date.log* file in the set directory (**Start in**). From now on, another line with the current time should be added to this file every hour.

11.3.1 Troubleshooting

From experience, automated script execution does not always work right away. For troubleshooting purposes, your first step should be to enable the **Enable All Tasks History** command in Microsoft Windows Task Scheduler. Behind this somewhat cryptic description is a logging function. Microsoft Windows Task Scheduler can log when actions are started and why, when they end, and more.

You can also use the **Run** command to start a script manually at any time, regardless of the selected trigger time. In the action list, in the **Next Run Time** column, you can see what the next regular start time of your script is.

On one of my test machines, Microsoft Windows Task Scheduler was completely unable to find `pwsh`, despite (presumably) correct `PATH` settings. In the event logging, only *file not found* was logged, without a clear indication as to which file was not found (`pwsh`, the script, another file?). Ultimately, I uninstalled PowerShell entirely, reinstalled it using `winget`, and rebooted the machine. After that, it worked.

11.3.2 Setting Up Tasks via cmdlets

Fortunately, Microsoft Windows Task Scheduler can also be controlled by cmdlets. `Get-ScheduledTask` returns a seemingly endless list of all actions stored in the system. If you've ever wondered why Windows often feels so sluggish, now you know the reason. On my test computer, the cmdlet returned 165 active tasks!

The Windows Task Manager UI always shows only the actions for a specific path—by default, those for the \ path, that is, for the root directory of the *task library*. You can view all other actions when you select a subdirectory, for example, *Microsoft\Windows\Bitlocker*.

```
> Get-ScheduledTask | Where-Object { $_.State -ne 'Disabled' }

  TaskPath                TaskName                      State
  --------                --------                      -----
  \                       GoogleUpdateTaskMachine...    Ready
  \                       log date                      Ready
  \                       start syncthing               Running
  \Microsoft\Windows\...  .NET Framework NGEN v4.0...   Ready
  ...
```

For Windows Only!

All cmdlets presented in this section are available only when you run PowerShell scripts on Windows. On Linux and macOS, no task scheduler exists, but other mechanisms (i.e., cron, systemd-timer, and launchd) can be used instead, but these capabilities cannot be controlled via cmdlets.

`Get-ScheduledTaskInfo` allows you to determine when the task was last performed and when the next start is scheduled:

```
> Get-ScheduledTaskInfo 'log date'
  LastRunTime        : 02.28.2023 09:24:24
  NextRunTime        : 02.28.2023 11:20:20
  NumberOfMissedRuns : 1
  ...

> Get-ScheduledTask 'log date' | Get-ScheduledTaskInfo
  (same result)
```

By combining a few cmdlets, you can even set up a new task. Here `New-ScheduledTaskTrigger` creates an object for the schedule and `New-ScheduledTaskAction` creates an object for the task. `Register-ScheduledTask` saves the new job.

```
> $trigger = New-ScheduledTaskTrigger -Once -At '6:00am' `
             -RepetitionInterval (New-TimeSpan -Hours 1) `
             -RepetitionDuration (New-TimeSpan -Days 1000)
> $action = New-ScheduledTaskAction  -Execute 'pwsh' `
             -Argument '-File C:\Users\kofler\log-date.ps1' `
             -WorkingDirectory 'C:\Users\kofler'
> Register-ScheduledTask -TaskName 'log-date' `
             -Trigger $trigger -Action $action

  TaskPath   TaskName   State
  --------   --------   -----
  \          log-date   Ready
```

11.4 Example: Saving Exchange Rates

The European National Bank publishes official reference rates between the euro and other major currencies once a day at *https://www.ecb.europa.eu/stats/eurofxref/eurofxref-daily.xml*. A sample of the daily XML file is shown in the following example:

```
<?xml version="1.0" encoding="UTF-8"?>
<gesmes:Envelope
  xmlns:gesmes="http://www.gesmes.org/xml/2002-08-01"
  xmlns="http://www.ecb.int/vocabulary/2002-08-01/eurofxref">
  <gesmes:subject>Reference rates</gesmes:subject>
  <gesmes:Sender>
    <gesmes:name>European Central Bank</gesmes:name>
  </gesmes:Sender>
  <Cube>
    <Cube time="2023-03-01">
      <Cube currency="USD" rate="1.0684"/>
      <Cube currency="JPY" rate="144.82"/>
      <Cube currency="CHF" rate="0.9997"/>
      ...
```

The goal of the following example is to save the exchange rate between the Euro and the Swiss Franc (CHF) once a day in a comma-separated values (CSV) file, which should have the following format:

```
date;chf_rate
2023-03-01;0.9997
```

We don't want the current date logged but instead the date embedded in the XML file using the `<Cube time=...>` tag. Analyzing the file is relatively easy despite the strange `cube` nesting (see Chapter 10, Section 10.4). The only new feature at this point is the

Invoke-RestMethod cmdlet for downloading the XML file, which I'll introduce in more detail in Chapter 18.

```
# Sample file get-exchange-rate.ps1
# download and analyze XML document
$csv = "chf-rates.csv"
$url = "https://www.ecb.europa.eu/stats/eurofxref/
         eurofxref-daily.xml"
$ecb = Invoke-RestMethod $url
$date = $ecb.Envelope.Cube.Cube.time
$rate = ($ecb.Envelope.Cube.Cube.Cube |
          Where-Object {$_.currency -eq 'CHF'}).rate
# if needed, create CSV file
if (!(Test-Path $csv)) {
    "date;chf_rate" | Out-File $csv
}
# add current rate
Add-Content $csv "$date;$rate"
```

Now, you just need to register the script with Microsoft Windows Task Scheduler for the daily call. Since the rates are usually updated around 4 pm Central European Time, a convenient time for the daily call is between 5 pm and 6 pm.

Since the ECB calculates exchange rates only on business days, the CSV file will contain doubles if executed daily. If you want, you can enhance the script to check if there is already an entry for the date contained in $date before you use Add-Content.

11.5 Tracking File System Changes

Relatively often, a scenario arises where, instead of executing actions at a predefined time, they should be executed when files change or when new files are added. The script that runs most often in my daily work monitors all Markdown files in a local directory. As soon as a file changes, the script calls various commands to create an updated PDF from the Markdown file with a preview of the chapter I'm working on. This Bash script has the following structure:

```
# Sample file run-pandoc.sh
while true; do
    for mdfile in *.md; do
        pdffile=${mdfile%.md}.pdf
        if [ $mdfile -nt $pdffile ]; then
            echo $mdfile
            pandoc ... $mdfile -o $pdffile
        fi
    done
    sleep 1
done
```

This script is easy to understand: `while true` forms an infinite loop. As a result, the script runs until it is stopped via Ctrl + C. `for mdfile` runs through all `*.md` files and then checks with the `-nt` operator (*newer than*) whether the Markdown file is newer than the corresponding PDF file. In this case, the name of the Markdown file is output, and a new PDF file is created using `pandoc`, which is a command to convert documents between different formats (see *https://pandoc.org*).

A crucial component of the script is `sleep`, which causes the script to pause for 1 second after each run. (Depending on the purpose of monitoring the directory, a longer pause is also conceivable.) Without `sleep`, the script would completely utilize a CPU. If you use `sleep`, however, the CPU load caused by the script is negligible.

This task can be solved just as elegantly with PowerShell. The only difference is the `if` condition, which also contains an additional test that checks whether the PDF file exists at all. If the PDF file doesn't exist, the comparison of `LastWriteTimeUtc` would result in an error. Bash is a bit more laid back in this regard.


```
# Sample file run-pandoc.ps1
while($true) {
    foreach($mdfile in Get-ChildItem -Path *.md) {
        $pdffile = $mdfile.FullName.Replace(".md", ".pdf")
        if(!(Test-Path $pdffile) -or
            ($mdfile.LastWriteTimeUtc -gt
             (Get-Item $pdffile).LastWriteTimeUtc))
        {
            Write-Host $mdfile.Name
            C:\path\to\pandoc.exe $mdfile.FullName -o $pdffile
        }
    }
    Start-Sleep -Seconds 1
}
```

11.5.1 inotify

The scripts presented earlier are only useful if the number of files to be monitored is small. Isn't there any better solution? Yes, depending on the operating system and programming language you use.

At this point, I will focus on using the `inotify` function, which is a Linux kernel function for monitoring the file system. You can use this function to register a directory, and you will subsequently always be notified when changes occur in this directory.

To use `inotify` in Python scripts, you first must install the `pyinotify` module with the following command:

```
$ pip[3] install pyinotify
```

To this function, you must create a `WatchManager` object. By using `add_watch`, you can specify which file or directory you want to monitor, which events you want to process (in this case, `IN_CLOSE_WRITE`, that is, closing a file after a change) and which function will then be called. Then, you pass the `WatchManager` object to the `Notifier`. Using `loop`, you start the event processing. As in our earlier example, `loop` also initiates an infinite loop. So, the script runs until you stop it via [Ctrl] + [C].

The `runPandoc` function is responsible for calling the `pandoc` command. However, it must first be tested whether the modified file is a Markdown file at all. (Unfortunately, you cannot pass patterns like `*.md` to `add_watch`.) For this purpose, the `ev` parameter (like *event*) is analyzed, which contains details about the event that occurred.

```
# Sample file run-pandoc.py
import pyinotify, subprocess

# this function is called by pyinotify
def runPandoc(ev):
    if ev.name.endswith('.md'):
        mdfile = ev.name
        pdffile = mdfile.replace('.md', '.pdf')
        cmd = 'pandoc %s -o %s' % (mdfile, pdffile)
        print(cmd)
        subprocess.run(cmd, shell=True)

wm = pyinotify.WatchManager()
wm.add_watch('.', pyinotify.IN_CLOSE_WRITE, runPandoc)
notifier = pyinotify.Notifier(wm)
notifier.loop()
```

In Bash scripts, you can use the `inotify` functions with the `inotifywait` and `inotifywatch` commands, but you must first install the `inotify-tools` package. Some simple application examples are documented at *https://github.com/inotify-tools/inotify-tools/wiki#inotifywait*.

11.5.2 Alternatives to inotify

On macOS, the *file system events (FSEvents) API* provides similar functions. In scripts, the easiest way to use FSEvents is with the `fswatch` command. This command can be installed using `brew`, as described at *https://github.com/emcrisostomo/fswatch*.

Another monitoring option is provided by the `launchd` program. For a simple use case, see this Stack Overflow post: *https://stackoverflow.com/a/1516034*.

On Windows, you can use the `FileSystemWatcher` feature. However, using this .NET feature is quite complicated. A code example for PowerShell is available at *https://powershell.one/tricks/filesystem/filesystemwatcher*.

Chapter 12
SSH

Secure Shell (SSH) has been the preferred method on Linux and macOS for decades to work in text mode on another computer and execute commands there. Fortunately, Microsoft also jumped on the SSH bandwagon a few years ago, so SSH finally works across platforms. For scripting, SSH is important for two reasons:

- Using SSH, you can work on other computers, create scripts there, and finally execute them. SSH is an admin requirement, especially for server administration.

  But you don't always have to connect to a server! I often use SSH to work on my Raspberry Pi as well. The Raspberry Pi does not need a screen or keyboard for this connectivity—a network connection suffices. Likewise, this simplicity applies to the numerous virtual machines in my everyday work: I often don't need a graphical user interface (GUI) at all and can enter the relevant commands or scripting programming in a terminal with an SSH connection.

  In addition, the Visual Studio Code (VS Code) editor and SSH make a good team. You can learn more about VS Code in Chapter 13.
- For many scripts, the ability to transfer files or entire directories securely between different computers is at least as important. The `scp` and `rsync` commands and the Secure FTP (SFTP) protocol use SSH. Backup and upload scripts therefore often require SSH access. You also need to know how authentication works with SSH keys. The handling of such keys is therefore an important topic in this chapter.

Prerequisites for This Chapter

As far as scripting is concerned, no content-related prerequisites must be fulfilled, which means you can read this chapter independently from all other chapters. The sample scripts assume that you have basic knowledge of Bash and PowerShell. You should also be familiar with the `find` command (see Chapter 6, Section 6.2). As far as you work on Linux, basic admin knowledge is of course always an advantage.

12.1 Installing the SSH Client and Server

To establish an SSH connection from local computer A to a second computer B, an SSH client must be available on computer A (usually the `ssh` command), and an SSH server must be running on B. This section describes the prerequisites you must fulfill before you can use SSH.

12.1.1 Linux

On Linux, the ssh command is part of the basic vocabulary, so to speak, and is almost always installed. You can see for yourself via ssh -V in the terminal. This command displays the installed version.

```
$ ssh -V

  OpenSSH_9.2p1, OpenSSL 3.0.8 7 Feb 2023
```

If the ssh command is indeed not installed, you can install the ssh command in the following ways:

```
$ sudo apt update                     (Debian, Ubuntu)
$ sudo apt install openssh-client

$ sudo dnf install openssh-client     (Fedora, Red Hat)
```

The operation of an SSH server is not quite as self-evident. The following short test can provide clarity:

```
$ systemctl status sshd

  sshd.service - OpenSSH Daemon
     Loaded: loaded (...)
     Active: active (running) since ...
```

If the sshd service is not known or not running, the installation will succeed in no time. I have again summarized the commands for the most important distributions here:

```
$ sudo apt update                     (Debian, Ubuntu)
$ sudo apt install openssh-server

$ sudo dnf install openssh-server     (Fedora, Red Hat)
$ systemctl enable --now sshd
```

12.1.2 macOS

On macOS, the SSH client and server are already installed. However, the SSH server must be explicitly enabled. For this task, open the **General • Share** module in the **System Preferences** and enable the **Remote login** option. Done!

12.1.3 Windows

In current Windows versions, the SSH client (i.e., the ssh command) is installed by default, whereas the SSH server is not. To install missing components, you must open the **Settings** program. You can find the *OpenSSH client* and the *OpenSSH server*—well hidden—under **Apps • Optional features • Add an optional feature**. (Why the program can't simply be installed via the Microsoft Store defies any logic. But I won't complain here; it's great that Microsoft finally offers an official SSH client and server, making the installation of the dreadfully outdated PuTTY program unnecessary.)

You can run the SSH client with the `ssh` command in the terminal after the installation. With regard to the SSH server, one more step is necessary. The program is installed but is not yet running as a service. The solution is the **Services** program, which you can find in the **Start** menu. Search for the *OpenSSH Server* item and double-click to open the settings dialog. Then, click the **Start** button to start the server service for the first time. You also must set **Startup type = Automatic** to always activate the service when the computer boots up in the future.

Instead of clicking through settings dialogs, you can also perform the installation and service startup in the terminal with the following commands:


```
> Add-WindowsCapability -Online -Name OpenSSH.Client
> Add-WindowsCapability -Online -Name OpenSSH.Server
> Start-Service sshd
> Set-Service -Name sshd -StartupType 'Automatic'
```

If you then log on to your Windows computer from an external computer via SSH, you'll abruptly land in the IT Stone Age. Inexplicably, the SSH server uses `cmd.exe` as the default shell. To enable you to use PowerShell within the SSH session, you must run `pwsh`.

For PowerShell to be used automatically on every SSH login, you must modify a registry entry. You can achieve this task using the following three commands, which must be executed with admin rights in a terminal:

```
> $PSPATH = (Get-Command -Name pwsh).path
> New-Item "HKLM:\Software\OpenSSH" -Force
> New-ItemProperty "HKLM:\SOFTWARE\OpenSSH"  -Name DefaultShell `
    -Value "$PSPATH" -PropertyType String -Force
```

Suddenly "Permission Denied" Displays at SSH Login

If the location where *pwsh.exe* is stored changes during a PowerShell update or during a new PowerShell installation, the SSH server can no longer start PowerShell. However, the error message in such cases is meaningless: *Permission denied*.

This problem can stem from countless reasons, from the wrong password to the incorrect configuration of *opensshd_config*. However, one possible cause of errors is a changed path to *pwsh.exe*.

Automatically Administrator

If you perform an SSH login for a user who has admin rights, then you get these rights immediately in the SSH session.

An important difference arises with interactive work: Usually, you work with reduced rights and only perform actions with admin rights when necessary—for example, by explicitly starting a terminal with admin rights. In this regard, Windows also behaves differently from Linux or macOS, where you must explicitly request administrator rights for individual commands via sudo.

12.1.4 Using an Editor in an SSH Session

On Linux or macOS, the matter is trivial: To modify a file directly in an SSH session, you simply need to launch an editor. nano and vim are almost always available. If required, you can separately install countless other editors such as emacs, joe, or zile.

On Windows, however, the concept of an editor without a GUI is still unknown today, and no suitable program is available by default. Things change once you install Git because Git Bash with the vim and nano editors usually is installed as well. Starting the two programs can be done in the following ways:

```
> & "C:\Program Files\Git\usr\bin\nano.exe" myscript.ps1
> & "C:\Program Files\Git\usr\bin\vim.exe" myscript.ps1
```

By the way, including C:\Program Files\Git\usr\bin in Path variables is not recommended. In this directory, countless Linux tools like cd, ls, cp, and so on are installed, and since these names are also commonly used as PowerShell aliases, this duplication can cause problems. Better to include a function in the profile file to call your editor (see $PROFILE for the path):

```
# in the $PROFILE file (usually C:\Users\<name>\
# Documents\PowerShell\Microsoft.PowerShell_profile.ps1)
function nano {
    & "C:\Program Files\Git\usr\bin\nano.exe" $args
}
```

You may need to adjust the installation path. As a result, to modify a script file, you can then run nano in an SSH session in the following way:

```
> nano myscript.ps1
```

A conceivable alternative is to use VS Code through an SSH connection (see Chapter 13, Section 13.3).

12.1.5 Securing an SSH Server

The SSH server is a popular target for hackers who often try to guess a combination of login name and password. (The attack is not carried out manually, of course, but by automated tools.) The most popular attack target on Linux servers is the `root` account.

Some elementary safeguards you should keep in mind include the following:

- Use good passwords (at least 10 characters) for *all* accounts.
- Block the `root` login (`PermitRootLogin no` in `/etc/ssh/sshd_config`).
- Install the *Fail2ban* program, which blocks IP addresses for a few minutes after several failed login attempts.
- Use an authentication with keys instead of passwords, which we will discuss further in Section 12.4.

12.2 Working with SSH

Unless you have some practical experience, you should first familiarize yourself with the `ssh` command (the SSH client). For this task, open a terminal and execute the following command:

```
> ssh user@hostname

  The authenticity of host 'hostname (123.124.125.126)'
  can't be established. ECDSA key fingerprint is
  SHA256:E3IH3027Bc+5DvsvtenJkma1v5nI3owg08ZZqUR2BYk.
  Are you sure you want to continue connecting? yes
  Warning: Permanently added 'hostname,123.124.125.126' (ECDSA)
  to the list of known hosts.

  user@hostname's password: **********
user@hostname$ grep VERSION /etc/os-release

  VERSION="20.04.5 LTS (Focal Fossa)"
  VERSION_ID="20.04"
  VERSION_CODENAME=focal

user@hostname$ exit
```

Replace `user` with the account name on the relevant computer and `hostname` with the network name of the computer or its IP address. If the account names on the local machine and the remote host match, you can omit this step and just run `ssh hostname`. For authentication, you must enter the password of the account on the remote computer (not your local password!).

To get familiar with SSH, simply specify localhost instead of the hostname (i.e., ssh localhost). This step establishes an SSH connection to the local machine, testing both the SSH client and the local SSH server.

After successful login, you can run commands on the external computer. In the previous listing, I used grep to get the version of the installed Linux distribution. Entering exit or pressing Ctrl + D will terminate the SSH session.

12.2.1 Host Verification

The first time you connect to a host, the SSH client asks if you trust that host (see the previous listing). To be honest, you don't have many options there because only if you agree can you continue with the login process. If you have set up the external computer yourself or know the administrator, you could check if the "fingerprint" (i.e., the short form) of the server's SSH key matches. To get the fingerprint of a server, you must run the following command there, again replacing hostname with the actual computer name:

```
$ ssh-keyscan hostname | ssh-keygen -lf -

  256 SHA256:Sma6TJ79bONK8PMISjxPIYUi...MK3HQ hostname (ED25519)
 2048 SHA256:i9FlmpRieIFIEHNfHSzFgjp4...Y3ZmO hostname (RSA)
  256 SHA256:E3IH3027Bc+5DvsvtenJkma1...R2BYk hostname (ECDSA)
```

12.2.2 Potential Issues and Their Cause

On many Linux distributions, SSH login for root is blocked for security reasons or only allowed if authentication is done with keys (Section 12.4). The recommended procedure for doing admin work via SSH is to login with a different account and then use sudo in the session. As an alternative, you can explicitly allow root login by making an adjustment in the */etc/ssh/sshd_config* file on the computer that runs the SSH server. Changes to this file won't take effect until you ask the SSH server to reload the file (systemctl reload sshd on Linux).

SSH logins to local virtual machines may fail due to network connectivity. Oracle VM VirtualBox in particular causes problems in this regard. With VirtualBox, virtual machines are connected to the local network via *Network Address Translation (NAT)*, while SSH is blocked. The solution is port forwarding. You find a good tutorial on this topic at *https://www.simplified.guide/virtualbox/port-forwarding*.

The SSH client remembers the hostname or IP address of the server and the key used by the server each time it logs in. If the key changes (e.g., in the course of a new installation of the server), the ssh command displays a drastic error message and blocks the login:

```
WARNING: REMOTE HOST IDENTIFICATION HAS CHANGED!
IT IS POSSIBLE THAT SOMEONE IS DOING SOMETHING NASTY!
Someone could be eavesdropping on you right now
(man-in-the-middle attack)!
```

If you know that the affected server has been newly set up, the warning does not apply. However, you must find and delete the line for the relevant hostname or IP address in the local *.ssh/known_hosts* file. The next time you log in, you'll be asked whether you trust the server.

12.2.3 Running Linux and macOS Commands

Instead of using `ssh` interactively, you can run a command directly on the remote computer. The command and its parameters are passed as parameters to `ssh`. `grep` is not executed on the local machine here, but on a remote Linux or macOS host.


```
> ssh user@linuxhost 'grep VERSION /etc/os-release'

  user@linuxhost's password: **********

  VERSION="20.04.5 LTS (Focal Fossa)"
  VERSION_ID="20.04"
  VERSION_CODENAME=focal
```

Far-reaching possibilities arise from this seemingly trivial function: For example, you can now run `tar` on the remote machine or forward the archive of the `data` directory to standard output (specify a hyphen `-` after the `-f` option, such as `-f -`). You can forward the standard output using `|` as input for a second `tar` command that runs locally. This capability allows you to transfer an entire directory tree securely from one machine to another via SSH.

```
$ ssh user@hostname 'tar -czf - data' | tar -xzC ~/copy/ -f -
```

To execute multiple commands via `ssh` in a Bash script, the best approach is to use the heredoc syntax (see Chapter 3, Section 3.9). The `-T` option prevents `ssh` from opening a pseudo-terminal, which is not desirable in this case because the execution of commands should not be interactive.

```
ssh -T root@host <<ENDSSH
rm -f /etc/file1
cp /root/file2 /userxy/file3
...
ENDSSH
```

The first time you establish an SSH connection to a new host, `ssh` asks if you trust the host. Normally, this query is useful. However, if you want to use `ssh` to perform automated work on multiple hosts or virtual machines, this query is interference. The solution in such cases is the `-oStrictHostKeyChecking=no` option.

12.2.4 Running Windows Commands

Command execution also works for Windows hosts, although the syntactic varieties are much smaller for Windows. Provided that you have set PowerShell as the default shell (Section 12.1), you can run a command via SSH.

```
$ ssh user@winhost 'Get-ChildItem C:\\'

  user@winhost's password: **********

  Directory: C:\

  Mode          LastWriteTime        Name
  ----    --------------------       ----
  d-r--    02.17.2023    08:20       Program Files
  d-r--    02.17.2023    08:20       Program Files (x86)
  d-r--    07.13.2022    04:02       Users
  d----    02.20.2023    04:13       Windows
```

12.2.5 SSH Remoting in PowerShell

You can use the `Enter-PSSession` or `New-PSSession` commands to run commands on external Windows computers via *Windows Remote Management*. Since PowerShell 6, this feature is also available for SSH connections and is accordingly referred to as *SSH remoting*. Previously, however, some preparatory work was required on the server side.

To use SSH remoting on an external Windows machine, a new `Subsystem` line must be added to the respective *sshd_config* file. The `Subsystem` statement is spread over two lines in our case with \ only for space reasons. (It must be specified in one line and without the \ character!) According to the documentation, the `-nologo` option will no longer be required as of PowerShell version 7.4.

```
# Windows host: File $env:ProgramData\ssh\sshd_config
...
Subsystem powershell c:/progra~1/powershell/7/pwsh.exe \
  -sshs -nologo
```

The easiest way to open the file is to start the editor from the terminal (e.g., using `code $env:ProgramData\ssh\sshd_config`). This approach will automatically replace `$env:ProgramData` with the appropriate path on your machine (usually `C:\ProgramData`).

The strange Subsystem setting c:/progra~1/powershell/7/pwsh.exe is the usual path to the PowerShell installation in DOS notation (i.e., with a maximum of 8 plus 3 characters per filename or directory name). This ancient notation is necessary because OpenSSH cannot handle Windows filenames with spaces.

Possibly the correct path is also c:/progra~2! The following commands show how you can find out the short notation. First, you want to use Get-Command to determine the installation location of PowerShell. Then, you must run cmd.exe to get the short notation of the program directory:

```
> (Get-Command pwsh).Path
  C:\Program Files (x86)\PowerShell\7\pwsh.exe
> cmd /c 'for %X in ("C:\Program Files (x86)") do @echo %~sX'
  C:\PROGRA~2
```

Finally, you need to restart the SSH server:

```
> Restart-Service sshd
```


The preparatory work for using a Linux machine for SSH remoting looks quite similar. On Linux, you must also add a Subsystem line to sshd_config. However, instead of /usr/bin/pwsh, you must use the path to PowerShell that is valid in your distribution. You can determine the path via which pwsh.

```
# Linux host: File /etc/ssh/sshd_config
...
Subsystem powershell /usr/bin/pwsh -sshs -nologo
```

The following command restarts the SSH server:

```
$ sudo systemctl restart sshd
```

Once you have completed this preparatory work, you can use New-PSSession to establish an SSH connection and use it as a parameter for Invoke-Command. For the following example, I worked locally on a Windows machine, connecting to the Linux machine on the network and running Get-ChildItem there. You can use Remove-PSSession to terminate the SSH connection.

```
> $session = New-PSSession linuxhostname -Username kofler
> Invoke-Command -Session $session { Get-ChildItem /etc/*.conf }

  Directory: /etc
  Mode           LastWriteTime     Length Name
  ----           -------------     ------ ----
  --r--  02/10/2023     22:08        833 appstream.conf
  --r--  01/27/2023     19:44          0 arptables.conf
  --r--  12/06/2021     13:27       1438 dhcpcd.conf

> Remove-PSSession $session
```

Further configuration tips and application examples can be found at the following links:

- *https://learn.microsoft.com/en-us/powershell/scripting/learn/remoting/ssh-remoting-in-powershell-core*
- *https://github.com/PowerShell/Win32-OpenSSH/issues/1498*

12.3 scp and rsync

scp enables you to copy a file back and forth between a local computer and a remote computer. The following lines summarize the main syntax variants of scp. Unlike the ssh command, the hostname must always be followed by a colon! Remember: The dot (.) is the short notation for the current directory.

```
# copy local file to an external host (upload)
$ scp filename user@host:
$ scp filename user@host:path/newfilename

# copy the file of the external host into the local
# file system (download)
$ scp user@host:filename .
$ scp user@host:path/filename .

# copy entire directory trees recursively
$ scp -r localdir/ user@host:
$ scp -r user@host:remotedir .
```

Annoying Password Specification

Even if not included in our listings for space reasons, each scp command must be acknowledged by entering a password, which is, of course, annoying. The solution in this case is to use an SSH key (Section 12.4).

As with the interactive use of ssh, the communication is encrypted. Even if an attacker succeeds in intercepting and recording data packets, they could not decrypt the data (according to current knowledge) without a password.

12.3.1 Copy-Item with SSH Remoting

scp is a conventional command (an **.exe* file) on Windows. Calling such commands always appears as something foreign in PowerShell scripts. An alternative is to set up SSH remoting (Section 12.2). Under this condition, you can first establish an SSH connection via New-PSSession and then pass the session object to Copy-Item:

```
> $session = New-PSSession linuxhostname -Username kofler
> Copy-Item localfile /home/kofler/somesubdir -ToSession $session
> Remove-PSSession $session
```

Note that you must always specify an absolute path when using `Copy-Item` in this way. (In contrast, `scp` automatically works relative to the home directory of the account of the SSH connection.)

12.3.2 rsync

Linux and macOS computers can synchronize directories via `rsync`, which works for local directories as well as for directories on remote computers that are accessible via SSH. In this case, the basic syntax is exactly the same as for `scp`; that is, simply replace `scp` with `rsync`. (You can control the detailed behavior of `rsync` via numerous additional options, but I won't go into detail in this book. Review the manual by using `man rsync`.)

Compared to `scp`, three main differences exist:

- The `rsync` command/package must be installed both on the local computer and on the external computer. The SSH client or server is not enough.
- `rsync` checks which files have already been transferred and copies only new or changed files. For large directory trees, this approach (really) saves a lot of time.
- `rsync` can also delete files and directories and thus synchronize deletions. Since this action can also cause a loss of data, you must explicitly enable this behavior using the `--delete` option.

rsync and Windows

`rsync` is not available on Windows. The easiest way to use `rsync` is via the *Windows Subsystem for Linux (WSL)*. After installing a distribution, you can easily use `rsync` on the client side within WSL, thereby accessing all Windows files.

A good (but not SSH-compatible) variant to `rsync` is the `robocopy` command, which I will introduce in Chapter 15 on backups.

12.4 SSH Authentication with Keys

The SSH server knows numerous different authentication methods: The most common one is the password login used so far in this chapter. Alternatives include two-factor authentication (2FA) and SSH authentication with keys, which I will discuss in this section. This type of authentication requires some preparatory work that can be done quickly. As a result, `ssh` or `scp` can be used without a password, which is ideal for implementing automation in scripts.

A pair of files serves as the "key." The public component of the key is stored on the SSH server while the private component remains on the machine where you want to use the ssh, scp, or rsync commands. When establishing an SSH connection, the SSH server can use the public key to check whether the locally stored private key matches it. If such a suitable key pair is found, this key pair will be considered sufficient authentication, and the password query will be omitted.

12.4.1 Generating a Key Pair

To generate a key pair on the client machine, you must run ssh-keygen once. This command is available on Windows, Linux, and macOS if an SSH client is installed. If the command displays a warning that a key already exists, you must abort the process or specify a new name if you need a second key pair.

```
$ ssh-keygen

  Generating public/private rsa key pair.
  Enter file in which to save the key
     (/home/kofler/.ssh/id_rsa): <Return>
  Enter passphrase (empty for no passphrase): <Return>
  Enter same passphrase again: <Return>
  Your identification has been saved in /home/kofler/.ssh/id_rsa
  Your public key has been saved in /home/kofler/.ssh/id_rsa.pub
```

ssh-keygen asks if it should secure the key with a *passphrase* (with a password). For security reasons, doing so is recommended. If your private key falls into the wrong hands, the thief cannot do anything with the key without a password. At this point, however, we are talking about the use of keys in scripting, and in this context, I recommend that you do *not* specify a passphrase, but just press [Enter]. This approach is the only way to automate the execution of your scripts with ssh or scp commands without any user intervention.

By default, the key pair is stored in the *.ssh* directory and consists of two files that have different names depending on the encryption algorithm. Many SSH installations still use the algorithm of *Rivest-Shamir-Adleman (RSA)*. Newer versions use methods such as the *Elliptic Curve Digital Signature Algorithm (ECDSA)* and the variant *Curve25519*. In the context of this book, the procedure is irrelevant; what you need to know is that the key files have different names depending on the SSH version.

Algorithm	Private Key	Public Key
RSA	id_rsa	id_rsa.pub
ECDSA	id_ecdsa	id_ecdsa.pub
Curve25519	id_ed25519	id_ed25519.pub

Table 12.1 Names of the Key Files Depending on the Algorithm

Never Share Your Private Key!

SSH keys are also required by many hosting providers to set up new servers or virtual machines, by Git portals to authenticate Git commands, and so on. Always be sure you only pass or upload the public component of the key (**.pub* identifier)—and never the private component!

The keys that consist of two components do not correspond to our human imagination. The following analogy fits better:

- The private SSH key is equivalent to a conventional key.
- The public SSH key, on the other hand, corresponds to a lock.

Thus, you have an unlimited supply of locks (copies of the public key) that you can place in any place you can think of, especially on foreign servers. However, you never let the corresponding key—the private key file—out of your hand.

12.4.2 Storing the Public Component of the Key on the Server (macOS and Linux)

If you work on a Linux or macOS client, the second step is also quite simple: You can use `ssh-copy-id` to copy the public component of your key to the user directory of the desired account on the server. Then, replace `name` with the account name (login name) and replace `hostname` with the computer name.

```
$ ssh-copy-id name@hostname

  name@hostnames's password: ********
```

Subsequently, you can try out whether everything has worked. SSH login should now be possible without going through a password request:

```
$ ssh name@hostname        (login without password!)
```

12.4.3 Storing the Public Component of the Key on the Server (Windows)

On Windows, the `ssh`, `scp`, and `ssh-keygen` commands are available, but `ssh-copy-id` is missing. This omission has a simple reason: `ssh-copy-id` is not a compiled program, but a Bash script. Thus, a port to Windows would require more effort. Fortunately, not a problem: You can copy the public component of the key manually to the server and add it to the *.ssh/authorized_keys* file in the home directory of the desired account.

The following listing summarizes the required commands. I have prefixed the prompt with a string indicating where the command is to be executed: on the local Windows machine or as part of an SSH session on the external host. I assume in this case that the host is running Linux or macOS. You must replace `name` with the account name; `host`, with the name of the external host; and `id_rsa.pub` (or `id_ecdsa.pub`), with the name for the public part of your key.

```
Windows> scp .ssh/id_rsa.pub name@host:
Windows> ssh name@host

host$ mkdir .ssh
host$ touch .ssh/authorized_keys
host$ cat id_rsa.pub >> .ssh/authorized_keys
host$ chmod 700 .ssh
host$ chmod 600 .ssh/authorized_keys
```

The `mkdir` and `touch` commands are only necessary if the *.ssh/authorized_keys* file does not yet exist. `cat` adds the key (which is simply a few lines of text with a hexadecimal code) to the end of this file. The two `chmod` commands ensure that the access rights for the `.ssh` directory and the *authorized_keys* file are correct; otherwise, the file will be ignored by the SSH server.

If the SSH server runs the SELinux security system, as is common on Fedora, Red Hat, and so on, you must also ensure that the SELinux context is correct:

```
host$ restorecon -R -v .ssh
```

Finally, in the terminal of your Windows computer, you must ensure that the SSH connection setup via `ssh user@host` now works without a password.

12.5 Example: Uploading Images to a Linux Web Server

The goal of this first example is to use a script to upload all new or modified images from a local directory via `scp` to an appropriately prepared directory on a web server.

12.5.1 Preparatory Measures

In this example, I assume that the web server is running on Ubuntu Linux and that the image directory is to be embedded in an existing WordPress installation. In principle, of course, the example also works without WordPress and for any other distribution. However, you may need to adjust paths and, for Red Hat-based distributions, make sure that the SELinux context of the image directory is set correctly.

Image upload should be allowed to multiple users/accounts. For this reason, the `imageupload` group is created on the server. All users who are allowed to upload will be added to this group.

In addition, the `myimages` directory is created on the server. `chown` assigns this directory to the `www-data` user (which is the system account of the web server in Debian and Ubuntu) and also to the `imageupload` group. The `chmod` command causes all members of the `imageupload` group to be allowed to work, read, and write in the directory and that newly uploaded files are automatically assigned to this group.

All commands in the following listing are to be executed on the Linux server and require root privileges on that server (hence, the # prompt character):

```
$ sudo -s
# addgroup imageupload
# usermod -a -G imageupload username1
# usermod -a -G imageupload username2
# usermod -a -G imageupload username3
# mkdir /var/www/html/wordpress/myimages
# chown www-data:imageupload /var/www/html/wordpress/myimages
# chmod 2775 /var/www/html/wordpress/myimages
```

Finally, I assume that the users (username1, etc.) have uploaded their SSH keys, so scp works without an interactive login. Before you start developing the script, you should test it interactively, for example, as with the following command:

```
$ scp tst.jpg username1@hostname:/var/www/html/wordpress/myimages
```


12.5.2 Bash Script

In this example, I first assume that the local machine is running Linux or macOS. For this case, the Bash script initializes some variables first. If the *last-run* file does not exist, it will be created in the current directory with a date of early 2000. This file serves as a reference for find, which only considers files that are newer. *last-run* is updated at the end of the script with the time when the script was started (the now file). This somewhat cumbersome procedure ensures that the script does not miss any files on the next run that were added exactly during the execution of find. Admittedly, this mistake is unlikely, but not impossible.

The find command processes the *.png, *.jpg, and *.jpeg identifiers. If you want to include additional identifiers—if necessary also in uppercase notation—you must add further options in the form -o -name .... In this case, -o means a logical OR. -maxdepth 1 causes find not to search any subdirectories. Of course, you can omit this option. Note, however, that the directory structure is lost during the upload (i.e., all files end up directly in myimages). If you don't want the directory structure to be lost, you should use rsync instead of scp.

The -exec option calls the scp command for each file found and passes the filename instead of {}. This feature also works for filenames with spaces. \; specifies where the command for -exec ends.

```
# Sample file upload-images.sh
LOCALDIR=$(pwd)
REMOTEDIR=/var/www/html/wordpress/myimages
REMOTEHOST=hostname
REMOTEUSER=username1
```

```
LASTRUN=$LOCALDIR/last-run
NOW=$LOCALDIR/now
# Create file last-run if it does not exist yet;
# use an old date (2000-01-01).
if [ ! -f $LASTRUN ]; then
  touch -m -t 200001010000 $LASTRUN
fi
# create file now with current date and time
touch $NOW

# upload all files that have changed after last-run
find $LOCALDIR -maxdepth 1 \( -name "*.jpg" -o -name "*.jpeg" \
   -o -name "*.png" \) -newer $LASTRUN \
   -exec scp {} $REMOTEUSER@$REMOTEHOST:$REMOTEDIR \;

# update last-run
mv $NOW $LASTRUN
```

12.5.3 PowerShell Script

If your images are located on a Windows computer, it makes sense to implement the script using PowerShell. The following code has a similar structure to the Bash script, so I'll leave it at some comments. For `New-Item`, `Out-Null` prevents the otherwise mandatory output of the filename.

```
# Sample file upload-images.ps1
$localdir = (Get-Location).Path
$remotedir = "/var/www/html/wordpress/myimages"
$remotehost = "hostname"
$remoteuser = "username"
$lastrun = "$localdir/last-run"
$now = "$localdir/now"

# Create file last-run if it does not exist yet;
# use an old date (2000-01-01).
if (-not (Test-Path $lastrun)) {
    (New-Item $lastrun).LastWriteTime = Get-Date "2000-01-01"
}
# create file now with current date and time
New-Item $now -Force | Out-Null

# upload all files that have changed after last-run
$lastruntime = (Get-Item $lastrun).LastWriteTime
Get-ChildItem -Path $localdir/* `
```

```
    -Include "*.jpg", "*.jpeg", "*.png" |
Where-Object { $_.LastWriteTime -gt $lastruntime } |
ForEach-Object {
    scp $_.FullName $remoteuser@${remotehost}:$remotedir
  }

# update last-run
Move-Item -Force $now $lastrun
```

I called scp directly in this script because a typical Linux server rarely has PowerShell installed, let alone the required configuration of sshd_config for SSH remoting. But should these requirements be met, you can of course also use SSH remoting. You can find the complete script in the sample files. Only the few lines that change in the course of this kind of approach are shown in the following excerpt:

```
# Sample file upload-images-remoting.ps1
...
$session = New-PSSession $remotehost -Username $remoteuser
Get-ChildItem -Path $localdir/* `
    -Include "*.jpg", "*.jpeg", "*.png" |
Where-Object { $_.LastWriteTime -gt $lastruntime } |
ForEach-Object {
    Copy-Item -ToSession $session $_ $remotedir
}
Remove-PSSession $session
```

12.6 Example: Analyzing Virtual Machines

Our second example is about reading information from a group of similar virtual machines. In this specific case, the virtual machines formed the basis of a laboratory exercise at a technical college. Each student had access to a virtual machine. When setting up these virtual machines, I made sure I put the public part of my SSH key there. The virtual machines are accessible under the hostnames host<nn>.mylab.com.

For a quick overview of how virtual disks and file systems are organized, I want to run the lsblk command on each instance, which can be done using a Bash one-liner (but is printed over four lines for space and readability). Due to the -o StrictHostKeyChecking=no option, ssh does not ask whether the host should be trusted the first time a connection is established.

```
$ for i in {01..25}; do
    echo "\n\nVM: $i";
    ssh user@host$i.mylab.com -o StrictHostKeyChecking=no lsblk;
  done
```

```
VM: 01
NAME               MAJ:MIN RM  SIZE RO TYPE MOUNTPOINTS
sr0                 11:0    1 1024M  0 rom
vda                252:0    0    5G  0 disk
  vda1             252:1    0    1G  0 part /boot
  vda2             252:2    0    4G  0 part
    almalinux-root 253:0    0  3,5G  0 lvm  /
    almalinux-swap 253:1    0  512M  0 lvm  [SWAP]
vdb                252:16   0    1G  0 disk
...
```

If more information is to be determined for each virtual machine and stored in result files, programming a small script could be worthwhile:

```
# Sample file gather-vm-data.sh
VMNAMES=$(echo host{01..25})
VMHOST=mylab.com
USER=username
CMDS='hostnamectl; echo; ip addr; echo; lsblk'

for vm in $VMNAMES; do
    echo $vm
    ssh $USER@$vm.$VMHOST -o StrictHostKeyChecking=no "$CMDS" \
      > result-$vm.txt
done
```

The script traverses all virtual machines contained in `VMNAMES`, executes the commands listed in `CMDS` there, and saves the results in files with names like `result-<vmname>.txt`.

I use a strongly extended variant of this script for evaluating exams for my "Linux System Administration" course. Students must perform all possible admin tasks in a freshly set up virtual machine as part of the exam. Correcting the exam tasks cannot be fully automated, but the script nevertheless greatly relieves me of tedious grading work.

Of course, you can also use comparable scripts away from teaching, for example, for the central monitoring or administration of large groups of servers or virtual machines.

Other Tools

The use of "hand-knitted" scripts is only recommended if the work to be performed is manageable. The more complex the task, the more likely you should look for remote administration or server pool monitoring programs. Proven configuration tools include *Ansible* or *Puppet*; you can manage comprehensive monitoring using *Grafana*, *Prometheus*, or *Nagios*.

If you're only interested in running commands via SSH on many computers as efficiently as possible, *Cluster SSH* or *Parallel SSH* might be worth trying out.

Chapter 13
Visual Studio Code

Visual Studio Code (VS Code), sometimes simply *Code*, is currently the most universally popular editor for software developers. The strengths of this program developed by Microsoft include support for all conceivable programming languages and platforms, a huge range of extensions, comprehensive configuration options, and excellent integration with the Git version management system.

Although VS Code is by no means the only editor in my everyday work environment, I wouldn't want to miss out on its strengths. From the perspective of this book, VS Code scores points for its consistency of use, whether you work on a Bash, Python, or PowerShell script. This is an advantage compared to dedicated development systems such as *PyCharm* for Python, for example, where you must memorize different working techniques and keyboard shortcuts.

An introduction to VS Code seems superfluous in this book as you probably already know about the editor. If not, you can find loads of tutorials and videos on the internet to get you started. This short chapter focuses instead on the scripting-specific features of VS Code—in particular, the Bash, PowerShell, Python, and Remote – SSH extensions.

Prerequisites for This Chapter

You can read this chapter separately from the rest of the book. However, using the remote SSH extension requires that you're familiar with SSH (see Chapter 12).

13.1 Introduction

Installing VS Code on Windows and macOS is quite easy. Simply download the installation program or the corresponding ZIP file from *https://code.visualstudio.com/download*. On Windows, run the program; on macOS, you must move the editor from the ZIP archive to the *Programs* folder.

For Linux, Microsoft provides Debian and RPM packages. When you install the Debian package, a package source gets automatically set up so that you'll also receive updates for VS Code as part of the system updates in the future. If, on the other hand, you run Fedora, openSUSE or a Red Hat compatible distribution, you'll have to take care of the updates yourself. To do this, you should visit the download page once every few months, download the latest version of the RPM package, and repeat the installation.

If you use Arch Linux, you can install VS Code as an AUR package, which allows you to choose between an Arch Linux variant or the official Microsoft binary. The best way to do this is to use an AUR helper, such as `yay`. If you do, then the VS Code installation will succeed by using `yay -S code-git` or `yay -S visual-studio-code-bin`.

13.1.1 Comparing VS Code, VSCodium, and Visual Studio

Although the code for VS Code is subject to an open-source license and is located in a public GitHub repository, the binary version offered for download by Microsoft is subject to a different license and contains telemetry functions. If these functions bother you, search for "Telemetry" in the settings and disable the corresponding options.

If you're unhappy with the license for the VS Code downloaded from Microsoft or you're generally suspicious, you can install the *VSCodium* variant instead (see also *https://vscodium.com*). VSCodium uses the same GitHub code as VS Code, but the telemetry features are disabled, the program has a different icon, and the liberal MIT license applies to its use.

VS Code or VSCodium have nothing (or at least very little) to do with the *Visual Studio* development environment. This commercial Microsoft product is specifically designed for developing programs in C#, C++, and Visual Basic.

13.1.2 Think in Terms of Directories, Not Files!

In traditional editors like Notepad++, you can simply open files from any location and edit them. While this access is also possible in VS Code, it is not the ideal way of working. In VS Code, you open a directory via **File • Open Folder**. The files contained therein will then be displayed in the sidebar and can be opened and edited by double-clicking them.

Why is the directory paradigm of VS Code so important? VS Code provides extensions for most programming languages. In this way, VS Code can "understand" your code better and supports you during input. At the same time, scripts can be run directly from the editor via a **Run** button. The active directory is then the directory last opened in VS Code, not the directory where the script file is located!

Let's suppose you have developed a script that opens and processes a CSV file located in the same directory. However, when running the script, an error occurs because the script does not find the file. If this error arises, you have fallen into the VS Code directory trap. The solution is pretty straightforward: Either run the script manually where the easiest way is in the terminal section of VS Code or, even better, use **File • Open Folder** to change to the directory where your script is located.

VS Code's preference for directories may force you to question specific ways of working. Editing scripts that are scattered across countless directories is tedious in VS Code. On the other hand, it's probably a good idea to place scripts that are related in content in one directory anyway.

13.2 Language-Specific VS Code Extensions

As soon as you edit a PowerShell or Python file in VS Code for the first time, the editor asks you whether it should install the corresponding extension(s). You should always follow this recommendation! VS Code then performs syntax highlighting, completes keywords, indents your code correctly, and helps test and debug your scripts.

13.2.1 PowerShell Extension

The most interesting features of the PowerShell extension include the following:

- **Run button**
  The toolbar of VS Code contains two **Run** buttons. One of them runs your script, while the other button runs only the previously marked lines of code.
- **Navigation**
  By pressing Ctrl while clicking, you can navigate directly to the definition of the variable or function under the mouse cursor.
- **PSScriptAnalyzer**
  This tool analyzes your code for obvious weaknesses or violations of *best practices*. The tool also takes care of indenting your code. After major rebuilds, you can restore the correct indentations using Ctrl + A and then Ctrl + I.
- **Debugging functions**
  This feature helps you to debug PowerShell scripts. You can find relevant instructions at *https://devblogs.microsoft.com/scripting/debugging-powershell-script-in-visual-studio-code-part-1*.

13

13.2.2 Python Extension

The active Python extension makes entering Python code really fun. VS Code automatically performs syntax checking, helps with code indentation, and completes the names of installed modules as well as the functions in imported modules. You can collapse comments and functions and view an overview if a script does run out of time.

Using what are called *refactoring functions* can help you restructure your code later. For example, if you rename a variable or function by pressing F2, VS Code automatically implements this change in all places in the code.

VS Code displays the number of the Python version installed on the computer in the bottom-right corner of the status bar. If you have multiple installations, you can select the version you want to use for code execution by clicking on the version number. (I strongly advise against having parallel installations, though, because they often cause trouble with module management and pip!)

On macOS and Windows, VS Code will also help you to install Python, especially if it cannot find a Python interpreter. I'm sure that's well-intentioned, but a better approach is to perform the Python installation by yourself. In this way, you can keep control over your Python installations and avoid multiple installations.

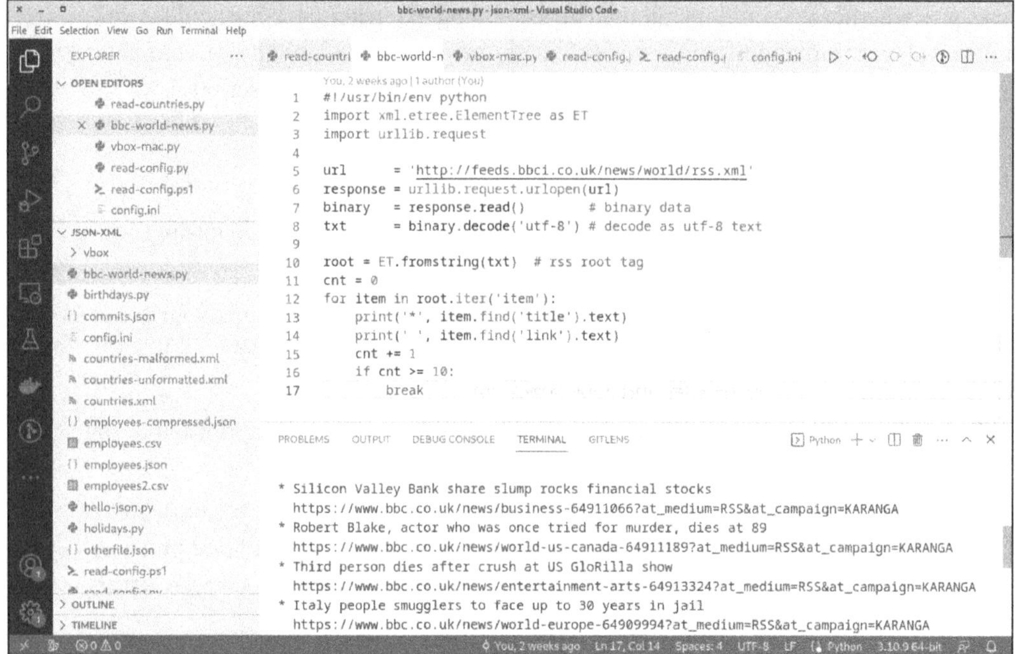

Figure 13.1 Visual Studio Code with the Python Extension

13.2.3 Bash/Shell Extensions

Unlike PowerShell and Python, no definitive VS Code extension exists for Bash scripts. VS Code also does not take the initiative and offer to install an extension when you write a Bash or Zsh script. Nevertheless, some extensions can make your life as a Bash developer easier. It's up to you which you install. (If you search for "bash" or "shell" in the **Extensions** sidebar, you'll find even more extensions, but some are of questionable benefit).

Some common extensions include the following:

- *Bash Debug* helps with debugging Bash scripts.
- *shellman* is aimed specifically at Bash beginners and helps with entering Bash structures, such as `if` or `for`.
- *ShellCheck* analyzes your code and suggests syntactic improvements and corrections. Personally, though, I find the tool too picky and not configurable enough.
- *Code Runner* adds a button for the direct execution of shell scripts to the VS Code toolbar.

13.3 Remote – SSH Extension

The biggest drawback of VS Code is its graphical user interface (GUI). This statement may seem absurd to you: After all, you use VS Code precisely because of how its intuitive operations and its many functions are elegantly integrated into its UI. As long as you work locally, that is, as long as your scripts are on your laptop, the benefits of VS Code really do come into their own.

However, in everyday scripting, you'll often write scripts that run on external servers or in virtual machines. Often, only a SSH connection exists to these computers or servers, and you must work in text mode. Linux fans then mostly rely on editors such as *vi* or *Emacs*, which unlock their full functionality in text mode and therefore remain applicable even in an SSH session. (Personally, I mostly use `jmacs` or `zile` in such cases. These minimalist editors are Emacs compatible in their basic commands.)

However, I don't blame you if you don't feel like learning the countless keyboard shortcuts for these dinosaurs from the Unix past. Instead, I want to present to you an elegant alternative: You can also use VS Code through an SSH connection to edit code on another machine! This method of operation is associated with certain limitations, but in principle, it works great.

13.3.1 Applying the Remote – SSH Extension

To combine VS Code with SSH, you must install the *Remote – SSH* extension developed by Microsoft. You should also copy your SSH public key to the remote machine (`ssh-copy-id`, see Chapter 12, Section 12.4). In this way, you can avoid repeatedly entering the password for your account on the remote computer.

To set up a new connection to an external computer, you must run [F1] *Remote-SSH: Add new ssh host* and then—in a terminal—enter the `ssh user@hostname` command. VS Code stores the data in *.ssh/config* but does not establish a connection for the time being.

The connection is established via [F1] *Remote SSH*: *Connect to host* or via the green **Remote** area in the status bar. VS Code uses the `ssh` command to establish a connection and accordingly analyzes the keys stored in the *.ssh* directory.

Once the connection has been successfully established, VS Code opens a new window, with the green area in the status bar making it clear that non-local data is being processed. From that moment on, VS Code will work as usual: You can select a directory, edit the files it contains, save your changes, and so on. The terminal area of VS Code is also extremely useful in remote operation. The terminal also runs *remotely*, so you can execute commands on the remote computer in it just like in an SSH session.

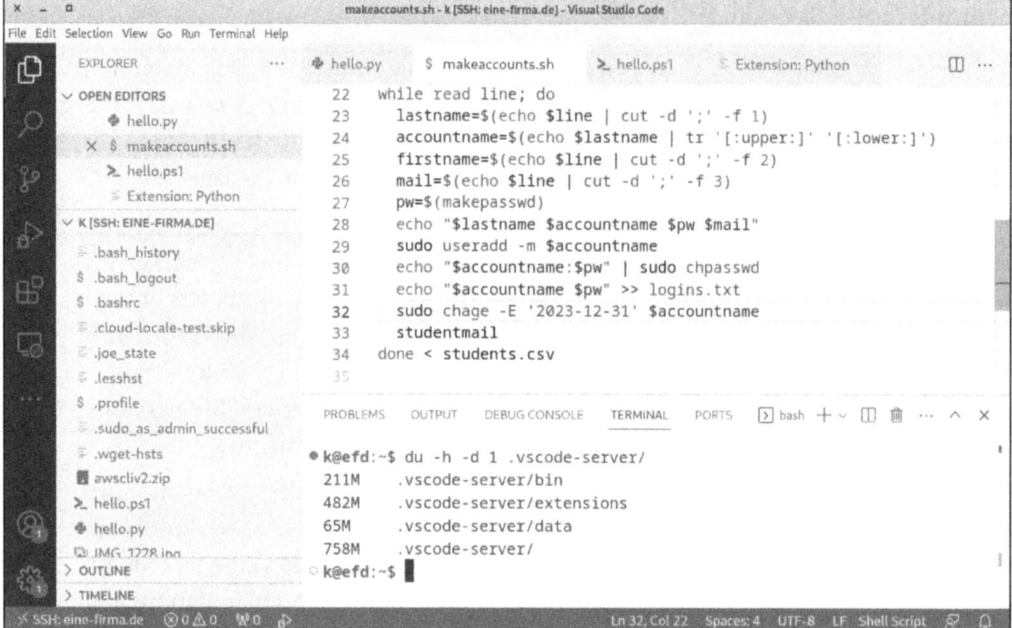

Figure 13.2 Editing a Bash Script in VS Code on the External Linux Server (eine-firma.de)

13.3.2 Limitations

Now, before you start thinking this is too good to be true, I must point out two limitations:

- VS Code installs a large amount of code (typically several hundred MBs!) on the remote machine into the *.vscode-server* directory and executes this code in that directory. For syntax checking and debugging, VS Code on your notebook communicates with the extension code on the remote machine.

  For this process to work smoothly, the remote computer requires sufficient storage space (both disk space *and* RAM), enough computing power, and an excellent network connection. Otherwise, working in VS Code is not much fun.

- VS Code also reaches its limits when you want to edit system files. No function is comparable to `sudo`. Thus, VS Code only allows access to the files that an SSH user is also allowed to read. For scripting, this access is sufficient, but for changing a configuration file in the */etc* directory, you still need an editor, which you can run in text mode using `sudo`.

Chapter 14
Git

Git is a version control system typically used when many people collaborate on a complex project. Thanks to Git, multiple branches of a program can then be managed, and changes can be tracked and reverted if necessary.

At first glance, scripting and Git do not go together: Scripts are small files that are often created by just one developer. Version management with Git seems therefore superfluous.

But this impression is not quite true. Scripting and Git can be combined wonderfully:

- Git can document the development process for small script collections: It serves as a backup, and it helps distribute scripts across multiple target machines in a straightforward manner.
- Some development operations can be automated by calling the `git` and `gh` commands in scripts.
- Git can execute what are called *hooks* for certain operations. Hooks are scripts you create that, for example, perform basic testing before a commit or take care of deployment after a commit.

Prerequisites for This Chapter

To get the most out of this chapter, you should already be familiar with SSH keys (see Chapter 12). Such keys are used for authentication in this chapter (for example, at GitHub or GitLab). As far as scripting examples go, this chapter is pretty Bash and Linux heavy.

This chapter begins with a crash course on Git that shows you how to version and back up a directory with some scripts using Git. However, you should really consider this section only as a starter! For a complete guide to Git, see *Git: Project Management for Developers and DevOps Teams* by myself and Bernd Öggl (Rheinwerk Computing, 2023), which covers advanced topics, special cases, variants, and best practices.

I will also describe how you can keep sensitive information in your scripts out of the Git repository. All too often, passwords to cloud services or FTP access are contained in scripts that have led to massive security breaches. This problem must be avoided at all costs.

14.1 Git Crash Course

This crash course is designed to help you get started with Git. If you already know Git, just scroll on to the next section!

I will restrict myself to the absolute basics in this chapter: You won't learn about branches or merge conflicts, let alone best practices for team deployment. The only authentication method I will describe is SSH. In short, this crash course could be called "Git for minimalists." Nevertheless, the knowledge I impart should be sufficient to manage a collection of scripts using Git. To learn more about Git, you can find comprehensive documentation online including videos at *https://git-scm.com/doc*. And did I mention that there are also some pretty good books on Git?

14.1.1 Preparation Tasks

First, you must install Git. On Linux, the best approach is to use the Git package of your distribution. If you run Debian or Ubuntu, `sudo apt install git` will do the job. For macOS and Windows, you can find installation packages at *https://git-scm.com/downloads* that are straightforward to use. In the terminal, you should verify that the `git` command can be executed. If that command does not work, you must check if the Git installation directory is included in the `PATH` variable!

```
> git --version
  git version 2.39.2
```

Windows, Linux, or macOS

I use the > PowerShell prompt in this section. The few screenshots I've included were taken on a Windows system. However, the procedure does not change whether you use Windows, Linux, or macOS or whether you run `git` in PowerShell, Bash, or Zsh.

Basically, you can use Git *standalone*; that is, you can manage the code of your project exclusively locally on your computer. However, I strongly recommend that you set up a free account with a Git host of your choice. I refer to GitHub in the following examples, but alternatives like GitLab work just as well.

To allow the local `git` command to authenticate with the Git host, you must store your public SSH key there (i.e., usually in the *.ssh/id_xxx.pub* file). On GitHub, you can find the corresponding upload dialog under **Settings • SSH and GPG keys**. The easiest way is to load the key file into an editor, copy all the text, and paste it into the web dialog.

Because this information is stored in every commit, Git needs to know your name and email address. (I'll explain what a commit is later.) You don't need to provide your real email address. If you use GitHub and you want your email address to remain anonymous, you should proceed as follows and replace `aname` with your GitHub account name:

```
> git config --global user.name  "Michael Kofler"
> git config --global user.email "aname@users.noreply.github.com"
```

14.1.2 The First Repository

In the GitHub web interface, you can now create a new repository. A *repository* is a collection of all the files in a project that you are managing using Git—including all the changes that come together during the course of the project. You must assign a name to the repository, and you should set its visibility to **Private**. (Your first tests are not meant to be seen by the entire world.) To ensure that the repository is not completely empty, I recommend activating the **Add a README file** option and leaving all the other options as they are.

Then, go back to your terminal. On my computers, I usually have a separate directory for repositories. (`git` is obvious.) In that directory, you can now run `git clone` and then change to the new directory with the repository, as in the following example:


```
> mkdir git
> cd git
> git clone git@github.com:MichaelKofler/test1234.git
> cd test1234
```

`git clone` downloads the repository from GitHub and sets up a copy in the `test1234` directory on your machine. Needless to say, you need to replace `MichaelKofler/test1234` with your own GitHub account name and the name of your repository. You can find the entire repository address in the GitHub web interface by clicking the green **Code** button and selecting the SSH variant.

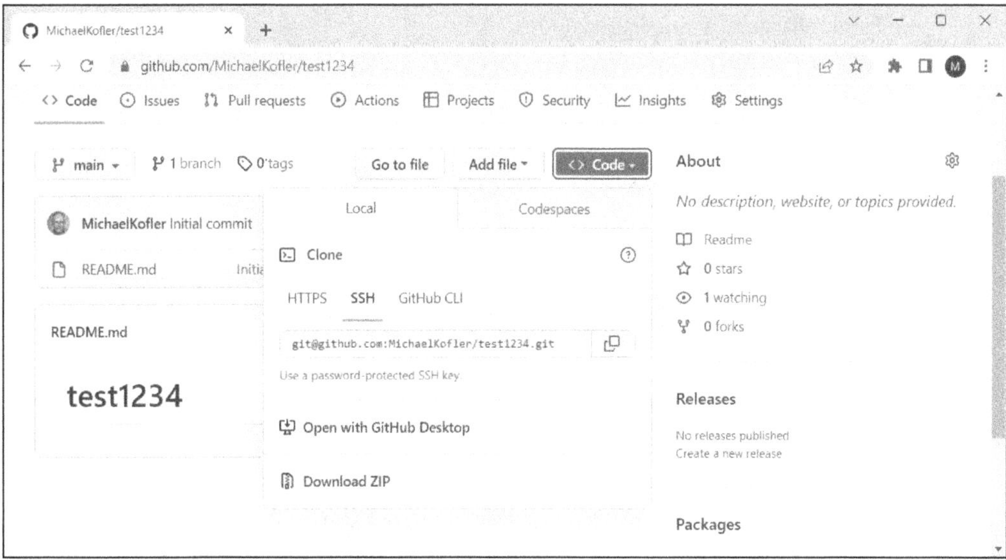

Figure 14.1 A Test Repository in the GitHub Web Interface

Internal Affairs

The repository directory—in our case, `git\test1234\`—reflects the current state of your project. Old versions of your code as well as other internal data (a kind of "Git database" for your project) are hidden in the `.git` subdirectory. These compressed files have names that are composed of hexadecimal characters. You should use only the `git` command to edit or read your repository. Do not touch the *.git* subdirectory!

14.1.3 The First Commit

The work you do now takes place in the directory of the repository—in the logic of this example, in `git\test1234\`. If you use Visual Studio Code (VS Code), you must open this directory. Let's assume you create three new scripts in this directory: *script1.ps1* to *script3.ps1*.

At the end of the day—or when you've reached a satisfactory intermediate state to take a break—you'll want to add these three scripts to the Git repository. To put it a little more precisely: You want to store a copy of these files in their current states in the Git database and then synchronize these changes with the external repository on GitHub. This process requires three steps or three commands, all of which must be run in the repository directory (`git\test1234`, in this example):

```
> git add script1.ps1 script2.ps1 script3.ps1

> git commit -m 'script1 to script3: basic functions work'

  [main cd35ac9] script1 to script3: basic functions work
  3 files changed, 3 insertions(+)
  create mode 100644 script1.ps1
  create mode 100644 script2.ps1
  create mode 100644 script3.ps1

> git push

  Writing objects: 100% (5/5), 399 bytes | 199.00 KiB/s, done.
  To github.com:MichaelKofler/test1234.git
     015ed58..cd35ac9  main -> main
```

Let's start with `git add`. This command does two things: First, Git now knows that these files belong to the project and are under version control. Second, Git stores the current state of these files in the local Git database (i.e., in the `.git` directory).

`git commit` generates a commit that saves the current status of the project—all changes marked up to the time of `git add`—in a kind of intermediate release. The *message* passed with `-m` usually contains a short description of the last changes made. Also, `git` `commit` is only processed locally; that is, the remote repository (GitHub, in our example) does not know anything about the local changes until now.

Only `git push` transfers the changes made to the remote repository (in our case, to GitHub). After running the command in the terminal, you should take another look at the GitHub web interface. You should see that both the commit and the three files (*script1.ps1* to *script3.ps1*) are now visible.

Git in VS Code

Instead of running the `git add`, `git commit`, and `git push` commands in a terminal, you can also trigger these actions from the VS Code user interface (UI). VS Code features excellent support for Git. However, you should refrain from this approach during your first attempts. First, try to get to know and understand the `git` command!

To learn more about Git in VS Code later, a good overview including a video tutorial is available at *https://code.visualstudio.com/docs/sourcecontrol/overview*.

14.1.4 Additional Commits

You've earned a break! The next day, you start with the documentation in the *README.md* file and make a few more improvements in *script2.ps1*. Now, it's time for the next commit. But instead of marking the changed files using `git add` again, this time you can use a shortcut: Run `git commit` with the `-a` (*all*) option, which automatically commits all changes to files that were already under Git control. Don't forget `git push` to upload the changes to the remote repository as well.

```
> git commit -a -m 'improved script2.ps1, started documentation'
> git push
```

For New Files, git add Is Required!

The `git commit -a` command is so convenient that using the `-a` option quickly becomes a matter of course. However, keep in mind one important caveat: The command only includes files that are already under Git control. If you create new files like *script4.ps1* or *configuration.ini* in your editor, don't forget to add them to the repository once using `git add`!

14.1.5 Setting Up the Repository on a Second Computer

Your scripts are working satisfactorily so far. But now, these scripts need to be run on a second computer. For this task, you can install Git on the second computer and then repeat the `git clone` command in the directory where you want to use the scripts:

```
computer2> cd some\directory
computer2> git clone git@github.com:MichaelKofler/test1234.git
computer2> cd test1234
```

When running tests on computer 2, perhaps you notice two more problems. You can fix the errors and then commit these changes to computer 2 as well:

```
computer2> git commit -a -m 'bugfixes in script1.ps1'
computer2> git push
```

The bugfixes are thus on computer 2 and in the remote repository (GitHub in our example), but not yet on computer 1. To synchronize computer 1's repository with GitHub, you need to run `git pull` to transfer new commits from the remote repository to computer 1:

```
computer1> git pull
```

git pull before git push

As soon as code is changed in multiple places or by multiple developers, you should get into the habit of regularly running `git pull` to bring your local repository up to date. In general, you should always run `git pull` before `git push`. If you forget to `git pull` and Git detects that commits are missing from the local repository, `git push` results in the following error message: *failed to push some refs to remote repository xxx*. The solution is to run `git pull` first.

Figure 14.2 shows—admittedly in a highly simplified manner—the effect of basic Git commands. The "staging area" is a special area of the Git database that stores files added via `git add` that are not yet part of a commit.

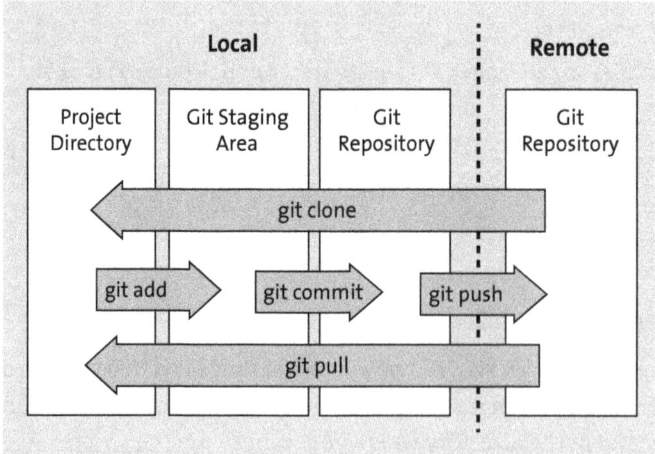

Figure 14.2 Basic Git Commands

14.1.6 Git Status

As your project grows, so does the risk of losing track of your Git repository. The solution to this problem is provided by `git status`. This command summarizes which files have been changed since the last commit, which ones have been added, and so on.

Another useful command is `git log`, which outputs a summary of the latest commits (with the newest commit first). With `git log`, myriad options control how many details are displayed for each commit. You can get the shortest version using `--oneline`: Then, only a hexadecimal identification code (the first digits of the hash code) and the commit message are displayed:

```
> git log

  f2665d9 (HEAD -> main, origin/main, origin/HEAD) more bugfixes
  5d3225d bugfixes in script1.ps1
  679ca1a improved script2.ps1, started documentation
  cd35ac9 script1 to script3.ps1: basic functions work
  015ed58 Initial commit
```


Instead of getting used to using `git log`, you can also use the GitHub web interface where you can click through the commits, view the changes made with the commits, and more.

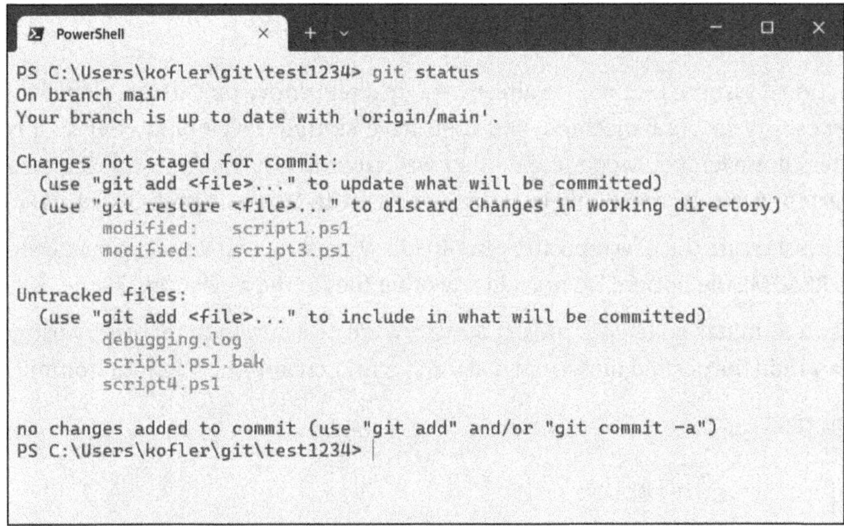

Figure 14.3 The State of the Local Repository

14.1.7 Excluding Files from Git (.gitignore)

Often, some files in your project directory should not be included in the repository, such as backups of your scripts created by the editor, files for logging and debugging, and so on. To prevent `git status` from listing these files, you can set up the *.gitignore* file in the local directory. This file contains samples of files that `git` should not consider, for example, the following kinds of files:

```
*.bak
*.log
*~
tmp/*
```

The *.gitignore* file itself should of course be stored in the repository:

```
> git add .gitignore
```

If, as an exception, you want to add a file to the repository for which *.gitignore* contains a lock pattern, you should run `git add` with the `-f` (*force*) option:

```
> git add debugging.log

  The following paths are ignored by one of your .gitignore
  files: debugging.log.
  Hint: Use -f if you really want to add them.

> git add -f debugging.log
```

14.1.8 Transferring Existing Code to a New Repository

In this section, I assume that you've already set up a repository on GitHub, cloned an empty repository to your machine, and then have started developing your scripts there. Often, however, you've gone the other way around: You've been working on a new project for a few days and only later decide to use Git. That's no problem either!

First, you must create the new repository in GitHub. Make sure that you do not activate the **Add a README file** option! Do not add any other files to the repository.

Then, open a terminal, go to your project directory, create a new local repository using `git init`, and add the desired files to it. Finally, `git commit` creates the first local commit:

```
> cd my\project
> git init
> git add script*.sh readme.md
> git commit -m 'initial commit'
```

Next, you must connect the local repository to the new remote repository. `git branch` ensures that the main branch in the local repository is called `main`. In current versions of Git, this name is used by default—the command is then superfluous but does not interfere. Only if your Git installation is rather old can it still use the obsolete `master` designation.

git remote add origin defines the remote repository. Instead of MichaelKofler/test1235.git, you must specify your own GitHub account name and repository name again.

git push performs the first upload. The -u (*set upstream*) option ensures that the mapping between the external repository for the main branch is stored permanently. Therefore, in the future, git push without any further options will be sufficient.

```
> git branch -M main
> git remote add origin git@github.com:MichaelKofler/test1235.git
> git push -u origin main

  To github.com:MichaelKofler/test1235.git
   * [new branch]      main -> main
  branch 'main' set up to track 'origin/main'.
```

Thus, the first commit is stored both locally and remotely. From that moment on, the git add, git commit, git pull and git push, git status, and git log commands work as described earlier.

14

14.2 Handling Settings and Passwords Correctly

Hackers are always looking for passwords for mail, FTP, and database servers. All too often, they find what they are looking for on GitHub, GitLab, and other Git hosts. That's not because these platforms themselves are so insecure, but because code files stored there that are publicly accessible might simply contain the passwords in plain text. This vulnerability can arise if your code looks something like the following backup script:

```
# Attention, negative example!
... code
mysqldump -u root -ptopSecret wordpress > db.sql
lftp -u ftpuser,topSecret2 backupserver.example.com << EOF
cd remote/dir/
put db.sql
bye
EOF
... more code
```

In this example, mysqldump first creates a backup of the database. The password required for this step is passed directly with the -p option. Then, lftp connects to an FTP server to store the backup there. The password is passed with the -u option. If you store this backup script in a Git repository, everyone who has access to the repository knows the passwords to the MySQL and FTP servers.

By the way, you should avoid FTP altogether if possible. The protocol is inherently insecure. If anything, you should only store files on an FTP server that you have encrypted previously.

14.2.1 What's a Better Method?

Several best practices for preventing these types of security breaches include the following:

- **Storing passwords externally**
  Almost all programs that require a password for authentication can read the password from a file. For `mysqldump`, the *.my.cnf* is used; for `lftp`, the *.netrc* file is used; and so on. With some tools, you don't need passwords at all and can use key files instead (for example, SSH; see Chapter 12, Section 12.4).

  Of course, passwords or key files must not be included in the Git repository under any circumstances. However, you can point out in the documentation which password files your script requires, and which syntax is necessary.

- **Saving other settings in a separate file**
  In general, it's a good idea to specify any parameters that must be changed when using the script on a different machine or in a different context separately from the rest of the code. In simple cases without security risks, this specification can be done in the first lines of a script. I often name such parameters in capital letters to visually differentiate them from the rest of the variables.

  As a rule, it is still better to store all parameters in a separate file that is imported at the beginning of the script. JSON or INI files are well suited for this purpose (see especially Chapter 10, Section 10.7).

- **Including a sample of the settings file in the Git repository**
  Don't stop at passwords! Critical information also includes hostnames, port numbers, and the names of Amazon Web Services (AWS) buckets or virtual machines.

  Configuration files with these types of data should *not* be included in any Git repository! Without the configuration file, however, getting your script up and running becomes a guessing game for other people. For this reason, a useful approach is to include a sample configuration file in the repository. If the real configuration file is named *mybackup.conf*, you can name the sample file *mybackup.conf.sample*, for example. The purpose of this file is to explain the syntax of the configuration file. However, the file does not contain any real data, only freely invented sample data.

These security rules apply to *all* Git repositories, including private repositories or repositories that are located on their own, non-public GitLab instances. When you set up or use a repository, you can never predict who else will have access to it later. Passwords and other critical information must *never* be stored in repositories.

What Should You Do If a Password Ends Up in a Git Repository after All?

The concept of Git repositories is that any file can also be restored to an earlier state. For this reason, removing the file in question in the next commit or to overwriting the password in the file is of no use. The only safe approach is to change the password in the respective program or on the server in question. If this is impossible because the external system is not controlled by you, you still have the option of deleting the repository in its entirety—an unpleasant thought, I know.

14.2.2 Example

How can we make the fragmentary backup script from earlier in this section better and more securely organized? The script starts with the `. filename` import statement (a short notation for `source filename`). This statement will read the specified file into the script and process it via Bash.

```
# Sample file mybackup.sh
# load initial configuration settings
. mybackup.conf

# mysqldump reads the password from .my.cnf
mysqldump -u $MYSQLUSER $DBNAM > db.sql

# lftp reads the password from .netrc
lftp $FTPHOST << EOF
cd remote/dir/
put db.sql
bye
EOF
```

The corresponding configuration file looks as follows:

```
# mybackup.conf configuration file
MYSQLUSER=root
DBNAME=wordpress
FTPHOST=backupserver.example.com
```

To ensure that this file does not end up in the Git repository, *.gitignore* is extended with the following line:

```
# .gitignore file
mybackup.conf
```

On the other hand, to help users of the script, the following sample file is included in the Git repository:

```
# configuration file mybackup.conf.sample
# copy this file to mybackup.conf and
# replace the sample texts with applicable names!
# note that myscript.sh expects the MySQL password in .my.cnf
# and the FTP password in .netrc.
MYSQLUSER=mysqlaccountname
DBNAME=databasename
FTPHOST=ftphostname
```

PowerShell and Python

The source operator `.` also works in PowerShell. For Python scripts, the best approach is to save your settings in an INI file (see Chapter 10, Section 10.7).

14.3 Git Automation

Many `git` command sequences are repeated over and over again, for example, `git add`, `git commit`, `git pull`, and `git push`. Therefore, automating calls of these commands in scripts often makes sense.

To give you an idea of what such scripts might look like, the commands in the following listing check to see if the current directory is controlled by Git and if a remote repository has been set up. If these requirements are met, `git add . --dry-run` shows which files would be included in the next commit. `git add .` assumes that you have previously set up a *.gitignore* file that excludes all unneeded files from Git operations.

Now, you have the choice: If you specify a commit message, `git add` runs without the `--dry-run` option and performs a commit; the changes are synchronized with the remote repository using `git pull` and `git push`. Thus, the process can be aborted because of the `-e` option in the hash bang, which indicates the script should end as soon as a command causes an error.

```
#!/bin/bash -e
# Sample file git-acp.sh = git add/commit/push
# test if current directory is under Git control
if ! git rev-parse --is-inside-work-tree >& /dev/null; then
    echo "not in git repo, exit"
    exit 1
fi
# test if remote repository exists for current branch
if ! git ls-remote >& /dev/null; then
    echo "no git remote, exit"
    exit 1
fi
```

```
# list files for the commit
echo "Dry run:"
git add -A --dry-run

# abort or enter the commit message
echo "Do you want to add and commit all files listed above?"
echo "Enter commit message or press return to exit."
echo -n "> "
read msg

# run git add, commit, pull + push
if [[ $msg ]]; then
    git add -A
    git commit -m "$msg"
    git pull
    git push
else
    echo "exit"
fi
```


The following lines show a sample run of the script. I have run the script in the working directory of this book. (Of course, I've managed all text, images, layout, and code files for this book using Git.)

```
$ ./code/git/git-acp.sh

  Dry run:
    add '.gitignore'
    add 'bash.md'
    add 'code/git/git-acp.sh'
  Do you want to add and commit all files listed above?
  Enter commit message or press return to exit.
  > git scripting sample, work in progress
  ...
  To github.com:MichaelKofler/scripting-buch.git
     a0ff68f..a60f1d8  main -> main
```

If you work on Windows, you can run the script in Git Bash, or you'll need to develop a PowerShell variant of the code.

A Pinch of Skepticism

You'll find countless Bash and PowerShell scripts on the internet that are structured similar to the previous example. I'm a fan of automating processes; otherwise, I wouldn't have written this book. However, our example is only for demonstration purposes; I don't normally use it myself.

I use Git on a daily basis. I know by heart the few commands I need all the time, and thus, typing effort for me is minimal. No automation is worthwhile, or at best a few aliases are sufficient, such as those contained in the Zsh extension Oh My Zsh.

Also, my Git repositories are quite different in character: Some repositories have only one branch, and I am the only user. With other repositories, many users are involved in multiple branches, with various special cases. Before something goes wrong, I prefer to run `git` manually and not rely on automatisms!

14.3.1 Controlling GitHub Remotely Using gh

The `git` command works for any Git repository. However, this command cannot perform operations that are specific to GitHub, for example, setting up a new repository on GitHub, performing a pull request, and so on. For such purposes, GitHub provides the `gh` command. You can find related downloads and installation instructions at *https://github.com/cli/cli/releases*.

After installation, you would perform a one-time authentication via `gh auth login`, which must be done in a web browser. `gh` takes care of starting the web browser and navigating to the correct page.

Then, you can use `gh repo list` to list your repositories on GitHub, `gh repo create` to set up a new repository, `gh pr create` to add a pull request, `gh pr status` to query the status of a pull request, and so on. You can call `gh` like `git` in your scripts. A reference of all `gh` commands can be found at *https://cli.github.com/manual/gh*.

GitLab Remote Control

As the name suggests, `gh` is only suitable for GitHub. For GitLab, an analogous project exists (the `glab` command); see *https://gitlab.com/gitlab-org/cli*.

14.4 Git Hooks

Git hooks are scripts that are automatically executed before or after certain Git actions. In each new Git repository, you'll find a collection of script patterns for various actions in the `.git/hooks` directory:

```
$ ls .git/hooks

  applypatch-msg.sample      prepare-commit-msg.sample
  commit-msg.sample          pre-push.sample
  fsmonitor-watchman.sample  pre-rebase.sample
  post-update.sample         pre-receive.sample
```

```
pre-applypatch.sample       push-to-checkout.sample
pre-commit.sample           update.sample
pre-merge-commit.sample
```

The sample files are well documented shell scripts. A look into these files not only reveals the purpose of the respective hook, but also immediately shows working sample code.

To activate a hook, you must remove the `.sample` identifier. (Unlike the sample files in this book, the `.sh` identifier is also taboo. The scripts are executed only if they have no identifier at all!)

On Linux and macOS, you also must ensure that the execute bit is set, which means you need to run `chmod +x script.sh`. On Windows, the script is executed by Git Bash. For more basic information on Git hooks, see the Git manual at *https://git-scm.com/book/en/v2/Customizing-Git-Git-Hooks*.

GitHub Actions and GitLab Pipelines

As an alternative to Git hooks, the major Git platforms provide alternative mechanisms to automatically perform actions when commits are executed, for example, for automated testing or for automatic deployment to other systems.

The configuration files for these mechanisms contain script sections where you can specify code in turn. Basic scripting knowledge thus helps even if you don't want to use hooks but do want to use certain advanced GitHub or GitLab features.

14

14.4.1 Example: Detecting Unversioned Files Before the Commit

The `.git/hooks/pre-commit` script is executed before each commit. This script can be used to guarantee compliance with certain rules of for a commit. If the script returns an error code (i.e., an exit code not equal to 0), `git commit` aborts, and the user must fix the detected defect.

The following example comes from my book with Bernd Öggl, *Git: Project Management for Developers and DevOps Teams* (Rheinwerk Computing, 2023). `pre-commit` tests if changed or new files exist that are not included in the commit and also not excluded by *.gitignore*. If so, these files will be listed by `git status`.

`exit 1` prevents you from forgetting a file during a commit. But at the same time, the script forces you to explicitly enumerate in *.gitignore* all the files that should be disregarded. This requirement can be quite annoying.

```
#!/bin/sh
# Sample file pre-commit, must be copied into the
# .git/hooks directory
untracked=$(git ls-files --others --exclude-standard | wc -l)
```

```
if [ $untracked -gt 0 ]; then
    git status
    echo
    echo "Pre commit fail! There are untracked files. Either run"
    echo "'git add' or add an entry to .gitignore."
    exit 1
fi
```

PART III

Applications and Examples

Chapter 15
Backups

The automated creation of backups is *the* classic scripting application. In this chapter, I will show you some concrete examples:

- Synchronization of directories of a desktop computer
- Backup of a WordPress system on a Linux computer
- Backup of SQL Server databases on Windows

Prerequisites for This Chapter

The examples in this chapter are formulated in the Bash and PowerShell languages. In addition to the language basics, I assume that you know how to use Microsoft Windows Task Scheduler and cron (see Chapter 11) and are familiar with SSH (see Chapter 12). Furthermore, you should be familiar with commands like `rsync`, `scp`, and `tar` or cmdlets like `Compress-Archive`.

Instead of your own scripts, you can of course also use ready-made backup solutions. You can find countless backup tools on the internet that run the gamut from simple, free scripts to expensive, commercial applications. If the task is relatively simple, as in the examples in this chapter, your own scripts are definitely sufficient. But, of course, that advice doesn't apply if you need company-wide redundant backups that should account for every conceivable location such as active directories, cloud storage, or employee notebooks located outside the company network.

15.1 Synchronizing Directories to External Storage

You probably use the cloud as a backup storage in some way or other: As a developer, you probably use Git to synchronize your code to a remote repository, combining the benefits of version control with those of an external backup. As an "ordinary" user, you simply save important files to a OneDrive, NextCloud, Dropbox, or iCloud Drive directory. All of these procedures are both useful and secure when applied correctly.

The starting point for this example is the desire to *additionally* synchronize important directories of the notebook to an external data medium. The advantage of this old-fashioned backup method is that stored files are available even if cloud access is not possible at any given time for whatever reason. Local backups also come in handy when data volumes are too large for cloud storage, for example, when virtual machines, video projects, and so on are involved.

I would also like to point out the most important disadvantage right away: "Synchronizing" means that files deleted on your notebook will also be deleted on the external disk. Thus, this backup procedure does not provide the option to restore deleted or overwritten files. In this respect, the Bash or PowerShell scripts presented in this chapter should not represent your sole means of backup but should instead complement other methods.

Be Careful with Backups of Files Currently Used

If you use the script to synchronize files that are currently open and change during copying, the backup is worthless most of the time. This limitation applies, for example, to image files of virtual machines or to databases.

Unfortunately, no universal solution exists for this problem. Ideally, you should run the script at a time when as few files as possible are actively in use. Most database servers provide features to perform consistent backups even while the database is running, but mostly not at the file level. (Two examples of this will follow in the other sections of this chapter.) You could shut down virtual machines in your script for the time of the backup and restart them afterwards. However, such approaches depend quite specifically on the software running on your computer.

Depending on the operating system, file system snapshots represent another solution: In this context, you can temporarily freeze a copy of the file system and use this static copy as the basis for the backup. On Linux, the *Logical Volume Manager (LVM)* or the Btrfs file system provides such options.

15.1.1 PowerShell Script with robocopy

`robocopy`, which stands for *robust file copy*, is a Windows command that has been shipped with all versions of Windows since 2008. Even though the command cannot be called as a cmdlet, it integrates well into PowerShell scripts. The command's myriad options are documented at the following links:

- *https://en.wikipedia.org/wiki/Robocopy*
- *https://learn.microsoft.com/en-us/windows-server/administration/windows-commands/robocopy*

The following script starts with the initialization of three parameters that specify which directories should be synchronized to which destination.

`Get-Volume` retrieves a list of all file systems. If the target disk is not recognized in it, the script will end. For `Where-Object`, note that although `Get-Volume` displays the file system name in the `FriendlyName` column, the property is actually called `FileSystemLabel`—which is hardly comprehensible with what the developers of `Get-Volume` had in mind!

When the target file system is detected, the corresponding drive letter is determined. This letter does not always have to remain the same, depending on which data carriers are currently in use.

The script logs all `robocopy` outputs to a file whose name has the following format: `robocopy-2023-12-31--17-30.log`. This file and a logging directory are set up automatically.

Finally, the script loops through all the directories listed in `$syncdirs` and runs `robocopy`. The options used in this process have the following meaning:

- `/e`: Traverse directories recursively
- `/purge`: Delete locally deleted files and directories also in the backup (caution!)
- `/xo`: Copy only files that have changed; this last option speeds up the synchronization process enormously from the second pass onwards
- `/log+:filename`: Adds logging output to the specified file

```
#!/usr/bin/env pwsh
# Sample file sync-folders.ps1
# $destvolume: name of the backup data medium (such as a USB flash drive).
# $destdir:   name of the target directory on this data medium
# $logdir:    name of the logging directory on the data medium
# $syncdirs: list of directories to be synchronized
#             (relative to the personal files)
$destvolume = "mybackupdisk"
$destdir    = "backup-kofler"
$logdir     = "$destdir\sync-logging"
$syncdirs   = "Documents", "Pictures", "myscripts"
# determine drive letter of the target file system
$disk = Get-Volume |
        Where-Object { $_.FileSystemLabel -eq $destvolume }
if (! $disk) {
    Write-Output "Backup disk $destvolume not found. Exit."
    Exit 1
}
$drive = ($disk | Select-Object -First 1).DriveLetter
Write-Output "Syncing with disk ${drive}:"

# create target directory if it does not exist yet;
# | out-zero prevents the directory name from being displayed
New-Item -ItemType Directory -Force "${drive}:\${destdir}" |
  Out-Null

# create logging directory and logging file
New-Item -ItemType Directory -Force "${drive}:\${logdir}" |
  Out-Null
$logfile = `
```

```
  "${drive}:\${logdir}\robocopy-{0:yyyy-MM-dd--HH-mm}.log" `
  -f (Get-Date)
New-Item $logfile | Out-Null

# loop through the sync directories
foreach ($dir in $syncdirs) {
    $from = "${HOME}\$dir"
    $to = "${drive}:\${destdir}\$dir"
    Write-Output "sync from $from to $to"
    robocopy /e /purge /xo /log+:$logfile "$from" "$to"
}
```

In my tests, the script kept throwing the *access denied* error (error code 5) when writing the files to the USB drive. Countless reports exist about this error on the internet and almost as many suggested solutions. Apparently, only running the script with admin privileges works reliably. You can simply run initial tests in a terminal window with administrator rights. After that, you must set up the script in *Microsoft Windows Task Scheduler* to run once a day with admin rights (**Run with highest privileges** option in the **General** dialog sheet).

15.1.2 Ideas for Improvement

Before you entrust your data to the script, I would like to point out a few restrictions and describe how you can optimize the script:

- **Warning in case of error or non-execution**
  The script simply aborts if the external data drive is not available at the moment. A better approach would be to display or send a warning in some form after several unsuccessful attempts.
- **Exclusion rules**
  The script can synchronize directories either completely or not at all. In practice, exclusion criteria would be helpful for files or directories that should not be included in the backup.

15.1.3 Bash Script with rsync

If you work on Linux or macOS, the best way to realize comparable synchronization tasks is to use a Bash script with `rsync`. The following script has the same structure as the PowerShell script described earlier. It tests whether the backup volume is available at a particular `mount` point and then runs the `rsync` command for a list of local directories.

As described in Chapter 12, Section 12.3, `rsync` also works in conjunction with SSH. Thus, you can adapt the script relatively easily so that your directories are not synchronized with an external data medium but with another computer.

```
# Sample file sync-folders.sh
# what is to be synchronized  where
DESTVOLUME="/run/media/kofler/mybackupdisk"
DESTDIR="backup-kofler"
LOGDIR="$DESTDIR/sync-logging"
SYNCDIRS=("Documents" "Pictures" "myscripts")

# is the backup file system available?
if ! mount | grep $DESTVOLUME --quiet; then
    echo "Backup disk $DESTVOLUME not found. Exit."
    exit 1
fi

# create destination and logging directories
mkdir -p "$DESTVOLUME/$DESTDIR"
mkdir -p "$DESTVOLUME/$LOGDIR"

# compose file name for logging
logfname=$(date "+rsycn-%Y-%m-%d--%H-%M.log")
log="$DESTVOLUME/$LOGDIR/$logfname"

# loop through all directories
for dir in "${SYNCDIRS[@]}"; do
    from=$HOME/$dir
    to=$DESTVOLUME/$DESTDIR/$dir
    echo "sync from $from to $to"
    rsync -a --delete -v "$from" "$to" >> $log
done
```

The rsync options have the following effect:

- -a (*archive*): Process directories recursively, get file information (owner, access rights)
- --delete: Delete locally deleted directories and files also in backup (caution!)
- -v (*verbose*): Output in detail what is currently going on

To have the script called automatically once a day at 12:30 pm, I added the following entry to */etc/crontab*. You can simply adjust the desired time, account name, and path to the backup script to suit your particular requirements:

```
# in file /etc/crontab
30 12 * * * kofler /home/kofler/myscripts/sync-folders.sh
```

macOS

I have tested this script only on Linux. For macOS, small adaptations are required, especially regarding the test that checks whether the backup disk is currently connected to the computer.

15.2 WordPress Backup

The starting point for the second example is a Linux machine running a web server and a database server to implement a web presence using WordPress. The content of the wp database, the /var/www/html/wordpress directory, and the entire server configuration, i.e., the /etc directory, are supposed to be backed up once a day. Compressed backups of the last 7 days should always be kept both locally and on a second server accessible via SSH.

The implementation is created by a Bash script that runs with root privileges. The mysqldump command is used to back up the MySQL database by connecting to the MySQL server with the wpbackupuser account. This account, which only includes rights to perform backups, can be set up in MySQL in the following way:

```
CREATE USER wpbackupuser@localhost IDENTIFIED BY 'TopSecret123';
GRANT Select, Lock Tables, Show View
   ON wp.* TO wpbackupuser@localhost;
GRANT Process, Reload ON *.* TO wpbackupuser@localhost;
```

To make sure that the script does not contain the password in plain text, it is stored in the */root/.my.cnf* file. mysqldump automatically searches for this file and analyzes the data it contains. You should use chmod 600 .my.cnf to make sure that nobody except root is allowed to read this file!

```
# in file /root/.my.cnf
[mysqldump]
user = wpbackupuser
password = TopSecret123
default-character-set = utf8
```

Once all the prerequisites have been met, you can start programming. Various configuration parameters are summarized in the first lines of the script. For better readability, I have used capital letters for these variables.

date +%u generates a consecutive number for the day of the week (1 for Monday to 7 for Sunday). This number will be integrated into the names of the backup files.

mysqlopt contains options for performing the backup. The behavior of mysqldump can be controlled via countless options. I have limited myself in this case to --single-transaction. This option ensures that the database cannot change during the backup. The output of mysqldump is passed to gzip, compressed, and finally stored in the *$dbfile* file. If the file already exists, it will be overwritten. (This process happens for the first time when the script runs for 8 consecutive days. So, you always have backup versions of the last 7 days.)

To perform the backup of a WordPress installation, a short tar command is sufficient (see also Chapter 5, Section 5.3). The WordPress directory also contains all installed plugins, all uploaded images, and so on. As a rule, the file created using tar is much larger than the MySQL backup.

The last line of the script copies the backups, which are only stored locally for the time being, to a second computer. Thus, all backup files are redundantly located in two different places.

```
# Sample file lamp-backup.sh
BACKUPDIR=/localbackup
DB=wp
DBUSER=wpbackupuser
WPDIR=/var/www/html/wordpress
SSH=user@otherhost:wp-backup/
# MySQL-Backup
weekday=$(date +%u)
dbfile=$BACKUPDIR/wp-db-$weekday.sql.gz
mysqlopt='--single-transaction'
mysqldump -u $DBUSER $mysqlopt $DB | gzip -c > $dbfile

# backup of the WordPress installation including plugins and uploads
htmlfile=$BACKUPDIR/wp-html-$weekday.tar.gz
tar czf $htmlfile -C $WPDIR .

# backup of the /etc directory
etcfile=$BACKUPDIR/etc-$weekday.tar.gz
tar czf $etcfile -C /etc .

# copy backup files to a second computer
scp $dbfile $htmlfile $etcfile $SSH
```

After you have executed the script manually, you still need to take care of the automated call. You can design the required line in */etc/crontab* based on the following pattern:

```
# in /etc/crontab
# run script every night at 3:00 am with root privileges
00 3 * * * root /path/to/lamp-backup.sh
```

Once you have set up the backup system, you should observe it for a few days. Does the automatic cron call work? A common cause of errors is that cron jobs often have a different PATH setting than the root account in which you ran your tests. This possibility is especially true if you use commands in the script that were manually installed off the usual paths. For such commands, you may need to specify the full path.

Be sure you also test if you can restore a WordPress installation from the backup files on another computer or in a virtual machine. What's the use of the nicest scripts if you don't realize until disaster strikes that the backup is incomplete for some reason?

Extension: Uploading Encrypted Backups to Amazon Web Services (AWS)

Keeping backup files on external computers is often less secure than on the local server with regard to their accessibility by attackers. Thus, a good idea is to encrypt backup files before uploading them to other hosts.

I'll show you how to encrypt files and then use Simple Storage Service (S3), Amazon's cloud storage service, as a storage location in Chapter 20, where we'll extend our most recent example in this respect.

15.3 SQL Server Backup

The goal of the following script is to back up all the databases of SQL Server as compressed files in a specified directory. For this purpose, I assume that you work on Windows. (SQL Server can also be installed on Linux, but I did not test that scenario for this example.)

For the administration of SQL Server via PowerShell scripts, you can use the `SqlServer` module developed by Microsoft and available in the PowerShell Gallery:

```
> Install-Module SqlServer
```

A reference for all the cmdlets in this module can be found at *https://learn.microsoft.com/en-us/powershell/module/sqlserver*.

Using `Backup-SqlDatabase` it is quite simple to create a backup of a database:

```
> Backup-SqlDatabase -ServerInstance "localhost\SQLEXPRESS01" `
                     -Database "dbname"
```

In this command, we use `-ServerInstance` to specify the name under which the SQL Server is accessible. Of course, the command can be executed only if your Windows account has access rights to the database server. By default, the backup ends up in the server's backup directory, which is usually at the following location:

```
C:\Program Files\Microsoft SQL Server\MSSQLn.n\MSSQL\Backup
```

Alternatively, you can specify the desired backup filename by using the `-BackupFile` option. (Numerous other options enable you to control how `Backup-SqlDatabase` works. Just take a look at the documentation!) The files created by `Backup-SqlDatabase` are in a binary format that can be compressed well.

dbatools

A useful alternative to the `SqlServer` module is the `dbatools` (see *https://dbatools.io/commands*). This module is much more extensive and includes many more cmdlets. If you specialize in the administration of SQL Server instances, you should definitely familiarize yourself with `dbatools`!

15.3.1 Backing Up and Compressing all Databases via Script

With this introductory information, you should have no problem understanding the next script. It starts with the declaration of some parameters that you'll need to adjust according to your own setup. `$exclude` contains a list of databases that should *not* be backed up. This list must necessarily contain `tempdb`. Attempting to apply `Backup-SqlDatabase` to this internal SQL server database will result in an error.

`Get-SqlDatabase` determines all databases available on SQL server. A loop then processes all databases. Each backup file is immediately packed into its own archive file. (Of course, you could conceivably save all databases together in one archive. But since databases can get huge, this approach is not a good idea.) With the `-Force` option, already existing ZIP files are overwritten without an error message. The original backup file will be deleted as a result.

```
# Sample file backup-all-dbs.ps1
$instance = "localhost\SQLEXPRESS01"
$backupdir = "C:\sqlserver-backups"
$exclude = "tempdb", "other", "tmp"

# create backup directory if it does not exist yet
New-Item -ItemType Directory -Force $backupdir | Out-Null

# loop through all databases
$dbs = Get-SqlDatabase -ServerInstance $instance
foreach($db in $dbs) {
    # skip databases from $exclude
    if ($db.name -in $exclude) { continue }

    # compose names of backup files
    $backupname = "$backupdir\$($db.name).bak"
    $archivename = "$backupdir\$($db.name).zip"
    Write-Output "Backup database $($db.name) to $archivename"

    # backup, create archive (-Force to overwrite existing),
    # delete original backup file
    Backup-SqlDatabase -ServerInstance $instance `
      -Database $db.name -BackupFile $backupname
    Compress-Archive -Force $backupname $archivename
    Remove-Item $backupname
}
```

Chapter 16
Image Processing

In my day-to-day work, scripts often help me to keep the flood of digital images under control. The scripts presented in this chapter perform the following tasks:

- Converting images from one format to another and downsizing and watermarking them if necessary
- Sorting photos into directories based on the date they were taken, using exchangeable image file format (Exif) data
- Entering metadata from photos into a database

For these purposes, the *ImageMagick* and *ExifTool* open-source tools are used.

Prerequisites for This Chapter

To read this chapter, you only need basic knowledge of the Bash, PowerShell, and Python languages.

16.1 Manipulating Image Files

Whether you want to convert PNG images to JPG format (or vice versa), include watermarks or take transparency effects into account, limit the maximum resolution, or crop a partial image—the free tools of the ImageMagick library will be helpful. The only obstacle is the non-trivial control of the commands through its countless options.

16.1.1 Installing ImageMagick

Most Linux distributions provide ImageMagick as a package. On Ubuntu, you must run `apt install imagemagick` to install it. On macOS, the easiest way to install it is to use Homebrew (i.e., `brew install imagemagick`).

For Windows, you can find an installation program at *https://imagemagick.org/script/download.php*. If you want to update an already installed version, you should uninstall it beforehand; otherwise, the old and the new versions will be installed in parallel, which is rarely useful. The setup program suggests adding the installation directory to the `PATH`, so be sure to leave this option checked. In general, it's mostly appropriate to leave the preselected options.

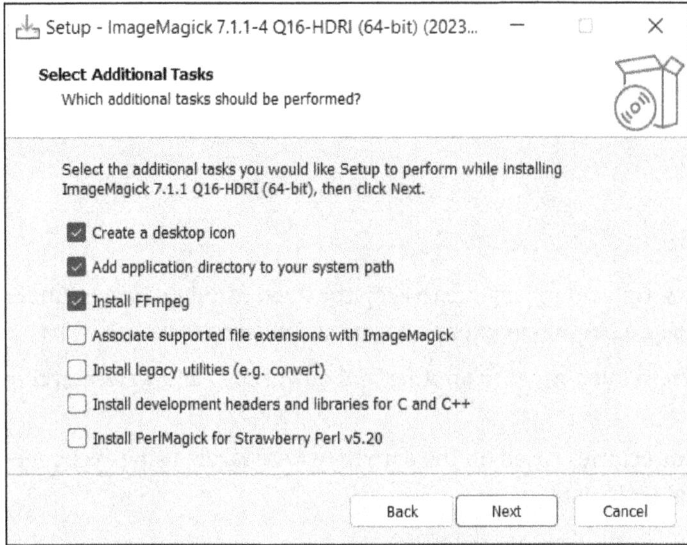

Figure 16.1 Installing ImageMagick on Windows

Use `magick --version` in a terminal to verify that the installation was successful and that the command is found:

```
$ magick --version
  Version: ImageMagick 7.1.1-4 Q16-HDRI x86_64 ...
```

If you also want to read PostScript, PDF, or Encapsulated PostScript (EPS) files with ImageMagick, you must also install the PostScript interpreter Ghostscript. On Linux and macOS, you can install appropriate packages via `apt`, `dnf`, or `brew`. Windows downloads can be found at *https://ghostscript.com/releases/gsdnld.html.*

16.1.2 Trying Out ImageMagick

ImageMagick provides the `magick` command, which is very versatile. However, several hundred options are available to control the behavior of this command, as described at *https://imagemagick.org/script/magick.php.*

Do not let all this choice confuse you! In many cases, `magick` can be applied easily. To convert an existing file to another format, simply specify the filename of the source file and that of a new result file. `magick` recognizes the desired data type by its identifier:

```
$ magick in.bmp out.png
```

ImageMagick 6: Use convert instead of magick

Many Linux distributions still rely on ImageMagick 6. This version does not provide the `magick` command. Instead, you must use `convert`. However, beginning with version 7, `convert` is deprecated in favor of `magick`.

The following command reduces a PNG image to a maximum size of 1024×1024 pixels. The image proportions are preserved. An image with originally 6000×4000 pixels is scaled to 1024×683 pixels. The > character after `1024x1024` causes small images to *not* be scaled up. 1024×1024 pixels are therefore the upper limit. The result will be saved in JPG format.

Transparent areas of the PNG image are displayed in light pink. The color code corresponds to the familiar CSS syntax. `-flatten` merges all image layers. `-quality 75` reduces the quality of the JPEG compression to 75 percent. This option reduces quality but also reduces the size of the image file. (By default, a quality level of 92 percent applies.)

```
$ magick in.png -resize '1024x1024>' -background '#ffdddd' \
    -flatten -quality 75 out.jpg
```

In the third example, `magick` adds a diagonal watermark text with a copyright notice in the middle of the image:

```
$ magick in.png -gravity center \
    -pointsize 40 -font Arial -fill black \
    -draw "rotate 45 text 0,0 '(c) Michael Kofler 2023'" out.png
```


Unlike many other commands, `magick` does not care about the order of the options. Rather, they are executed in the specified order or refer to the currently active image (if multiple image files are merged).

If you want to process multiple images at once, it is usually advisable to program a script. Creating a script has an advantage in that the often laboriously compiled options will be available again the next time. However, you can of course perform simple tasks directly in the terminal.

The final example in Bash syntax runs through all `*.jpeg` files in the current directory and turns them into *thumbnails* (i.e., greatly reduced images). Watch out though because since the following command uses the same source and destination filename, the original images will be overwritten! If you don't want that to happen, you must use another destination filename (e.g., `"thumb-$file"`).

```
$ for file in *.jpeg; do magick "$file" -resize '320x320' \
    -quality 80 "$file"; done
```

As far as the destination file format supports Exif data, this data will be preserved. Exif data is metadata that, among other things, provides information about the place and time the image was taken. Exif data is the focus of the remaining sections of this chapter. If you want to remove Exif data, you can call `magick` with the `-strip` option. A safer choice is to use the `exiftool -all:all= file.jpg` command presented in the next section.

Quoting Special Characters

Note that the magick syntax provides for various special characters that have a special meaning in Bash and PowerShell. You should either enclose the strings in quotes, as in the previous examples, or use the quotation mark \ (Bash) or ` (PowerShell).

Artificial Intelligence (AI) Help

AI tools like ChatGPT also know ImageMagick. If you have a specific task, it's at least worth trying to determine the required combination of options with AI support. In my attempts, the hit rate was about 50 percent. The result did not always correspond to my expectations, but often, ChatGPT put me on the right track. Note that both ChatGPT and many proposed solutions on the internet use the convert command instead of magick.

16.1.3 Example: convert2eps (Bash Variant)

To make printable PostScript files from the text files of my books in Markdown or LaTeX formats, I need an equivalent EPS file for each screenshot in PNG format, which is exactly what our next script takes care of.

This example loops through all PNG files in the current directory. If no <name>.eps file exists for <name>.png or if the PNG file is newer than the EPS file (comparison operator -nt; i.e., *newer than*), magick creates a new EPS file.

The magick options or parameters have the following meaning: -quiet suppresses the display of warnings and status messages. -background white uses a white background for the transparent areas of the image. -flatten merges the image layers.

eps2:$epsfile specifies that the PostScript Level 2 specifications should apply when writing the EPS file. This choice has a big impact on image size because the file is compressed much better (without quality loss) than in default level 1. Level 3 (i.e., eps3:$epsfile) promises even more compact files. However, this level places higher demands on the printer or exposure software and can cause compatibility problems.

```
# Sample file convert2eps.sh
for pngfile in *.png; do
    # replace .png identifier with .eps
    epsfile=${pngfile%.png}.eps
    if [ $pngfile -nt $epsfile ]; then
        echo "$pngfile -> $epsfile"
        magick "$pngfile" -quiet -background white \
           -flatten "eps2:$epsfile"
    fi
done
```

16.1.4 Example: convert2eps (PowerShell Variant)

You can use the last script as a pattern for various uses of magick—whether you want to resize hundreds of images, watermark them, or convert them to a different format. If you work in Windows, the script in the next listing serves the same purpose:

```
# Sample file convert2eps.ps1
$pngfiles = Get-ChildItem *.png
foreach ($pngfile in $pngfiles) {
    $pngname = $pngfile.Name
    $epsname = $pngname -replace ".png", ".eps"
    # skip if there is already an up-to-date EPS file
    if ( (Test-Path $epsname) -and
         (Get-ChildItem $epsname).LastWriteTime
                        -gt $pngfile.LastWriteTime )
    {
        continue
    }
    Write-Host "$pngname -> $epsname"
    magick $pngname -quiet -background white -flatten `
      eps2:$epsname
}
```


Editing Images on Windows without ImageMagick

Of course, various classes exist in the .NET framework that include elementary functions for image processing that you can apply in PowerShell scripts. None of these classes can even come close to matching ImageMagick's capabilities. This limitation is offset by the advantage of not needing to install external tools. A good example of using the System.Drawing.Bitmap class can be found at *https://stackoverflow.com/questions/47602716*.

16.2 Sorting Photos by Date Taken

The starting point of this example is a large collection of photos in the JPEG format. These files are supposed to be moved to directories that indicate the month of the date on which they were taken. Thus, a photo taken in July 2023 should be moved to the 2023-07 directory. If this directory does not exist yet, it should be created.

The solution to this task succeeds through the analysis of Exif data. This data is metadata built into the JPEG file by the camera. Depending on the smartphone or camera model, the Exif data contains the date the photo was taken; the location (GPS coordinates); various camera parameters (aperture, exposure time); the orientation (image rotation, e.g., *portrait* or *landscape*); and so on.

16.2.1 Installing and Trying Out ExifTool

The best tool for analyzing Exif data is *ExifTool*. This package consists of a Perl library and the `exiftool` command. On Linux, you can install ExifTool from the package sources. The package name varies depending on the distribution. `exiftool -ver` then determines the version number.

```
$ sudo apt install exiftool                 (Debian, Ubuntu)
$ sudo dnf install perl-Image-ExifTool      (Fedora)
$ sudo pacman -S perl-exiftool              (Arch Linux)

$ exiftool -ver
  12.50
```

Installation on Windows is a bit more tedious: At *https://exiftool.org*, you can find a ZIP file for download. However, that file does *not* contain any setup program. Instead, you must manually copy the `exiftool(-k).exe` file contained in the archive to a directory listed in the `PATH` variable. The easiest way is to use `C:\Windows` (which requires administrator rights, however). Then, you must rename the file to `exiftool.exe`.

Microsoft Defender blocks the first attempt to run ExifTool on Windows because the publisher is unknown. Click **More information** and **Run anyway**. As a result, the startup succeeds without a problem, even from the terminal.

You also must overcome some small hurdles on macOS: The DMG image contains a **.pkg* file with an installer. However, the execution is blocked by macOS because the installer is not signed. You must open the **Privacy** module in the system settings. Then, click on **Open ExifTool n.n.pgk anyway**.

Once the installation is done, using the `exiftool` command is quite simple: You can pass a filename and get a seemingly endless list of Exif values as a result:

```
$ exiftool cimg2647.jpg

  ExifTool Version Number       : 12.50
  File Name                     : cimg2647.jpg
  ...
  Date/Time Original            : 2008:08:28 12:53:22
  ...
  Shutter Speed                 : 1/250
  Circle Of Confusion           : 0.005 mm
  Field Of View                 : 50.7 deg
```

To sort the images by the date on which they were taken, only the `Date/Time Original` entry is relevant. The option of the same name, in combination with the desired format for the date (`-d`) and the `-s3` option (for *shortest*), reduces the output to the desired information:

```
$ exiftool -d '%Y-%m' -s3 -DateTimeOriginal cimg2647.jpg

  2008-08
```

Exif data can reveal a lot of information about the origin of the images. ExifTool therefore provides the option to remove the Exif data from a file. The recommended command is `exiftool -All= image.jpg`. This command removes almost all metadata but leaves the APP14 Adobe block of color information. This data block is necessary so that the colors of the image can be displayed correctly. However, the data has no privacy relevance. Concerning deleting Exif data, we also recommend reading the following post on the ExifTool forum: *https://exiftool.org/forum/index.php?topic=13034.0.*

ExifTool has countless other options, which I will not go into here. Refer to the manual, if necessary, at *https://exiftool.org/exiftool_pod.html.*

16.2.2 Bash Example

The following lines show an implementation of the `sort` script in Bash. The code should be understandable without further explanation.

```
# Sample file sort-photos.sh
# loop through all filenames passed as parameters
for file in "$@"; do
    yearmonth=$(exiftool -s3 -d '%Y-%m' -DateTimeOriginal $file)
    if [ $yearmonth ]; then
        echo "$file -> $yearmonth/"
        mkdir -p $yearmonth
        mv "$file" $yearmonth/
    fi
done
```

To facilitate trying out the script, you'll find an archive with some small photos in the sample files at *https://rheinwerk-computing.com/5851.*

```
$ ./sort-photos.sh *.jpg

  cimg2372.jpg -> 2007-12/
  cimg2374.jpg -> 2007-12/
```

The script ignores all files without Exif data or with missing recording time and leaves them at the previous location. To test this process, `photos.zip` contains some special cases: `z-empty.jpg` is simply an empty file (0 bytes). `z-almost-no-metadata.jpeg` was taken with an iPhone, then downsized, and finally stripped of almost all Exif data by using `exiftool -All=`. Then, `z-gimp-metadata.jpeg` was inserted as a screenshot into the image processing program Gimp and then saved. The file therefore contains only the metadata provided by Gimp for newly created images.

16.2.3 PowerShell Example

The code for the PowerShell implementation looks almost the same as the one for the Bash script. The biggest difference is the nested loop. This nested loop is required because PowerShell does not perform *globbing*, that is, it does not convert patterns like `*.jpg` into a list of filenames. You must do this step yourself!

The first loop runs through all parameters. The second loop executes `Get-Item` for each parameter. With a filename like `myimg.jpg`, `Get-Item` simply returns the file. If, on the other hand, an expression was passed, then `Get-Item` returns the list of matching files. The two loops ensure that a call of `.\sort-images.ps1 *.jpg *.jpeg` is also processed correctly.

```
# Sample file sort-images.ps1
# loop through all parameters
foreach ($arg in $args) {
    # loop through the Get-Item results
    foreach ($file in Get-Item $arg) {
        $yearmonth = exiftool -s3 -d '%Y-%m' `
                              -DateTimeOriginal $file
        if ($yearmonth) {
            Write-Output "$($file.Name) -> $yearmonth/"
            $targetdir = New-Item -ItemType Directory `
                                  -Path $yearmonth -Force
            Move-Item $file $targetdir
        }
    }
}
```

Speed Problems

When it comes to sorting "only" a few hundred images, the approach presented in this section is good enough. However, when dealing with thousands of images, a more efficient approach is to use the scripting features built into ExifTool, which requires a detailed study of the manual. With ExifTool scripting, ExifTool needs to be started only once and not thousands of times. This feature is crucial because ExifTool uses the Perl programming language. Whenever ExifTool is started, a complex Perl environment needs to be loaded. By starting ExifTool only once and then processing many commands within the environment, a lot of time can be saved. You can find a code example at *https://exiftool.org/mistakes.html#M3*.

16.3 Converting Exif Metadata to SQL Commands

The goal of the next example is to process a pool of photos and enter the most important metadata of each image into a database. Among other things, the name, file size, modification date, and GPS coordinates should be saved. The somewhat higher complexity of this task suggests the use of Python in this case.

16.3.1 PyExifTool

Various Exif modules are available for Python. The *PyExifTool* presented in this section uses the `exiftool` command. Thus, you must install the ExifTool first (Section 16.2) and then run the following `pip` command:

```
$ pip  install pyexiftool     (Windows, new Linux distributions)
$ pip3 install pyexiftool     (macOS, old Linux distributions)
```

The following listing shows the application of the module. `ExifToolHelper` establishes the connection to the `exiftool` command. For efficiency reasons, this connection will be maintained until it is no longer needed, so `exiftool` doesn't need to be called again for each image. The `with` construct takes care of closing the connection in any case, either at the end of the code block or when an error occurs.

Now, you can pass a list of filenames to the `get_metadata` method. The method responds with a list of dictionaries, each dictionary containing all the metadata available for that image. In the sample script, only a few selected Exif parameters are read.

16

```
# Sample file hello-pyexiftool.py
# call: ./hello-pyexiftool.py file1.jpg file2.jpg
import exiftool, sys
filenames = sys.argv[1:]
keys = ['SourceFile', 'EXIF:Model', 'EXIF:ExposureTime',
        'EXIF:ISO', 'EXIF:DateTimeOriginal']

with exiftool.ExifToolHelper() as exifhelper:
    # returns a list with dictionaries, one dictionary for
    # every filename
    metadatalst = exifhelper.get_metadata(filenames)
    # show selected EXIF elements for each photo
    for metadata in metadatalst:
        print()
        for key in keys:
            # does the key exist at all?
            if key in metadata:
                print('%25s : %-30s' % (key, metadata[key]))
```

The following lines present a test run for two files:

```
$ ./exif-to-sql.py IMG_3798.jpg IMG_3799.jpg

               SourceFile : IMG_3798.jpg
               EXIF:Model : Canon IXUS 210
```

```
     EXIF:ExposureTime : 0.0008
              EXIF:ISO : 100
  EXIF:DateTimeOriginal : 2012:11:03 08:44:32

           SourceFile : IMG_3799.jpg
           EXIF:Model : Canon IXUS 210
     EXIF:ExposureTime : 0.0008
              EXIF:ISO : 125
  EXIF:DateTimeOriginal : 2012:11:03 08:44:39
```

Note that different Exif data is available depending on the smartphone or camera model. For this reason, you should always secure access to individual entries. (In the last code listing, this secure access is created via `if key in metadata`.)

The `exifhelper.get_metadata(filenames)` statement in the last example unfortunately has its pitfalls, such as the following:

- If even a single file contains incorrect Exif metadata or is missing entirely, then an `ExifToolExceptionError` will occur. The error makes it impossible to analyze the results of the remaining files.
- A second problem is that `get_metadata` reads all metadata, even metadata you're not interested in. Depending on the operating system (Windows!) the *charmap: codec can't decode byte xxx in position nnn* error may occur. Apparently the PyExifTool chokes on UTF-8 strings in the metadata. In my tests, the error occurred only on Windows and only in PyExifTool, not when `exiftool` was called directly.

In this respect, a better approach is to process each image file individually and to secure the analysis by using `try-except`. Also, instead of `get_metadata`, you should use the `get_tags` method, which processes only selected Exif keys. I will demonstrate this procedure in the next script, `exif-to-sql.py`.

16.3.2 EXIF2SQL

The first subtask of the `exif-to-sql.py` script is *globbing* (i.e., the analysis of patterns like `*.jpg`). On macOS and Linux, this step is not needed because, in those cases, the shell generates the corresponding list of files from `*.jpg` and passes it to the script.

On Windows, on the other hand, the `*.jpg` parameter ends up unchanged in the parameters list. If the script determines that it is running on Windows by analyzing `platform.system()`, it must determine the appropriate filenames itself. This task is performed by the `glob` function from the module of the same name. The loop through `argv[:1]` ensures that globbing works correctly even if multiple file patterns are passed (so, for example, `.\exif-to-sql.py *.jpg *.jpeg`).

The keys list is initialized with the names of all Exif parameters the script is supposed to analyze. Note that you must use the two-part name structure of PyExifTool. (ExifTool, on the other hand, uses shorter names without preceding group names.)

The sql variable contains the SQL command to be run. inspect.cleandoc removes the indentations from the multiline string. The INSERT command requires that the database contain a corresponding table. I will show you how to set up the table, if needed, in Chapter 19, Section 19.3.

```
# Sample file exif-to-sql.py
import exiftool, inspect, platform, sys
from glob import glob

# Globbing (only necessary on Windows)
if platform.system() == 'Windows':
    filenames = []
    for arg in sys.argv[1:]:
        filenames.extend(glob(arg))
else:
    filenames = sys.argv[1:]

# analyze only these EXIF parameters
keys = ['File:FileName', 'File:FileSize', 'EXIF:Orientation',
        'EXIF:DateTimeOriginal', 'EXIF:GPSLatitude',
        'EXIF:GPSLongitude', 'EXIF:GPSAltitude']

# SQL command to insert a data record;
# cleandoc removes the indentation
sql = inspect.cleandoc("""
  INSERT INTO photos (name, size, orientation, datetimeoriginal,
                      latitude, longitude, altitude)
  VALUES (%s, %s, %s, %s, %s, %s, %s);""")
```

After this preparatory work, ExifToolHelper establishes the connection to the locally installed ExifTool.

The for loop processes all image files. get_tags reads only the Exif tags specified by keys. These keys are then collected in the results list, with missing tags replaced by NULL. For the DateTimeOriginal tag, the format of the date must also be changed from 2023:12:13 to the International Organization for Standardization (ISO) format-compliant syntax 2023-12-13. For this purpose, replace replaces the first two colons with hyphens.

Finally, the results gathered in this way are converted into a tuple and incorporated into the SQL string using the % formatting operator.

```
# ... Continued, connect to exiftool
with exiftool.ExifToolHelper() as exifhelper:
    # loop through all image files
    for file in filenames:
        # gather EXIF data
        results = []
        try:
            # get_tags reads only selected keys
            metadata = exifhelper.get_tags(file, keys)[0]
            for key in keys:
                if key in metadata:
                    if key == 'EXIF:DateTimeOriginal':
                        # 2023:12:13 -> 2023-12-13
                        date = str(metadata[key]).\
                                 replace(':', '-', 2)
                        results += [ "'%s'" % (date) ]
                    else:
                        results += [ "'%s'" % (metadata[key]) ]
                else:
                    results += ['NULL']
            print(sql % tuple(results))
        except Exception as e:
            print("-- skipped %s" % (file))
```

If you call the script and pass some JPEG files, the output will look as follows:

```
$ ./exif-to-sql *.jpg *.jpeg

  INSERT INTO photos (name, size, orientation, datetimeoriginal,
                      latitude, longitude, altitude)
  VALUES ('IMG_3422.jpeg', '23521', '1', '2022-01-07 15:54:01',
          '47.1209027777778', '13.6318833333333', '2033.231752');
  ...
```

Of course, you can also redirect the output to an SQL file:

```
$ ./exif-to-sql *.jpg *.jpeg > photos.sql
```

Missing GPS Data

Photos that you take with a smartphone always contain geographical data unless you have explicitly disabled this function. Note, however, that for privacy reasons, some photo programs remove the location information when photos are exported. For example, if you use Apple Photos, make sure to set the **Include • Location Information** option when exporting!

16.3.3 Options for Enhancement

Naturally, you can adapt the script according to your own ideas, depending on what Exif data you want to store in the database.

Instead of displaying the SQL commands on the screen or redirecting them to a file, the script could also connect to a database server and run the commands there. I present a corresponding extension of the script in Chapter 19.

Assuming a database connection, the script could also perform a duplicate check, that is, replace entries instead of adding them, if only the filename or the combination of filename and file size matches.

Chapter 17
Web Scraping

Web scraping refers to the targeted extraction of data from a webpage. The basic idea is to load the HTML code of a page and search for the desired data there. With web scraping, you can automatically determine the price of a product on shopping websites, the current temperature in Hawaii on a weather website, the latest headlines on a news website, or the latest security vulnerabilities for software you use on a security site.

In this chapter, I'll describe some techniques around web scraping:

- I am going to start with the `wget` command: This command allows you to download entire websites including all linked images, CSS files, and so on. Technically, this command has little to do with web scraping and goes more in the direction of *web crawling*. (I will explain the term shortly.) An advantage of using `wget` is that you can solve complex tasks with a single command without having to develop a script at all.
- Using regular expressions, you can analyze the HTML code of documents and in this way determine the desired data. However, this approach only works satisfactorily in simple cases.
- A better approach is to use a library that represents an HTML document as an object tree. The technical term for this library is *Document Object Model (DOM)*. In this chapter, I will introduce the Python modules *Beautiful Soup* and *Requests-HTML* as well as the PowerShell module, called *PowerHTML*, will allow you to navigate through complex HTML documents with ease. The resulting code is clearer and more reliable than using regular expressions.

17

Prerequisites for This Chapter

Most of the scripts in this chapter use the Python programming language. Therefore, you should know how to use regular expressions. You also need basic HTML knowledge, but I can't teach you that in this book.

17.1 Limitations

Web scraping is a popular scripting concept, but it comes with numerous limitations:

- The structure of a web page changes frequently. Web scraping script must thus be adjusted often.

- Modern websites use JavaScript on the client side, which can cause a simple readout of the HTML code to fail. (You're lucky if JavaScript is only responsible for displaying the ubiquitous ads.)
- Basically, it's not permitted to use data collected via web scraping for commercial purposes. Let me illustrate this rule with a simple example: You can't collect weather data from a popular weather website, share it with your customers in some form, and possibly make money from advertising in the process.

  Of course, not *everything* is forbidden: After all, the basic idea of the internet is that information is shared publicly. A popular permitted application of web scraping is price comparison sites such as *https://www.pricegrabber.com/*. But even for such services, rules of the game apply, for example, regarding the use of product photos.

  Legally, we're navigating rocky terrain. I will let this warning stand and focus on technical details in this chapter. However, an essential task is that you clarify the legal requirements before using web scraping beyond the purely private sphere!

The solution to these limitations are *application programming interfaces (APIs)*, which provide an ordered access to data. While webpages are optimized in terms of beautiful layout, APIs allow for an efficient data exchange without overhead, with some APIs even allowing data changes. In addition, API usage rules provide clarity as to which data may be used and how, or what costs are incurred in the process.

To cut a long story short: If the website whose data you want to use provides an API, you should skip ahead to Chapter 18.

17.2 Web Scraping, Web Crawling, and Data Mining

Two other terms are often used along with *web scraping* that have similar meanings. While *web scraping* extracts data from a website, *web crawling* tracks the links of a website. Through web crawling, you can create a directory of all pages on a website and, when tracking links to other pages, even a directory of large parts of the internet. Search engines like Google or Bing are based on the concept of web crawling.

Data mining also goes a step further than web scraping: In this context, we are combining and statistically analyzing information from different data sources and over longer periods of time. Many reasons exist for data mining, such as marketing studies or scientific tasks.

17.3 Downloading Websites Using wget

In its simplest usage, you can use the `wget` command to download a file via HTTP(S) or FTP. The following command downloads an image of the cover of this book from my website and saves it in the local directory:

```
$ wget https://kofler.info/wp-content/uploads/scripting-en.jpg
```

Most of the time, wget is installed by default on Linux; if not the case, apt/dnf install wget will help you get set up. On macOS, the best way to install the command is to use brew install wget (see *https://brew.sh*). A variant compiled for Windows can be downloaded from: *https://eternallybored.org/misc/wget*. However, you must take care of saving the program yourself in one of the directories listed in PATH.

wget can be controlled by dozens of options documented in its man page or at *https://linux.die.net/man/1/wget*.

17.3.1 Example 1: Downloading Directly Linked Images

I will refrain from an encyclopedic description here, but instead show you three typical cases of using wget.

The first command, which I have specified once with the more readable long options and a second time in a more compact way with equivalent short options, downloads all image files with the extensions *.jpg, *.jpeg, *.png, and *.gif that are used directly on the home page of *https://example.com*. However, the command does not take into account images used in other pages of *https://example.com*.

```
$ wget --no-directories --span-hosts --page-requisites \
       --accept jpg,jpeg,png,gif --execute robots=off example.com

$ wget -nd -H -p -A jpg,jpeg,png,gif -e robots=off example.com
```


Let's briefly explain the meanings of these options next:

- --no-directories does not create image directories on your computer that represent the location of images on the website. Rather, all images are stored in the currently active directory.
- --span-hosts also takes into account links to images located on websites other than the home page (here *https://example.com*).
- --page-requisites tells wget to download not only the HTML start page, but also all additional files linked there (images, but also CSS files, etc.).
- --accept restricts the previous option: We are only interested in files with the specified identifiers.
- --execute specifies that any rules formulated on the website in the robots.txt file should be ignored for search engines. That's not the way to do it!

The command fails for images whose URL does not end with the identifier, such as in the following example:

```
https://example.com/images/img_1234.jpg?s=2b63769b
```

17.3.2 Example 2: Downloading all PDF Files Linked on the Website

The second command is a variant of the first. This time, PDF documents are downloaded instead of images. However, not only should the start page of *https://example.com* be taken into account, but also all other pages of this website, which wget can reach by analyzing links starting from the home page within four jumps.

```
$ wget --recursive -no-directories --level=4 --accept pdf \
       --execute robots=off example.com

$ wget -r -nd -l 4 -A pdf -e robots=off example.com
```

The command uses two new options:

- --recursive tells wget to continue following the links located on the home page and also to search the target pages. By default, the command only includes pages on the source domain. (I have omitted --span-hosts in this example. The explanation follows below).
- --level specifies how many link levels should be considered. You can use --level inf to really search a website in its entirety.

You need patience when running the command. Note that the command only considers PDF files stored directly on the specified website, not PDF documents located elsewhere (for example, in an Amazon cloud directory).

In contrast to the first example, using the --span-hosts option is not recommended here. Although wget will then also download PDF files located on other servers, at the same time the command will extend the search to the pages of other servers. Tips on how you can limit this problem, for example by listing selected external hosts, are provided by Stack Overflow: *https://stackoverflow.com/questions/16780601*.

Many Page Views and High Data Volumes

The --recursive option will cause you to download countless files from the specified website in a short time. This causes a relatively high load for the web server, depending on the network speed. For this reason, some administrators limit the maximum number of requests originating from an IP address. In the worst case, the crawling attempt in disregard of the robot rules can even be interpreted as an attack.

17.3.3 Example 3: Creating a Local Copy of the Website

The third command copies all files of a website to a local directory. Images and CSS files are also taken into account. The directory structure of the website is replicated locally. Finally (only once the download of *all* files is finished!) all links are replaced by links to local files.

Ideally, you can now view the local copy of the website in a browser without an internet connection. In real life, this does not always work that well. A major source of errors is JavaScript code that does not work as expected.

```
$ wget --mirror --convert-links --adjust-extension --no-parent \
  --page-requisites --max-redirect=3  https://example.com

$ wget -m -k -E -np -p --max-redirect=3  https://example.com
```

The options have the following meaning:

- `--mirror` activates the mirroring functions. These include recursive link processing and unlimited link tracking.
- `--convert-links` converts links within the website to local links. This action can be performed only once all downloads are finished.
- `--adjust-extension` adds the `.html` identifier to downloaded HTML files that have no extension.
- `--no-parent` traces links only "downward" (into subdirectories), but not "upward" (outside the starting point).
- `--max-redirect` limits the number of redirection statements from the web server.

The same warnings apply to the execution of the command as for the second example.

17.4 Web Scraping with Regular Expressions

In Chapter 9, I already warned against using regular expressions for processing HTML documents. Nevertheless, regular expressions are often used in practice for exactly this purpose—simply because using them is obvious and requires little effort. The following Python script is a good example of this use. The goal of the script is to download all images linked on an HTML page via `<img src=...>`.

The code is basically easy to understand: The script first creates the local directory `tmp`, if it does not exist yet, and then downloads the HTML document with the address specified in `url`. `findall` searches in it for expressions of the `<img src="..."` type and returns a list of the regex group as a result (i.e., in each case the address between the quotation marks).

The loop processes all links and prefixes relative addresses with the start address. It then extracts the actual image name from the often long URLs. In this step, `urllib.urlsplit` and `os.path.basename` are used. The following lines illustrate the use of the two functions:

```
import os
from urllib import parse
url = 'https://example.com/dir1/dir2/img.jpg?p1=123&p2=534'
path = str(parse.urlsplit(url).path) # '/dir1/dir2/img.jpg'
base = os.path.basename(path)        # 'img.jpg'
```

Finally, the script tries to download all images and save them in the temporary directory.

```
# Sample program load-images.py
from urllib import parse, request
import os, re

# create temporary directory
os.makedirs("tmp/", exist_ok=True)
# load HTML code
url = "https://sap-press.com"
with request.urlopen(url) as response:
    html = response.read().decode('utf8')
# search for <img src="..." using regular expression
imageUrls = re.findall(r'<img.*?src=\"(.+?)\"', html)
for imgUrl in imageUrls:
    # convert relative links to absolute links
    if not imgUrl.startswith('http'):
        imgUrl =  parse.urljoin(url, imgUrl)
    # extract destination filename
    path = str(parse.urlsplit(imgUrl).path)
    basename = os.path.basename(path)
    destination = 'tmp/' + basename
    try:
        # download and save image
        with request.urlopen(imgUrl) as response, \
             open(destination, 'wb') as f:
            f.write(response.read())
        print(basename)
    except:
        print("skipped", basename[:30])
```

For simple HTML pages, the script works perfectly, and you might get the impression that not too much can actually go wrong, which would be a big mistake:

- The script also recognizes the `<img src="..."` expression in HTML code that's commented out, in listings (`<pre>`), and in JavaScript code where parts of the filename are generated dynamically. This recognition results in download errors.
- The script fails if is a line break exists between `<img` and `src="..."`. `findall(..., re.MULTILINE)` does not help in such cases either without further ado because then `\n` must be explicitly built into the regular expression.
- The script cannot handle images whose content is embedded directly in the HTML code (for example, as in `<img src="data:image/png;base64 ...`).

The point remains: Although tempting, you should avoid using regular expressions in web scraping processes!

17.5 Web Scraping with Beautiful Soup

The "right" way to do web scraping is to use an HTML parser that builds a DOM from the HTML code. For Python, several HTML parsers have been optimized with regard to different properties (e.g., speed, error tolerance, ease of use). An initial overview is available at the following links:

- *https://elitedatascience.com/python-web-scraping-libraries*
- *https://html5-parser.readthedocs.io/en/latest/*

17.5.1 Beautiful Soup and Requests

The following examples rely on the Python module, Beautiful Soup, version 4, which is used in combination with Python's default HTML parser. You must first install this module using pip:

```
$ pip  install beautifulsoup4  (Windows, Linux)
$ pip3 install beautifulsoup4  (macOS, old Linux distributions)
```


Instead of the standard `urllib` Python module with the `request` function used in the previous examples, in this example, I will perform downloads via the `requests` module. This module must also be installed using pip:

```
$ pip  install requests        (Windows, Linux)
$ pip3 install requests        (macOS, old Linux distributions)
```

I will introduce `requests` in more detail in Chapter 18. For now, knowing how to download an HTML document and how to pass it to Beautiful Soup is sufficient:

```
import requests
from bs4 import BeautifulSoup
response = requests.get('https://example.com')
dom = BeautifulSoup(response.content, 'html.parser')
```

17.5.2 Hello, Beautiful Soup!

Beautiful Soup provides countless functions to navigate to a specific point within the DOM, analyze attributes of the DOM, and loop through subelements. I will limit myself, in this section, to presenting the most important basic functions. In our example, the `x` variable contains either the DOM root object or another previously determined HTML object.

The basic functions of Beautiful Soup include the following:

- `x.attrs('attributename')` or simply `x['attributename']` returns the desired attribute as a string.
- `x.contents` returns the contents as a string array (as an array because there can be multiple parts).
- `x.find('elementname')` finds the first HTML element of the specified type, such as `x.find('<table>')`, starting from the current position in the DOM.

  Note that `find` searches only *within* the current subtree. If `x` is a `<table>` element, `x.find('th')` searches only within this one table, but not in other tables in the document.
- `x.find('name', aname='value')` searches for the first HTML element where an attribute has the desired value, such as `x.find('div', id= '1234')`. For CSS classes, you must use the `class_` attribute name, for instance, `x.find('p', class_='intro')`.
- `x.find_all(...)` works like `find` but returns all matching elements starting from the starting point. The result can then be looped through.
- `x.select('css selector')` works similar to `find_all` but processes a CSS selector as a parameter.

Countless other functions are documented with many application examples at *https://www.crummy.com/software/BeautifulSoup/bs4/doc/*.

The following introductory example searches an HTML page for all `img` elements and returns the associated `src` attributes:

```
# Sample file hello-beautifulsoup
import requests
from bs4 import BeautifulSoup
siteurl = "https://kofler.info/"
response = requests.get(siteurl)
dom = BeautifulSoup(response.content, 'html.parser')
images = dom.find_all('img')
for img in images:
    print(img['src'])
```

17.5.3 Example: Determining a List of Top Titles from Rheinwerk Publishing

The Rheinwerk Publishing website (*https://sap-press.com*) serves as the starting point for our first example. Eight books—new releases or bestsellers—are presented centrally every month. The goal of the script is to extract these eight titles as well as the links to their detail pages.

To navigate within the HTML code, you must open the website in a web browser and activate the development tools there. With just a few mouse clicks, you can then navigate through the nested structure of the HTML elements until you find the section that is relevant to you.

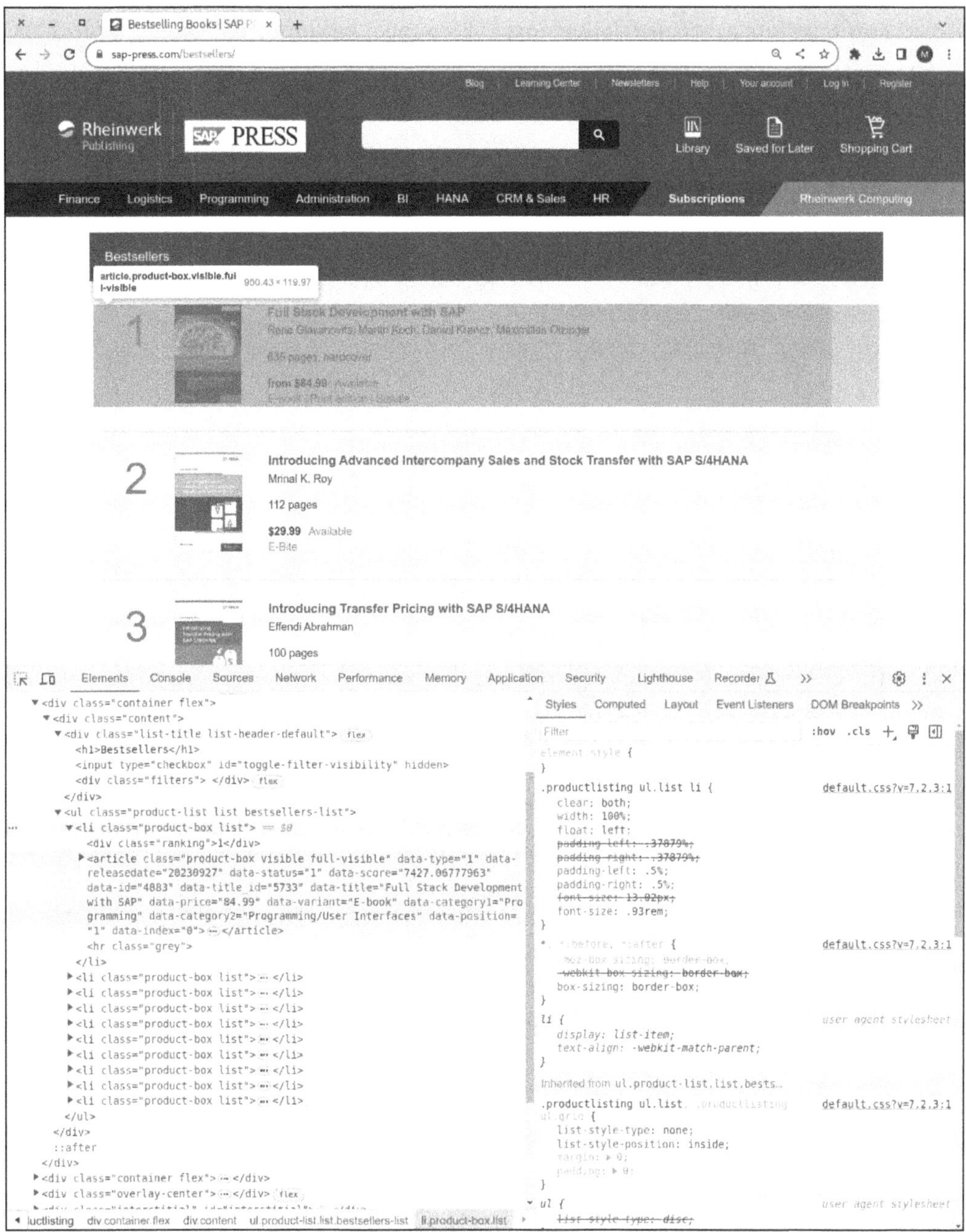

Figure 17.1 The Rheinwerk Publishing Website in a Web Browser in Development Mode

Now, it's just a matter of replicating the analyzed structure in Python code, which, in this case, is quite simple: First, `dom.find` looks for the `<ul>` element that has the bestsellers-list class. Within this element, a loop through find_all results runs through all <article> objects. For each article, the data-title attribute shows the book title. The first link (<a>) references the detail page of the book. However, the href attribute contains relative links, which must be completed using urljoin.

```
# Sample file sap-press-bestsellers.py
import requests
import urllib.parse
from bs4 import BeautifulSoup

# parse HTML content using BeautifulSoup
siteurl = " https://www.sap-press.com/bestsellers/"
response = requests.get(siteurl)
dom = BeautifulSoup(response.content, 'html.parser')


# find the section that contains the bestsellers
bestsellers = dom.find('ul', class_ = 'bestsellers-list')

# extract the titles and their detail page links
articles = bestsellers.find_all('article')
for article in articles:
    print('*', article['data-title'])
    link = article.find('a')['href']
    bookurl = urllib.parse.urljoin(siteurl, link)
    print(' ', bookurl)
```

In November 2023, a test run produced the following results:

```
* Full Stack Development with SAP
  https://www.sap-press.com/full-stack-development-with-sap_5733/
* Introducing Advanced Intercompany Sales and Stock Transfer with SAP S/4HANA
  https://www.sap-press.com/introducing-..._5743/
* Introducing Transfer Pricing with SAP S/4HANA
  https://www.sap-press.com/introducing-..._5790/
...
```

Error during Relaunch

Web scraping relies on the structure of a website. As soon as the layout of a website changes, the script must be adapted accordingly. This fact is also true for our example. It worked beautifully when I developed the code in November 2023. But if the publisher decides to relaunch the site or even to change the layout, the script will probably return only error messages instead of the title list.

17.6 Web Scraping with Requests-HTML

With some websites, the devil is in the details. When viewing the page in a web browser, you can see the finished HTML code and probably would not expect any problems. But when you try to process the same page as a DOM, important components are suddenly missing. (You can also try just downloading the page via curl. Then, compare the downloaded code with the HTML code you see in the browser.)

The reason for this strange behavior has to do with JavaScript: Many modern websites deliver a half-finished HTML document. Portions of the page are only completed in the web browser through the local execution of embedded JavaScript code.

For this type of webpage, you cannot simply download the HTML document; the JavaScript code it contains must also be executed by Python. To make this work, you must use the much more powerful requests-html module instead of the requests module. As usual, this module must be installed in advance via pip, with the following commands:

```
$ pip  install requests-html   (Windows, Linux)
$ pip3 install requests-html   (macOS, old Linux distributions)
```

The following lines show the application of the module:

```
from requests_html import HTMLSession
url = "https://www.githubstatus.com/"
session = HTMLSession()
# download HTML code including JavaScript
response = session.get("https://example.com")
# run embedded JavaScript code
response.html.render()
```

The first time render is run, a local copy of Chromium is downloaded. (The download is larger than 100 MB, so it takes a while.) Chromium then takes care of processing the JavaScript code and, fortunately, also works without a problem on Windows. However, Chromium must be run again with every script start, which noticeably delays the render call. You should therefore use render only when truly necessary!

17.6.1 Example: Analyzing the GitHub Status

On the *https://www.githubstatus.com* page, the GitHub company summarizes the current status of its services. The goal of this example is to read this status information into a dictionary. At first glance, the task looks straightforward.

However, the finished HTML code is only generated on the client side by JavaScript. Web scraping does not work until you load the page via the Requests-HTML module and run it using render.

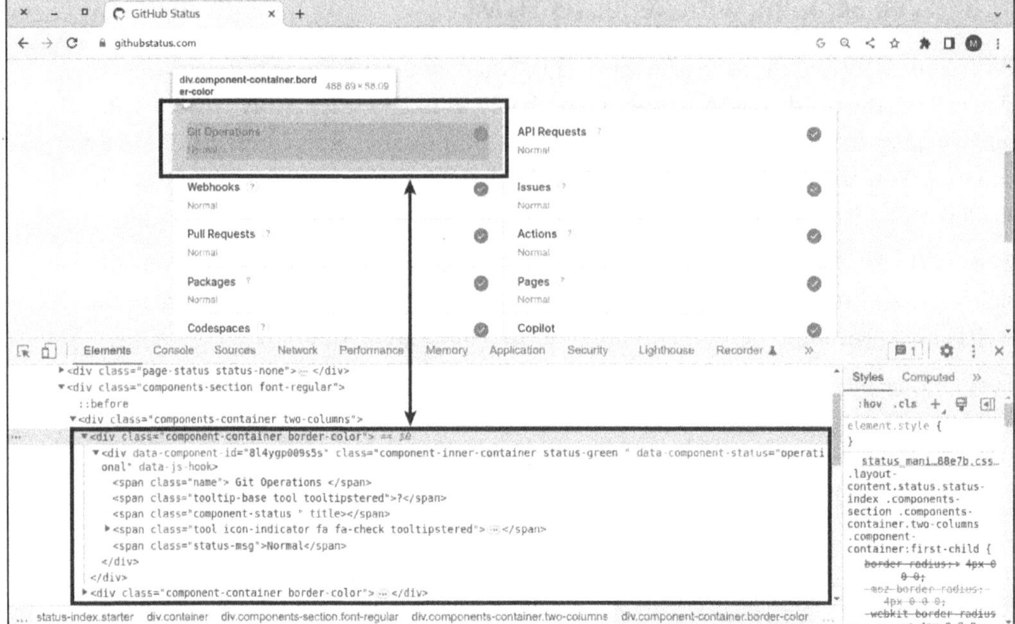

Figure 17.2 GitHub Status

Now, you have a choice: `response.html` provides access to a DOM similar to Beautiful Soup. The methods have slightly different names than in Beautiful Soup but are intuitive to use after a quick look at the documentation (see *https://requests.readthedocs.io/projects/requests-html*). The following lines show the first variant of the GitHub example, which uses only the Requests-HTML module:

```
# Sample program github-status1.py
from requests_html import HTMLSession
url = "https://www.githubstatus.com/"
session = HTMLSession()
response = session.get(url)  # response object
response.html.render()

# to save the results
dict = {}

# loop through all component-container elements
containers = response.html.find('div.component-container')
for container in containers:
    # skip invisible containers
    if 'style' in container.attrs and
      container.attrs['style'] == 'display: none;':
        continue
```

```
    # parse the remaining containers, save results
    name = container.find('span.name', first=True).text.strip()
    status = container.find('span.status-msg',
                            first=True).text.strip()
    dict[name] = status

# display the result
print(dict)
```

Provided the GitHub services are all running without an error right now, the script result should look as follows:

```
{'Git Operations': 'Normal', 'API Requests': 'Normal',
 'Webhooks': 'Normal', 'Issues': 'Normal',
 'Pull Requests': 'Normal', 'Actions': 'Normal',
 'Packages': 'Normal', 'Pages': 'Normal',
 'Codespaces': 'Normal', 'Copilot': 'Normal'}
```

If you don't feel like dealing with the DOM functions of `requests-html`, you can also process the HTML code using Beautiful Soup. The `.html.html` duplication is not an error in this case. `response.html` references the DOM, `response.html.html` on the other hand provides the corresponding HTML code.


```
# Sample program github-status2.py
# the first lines are as in github-status1.py ...
# parse HTML content using BeautifulSoup
dom = BeautifulSoup(response.html.html, 'html.parser')
dict = {}

# loop through components
containers = dom.find_all('div', class_ = 'component-container')
for container in containers:
    # skip invisible containers
    if container.has_attr('style') and container['style'] == 'display: none;':
        continue
    name = container.find('span', class_='name').contents[0].strip()
    status = container.find('span', class_='status-msg').contents[0].strip()
    dict[name] = status
```

17.7 Web Scraping with PowerShell

Of the three programming languages covered in this book, Python is best suited for web scraping. However, simple tasks can also be solved using PowerShell. The `Invoke-WebRequest` cmdlet returns a `BasicHtmlWebResponseObject`, which provides access to selected properties of the response to the request. This cmdlet does not give you a full DOM, but for some tasks, the included properties are sufficient.

Property	Meaning
Content	HTML code (string)
Headers	The returned headers (dictionary with strings)
Status	The HTML status code of the response (integer)
Images	List of all images contained in the HTML code
InputFields	List of all input fields in the forms of the HTML page
Links	List of all included links

Table 17.1 The Most Important Properties of the BasicHtmlWebResponseObject

The following script downloads all images linked on a web page into a temporary directory. The download is performed in a loop with `Invoke-WebRequest` and the `-OutFile` option. To suppress the status outputs produced by this cmdlet, the `ProgressPreference` variable is temporarily set to `'SilentlyContinue'`.

```
# Sample file load-images.ps1
New-Item -ItemType Directory -Force tmp | Out-Null

$url = 'https://sap-press.com/'
$response = Invoke-WebRequest $url

# loop through all images on the home page of the website
foreach($image in $response.Images) {
    $src = $image.src
    if ($src.StartsWith('//')) {
        # prefix protocol-relative links with 'https:'
        $src = "https:" + $src
    } elseif (! $src.StartsWith('http')) {
        # prefix the base URL for relative links
        $src = $url + $src
    }
    $filename = 'tmp/' + (Split-Path $image.src -Leaf)
    Write-Output ($src + " -> " +  $filename)
    $ProgressPreference = 'SilentlyContinue'  # no status
    Invoke-WebRequest $src -OutFile $filename # output
    $ProgressPreference = 'Continue'
}
```

17.7.1 PowerHTML Module

To convert an HTML page into a proper DOM, the best approach is to use the `ConvertFrom-HTML` cmdlet from the *PowerHTML* module. Note that you must install the module in advance:

```
> Install-Module PowerHTML
```

This module has not been changed since 2019 and lacks JavaScript functions comparable to *Requests-HTML*. In addition, *PowerHTML* is poorly documented. Internally, the module uses the *Html Agility Pack* (HAP), described at *https://html-agility-pack.net*.

The following script reads the Wikipedia page for PowerShell and extracts all `<h2>` headings from it. Since each headline is built from several components, the `<span>` element of the `mw-headline` class is determined within the headline.

```
# Sample file wikipedia.ps1
$url = 'https://en.wikipedia.org/wiki/PowerShell'
$response = Invoke-WebRequest $url
$dom = ConvertFrom-Html $response
# <div id='bodyContent'> search
$content = $dom.SelectSingleNode("//div[@id='bodyContent']")
# search all <h2> headings in it
$headers = $content.SelectNodes("//h2")
foreach ($header in $headers) {
    $headline =
      $header.SelectSingleNode("span[@class='mw-headline']")
    Write-Output $headline.InnerText
}
```

Alternatives to PowerHTML

The PowerHTML module works across different platforms, even in PowerShell scripts on Linux. An alternative is to use the `HTMLFile` class, but this class is only available on Windows, and even then, it is a pain to use in PowerShell scripts. You can find an example on Stack Overflow at *https://stackoverflow.com/a/71855426*.

Chapter 18
Using REST APIs

In the introduction to Chapter 17, I made it clear that web scraping is only a stopgap measure. The exchange of information between websites or with external services is much more reliable if an *application programming interface (API)* can be used for this purpose. REST APIs have become established in recent decades. *Representational state transfer (REST)* is based on data exchange via established HTTP requests such as GET, PUT, or POST. The data is predominantly transferred in JSON format or, fortunately much less frequently, as XML. Some APIs also require authentication, with various methods to choose from (Basic, Bearer, Digest, OAuth, and so on).

In this chapter, I will demonstrate how you can use REST APIs, and I will show you some elementary programming techniques.

Prerequisites for This Chapter

The sample scripts use all three programming languages covered in this book. In addition, an important prerequisite for reading this chapter is Chapter 10. JSON is ubiquitous as a REST data format.

You'll benefit from this chapter only if you have a basic knowledge regarding HTTP and REST. If you're not familiar with typical request types such as GET, PUT, or POST, or have never heard of *Bearer authentication*, you should first do some research.

18.1 Tools

As I will show you momentarily, the `curl` or `wget` commands are sufficient to test REST APIs. But it's not exactly fun. You should definitely install a graphical user interface (GUI) for running HTTP requests to analyze foreign APIs as well as for debugging. My recommendation is *Postman* (*https://postman.com*), but *Swagger UI*, the *Insomnia REST client*, or *RapidAPI* (formerly *Paw*, for macOS only) are also good alternatives. Various browser extensions also exist to try out REST APIs in a web browser.

18.2 Sample APIs to Try Out

To practice using REST APIs, you'll need a playground. On the following pages, you'll find APIs that you can try out for free (although some only free to a limited extent):

- *https://httpbin.org*
- *https://restcountries.com*
- *https://www.postman.com/explore*
- *https://apipheny.io/free-api*
- *https://github.com/public-apis/public-apis*

To simulate a real API in a straightforward way, you can use *WireMock* (*https://wiremock.org*). Basically, WireMock is an open-source project. However, the use of the associated cloud service is only free of charge with major restrictions and is aimed more at large companies that want to test APIs away from productive operation.

18.3 Implementing Custom REST APIs

Using Bash or PowerShell, implementing your own REST APIs is nearly impossible. The situation is different for Python, where *Flask* and *Django* are two widely used frameworks for server programming. Possible alternatives include *FastAPI*, *Pyramid*, or *Bottle*. However, both designing and implementing APIs are well beyond the scope of this book, with its focus on typically short scripts.

18.4 curl and wget

Linux users especially are familiar with the `curl` and `wget` commands. These commands are primarily used to download files in the terminal. `curl` displays the contents of the downloaded file by default; however, the output can be saved to a file by using `-o` (an "oh"/not a "zero"). `wget` saves the file to the local directory by default. If the filename is not clear from the URL, the site's default home page filename is used (often `index.html`). To display the file in standard output, you should use `-O` ("oh" again) followed by the desired filename or - for standard output.

```
$ curl https://example.com/some/file.txt -o file.txt
$ wget https://example.com/some/file.txt
```

Installation

On Linux and macOS, `curl` is available by default. `wget` can be installed using the usual package management tools (i.e., `apt/dnf/brew install wget`).

`curl` for Windows can be downloaded from *https://curl.se/windows*; `wget`, from *https://eternallybored.org/misc/wget*.

18.4.1 curl

curl and wget execute a GET request by default and do not require authentication. However, both commands can also upload local data (PUT/POST), support various authentication types, and so on. In this section, I will focus on curl and briefly summarize the most important options in the REST context:

- -X or --request GET/POST/PUT... specifies the desired request type (GET by default).
- -H or --header 'txt' passes the desired HTTP header, for example, -H "Content-Type: application/json". The option can be repeated if multiple headers are required. -H @file.txt reads the headers from a file.
- -d or --data 'data' sends the specified data with the request. For --data, the following alternatives are available: --data-binary, --data-raw, and --data-urlencode. In any case, the data can also be read from the specified file via @file.
- -u or --user name:pw passes a username and the corresponding password.
- -n or --netrc tells curl to read the login information from the *.netrc* file. Using --netrc-file file.txt, you can alternatively specify a different location for this file. Both variants are more secure than the password transfer via -u.
- --oauth2-bearer 'token' sends the specified Bearer token along with the request.
- -L or --location allows curl to run an HTTP redirect. So if the server indicates that the page is now in a different location, this redirection will be followed.
- -k or --insecure does not check the SSH or HTTPS certificates. (This is unsafe!)
- -v or --verbose displays comprehensive debugging information during the execution of the request.
- -I or --head returns only the header of the response as a result. This option is convenient, for example, if you're only interested in the HTTP status code, not in the other data from the response.

The following examples refer to *https://httpbin.org*. The purpose of this website is to test REST tools or scripts. For example, a GET request of the /headers address returns a JSON document with all transferred headers:

```
$ curl https://httpbin.org/headers -H 'myheader1: lorem' \
                                    -H 'myheader2: ipsum'

  {
    "headers": {
      "Accept": "*/*",
      "Host": "httpbin.org",
      "Myheader1": "lorem",
      "Myheader2": "ipsum",
      "User-Agent": "curl/8.0.1",
```

```
    "X-Amzn-Trace-Id": "Root=1-64228236-74fe..."
  }
}
```

In the second example, you first create the tiny local JSON file called `mydata.json`. Then, you use PUT to transfer this file to the `/put` address. The website responds with the sent data, so you can control if everything works:

```
$ cat > mydata.json << EOF
{
    "firstName": "John",
    "lastName": "Doe"
}
EOF

$ curl -X PUT https://httpbin.org/put?para=123 -d @mydata.json  \
       -H "Content-Type: application/json"

  {
    "args": {
      "para": "123"
    },
    "data": "{ \"firstName\": \"John\",  \"lastName\": \"Doe\"}",
    "json": {
      "firstName": "John",
      "lastName": "Doe"
    }, ...
  }
```

For debugging purposes, an often useful approach is to compile requests in a GUI.

In the final example, you'll test the *basic authentication*. In this test, you specify the login data with `/basic-auth/name/pw`. Then, the website checks if this data matches that of `-u 'name:pw'`. With `-I`, the status code of the response will be displayed: In the first case, that's 200 (*successful authentication*); in the second case, 401 (*unsuccessful authentication*).

```
$ curl -X GET "https://httpbin.org/basic-auth/maria/topsecret" \
       -u 'maria:topsecret' -I

  HTTP/2 200

$ curl -X GET "https://httpbin.org/basic-auth/maria/topsecret" \
       -u 'maria:wrong' -I

  HTTP/2 401
```

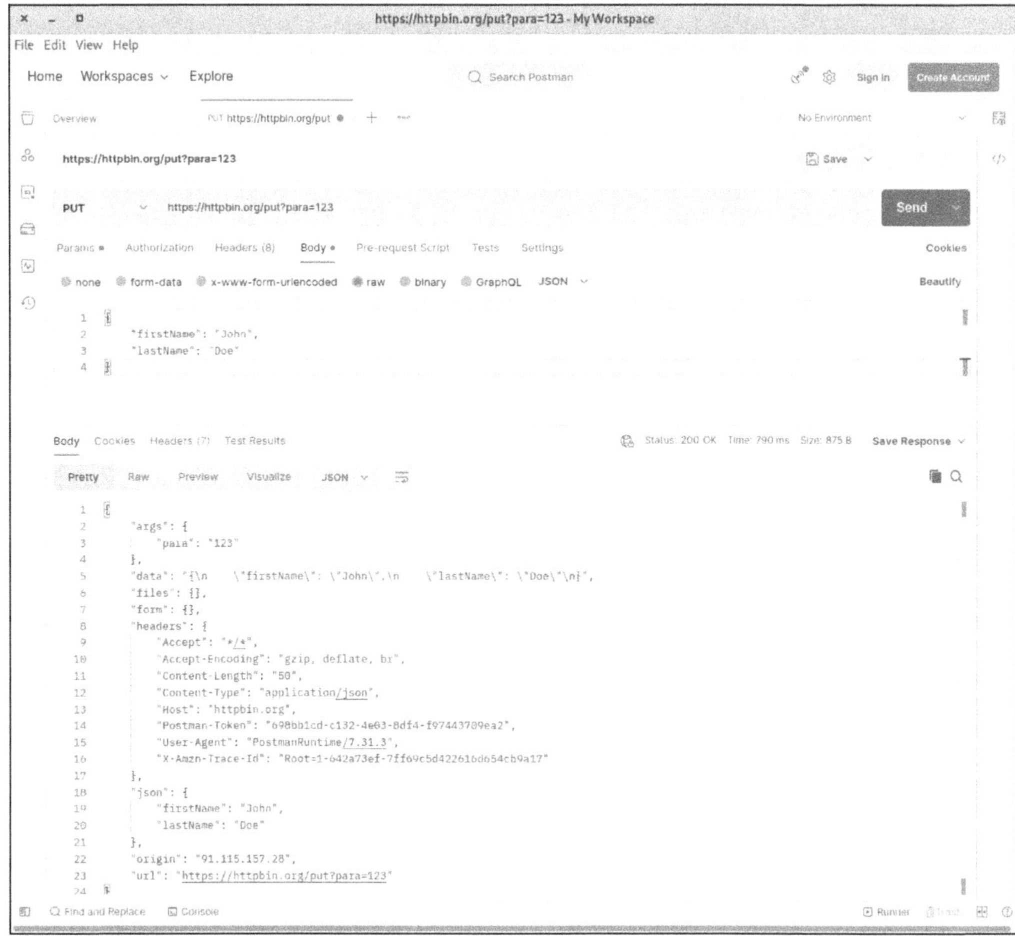

Figure 18.1 PUT Request Executed Using Postman

A reference of all *httpbin.org* functions and more `curl` examples can be found at the following links:

- *https://httpbin.org*
- *https://www.naleid.com/2017/11/26/using-http-apis-on-the-command-line-1-curl.html*

18.4.2 wget

`wget` basically supports the same functions as `curl`, but the options have different names. It is a matter of personal preference whether you prefer using `wget` or `curl`. I will refrain from describing the options in this section (you can read `man wget` if needed!) and just describe two examples. The first command is a simple `GET` request. *httpbin.org* responds with a UUID wrapped in a JSON document. Because of `-O -`, the return is directly displayed in the terminal. In turn, `-q` (*quiet*) prevents the output of status information.

```
$ wget https://httpbin.org/uuid -O - -q

  {
    "uuid": "9672f6c6-a27e-4059-8d87-35f0dc171bc7"
  }
```

The second example tests the transfer of JSON data by means of a POST request:

```
$ wget --header "Content-Type: application/json" \
       --post-data '{"firstName": "John", "lastName": "Doe"}' \
       https://httpbin.org/post -O -

  { ...
    "json": {
      "firstName": "John",
      "lastName": "Doe"
    }, ...
  }
```

18.4.3 Using REST APIs in Bash Scripts

Bash is not the ideal scripting language for REST applications. Using Python or PowerShell, you can formulate your scripts better, more efficiently, and more reliably. For simple tasks, however, the combination of curl/wget plus jq (see Chapter 10) is sufficient.

The following example uses the *https://ipinfo.io* website. This website responds to GET requests with a JSON document that contains an approximate geographic mapping in addition to the original IP address. (Do not rely on the accuracy of the answer!)

```
$ curl https://ipinfo.io

  {
    "ip": "91.115.157.28",
    "hostname": "91-115-157-28.adsl.highway.telekom.at",
    "city": "Graz",
    "region": "Styria",
    "country": "AT",
    "loc": "47.0667,15.4500",
    "postal": "8041",
    "timezone": "Europe/Vienna", ...
  }
```

The *get-location.sh* script uses jq to extract the city, the region, and the country from the response:

```
# Sample file get-location.sh
json=$(curl https://ipinfo.io -s)
for key in city region country; do
    echo -n "$key: "
    echo $json | jq .$key
done
```

At my location, the script then returns the following output:

```
city: "Graz"
region: "Styria"
country: "AT"
```

18.5 Using REST APIs in PowerShell

PowerShell provides two cmdlets to choose from to perform HTTP requests:

- You learned about `Invoke-WebRequest` in the previous chapter (see Chapter 17, Section 17.5). The cmdlet can also be used for REST methods.
- `Invoke-RestMethod` has certain advantages and disadvantages compared to `Invoke-WebRequest`: A convenient aspect is that the cmdlet converts responses in a flat (non-nested) JSON format directly into a `PSCustomObject`. If the web service returns responses in XML format, `Invoke-WebRequest` directly returns an object of the `XmlDocument` type. This relatively intelligent handling of typical REST data types simplifies the continued analysis.

  On the other hand, annoyingly, the cmdlet does not return the HTTP status code. If the request is successful (code 2xx), you'll receive result data; otherwise an error will occur. In some REST applications, this approach is too minimalistic.

From my point of view, `Invoke-RestMethod` has more disadvantages. In most applications, I prefer `Invoke-WebRequest` and then convert the `Content` string into a JSON object in the following way:

```
> $json = (Invoke-WebRequest `
     'https://httpbin.org/headers').Content | ConvertFrom-Json

> $json.headers.host
  httpbin.org
```

In my tests, some REST services returned HTML code instead of JSON code on requests made using `Invoke-RestMethod` or `Invoke-WebRequest`. The solution in this case is to specify the user agent `curl` in the header so that the service does not erroneously assume that the user agent is a web browser:

```
> Invoke-RestMethod 'https://ipinfo.io'

  <!DOCTYPE html><html lang="en"> ... (HTML code extends over multiple pages)

> Invoke-RestMethod 'https://ipinfo.io' `
      -Headers @{'User-Agent' = 'curl'}

  ip       : 91.115.157.28
  hostname : 91-115-157-28.adsl.highway.telekom.at
  city     : Graz
  region   : Styria
  country  : AT
  ...
```

18.5.1 Options

Not only do the two Invoke cmdlets provide different result data types, but there are also various special options that differ from each other. Fortunately, at least the options for the basic settings match:

- -Uri passes the address. This option does not have to be specified (i.e., the address can also be passed directly to the cmdlet).
- -Method specifies the desired request. Allowed settings are Get, Put, Post, and so on.
- -Authentication selects the desired authentication method (None, Basic, Bearer, or OAuth).
- -Credential passes data for Basic authentication to the request. The pair of login name and password must be passed as a PSCredential object. You can initialize such an object interactively via Get-Credential. Alternatively, you can initialize such an object by using the following code:

  ```
  $password = ConvertTo-SecureString 'topSecret' -AsPlainText `
                                                 -Force
  $credential = New-Object `
     System.Management.Automation.PSCredential('loginname',
                                               $password)
  ```
- -Token passes a string to the cmdlet for Bearer and OAuth authentication.
- -Body passes the data to be transferred to the web server (upload). If necessary, you can use -ContentType to specify the format and character set of this data.
- -Header expects a hash table with the header settings.

The following lines show how you can transfer your own data to a server using Invoke-WebRequest:

```
$data = @{ firstName = 'John'; lastName = 'Doe'}
$jsondata = $data | ConvertTo-Json
$url = 'https://httpbin.org/put'
$response = Invoke-WebRequest -Method Put $url -Body $jsondata
$response.Content

  {
    "headers": {
      "Content-Length": "46",
      "Host": "httpbin.org",
      "User-Agent": "Mozilla/5.0 (Linux; ...) PowerShell/7.3.2",
      "X-Amzn-Trace-Id": "Root=1-6426e776-337f635051c3c6753..."
    },
    "json": {
      "firstName": "John",
      "lastName": "Doe"
    }, ...
  }
```

Since a request call typically requires many options and parameters, a good idea is to first collect the data in a hash table and pass it to the cmdlet via *splatting* (see Chapter 4, Section 4.3):

```
$data = @{ firstName = 'John'; lastName = 'Doe'}
$para = @{ Uri = 'https://httpbin.org/put';
           Method = 'Put';
           Body = $data | ConvertTo-Json}
$response = Invoke-WebRequest @para
```

18.6 Example: Determining the Current Weather

The following script combines two REST APIs:

- First, the *https://ipinfo.io* geolocation service is used to determine the presumed location for the current IP address. This doesn't always work precisely and can go completely wrong if you use a VPN connection. But in most cases, the returned coordinates are reasonably good.
- In the second step, the current weather is determined for the identified location. The API at *https://api.weatherapi.com* is available free of charge with certain restrictions. However, you must get an API key. (Providing your email address is sufficient; you don't need to provide a credit card number or any other personal information.)

For the first step, I used Invoke-RestMethod, which is the most convenient way to analyze the data submitted by *ipinfo.io*. In addition, I explicitly converted the much more complex JSON structure of *weatherapi.com* into PowerShell data structures using ConvertFrom-Json.

```
# Sample file get-weather.ps1
# Use your own key!
$key = "7901..."

# determines longitude and latitude from the current IP address
$location = (Invoke-RestMethod "https://ipinfo.io" `
          -Headers @{'User-Agent' = 'curl'}).loc

# determines the weather for this location
$base = "https://api.weatherapi.com/v1/current.json"
$url = "${base}?key=$key&q=$location&aqi=no"
$response = Invoke-WebRequest $url
$content = $response.Content | ConvertFrom-Json
$city = $content.location.name
$temp = $content.current.temp_c
$text = $content.current.condition.text
Write-Output "Current weather in ${city}: $text at $temp °C"
```

When you run the script, the result looks something like the following line:

```
Current weather in Graz: Partly cloudy at 5 °C
```

For another example of using Invoke-RestMethod to save exchange rates, see Chapter 11, Section 11.4. In this example, the cmdlet directly returns an XML object that is subsequently evaluated.

18.7 Using REST APIs in Python

The linchpin of REST scripts in Python is the requests module, which I already briefly introduced to you in Chapter 17. The module has a disadvantage in that, unlike the urllib module, it must be installed separately using pip:

```
$ pip  install requests        (Windows, Linux)
$ pip3 install requests        (macOS, old Linux distributions)
```

Instead, the function of the same name can be used to run all conceivable requests without syntactic contortions. The following lines show a simple Get request. The binary result (response.content) is converted to a UTF-8 string via decode and is then output:

```
import requests
# Get request
response = requests.get('https://httpbin.org/get?q=123')
print(response.content.decode('utf-8'))
# {
#   "args": {
#     "q": "123"
#   }, ...
```

When the REST API returns a JSON document, you turn it into a Python object tree using the built-in `json` method. (In this way, you don't need to use to the `json` module.) You can determine the HTTP status of the web server response using the `status_code` property.

```
data = response.json()
print(data)
# {'args': {'q': '123'}, 'headers': {'Accept': '*/*', ...
print(response.status_code)
# 200
```

Depending on what kind of request you want to run, you can use `put`, `patch`, `delete`, etc. instead of `requests.get` accordingly. You can pass various optional parameters to all methods:

- `header` expects a dictionary with the header data.
- To `data` you can pass either a dictionary with parameters (e.g., for a `POST` request) or a string with other data.
- Alternatively, you can pass a dictionary with the `json` parameter. Its content is transferred in JSON format.
- Using `files`, you can upload local files to the server.

The following lines show a `PUT` request where data is transferred to the server in JSON format:

```
data = {'firstName': 'John', 'lastName': 'Doe'}
response = requests.put('https://httpbin.org/put', json=data)
```

If you want to perform basic authentication on a request, you must pass the username and password to the `auth` option:

```
url = 'https://httpbin.org/basic-auth/maria/topsecret'
response = requests.get(url, auth=('maria', 'topsecret'))
print("Status Code", response.status_code)
```

Alternatively, if you prefer a simple Bearer authentication, the best approach is to pass the token as a header:

```
token = "234f1523werf"
headers = {"Authorization": "Bearer %s" % (token)}
url = 'https://httpbin.org/bearer'
response = requests.get(url, headers=headers)
print("Status Code", response.status_code)
```

Countless other features of the `requests` module are documented at *https://requests.readthedocs.io*.

18.8 Example: Determining Electricity Prices and Displaying Them Graphically

The expansion of renewable energies means that electricity prices fluctuate more strongly today than before. The more the wind blows or the stronger the sun shines, the more electricity is available—sometimes even more than is actually needed. At such times, electricity is quite cheap on the power exchanges.

Against this backdrop, new electricity providers with hourly changing prices (aWATTar, Tibber, etc.) are currently establishing themselves. Such dynamic tariffs motivate people to carry out energy-intensive actions (charging an e-car, starting a dryer at a certain time) as far as possible when a lot of electricity is available, which benefits both customers and energy suppliers.

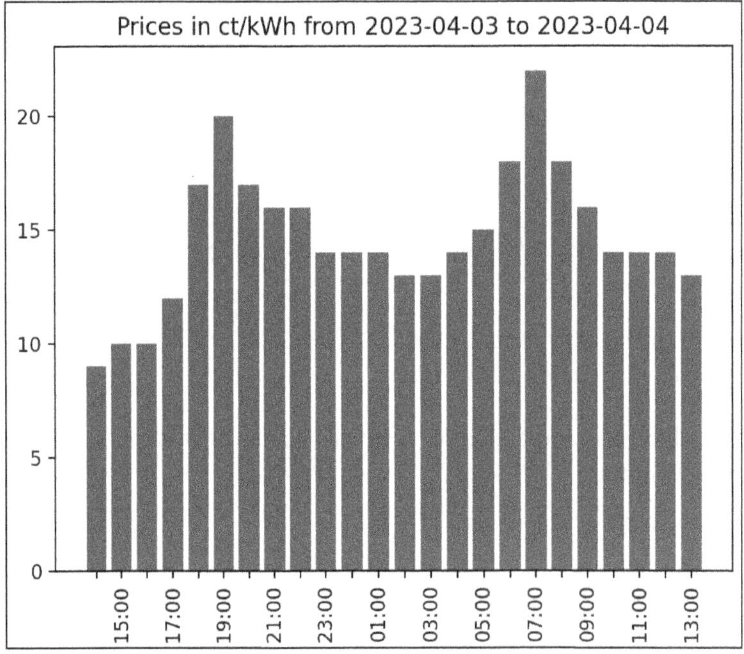

Figure 18.2 Electricity Prices for the Next 24 Hours (Pure Energy Prices Including VAT for Austria at the Beginning of April 2023)

Our example in this section refers to the company *aWATTar*. This company offers an API that informs consumers about electricity prices for the coming hours (maximum for 24 hours). The European EPEX SPOT power exchange serves as the data basis where these prices are calculated on the basis of supply and demand. Prices for the next day will be available from about 2 pm.

The script presented in this section turns this data into a graph. Note that, in addition to the prices shown in the diagram for the energy costs alone, data also includes the monthly basic fee, line costs, flat electricity meter charges, etc.

18.8.1 aWATTar API

The API is currently accessible free of charge, but with a maximum of 100 access events per day:

- *https://api.awattar.at/v1/marketdata* (prices for Austria)
- *https://api.awattar.de/v1/marketdata* (prices for Germany)

Unfortunately, the JSON result is not readable to humans. The time periods during which a given price is valid are expressed in epoch milliseconds. This time specification, common in Unix, calculates the seconds or milliseconds since January 1, 1970 UTC. Prices are quoted in euros per megawatt hour, but excluding VAT and the 3 percent surcharge charged by aWATTar.


```
{
   "object":"list",
   "data":[
      {
         "start_timestamp":1680508800000,
         "end_timestamp":1680512400000,
         "marketprice":107.11,
         "unit":"Eur/MWh"
      },
      {
         "start_timestamp":1680512400000,
         "end_timestamp":1680516000000,
         "marketprice":93.08,
         "unit":"Eur/MWh"
      },
      ...
```

18.8.2 Analysis of the Data

After initializing various variables, the script makes an API call and then analyzes the collected data in a loop. The conversion of the epoch time data into “ordinary”

DateTime objects can be done without much effort using fromtimestamp. VAT and aWATTar surcharge are added to the net prices.

```
# Sample file electricity-prices.py
import locale, requests
from datetime import datetime
import matplotlib.pyplot as plt
# use language according to system setting
locale.setlocale(locale.LC_ALL, '')
# basic settings
surcharge = 0.03   # Awattar surcharge on EXPO SPOT
vat = 0.20         # 20% VAT (Austria)
url = 'https://api.awattar.at/v1/marketdata'
# alternative for Germany
# vat = 0.19
# url = 'https://api.awattar.de/v1/marketdata'
# API call
response = requests.get(url)
jsondata = response.json()

# collect data
hours = []         # list for times
prices = []        # list for prices
dateStart = None   # start date of time span

# analyze data and present it in text form
for price in jsondata['data']:
    startDt = \
      datetime.fromtimestamp(price['start_timestamp'] / 1000)
    hour = startDt.strftime('%H:%M')
    day = startDt.strftime('%a')
    if not dateStart:         # initialize once
      dateStart = startDt.strftime('%Y-%m-%d')
    dateEnd = startDt.strftime('%Y-%m-%d')  # overwrite
    priceCentKw = round(price['marketprice'] / 10 * \
      (1 + surcharge) * (1 + vat))
    priceBar = '*' * int(priceCentKw)       # ASCII type bar
    print('%s %s %3d ct/kWh %s' % \
      (day, hour, priceCentKw, priceBar))
    hours += [hour]
    prices += [priceCentKw]
```

The script outputs the processed data as text first, for example:

```
Mo 19:00  20 ct/kWh ********************
Mo 20:00  17 ct/kWh *****************
Mo 21:00  16 ct/kWh ****************
...
```

18.8.3 Matplotlib

Python is also quite popular in the field of (natural) sciences. Accordingly, various modules support the drawing of technical diagrams, the most popular of which is Matplotlib. The following listing shows that a few lines of code are sufficient to design a simple diagram:

```
# Continuation of electricity-prices.py
fig, ax = plt.subplots()
ax.bar(hours, prices)
plt.xticks(rotation=90)
plt.title('Prices in ct/kWh from %s to %s' % \
  (dateStart, dateEnd))
# hide every second label point
for label in ax.xaxis.get_ticklabels()[::2]:
    label.set_visible(False)
fig.savefig('prices.png', dpi=200)
```

`subplots` returns *two* objects responsible for different aspects of the chart. `ax.bar` creates a simple bar chart from the X and Y values passed in two parameters. `plt.xticks(rotation=90)` causes a space-saving labeling of the X axis. `plt.title` takes care of the labeling of the chart.

The following loop hides every second label point on the X axis. `savefig` finally saves the diagram in a PNG file. The `dpi` parameter (*dots per inch*) determines the desired resolution. (The default value of only 100 DPI leads to quite pixelated diagrams.)

Unfortunately, not enough space is available in this book for an intensive discussion of Matplotlib. However, you can find countless examples as well as very useful cheat sheets on the project website at *https://matplotlib.org*.

For more information on diagrams using Matplotlib as well as other Python functions in the scientific field, see *Python for Engineering and Scientific Computing* (Rheinwerk Computing, 2024).

18.8.4 Controlling the Energy Consumption

What is even more exciting than the graphical representation of electricity prices is the automated operation of large consumers preferentially during the times when energy costs are lowest. A Raspberry Pi that regularly reads price data can, for example, switch an electric boiler on and off via a controllable switch at the ideal time in terms of price. For heat pumps, the *smart grid* interface provides a way to switch between normal, economy, or extra operation depending on electricity availability or price.

Unfortunately, due to a lack of my own experience, I cannot offer you any sample scripts in this regard.

Chapter 19
Databases

The topic of scripting and databases is almost inexhaustible. You can use scripts to enter data into a database, read and process information from it, change the structure of databases, and so on.

In detail, the procedure depends on the database management system (DBMS), programming language, library, or module you use. In this respect, a systematic treatment of all aspects is impossible here from the outset. Instead, this chapter focuses on some concrete examples that relate to SQL Server or MySQL:

- Modifying, maintaining, and reading similar databases (Bash, PowerShell)
- Setting up databases for new customers (Bash)
- Saving exchangeable image file format (Exif) data (Python)
- Importing JSON files (PowerShell)

Prerequisites for This Chapter

As usual, you need basic knowledge of Bash, Python, and PowerShell to read this chapter. You should also be able to handle JSON files (see Chapter 8). Finally, you need to have a basic understanding of how database servers work.

If you want to create backups of databases with your scripts, I recommend you look at Chapter 13.

To keep the examples clear, I have refrained from error-proofing and from swapping out the login data and other settings. For "real" database scripts, both points should be a matter of course. For tips on error-proofing, see the chapters on the basic principles of Bash, PowerShell, and Python. I have described how to handle settings and passwords securely in Chapter 14, Section 14.2.

The sample scripts from that chapter cannot be tried out easily. You must first install the appropriate database server, set up a suitable database with tables, take care of authentication with the database server, and so on.

19.1 Updating and Maintaining Databases

In my professional work, I maintain a MySQL server that hosts many similar databases. Each customer has a separate database. Although the content of these databases varies depending on the customer, the structure is always the same.

Now and then, it happens that—for example for troubleshooting—I want to apply the same SELECT commands to all databases. The required script is, according to the motto of this book, not even 10 lines long:

```
# Sample file apply-select.sh
# this file contains the names of all databases
DBLIST=dbs.txt
# this file contains the commands to be executed;
# the commands must be separated by ;.
SQLFILE=select.sql

for db in $(cat $DBLIST | sort) ; do
  echo "Database: $db"
  mysql $db < $SQLFILE
  echo "---"
done
```

The mysql command plays a central role in the script. It connects to the database specified by the db variable and executes all commands contained in the file read by input redirection. Establishing a connection to the database server requires that the active user has sufficient MySQL access rights and that authentication is performed either at the operating system level (auth_socket method for MySQL or unix_socket for MariaDB) or that the *.my.cnf* file contains the required password.

The results of the SELECT commands are displayed directly on the screen. Most of the time, I run the script in the ./apply-select.sh | less format, so I can conveniently scroll or search through the output.

Basically, *select.sql* could also contain commands to modify all databases, for example to add a column to a table in each database. But because such changes are much more dangerous than pure queries, I store such commands in a separate *updates.sql* file, which is processed by a second *apply-updates.sh* script. The script is identical to *apply-select.sh* except for the initialization of the SQLFILE variable.

19.1.1 PowerShell and sqlcmd

Of course, the same concept can be implemented via a PowerShell script. The script calls the sqlcmd command, which is the SQL Server counterpart to mysql. The code then looks as follows:

```
# Sample file apply-select.ps1
$dblist = "dbs.txt"         # list with database names
$sqlfile = "select.sql"     # SQL commands
$server = ".\sqlexpress01" # SQL Server instance

# loop through all databases
foreach($db in Get-Content $dblist) {
    Write-Output "Database: $db"
    sqlcmd -S $server -d $db -i $sqlfile
}
```

If SQL Server is not running on the local machine, you need to replace `.` with the host name. Again, I'm assuming here that the script is running in an account that has access to all the databases in question. Note that the SQL commands contained in *select.sql* must be separated by semicolons. The script requires that `sqlcmd.exe` be located in a directory listed in the `PATH` variable.

19.2 Creating a New Customer Account

The starting point for this example is a web server for customer accounts. When placing an order, customers receive their own database and can access the web application via their own address:

https://example.com/name

19

The following Bash script takes care of the initialization work required when a new account gets set up:

- Creating and initializing a new MySQL database
- Creating a new MySQL user and enabling it to access the database
- Setting up the */var/www/html/name* directory
- Creating a configuration file in that directory
- Sending an email to the customer with the login data

On a server I maintain, I actually use a script that works in this way. For didactic reasons, I have greatly simplified the code for this book. So, let me explain the basic procedure first.

No Testing Option

The code for the script can of course be found in the sample files for the book. However, you can't try out the script without further ado. For this purpose, you would need a Linux server (including web, database, and mail servers) as well as the code for a web application, a sample database, etc.

19.2.1 Account Data

accountdata contains the data of the new customer. The URL variable specifies the custom part of the web address (i.e., *https://example.com/sd-architects*). DB is used as the name for the new MySQL database and for the associated MySQL user. DB is maximum 16 characters long and may contain only letters, digits, and underscores.

```
# Sample file accountdata
FIRSTNAME='Maria'
LASTNAME='Smith'
COMPANY='Smith & Davis Architects'
EMAIL='maria.smith@example.com'
URL='sd-architects'
DB='sdarchitects'
```

19.2.2 Structure of the Script

The *make-new-account.sh* script must be run with root privileges. The mysql and mysqldump commands included in the script are based on the assumption that root has unrestricted access rights to the MySQL server or that the password for the MySQL root user is contained in the */root/.my.cnf* file.

The code starts by reading the account data of the new customer. The script first tests whether a database of that name already exists. In this case, the execution will be terminated:

```
# Sample file make-new-account.sh
# import account data
. accountdata
# abort if the database already exists
sql="SELECT SCHEMA_NAME FROM INFORMATION_SCHEMA.SCHEMATA
     WHERE SCHEMA_NAME='$DB'"
result=$(mysql -s -N -e "$sql")
echo "result = $result"
if [ "$result" ]; then
  echo "Database $DB already exists."
  exit
fi
```

The script uses the mkpasswd password generator to generate two random passwords:

- The dbpw variable contains the password for accessing the customer database. This password is only used internally and is stored in a configuration file on the server.
- loginpw contains the customer password for the web login. A hash code of this password is stored in the database. The password is sent to the customer by mail.

In the following lines, a new database is created and initialized using a sample database. Also, a MySQL account is created that has access to this database.

```
# database password (internal)
dbpw=$(makepasswd)
# customer password for web login
loginpw=$(makepasswd)

# create a database and compare it with a copy of the 'template' database
# initialize
mysqladmin create $DB
mysql $DB | mysqldump template

# set up an account for database access
sql="CREATE USER $DB@localhost IDENTIFIED BY '$dbpw';
     GRANT ALL ON $DB.* TO $DB@localhost"
mysql -e "$sql"
```

A hash code of the login password is stored in the customer database. The hash code is generated via htpasswd. Subsequently, the customer data is stored in the customer database created earlier:

```
# generate hash code of login password
hash=$(htpasswd -bnBC 10 "" $loginpw | tr -d ':\n')
# save customer data in the customer database
sql="INSERT INTO accounts (firstname, lastname, company,
                           email, hashcode)
     VALUES ('$FIRSTNAME', '$LASTNAME', '$COMPANY',
             '$EMAIL', '$hash')"
mysql $DB -e "$sql"
```


In the next step, the script sets up a new customer directory in */var/www/html* and stores the login data for database access in *dbconfig.php*. The chown and chmod commands ensure that the access rights to the files are correct:

```
# set up a web directory for the customer
cd /var/www/html/myapplication
mkdir $URL
cat > $URL/dbconfig.php << EOF
<?php
LocalConfig::set('dbname', '$DB');
LocalConfig::set('dbhost', 'localhost');
LocalConfig::set('dbuser', '$DB');
LocalConfig::set('dbpass', '$dbpw');
EOF
```

```
chown -R www-data:www-data $URL
chmod -R o-rwx $URL
chown root:www-data $URL/dbconfig.php
chmod 640 $URL/dbconfig.php
```

Finally, the script sends an email to the new customer. The `mail` command requires a working mail server.

```
# send email to the new customer
BODY="Dear customer,
\n
\nthis is your login data:
\n
\nLogin:         https://example.com/$URL
\nAccount:       $EMAIL
\nPasswort:      $loginpw
\n
\nPlease change your password after the first login!
"
echo -e $BODY | mail -s "your new account"  \
    -a "From: support@example.com" \
    -a "Content-Type: text/plain; charset=UTF-8" \
    $EMAIL
```

19.3 Storing Exif Metadata in a Database

In Chapter 16, Section 16.3, I described a Python script that extracts Exif metadata from photos in the current directory and generates SQL commands with corresponding `INSERT` commands. The SQL commands could be saved to a file via output redirection and later applied to a database (for example, using the `mysql` command).

But a much more elegant approach is if the script establishes a database connection and stores the metadata directly in the database. This approach avoids the detour with a SQL file. For the following example, I assume that the database is managed by a MySQL server and that the `photos` table exists there. The `CREATE TABLE` command documents the structure of the table:

```
CREATE TABLE photos(
  id INT NOT NULL PRIMARY KEY AUTO_INCREMENT,
  name VARCHAR(255) NOT NULL,
  size INT,
  orientation INT,
  datetimeoriginal DATETIME,
  latitude DOUBLE,
  longitude DOUBLE,
  altitude DOUBLE,
```

```
  -- ts contains the date and time of the last change
  ts TIMESTAMP NOT NULL DEFAULT CURRENT_TIMESTAMP()
     ON UPDATE CURRENT_TIMESTAMP()
);
```

19.3.1 PyMySQL

Several Python modules are available for accessing MySQL or MariaDB databases, but I want to focus on PyMySQL in this section. The module is easy to install, is easy to use, and has proven itself in my work. You can find more information about alternative MySQL or database modules at the following links:

- *https://stackoverflow.com/questions/372885*
- *https://wiki.openstack.org/wiki/PyMySQL_evaluation*

As usual, PyMySQL must be installed using pip:

```
$ pip  install requests        (Windows, Linux)
$ pip3 install requests        (macOS, old Linux distributions)
```

When you establish a connection using connect, you need to specify the hostname of the server (localhost if the database server is running on the same machine as your script), the username, password, and the name of the database you want to access.

MySQL and MariaDB support various UTF-8 variants. For the interaction with Python, utf8mb4 is the best solution. The cursorclass parameter controls the way PyMySQL returns SELECT results. The DictCursor cursor type wraps each data record in a dictionary, using the column names as keys. This facilitates further processing of the results.

Each time you want to run a SQL command, you need a cursor object. I recommend using such cursors with with because, in this way, you can ensure that you release the objects as soon as possible and do not block unnecessary resources.

The string with the SQL command must then be passed to the execute method. The command can contain any number of %s codes. execute replaces them with strings from the tuple, list, or dictionary passed in the second parameter. Note that no other codes are allowed here, such as %d for numbers, for example. If you want to store NULL, you must use the Python keyword None.

```
# Sample file hello-pymysql.py
conn = pymysql.connect(host='localhost',
                       user='username',
                       password='topsecret',
                       db='dbname',
                       port=3306,
                       charset='utf8mb4',
                       cursorclass=pymysql.cursors.DictCursor)
```

```
# read entries from the 'photos' table
with conn.cursor() as cur:
    sql = 'SELECT * FROM photos WHERE id < %s'
    cur.execute(sql, (1000))
    while row := cur.fetchone():
        print(row)
```

Using `execute`, you can also run `INSERT`, `UPDATE`, or `DELETE` commands. `commit` completes the transaction. You can then get the ID number of the new record from the `lastrowid` property.

```
sql = '''INSERT INTO photos (name, size, orientation)
         VALUES (%s, %s, %s)'''
with conn.cursor() as cur:
    cur.execute(sql, ('img_1234.jpg', 3231283, 0))
    conn.commit()
    print('ID of new record:', cur.lastrowid)
```

If your script continues to run once the database operations are complete, you should close the database connection:

```
conn.close()
```

More details on how to use PyMySQL can be found in the project documentation: *https://pymysql.readthedocs.io*.

19.3.2 Saving Exif Metadata

I have already explained how you can analyze the Exif data embedded in the image files of photos in Python using a script in Chapter 16, Section 16.3. At this point, it's just a matter of storing the metadata directly in a database. For this purpose, a database connection must be established at the beginning of the script. After that, all image files are run through in a loop.

```
# Sample file exif-to-mysql.py (shortened)
import ...
# establish connection
conn = pymysql.connect(host='localhost', ...)

# consider only the following EXIF keys
keys = ['File:FileName', 'File:FileSize', ...]

# analyze parameters (sys.argv)
filenames = ...

# INSERT command
```

```
sql = '''INSERT INTO photos (name, size, orientation,
            datetimeoriginal, latitude, longitude, altitude)
        VALUES (%s, %s, %s, %s, %s, %s, %s)'''

# connect to exiftool command, DB cursor
with exiftool.ExifToolHelper() as exifhelper, \
     conn.cursor() as cur:

    # loop through all files
    for file in filenames:
        # collect EXIF data in list
        results = []
        try:
            metadata = exifhelper.get_tags(file, keys)[0]
            for key in keys:
                if key in metadata:
                    if key == 'EXIF:DateTimeOriginal':
                        # adapt date to ISO syntax
                        date = str(metadata[key])
                        results += [ date.replace(':', '-', 2) ]
                    else:
                        results += [str(metadata[key])]
                else:
                    results += [ None ]   # corresponds to NULL
            # run INSERT
            cur.execute(sql, results)
        except Exception as e:
            print("-- skipped %s" % (file))

# save all changes (commit)
conn.commit()
conn.close()
```

For a collection of photos to try out the script, see the sample files for Chapter 14.

19.4 Importing JSON Data into a Table

The starting point for this section is the JSON file, *employees.json*, which has the following structure:

```
[
  {
    "FirstName": "Ruthanne",
    "LastName": "Ferguson",
```

```
    "DateOfBirth": "1977-06-04",
    "Street": "4 Dewy Turnpike",
    "Zip": "27698",
    "City": "Clifton Hill",
    "State": "NJ",
    "Gender": "F",
    "Email": "ruthanne_ferguson5693@fastmail.cn",
    "Job": "Junior Engineer",
    "Salary": "5201.45"
  }, ...
```

A PowerShell script is supposed to process this file and enter the records into a table of a SQL Server database. I am assuming that the JSON keys match the column names of the table. You can create a suitable table using the following command:

```
CREATE TABLE employees(
  id INT IDENTITY(1, 1) PRIMARY KEY,
  FirstName TEXT NOT NULL,
  LastName TEXT NOT NULL,
  DateOfBirth DATE,
  Street TEXT,
  City TEXT,
  State CHAR(2),
  Gender CHAR(1),
  Email TEXT,
  Job TEXT,
  Salary FLOAT);
```

The script uses the `SQLServer` module that we described in Chapter 15, Section 15.3. If you have not already done so, you must install the module using `Install-Module SQLServer`.

The code starts with the initialization of some variables. `Get-Content` reads the JSON file. `ConvertFrom-JSON` turns it into an array with `PSCustomObjects`. The outer `foreach` loop runs through all array elements. The inner loop runs through all columns and creates the `VALUES` part of the `INSERT` command. The resulting commands will look like the following example:

```
INSERT INTO employees (FirstName, LastName, DateOfBirth, ...)
VALUES('Sebastian', 'James', '1953-05-14', ...);
```

The script relies on the fact that data is available for all columns for each data record. If not the case, you must include appropriate tests and, if necessary, include `NULL` in the SQL command.

Finally, all collected commands are passed to SQL Server using `Invoke-Sqlcmd`.

```
# Sample file json-to-sql-server.ps1
Import-Module SQLServer

# connection to SQL Server
$connectionString = "Server=.\sqlexpress01;Database=mydb;" +
                    "Trusted_Connection=true;Encrypt=false"

# name of the table and columns
$tableName = "employees"
$columns = "FirstName", "LastName", "DateOfBirth", "Street",
           "City", "State", "Gender", "Email", "Job", "Salary"

$sql = "INSERT INTO $tablename (" +  ($columns -Join ", ") + ") "
$sqlcmds = ""

# read JSON file and convert it to PowerShell objects
$jsonFilePath = "employees.json"
$json = Get-Content $jsonFilePath | ConvertFrom-Json

# loop through all array elements (data records)
foreach ($record in $json) {
    $values = ""
    # loop through all columns
    foreach ($column in $columns) {
        if ($values) {
            $values += ", "
        }
        $values += "'" + $record.$column + "'"
    }
    $sqlcmds += $sql + "`nVALUES(" + $values + ");`n"
}

# run SQL commands
Invoke-Sqlcmd -ConnectionString $connectionString -Query $sqlcmds
```

19

Chapter 20
Scripting in the Cloud

The cloud is large and diverse—in this respect, the title of this chapter is presumptuous. One could write an entire book on the subject, covering different cloud models, providers, and programming variants.

At this point, I will focus on the *Simple Storage Service (S3)* of *Amazon Web Services (AWS)*. This service has established itself as a cost-effective way to store files. Two major options for usage exist: You can store files there that are publicly accessible (for example, to relieve the load on your own web server), or you can use S3 as a place for backups or rarely needed files. At the same time, you'll need to keep an eye on the costs: Depending on the offer, the transfer or the actual storage can be the decisive factor.

Two great libraries for controlling AWS S3 functions are available: the AWS command-line interface (CLI) for Bash scripts and the AWS module for PowerShell scripts. This chapter describes both variants.

Prerequisites for This Chapter

To benefit from this chapter, you'll need good knowledge of Bash or PowerShell. You'll also need some basic knowledge of AWS S3: In particular, you need to know what is meant by the term "buckets" and how user management, specifically *identity and access management (IAM)*, works.

The two examples presented in this chapter are based on techniques that are described in Chapter 15 and Chapter 17, respectively. In this respect, it is advisable you review these two chapters first.

20

20.1 AWS CLI

The AWS CLI enables you to control AWS functions at the command level. The CLI can basically be installed on all common platforms. However, in the following sections, I assume that you use Linux or macOS and want to develop your scripts in Bash.

Don't worry, PowerShell fans aren't shorted and can just scroll down to Section 20.3.

20.1.1 Installation on Linux and macOS

AWS CLI downloads and installation guides for all platforms can be found at *https://docs.aws.amazon.com/cli/latest/userguide/getting-started-install.html.*

On Linux, you must download the ZIP file, unpack the archive, and run the installation script. The `aws` command will be stored in the */usr/local/bin* directory and should be executable there without any changes to `PATH`. If you want to update an existing installation, you must pass the `--update` option to the `install` command.

```
$ curl https://awscli.amazonaws.com/awscli-exe-linux-x86_64.zip \
    -o "awscliv2.zip"
$ unzip awscliv2.zip
$ sudo ./aws/install
$ aws --version
  aws-cli/2.11.11 Python/3.11.2 ...
```

Trouble with cron

On some Linux distributions, `/usr/local/bin` is not included in the `PATH` variable relevant to cron jobs. In that case, calling `aws` in cron jobs will fail. One solution might be to create a link from */usr/bin/aws* to */usr/local/bin/aws*, or to always specify the full path of the `aws` command in the script.

For macOS, Amazon provides a PKG installer. The installation process can be completed with a few clicks. Again, the `aws` command is installed in the */usr/local/bin* directory.

20.1.2 Configuration

For the following examples, you'll need an AWS user that has access rights to one or more buckets. Once you've set up a user in the AWS web interface under **Identity and Access Management** and assigned an access key, you should run `aws configure`. This command asks for the credentials and stores them in the local configuration files *.aws/config* and *.aws/credentials*. The run `aws configure` in the account under which you want your scripts to run later. If these scripts are backup scripts that require `root` privileges, `aws configure` must also be run in the `root` account.

```
$ aws configure

  AWS Access Key ID [None]:     AKxxxxxxx
  AWS Secret Access Key [None]: xxxxxxxxxxxxxxxx
  Default region name [None]:   eu-central-1
  Default output format [None]: <Return>
```

You can leave the default region blank at the beginning. Later, you can use aws s3api get-bucket-location to determine the region of your buckets and then repeat aws configure:

```
$ aws s3api get-bucket-location --bucket my.bucket.name
  "LocationConstraint": "eu-central-1"
```

20.1.3 Getting Started

aws commands usually consist of three parts: the main aws command; the name of an AWS service (e.g., s3 or ec2); and finally, a subcommand for that service. To determine which buckets you can access in your configuration, you want to run the following command:

```
$ aws s3 ls

  2020-06-23 00:40:38 my.bucket.name
  2022-12-12 02:51:07 my.bucket.othername
```

If you pass s3://<bucketname> as another parameter to ls, aws displays the files in that bucket:

```
$ aws s3 ls s3://my.bucket.name

  2023-12-15 11:11:53      61431 test.txt
  2023-03-22 15:23:01      61431 test2.txt
```

By using aws s3 cp, you can copy a local file to a bucket, or vice versa:

```
$ aws s3 cp local-file.txt s3://my.bucket.name
$ aws s3 cp s3://my.bucket.name/local-file.txt copy.txt
```

Besides cp, you should be familiar with some other subcommands from your work in Bash, such as mv or rm. Many commands know the --recursive, --include 'pattern', and --exclude 'pattern' options, where pattern supports the ? and * characters, among others. The characters have the same meaning as in Bash (see Table 3.3 in Chapter 3, Section 3.8), not as in regular expressions.

Note that S3 buckets are aware of the concept of directories only with limitations. Although the name of a file stored in the bucket may be composed of several parts (dir1/dir2/file), there is no way to create a directory via mkdir or to delete a directory using rmdir.

One of the most important AWS S3 commands is aws s3 sync. This command allows you to synchronize a local directory and a directory in a bucket. This command is extremely useful especially for backups: For example, if a complete backup of your data is stored in a local directory, you can create redundancy with a regularly executed synchronization command. If the local backup is lost, you'll still have a copy in the cloud. (Note that, with AWS, you pay not only for the amount of data stored, but also for each transport in one direction or another. For cost reasons, it is convenient to organize the backup incrementally, so that only the changes saved from one day to the next are transferred.)

```
$ aws s3 sync my-local-backupdir s3://my.bucket.name
```

A reference for all AWS S3 commands can be found at *https://awscli.amazonaws.com/v2/documentation/api/latest/reference/s3/index.html.*

20.1.4 Encrypting Files

Even though Amazon advertises that your files are stored encrypted, this encryption does not improve the security of your data that much as long as Amazon has the key. If you don't want outside companies or intelligence agencies to read your organization or company's backups, you must encrypt all files before transferring them to the cloud. This basic rule is not specific to Amazon but applies to *any* storage of data on external servers or cloud services.

In the following sections, I will introduce you to the gpg command, which allows you to encrypt files symmetrically in an uncomplicated way and decrypt them later.

Symmetric versus Asymmetric

"Symmetric encryption" means that the same key is used for both encryption and decryption. In contrast, with asymmetric methods, a key pair is used (as with SSH): The public key is used for encryption; the private key, for decryption. This approach is especially advantageous if the encryption is supposed to take place at different locations (computers). The public key required for this setup can be distributed without hesitation.

Unfortunately, however, asymmetric methods are inefficient for large files. Nevertheless, to take advantage of asymmetric procedures, a common practice is to continue encrypting the files symmetrically. In addition, however, the keys are now also encrypted—namely, asymmetrically! This scenario is now referred to as a "hybrid encryption system" and is described at *https://en.wikipedia.org/wiki/Hybrid_cryptosystem.*

For our purposes (i.e., for the safekeeping of backup files in a cloud), a symmetric procedure is absolutely sufficient. You just need to ensure that the key you use does not fall into the wrong hands.

First, you need a key (i.e., just a binary file with random data). A good way to generate a new key is the openssl command, which is part of the package of the same name on Linux. The following command creates a key with a length of 32 bytes. (32 bytes seems small, but that's 256 bits. For symmetric methods, 128 bits are already considered sufficiently secure.)

```
$ openssl rand 32 > mykey
```

If openssl is not available to you, the following command will also work on Linux:

```
$ dd if=/dev/random of=mykey bs=16 count=1
```

As I have already clarified in a previous chapter: The key file is (pun intended) the key to security. On my servers, I keep such files in a directory that can only be read by the root user and use chown root:root mykey and chmod 600 to ensure that really nobody except root is allowed to read the file. (Also remember to keep a backup of your key in a safe place! Should your server including the key file get lost—for example due to a hardware defect—you can never decrypt the encrypted backup files in the cloud again.)

To encrypt or decrypt a key, you can use the gpg command. Because numerous options must be passed in each case, the best way is to wrap the call into two tiny scripts:

```
# Sample file mycrypt.sh
# usage: mycrypt.sh < plain > crypted
gpg -c -q --batch --cipher-algo AES256 --compress-algo none \
  --passphrase-file /path/to/mykey

# Sample file myuncrypt.sh
# usage: myuncrypt.sh < crypted > plain
gpg -d --batch --no-tty -q --cipher-algo AES256 \
  --compress-algo none --passphrase-file /path/to/mykey
```


Let's briefly explain some of these options:

- -c (*symmetric crypt*) encrypts standard input and writes to standard output.
- -d (*symmetric decrypt*) decrypts the standard input and writes to the standard output.
- -q (*quiet*) suppresses status messages.
- --batch activates the batch mode (no interactive queries).
- --cipher-algo sets the encryption algorithm.
- --compress-algo sets the compression algorithm.
- --passphrase-file specifies from which file gpg should read the key.

You can test the two scripts in the following way:

```
$ ./mycrypt < readme.txt > readme.crypt
$ ./myuncrypt < readme.crypt > readme.copy
$ diff readme.txt readme.copy
```

The first command encrypts `readme.txt`. The second command decrypts the file and saves the result as `readme.copy`. The third command compares the two files and lists all differences. If `diff` outputs nothing, the files are identical.

Compress First, Then Encrypt

If you want to compress *and* encrypt a file, you should always compress first and then encrypt. Doing it the other way round, compression fails to reduce the file size because already encrypted files look like a sequence of random data to the compression program. Compressing them is thus impossible.

20.2 Example: Uploading Encrypted Backup Files to the Cloud

In Chapter 15, Section 15.2, I introduced you to a script that stores backups of a MySQL server database and web server directory in a local directory. With just a little effort, you can improve this script to compress the local files first and then upload them to an AWS bucket. Because the script is quite short, I have printed the entire code again here. Let me also briefly point out a few special features:

- The encryption commands are wrapped in functions.
- The functions are called in a pipe: `mysqldump` creates the backup, `gzip` compresses it, and `mycrypt` encrypts it. Only the result is saved in a file. This approach avoids the time-consuming creation of intermediate files.
- Similarly, `tar` creates a compressed archive. `-f -` forwards it to standard output. `mycrypt` encrypts it and again saves the result to a file.
- When calling `aws`, I specified the full path of the command in each case, so that the script works without errors even when automated by cron.
- Unlike the usual `cp` command where you can copy multiple files to a destination directory (i.e., `cp file1 file2 file3 dir`), `aws s3 cp` accepts only one source file. For this reason, I must call the command for each file separately.

```
# Sample file lamp-backup-to-aws.sh
BACKUPDIR=/localbackup
DB=wp
DBUSER=wpbackupuser
WPDIR=/var/www/html/wordpress
BUCKET=s3://your.bucket.name

function mycrypt {
  gpg -c -q --batch --cipher-algo AES256 --compress-algo none \
      --passphrase-file /etc/mykey
}
function myuncrypt {
```

```
  gpg -d --batch --no-tty -q --cipher-algo AES256 \
      --compress-algo none --passphrase-file /etc/mykey
}

# MySQL backup
weekday=$(date +%u)
dbfile=$BACKUPDIR/wp-db-$weekday.sql.gz.crypt
mysqlopt='--single-transaction'
mysqldump -u $DBUSER $mysqlopt $DB | gzip -c | mycrypt > $dbfile

# backup of the WordPress files
htmlfile=$BACKUPDIR/wp-html-$weekday.tar.gz.crypt
tar czf - -C $WPDIR . | mycrypt > $htmlfile

# upload to an AWS bucket
/usr/local/bin/aws s3 cp $dbfile   $BUCKET
/usr/local/bin/aws s3 cp $htmlfile $BUCKET
```

Checking the Recovery

When your backup script is ready, you should make sure to test if you can restore your data from the backups!

20.3 AWS PowerShell Module

20

Basically, there is nothing wrong with calling the AWS CLI described earlier (i.e., the `aws` command) in PowerShell scripts. But an even more elegant way is available: Amazon provides several modules for various AWS services. These modules are referred to as *AWS Tools for PowerShell*. The modules are excellently maintained and usually updated once or twice a week. Because the AWS Tools for PowerShell return real PowerShell objects, you can often express your scripts more clearly than with by using AWS CLI.

You can easily install the tools using `Install-Module`, and not only on Windows, by the way, but also on Linux and macOS:

```
> Install-Module AWS.Tools.Common
> Install-Module AWS.Tools.S3
```

20.3.1 Getting Started

As with the AWS CLI, I assume in the following sections that there is an AWS user with sufficient access rights to one or more buckets. You must now specify its *access key* and *secret key* via `Set-AWSCredentials`. You can also specify a profile name. This step allows you to use separate access data for different scripts. By using -StoreAs default, you can create a default profile.

```
> Set-AWSCredential -AccessKey AKxxx -SecretKey xxxx `
   -StoreAs MyProfile
```

On Windows, access data is stored encrypted in the following file:

```
C:\Users\<name>\AppData\Local\AWSToolkit\RegisteredAccounts.json
```

On Linux and macOS, the location is .aws/credentials as for the AWS CLI; the keys are stored in plain text.

To test if the configuration worked, you must run Get-S3Bucket. The cmdlet lists your buckets.

```
> Get-S3Bucket -ProfileName MyProfile
> Get-S3Bucket                           # for the default profile
```

In the remaining examples, I will assume that you have set up a profile named default. If not the case, you must add the -ProfileName option with your profile name to all cmdlets. Alternatively, you can preset the desired profile at the beginning of a session or script using Set-AWSCredential:

```
> Set-AWSCredential -ProfileName MyProfile
```

If you want to know in which region your buckets are located, you must run Get-S3BucketLocation. Note that the cmdlet will return an empty result if the bucket is in the US-East (North Virginia) region (us-east-1).

```
> Get-S3Bucket | ForEach-Object {
    $name = $_.BucketName
    $region = Get-S3BucketLocation -BucketName $name
    Write-Output "$name : $region"
  }

  my.first.bucket : eu-central-1
  my.other.bucket : eu-west-2
  ...
```

The content of a bucket is displayed via Get-S3Object, which might be a bit more detailed than you need:

```
> Get-S3Object -BucketName my.first.bucket -Region eu-central-1

  ChecksumAlgorithm : {}
  ETag              : "b81e..."
  BucketName        : my.first.bucket
  Key               : duplicati1.png
```

```
LastModified      : 13.05.2019 21:36:35
Owner             : Amazon.S3.Model.Owner
Size              : 31729
StorageClass      : STANDARD

ChecksumAlgorithm : {}
ETag              : "ab98"
...
```

Probably you're only interested in the filenames (Key property). Also, only in rare cases will you really need *all* the files from a bucket. (In fact, the cmdlet returns a maximum of 1,000 hits.) The following command returns only the names of all files starting with dir1/:

```
> Get-S3Object -BucketName my.first.bucket -KeyPrefix 'dir1/' |
  Select-Object Key
```

Unfortunately, Get-S3Object does not provide a way to filter files by other criteria. As long as you do not exceed the 1,000-file limit, you must determine *all* filenames and then apply Filter-Object. The following command displays the names of all files ending with .txt:

```
> Get-S3Object -BucketName my.first.bucket |
  Select-Object Key |
  Where-Object { $_.Key -like '*.txt' }
```

Relatively often, you may find that Get-S3Object or various other cmdlets return the following error message: *The bucket you're attempting to access must be addressed using the specified endpoint.*

The error indicates that you forgot the -Region option and AWS does not know where your bucket is located. Since constantly specifying the -Region option is annoying, you can set the default region for the current session or for your script via Set-DefaultAWSRegion.

```
> Set-DefaultAWSRegion -Region eu-central-1
```

20.3.2 Copying Files

Probably the most common task when using AWS S3 is to upload and download files to and from the cloud. Write-S3Object and Read-S3Object are used for this purpose:

- The first command uploads a local file to a bucket. The key name in the bucket matches that of the local file.
- The second command uploads another file but assigns a different name to the file in the bucket (-Key option).

- The third command downloads the *readme.txt* file from the bucket and saves the file locally as *local-file.txt*.
- The fourth command downloads all files whose key starts with `dir1/` into the current directory.

```
> Write-S3Object -BucketName my.first.bucket -File local-file.txt
> Write-S3Object -BucketName my.first.bucket -File local.txt `
                 -Key dir1/tst.txt
> Read-S3Object  -BucketName my.first.bucket -Key  readme.txt `
                 -File local-file.txt
> Read-S3Object  -BucketName my.first.bucket -KeyPrefix dir1/ `
                 -Folder .
```

You can use `Remove-S3Object` to delete files in the bucket:

```
> Remove-S3Object -BucketName my.first.bucket -Key readme.txt
```

In addition to the cmdlets listed so far, the AWS Tools for PowerShell provide countless other functions to choose from. A reference of all S3 cmdlets can be found at *https://docs.aws.amazon.com/powershell/latest/reference/items/S3_cmdlets.html*.

In view of the abundance of cmdlets, the absence of a very important function is confusing: No cmdlet in AWS Tools for PowerShell corresponds to the `aws s3 sync` CLI command. If you want to synchronize a local directory with a bucket, I recommend you use the CLI in PowerShell scripts as well.

20.4 Example: Offloading Large Files from a Website to the Cloud

The starting point for the following example is your own website. The goal is to swap out the very large PDF files linked there to the cloud. Thus, the website should continue to be operated with its own server. However, when visitors click on a PDF download link, that file is should be downloaded from AWS S3. In this way, you can continue to manage the website yourself, while at the same time minimizing the load on your web server caused by large downloads.

The *migrate-pdf-to-aws.ps1* script works in the following way:

- It downloads the HTML code of a web page.
- It searches all links for those ending with `.pdf`.
- It first downloads the PDF documents to a temporary directory and then uploads them to a public AWS S3 bucket.
- In the HTML code, the links are adjusted, and a new version of the HTML page is saved locally.

20.4.1 Preparations

For this example, you need a bucket that is publicly accessible on the web. For this task, make several settings in the AWS Console:

- For security reasons, all public access to new buckets is blocked by default. The corresponding **Block all public access** option must be disabled.
- You need to set a *bucket policy* that allows access to all objects. In the console, you can complete this task by formulating a JSON document based on the following pattern:

  ```
  {
      "Version": "2012-10-17",
      "Statement": [
          {
              "Sid": "PublicReadGetObject",
              "Effect": "Allow",
              "Principal": "*",
              "Action": "s3:GetObject",
              "Resource": "arn:aws:s3:::my.public.bucket/*"
          }
      ]
  }
  ```

  In this code, replace `my.public.bucket` with the name of your bucket. The `version` date, on the other hand, must not be changed.
- Finally, you must enable the **Static website hosting** option. At this point you'll also learn at which HTTP address your bucket objects can be found. Next, specify a starting document for web hosting, usually `index.html`.

  Actually, this page is intended as a starting point for the static website. For this example, however, such a start page is not necessary at all. You can still upload a minimal HTML file explaining the purpose of the website (for example, *This site hosts PDF documents*).

20

20.4.2 Script

The script starts with the initialization of some variables. `Set-DefaultAWSRegion` and `Set-AWSCredential` set the region and profile for all other AWS cmdlets. It then creates a temporary directory where the PDF documents can be stored temporarily and uses `Invoke-WebRequest` to download the HTML code to be processed.

```
# Sample file migrate-pdf-to-aws.ps1
$bucket = "my.pdf.bucket"
$awsurl = `
  "http://my.pdf.bucket.s3-website.eu-central-1.amazonaws.com/"
$region = "eu-central-1"
```

```
$awsprofile = "MyProfile"      # profile for AWS credentials
$htmlsource = "https://example.com/page-with-pdf-links.html"
$htmldest = "updated.html"  # file name for new HTML code

# create .\tmp directory
New-Item -ItemType Directory -Force tmp | Out-Null

# set AWS default region and profile
Set-DefaultAWSRegion $region
Set-AWSCredential -ProfileName $awsprofile

# download HTML code
$response = Invoke-WebRequest $htmlsource
$html = $response.Content
```

Then, a loop now runs through all links in the HTML document. If the link ends with `.pdf`, the file is first downloaded to the local directory and then uploaded to the cloud. `Replace` then replaces the original link address with the new one. (Note that `Replace` is more appropriate here than the `-replace` operator, which processes regular expressions. A URL often contains dots, which have a special meaning in regular expressions.) Finally, the script saves the modified HTML code to a local file.

```
# (continued ...)
# loop through all links
foreach ($link in $response.links) {
    $href = $link.href
    if ($href -match '.*pdf$') {
        Write-Output $href
        # extract filename from URL
        $filename = $href.Substring($href.LastIndexOf("/") + 1)
        # download PDF
        Invoke-WebRequest $href -OutFile tmp\$filename
        # upload PDF to cloud
        Write-S3Object -BucketName $bucket -File tmp\$filename `
                       -Key $filename
        # assemble AWS URL for PDF
        $pdfAtAws = "$awsurl$filename"
        # update link in HTML document
        $html = $html.Replace("href=`"$href`"",
                              "href=`"$pdfAtAws`"")
    }
}
# save modified HTML code
$html | Out-File $htmldest
```

20.4.3 Limitations

Before you get the idea to apply this script to a real website, you should deal with the not insignificant limitations:

- Most modern websites are implemented via a *content management system (CMS)*. The HTML code of a page consists of various components. The script sees this HTML code in its entirety. But in fact, you usually want to change only parts of it. For this task, the script would need to have access to the single page within the CMS. Often, Markdown or a CMS-specific language is used instead of HTML.
- The direct links to the PDF files in the AWS S3 bucket use only HTTP, not the contemporary HTTPS protocol. This choice can be changed, but considerable configuration effort is needed. The details are documented at *https://docs.aws.amazon.com/AmazonS3/latest/userguide/WebsiteHosting.html.*
- The script itself could also be optimized. It should consider only PDF links referencing files of your own website. Foreign PDFs or PDFs that have already been swapped out should not be processed again.

  A duplicate check is also recommended to ensure that a document linked multiple times will only once be uploaded to the cloud.
- The script requires absolute links (i.e., `href="https://hostname/..."`). However, HTML also allows relative links (`href="mydocument.pdf"`). If necessary, you must supplement your script to this effect. Corresponding sample code—there, however, formulated in Python—can be found in Chapter 17, Section 17.2 .

In a nutshell, the implementation of the simple idea of this example faces several hurdles in practice.

20

Chapter 21
Virtual Machines

As long as you use virtual machines only sporadically, automation does not make any sense. You may want to consider using a tool for faster setup of new virtual machines (such as Vagrant).

The situation is completely different if you want to automatically create, configure, maintain, and analyze a large number of virtual machines, for example, for a lab (teaching), for cluster operation (science), or for scalable deployment (container or server operation). Of course, there are all kinds of special tools available for this type of use cases, from OpenStack to Kubernetes. However, getting used to these monster programs is complicated and requires intensive training. For simple tasks, a few small scripts are often sufficient.

The scripts in this chapter refer to the Kernel-based Virtual Machine (KVM) for Linux and Microsoft Hyper-V for Windows virtualization systems.

Prerequisites for This Chapter

In addition to a basic knowledge of Bash or PowerShell, you'll need a basic understanding of the relevant virtualization system and of the underlying network technology for this chapter.

One of the examples uses the `cut`, `grep`, and `sed` commands and applies regular expressions to modify network configuration files. I covered the related basic principles in Chapter 8 and in Chapter 9.

The SSH authentication with keys also plays a role in the examples. If necessary, you should take another look at Chapter 12.

21.1 Setting Up and Running Virtual Machines (KVMs)

The starting point for the following scripts is an Ubuntu server. The KVM virtualization system, the `virsh` command from the `libvirt-clients` package, and the `virt-clone` command from the package of the same name are installed there. The goal is to run multiple similar virtual machines cloned from an existing virtual machine named `vm-base`. The `vm-base` output system has three network interfaces and four virtual disks.

21.1.1 Cloning Virtual Machines

The `make-vms.sh` script expects two numeric parameters. It then loops from the start value to the end value and creates the virtual machines, `vm-<nn>`. Thus, the `make-vms.sh 10 29` command creates 20 virtual machines named `vm-10` to `vm-29`.

The script first tests whether two parameters have been passed. Before it starts cloning, the script makes sure that the original virtual machine (the clone base system, `orig` variable) is shut down. It analyzes the list of all running virtual machines generated via `virsh list`.

`virt-clone` automatically creates the required virtual disks using the filenames specified with `--file` and the *Media Access Control (MAC)* addresses specified with `--mac` (for identifying network devices). However, these disks always use the RAW image format. The `qemu-img` commands that follow convert the image files into the more efficient QCOW2 format.

```
# Sample file make-vms.sh
if [ $# -ne 2 ]; then
    echo "usage: make-vms.sh <start> <end>"
    exit 1
fi
vmstart=$1
vmend=$2
orig='vm-base'    # base VM to clone

# shut down clone base system
result=$(virsh list | grep $orig)
if [ ! -z "$result" ]; then
  echo "shutting down $orig"
  virsh shutdown $orig
  sleep 10
fi

# create VMs
for (( nr=$vmstart; nr<=$vmend; nr++ )); do
  echo "create vm-$nr"
  disk1=/var/lib/libvirt/images/vm-$nr-disk1.qcow2
  disk2=/var/lib/libvirt/images/vm-$nr-disk2.qcow2
  disk3=/var/lib/libvirt/images/vm-$nr-disk3.qcow2
  disk4=/var/lib/libvirt/images/vm-$nr-disk4.qcow2
  tmpdisk=/var/lib/libvirt/images/tmpdisk.qcow2
  virt-clone --name "vm-$nr" --original $orig \
     --mac 52:54:00:01:00:$nr --mac 52:54:00:02:00:$nr \
     --mac 52:54:00:03:00:$nr \
     --file $disk1 --file $disk2 --file $disk3 --file $disk4
```

```
  # convert RAW disks to QCOW2 disks
  qemu-img convert $disk1 -O qcow2 $tmpdisk
  mv $tmpdisk $disk1
  qemu-img convert $disk2 -O qcow2 $tmpdisk
  mv $tmpdisk $disk2
  qemu-img convert $disk3 -O qcow2 $tmpdisk
  mv $tmpdisk $disk3
  qemu-img convert $disk4 -O qcow2 $tmpdisk
  mv $tmpdisk $disk4
done
```

21.1.2 Starting and Shutting Down Virtual Machines

`make-vms.sh` only creates the `vm-<nn>` virtual machines; it does not start them. This task is carried out by another script (`start-vms.sh`), which again expects two numbers as parameters. It runs `virsh start <name>` to start the virtual machine in question.

```
# Sample file start-vms.sh
vmstart=$1
vmend=$2
for (( nr=$vmstart; nr<=$vmend; nr++ )); do
  echo "start vm-$nr"
  virsh start "vm-$nr"
done
```

In addition, there are two analogous scripts to shut down the virtual machines (`virsh shutdown`) and to delete them, deleting all virtual disks, respectively (`virsh undefine --remove-all-storage`).

21

21.1.3 Running Scripts on Multiple Virtual Machines

Once you have gotten 20 virtual machines up and running, you notice that you forgot a configuration detail. You could now log in to each of the virtual machines using SSH and complete the configuration. But of course, a more elegant solution exists: You can use `run-script-on-vms.sh` to run the commands stored in `myscript.sh` via SSH on all desired virtual machines.

`run-script-on-vms.sh` assumes that there is an SSH key pair on your local server and that the public key is known in the root account of the virtual machines. For this purpose, you must allow SSH logins for `root` on `vm-base` and copy the local key there with `ssh-copy-id root@basevm`. Needless to say, this step must be done before cloning! Instead of `basevm`, you specify the hostname or IP address of the virtual machine.

run-script-on-vms.sh is amazingly short. Basically, for each virtual machine in a loop, the ssh root@host < myscripts.sh > result.txt command is executed. Instead of host, the host name (here vm-<nn>.example.com) or the IP address of the virtual machine in question must be specified in the script. The -o StrictHostKeyChecking=no option causes SSH to forego asking whether to trust a host to which a connection is being made for the first time.

```
# Sample file run-script-on-vms.sh
vmstart=$1
vmend=$2
for (( nr=$vmstart; nr<=$vmend; nr++ )); do
    ssh -o StrictHostKeyChecking=no \
      root@vm-$nr.example.com 'bash -s' \
      < myscript.sh > results-$nr.txt
done
```

21.2 Automating the Network Configuration (KVMs)

"Cloning" a virtual machine means that all the properties of the source system are preserved. For this reason, all configuration files are also cloned. In most cases, that is exactly what you want, but there are exceptions. One of these exceptions is related to the static network configuration. As far as the network adapters do not obtain their addresses automatically via DHCP, the network configuration files of each virtual machine must be adjusted, as otherwise network conflicts will occur.

This task is performed by another script, which, however, is not located on the virtualization host, but *inside* the virtual machine. So, there must be a script in the clone base system (according to the names of the previous example in vm-base) that is executed when the virtual machine or its clones are booted.

In my setup for the Linux courses I teach, the virtual machines are compatible with Red Hat Enterprise Linux (RHEL) 9. (I use AlmaLinux, but RHEL 9, Oracle Linux 9 or Rocky Linux 9 work exactly the same way in this regard.) The vm-base virtual machine contains a script named /etc/myscripts/setup-vm-network, which is executed on every boot process. The file that is responsible for this task is /etc/rc.d/rc.local, which looks as follows:

```
#!/bin/bash
touch /var/lock/subsys/local
. /etc/myscripts/setup-vm-network
```

You must make this file executable using chmod +x /etc/rc.d/rc.local for it to be considered.

21.2.1 Starting Point

The setup-vm-network Bash script assumes that there are existing configuration files for two network adapters:

```
/etc/NetworkManager/system-connections/enp1s0.nmconnection
/etc/NetworkManager/system-connections/enp7s0.nmconnection
```

The files use the Linux NetworkManager syntax and contain the following lines, among others:

```
# static IPv4 configuration with 192.168.122.1 as gateway
address1=192.168.122.27/24,192.168.122.1
# static IPv6 configuration with 2a01:abce:abce::2 as gateway
address1=2a01:abcd:abcd::27/64,2a01:abce:abce::2
```

These files should be customized so that each virtual machine has a unique IPv4 and IPv6 address. For this purpose, the last two digits of the MAC address of the first network adapter are analyzed. For example, if the MAC address is 52:54:00:01:00:27, the virtual machine should use the following IP addresses:

- IPv4: 192.168.122.27
- IPv6: 2a01:abcd:abce::27

In the first lines of the script some variables are initialized. Then, the script analyzes the /sys/class/net/enp1s0/address system file, which contains the MAC address of the first adapter. cut extracts the sixth hexadecimal group from it. The if statement eliminates a leading 0, so it simply turns 07 into 7, for example.

The ipv4old or ipv4new variables as well as ipv6old or ipv6new contain a pattern for the previous IP address and the required correct IP address. If the script detects via grep that the current network configuration does not match the desired address, both configuration files will be modified using sed. Simply put, the sed commands have the following effect:

- conffile1: 192.168.122.*/24 gets replaced by 192.168.122.<nn>/24
- conffile2: 2a01:abcd:abcd::*/64 gets replaced by 2a01:abcd:abcd::<nn>/64

Next, the script deletes the /etc/machine-id file and then sets it up again with a random ID. This file as well has to do with the network configuration. It is analyzed by NetworkManager (a Linux system component) and used to generate IPv6 link local unicast addresses (fe80-xxx). If all virtual machines have the same internal ID number, then the unicast addresses are also identical and address conflicts will occur despite an otherwise correct IPv6 configuration.

If required, you can of course add more functions to the script, for example, to generate new keys for the OpenSSH server or to set the hostname.

```
# Sample file setup-vm-network.sh
NMPATH=/etc/NetworkManager/system-connections
IF1=enp1s0
IF2=enp7s0

# location of the network configuration files
conffile1=$NMPATH/$IF1.nmconnection
conffile2=$NMPATH/$IF2.nmconnection

# extracts the last 2 MAC digits, eliminates leading 0
mac=$(cut -d ':' -f 6 /sys/class/net/$IF1/address)
if [ ${mac:0:1} == 0 ]; then mac=${mac:1:2}; fi

# IPv4 and IPv6 addresses: old = previous, new = desired
ip4old="192\.168\.122\..*/24"
ip4new="192\.168\.122\.$mac/24"
ip6old="2a01:abcd:abcd::.*/64"
ip6new="2a01:abcd:abcd::$mac/64"

# if the configuration file uses a different address
# than ip4new: rectify configuration files using sed
if ! grep -q "address1=$ip4new" $conffile1; then
  sed -E -i.old  "s,$ip4old,$ip4new," $conffile1
  sed -E -i.old  "s,$ip6old,$ip6new," $conffile2
  # set up new /etc/machine-id
  rm /etc/machine-id
  systemd-machine-id-setup
  # restart virtual machine
  echo "reboot"
  reboot
else
  echo "no network changes"
fi
```

The script ends with a `reboot` statement. If you develop a script yourself like in this example, you must be extremely careful with `reboot`! If your script does not work properly, the virtual machine will restart continuously. So, make sure to test your script extensively before you include `reboot`!

Since the script processes the last two digits of the MAC address decimally (not hexadecimally), it is suitable for the administration of 100 virtual machines. 192.168.122.0 is reserved. 192.168.122.1 and 2a01:abce:abce::2 are used as gateway addresses. This leaves the address range 192.168.122.3 to .99 for IPv4. So, you can set up a maximum of 97 virtual machines. If necessary, you can work around this limit by analyzing the last two MAC digits hexadecimally or by considering multiple MAC digits.

Alternatives

Running a script within the init system is not the only way to configure virtual machines. Major virtualization frameworks such as OpenStack rely on cloud init (see *https://cloud-init.io*).

To configure running virtual (or real) machines, you can also use configuration tools such as Puppet or Ansible. However, these programs assume that all machines in the network are accessible, i.e., that the network configuration has already been completed.

21.3 Controlling Hyper-V

Hyper-V is to Windows what KVM is to Linux. It is therefore not surprising that Microsoft has added a comprehensive PowerShell module to its own virtualization system. If you have Windows Pro and have not yet enabled Hyper-V, the quickest way to do this is to use the following command:

```
> Add-WindowsFeature Hyper-V  -IncludeManagementTools
```

About 250 aliases and cmdlets can then be executed on Windows (but not on Linux or macOS) via the Hyper-V PowerShell module:

```
> Get-Command -Module Hyper-V

  CommandType  Name                    Version    Source
  -----------  ----                    -------    ------
  Alias        Export-VMCheckpoint     2.0.0.0    Hyper-V
  Alias        Get-VMCheckpoint        2.0.0.0    Hyper-V
  Alias        Remove-VMCheckpoint     2.0.0.0    Hyper-V
  Alias        Rename-VMCheckpoint     2.0.0.0    Hyper-V
  Alias        Restore-VMCheckpoint    2.0.0.0    Hyper-V
  Cmdlet       Add-VMAssignableDevice  2.0.0.0    Hyper-V
  Cmdlet       Add-VMDvdDrive          2.0.0.0    Hyper-V
  ...
```

Admin Rights Required

By default, the execution of Hyper-V cmdlets requires admin rights. This means you need to open a PowerShell terminal with admin rights.

Alternatively, you can add individual users or groups to the Hyper-V administrators. This type of settings can be done in the Group Policy Management Editor.

Get-VM lists all installed virtual machines and shows details about their current state:

```
> Get-VM

  Name    State     CPUUsage(%)   MemoryAssigned(M)     ...
  ----    -----     -----------   -----------------   -----
  alma9   Running   24            2024
  kali    Running   0             5976
  ...
```

Get-VM returns VirtualMachine objects. Get-Member shows that the underlying class has innumerable properties:

```
> Get-VM | Select-Object -First 1 | Get-Member

  TypeName: Microsoft.HyperV.PowerShell.VirtualMachine

  Name                          MemberType    Definition
  ----                          ----------    ----------
  CheckpointFileLocation        AliasProperty ...
  VMId                          AliasProperty ...
  VMName                        AliasProperty ...
  Equals                        Method        ...
  GetHashCode                   Method        ...
  AutomaticCheckpointsEnabled   Property      ...
  AutomaticCriticalErrorAction  Property      ...
  AutomaticStartAction          Property      ...
  AutomaticStartDelay           Property      ...
  ...
```

You can start or shut down all virtual machines by using two one-liners that call the Start-VM and Stop-VM cmdlets, respectively:

```
> Get-VM | Where-Object {$_.State -eq 'Off'} | Start-VM

> Get-VM | Where-Object {$_.State -eq 'Running'} | Stop-VM
```

The especially useful Set-VM cmdlet allows you to change various properties of virtual machines:

```
> $vm = Get-VM "alma9-clone1"
> Set-VM -VM $vm -MemoryStartupBytes 2GB -ProcessorCount 2
```

Changing the memory is impossible if the virtual machine uses a dynamically allocated memory area. In that case, you can set the upper and lower limits, as well as the initial memory size, which must not be larger than the upper limit. The -DynamicMemory option allows you to switch from static to dynamic memory management.

```
> Set-VM -VM $vm -DynamicMemory -MemoryStartupBytes 512MB `
    -MemoryMinimumBytes 512MB -MemoryMaximumBytes 1GB
```

As usual, a reference of all Hyper-V cmdlets with their myriad options can be found online: *https://learn.microsoft.com/en-us/powershell/module/hyper-v*.

21.3.1 Cloning Virtual Machines

The `Hyper-V` module does not provide its own cmdlet for cloning virtual machines. However, this task can be done by means of a workaround: For this purpose, you first need to export the virtual machine (`Export-VM`) and then create the new virtual machine by means of an import (`import VM`).

In real life, however, the process is more complex than this brief summary suggests. The following script creates `noOfClones` copies of an existing virtual machine. The script starts by shutting down the base virtual machine and deleting all snapshots. (You should remove `Remove-VMSnapshot` if you want to keep the snapshots! Note, however, that `Export-VM` also includes all snapshots and there is no option to prevent this.)

```
# Sample file clone-vm.ps1
$basename = "alma9"
$noOfClones = 3
$tmp = $env:TEMP  # Caution: $env:TEMP works only on
                  # Windows, but not on Linux/macOS

# the function tests if a directory exists, and
# then deletes it; be careful!
function delete-dir($path) {
    if (Test-Path "$path") {
        Write-Output "delete $path"
        Remove-Item "$path" -Recurse -Force
    }
}

# when VM is running: shutdown
$basevm = Get-VM $basename
if ($basevm.State -eq 'Running' ) {
    Write-Output "shutdown $basename"
    Stop-VM -VM $basevm
}
# delete all snapshots of the VM (be careful!)
Get-VMSnapshot -VM $basevm | Remove-VMSnapshot
```

The next lines use `Get-VMHardDiskDrive` to determine the location of the first disk of the base virtual machine. The disks of the cloned virtual machines will be created later in subdirectories relative to this.

If the temporary directory to which the export is to be done already exists (e.g., as a left-over from a previous script call), then it will be deleted.

`Export-VM` finally exports the base virtual machine. This creates a subdirectory in the temporary directory with the virtual machine name. The actual description of the virtual machine is contained in a `*.vmcx` file. `Get-ChildItem` gets the filename.

```
# (continued ...)
# determines the directory in which the first disk image
# is stored
$pathFirstDisk =  (Get-VMHardDiskDrive -VM $basevm |
                   Select-Object -First 1).Path
$dirFirstDisk = Split-Path $pathFirstDisk -Parent
Write-Output "Virtual disk directory: $dirFirstDisk"

# delete temporary export directory (if it exists)
delete-dir "$tmp\$basename"
# perform export
Export-VM -VM $basevm -Path $tmp
$vmcxfile = Get-ChildItem `
    "$tmp\$basename\Virtual Machines\*.vmcx"
Write-Output "VMCX file: $vmcxfile"
```

Several clones of the virtual machine are now created in a loop. The `-Copy` option means that this really creates a new virtual machine with its own files. `-GenerateNewId` gives the virtual machine its own Hyper-V identification number. The two `-XxxPath` options specify where to store the virtual machine files.

`Rename-VM` gives the virtual machine a new name. Hyper-V has no problem with multiple virtual machines having the same name, but virtual machines with the same name only cause confusion.

Hyper-V automatically assigns 2 CPUs and 2 GB of memory to new virtual machines. `Set-VM` reduces these values. In addition, `Set-VMNetworkAdapter` sets a static MAC address for each virtual machine. By default, Hyper-V uses dynamic MACs that are generated only when a virtual machine is started. The first six digits of the MAC should always be `00155d`. This part of the MAC was reserved by Microsoft for Hyper-V.

```
# (continued ...)
# create $noOfClones copies of the exported VM
for ($i = 1; $i -le $noOfClones; $i++) {
    $cloneName = "${basename}-clone${i}"
    Write-Output "setup $cloneName with MAC $mac"
```

```
    $clone = Import-VM -Path $vmcxfile -Copy -GenerateNewId `
        -VhdDestinationPath "$dirFirstDisk\$cloneName" `
        -VirtualMachinePath "$dirFirstDisk\$cloneName"

    # rename the clone
    Rename-VM -VM $clone -NewName $cloneName

    # set properties of the VM
    Set-VM -VM $clone -ProcessorCount 1 `
      -MemoryStartupBytes 1GB

    # set static MAC address
    $mac="00155d1234{0:d2}" -f $i
    Set-VMNetworkAdapter -VMName $cloneName -StaticMacAddress $mac
}

# delete temporary export directory
delete-dir "$tmp\$basename"
```

Note that the script must be run with admin rights. The script returns an error if the virtual machine files of a clone already exist, for example when the script gets executed a second time. If you want, you can extend the script to detect and delete existing clones within the script.

The Author

Dr. Michael Kofler is a programmer and Linux administrator. He studied electrical engineering/telematics at Graz University of Technology. He has been one of the most successful and versatile computing authors in the German-speaking world for many years. His current topics include Linux, Docker, Git, hacking and security, Raspberry Pi, and the programming languages Swift, Java, Python, and Kotlin. Michael Kofler also teaches at the Joanneum University of Applied Sciences in Kapfenberg, Austria.

Index

J

K

L

M

S

X

Z

- Build user interfaces with React.js, a frontend JavaScript library
- Work with classes, hooks, type systems, CSS, forms, and more
- Grow your skills in areas such as testing, debugging, server communication, and server-side rendering

Sebastian Springer

React

The Comprehensive Guide

React.js makes developing dynamic user interfaces faster and easier than ever. Learn how to get the most out of the library with this comprehensive guide! Start with the basics: what React is and how it works. Then follow practical code examples to build an application, from styling with CSS to maximizing app performance. Whether you're new to JavaScript or you're an advanced developer, you'll find everything you need to build your frontend with React!

676 pages, pub. 10/2023
E-Book: $54.99 | **Print:** $59.95 | **Bundle:** $69.99

www.rheinwerk-computing.com/5705